Promoting Democracy, Reinforcing Authoritarianism

Jordan is one of the highest recipients of US and European 'democracy promotion' funding and simultaneously demonstrates a remarkably stable authoritarian system. Against this backdrop, *Promoting Democracy, Reinforcing Authoritarianism* investigates what external 'democracy promoters' *actually do* when they promote democracy. By examining why Jordanian authoritarianism is so stable, not despite but in part because of external attempts at 'democracy promotion', Benjamin Schuetze demonstrates the depth of Orientalist attitudes among 'democracy promoters'. In highlighting the undermining of democratic values as they become circumscribed by the free market and security concerns, Schuetze suggests that although US and European policy in Jordan comes under the cloak of a universal morality which claims the surmounting of authoritarianism as its objective, its effect is not very different to traditional modes of imperial support for authoritarian regimes. As a result, this is a vivid illustration of what greater US and European policy presence in the Global South really means.

Benjamin Schuetze is a postdoctoral research fellow in the Department of Political Science at the University of Freiburg and a research associate at the Arnold Bergstraesser Institute (ABI). His research has been supported by the Friedrich Ebert Foundation (FES) and the German Academic Exchange Service (DAAD) and has appeared in journals including Cooperation and Conflict and Security Dialogue, as well as on Al Jazeera and Jadaliyya.

Cambridge Middle East Studies

Cambridge Middle East Studies has been established to publish books on the nineteenth- to twenty-first-century Middle East and North Africa. The series offers new and original interpretations of aspects of Middle Eastern societies and their histories. To achieve disciplinary diversity, books are solicited from authors writing in a wide range of fields including history, sociology, anthropology, political science, and political economy. The emphasis is on producing books affording an original approach along theoretical and empirical lines. The series is intended for students and academics, but the more accessible and wide-ranging studies will also appeal to the interested general reader.

A list of books in the series can be found after the index.

Promoting Democracy, Reinforcing Authoritarianism

US and European Policy in Jordan

Benjamin Schuetze

University of Freiburg and Arnold Bergstraesser Institute

CAMBRIDGE
UNIVERSITY PRESS

University Printing House, Cambridge CB2 8BS, United Kingdom

One Liberty Plaza, 20th Floor, New York, NY 10006, USA

477 Williamstown Road, Port Melbourne, VIC 3207, Australia

314–321, 3rd Floor, Plot 3, Splendor Forum, Jasola District Centre,
New Delhi – 110025, India

79 Anson Road, #06–04/06, Singapore 079906

Cambridge University Press is part of the University of Cambridge.

It furthers the University's mission by disseminating knowledge in the pursuit of
education, learning, and research at the highest international levels of excellence.

www.cambridge.org
Information on this title: www.cambridge.org/9781108493383
DOI: 10.1017/9781108623681

First published 2019

Printed in the United Kingdom by TJ International Ltd, Padstow Cornwall

A catalogue record for this publication is available from the British Library.

Library of Congress Cataloging-in-Publication Data
Names: Schuetze, Benjamin, 1986– author.
Title: Promoting democracy, reinforcing authoritarianism / Benjamin Schuetze.
Description: Cambridge, UK ; New York, NY : Cambridge University Press
2019. | Series: Cambridge Middle East studies | Includes bibliographical
references and index.
Identifiers: LCCN 2019019431
Subjects: LCSH: Democracy – Jordan. | Authoritarianism – Jordan. | Jordan –
Politics and government – 1999– | Democracy – Government policy – European
Union countries. | Democracy – Government policy – United States. |
European Union countries – Foreign relations – Jordan. | Jordan – Foreign
relations – European Union countries. | United States – Foreign relations –
Jordan. | Jordan – Foreign relations – United States.
Classification: LCC JQ1833.A91 S38 2019 | DDC 320.95695–dc23
LC record available at https://lccn.loc.gov/2019019431

ISBN 978-1-108-49338-3 Hardback

For Delphine and Félix

Contents

Figures

Figure 1.1 Map of Jordan.
© Peter Palm, Berlin.

Preface: In Jordan 'Reform Is Not a Strange Word'

Commissioning external reports that they then deliberately ignore, holding a political party fair at which participating youth end up celebrating the king, organising a 'score for democracy' football cup which is won by the Ministry for Political Development, holding graduation ceremonies at which participating students celebrate 'their commitment to democracy', mobilising voters for an utterly toothless parliament, teaching students proposal-writing skills so they can secure funds from the regime's own 'democracy promotion' initiative, assisting in the privatisation of public goods and linking the resulting socio-economic problems to the deficient 'nature of Jordanians', establishing a military training centre in which affluent customers learn how to best use a shotgun and hide in a fake refugee camp: the world of 'democracy promotion' is both full of contradictions and highly diverse, with activities spanning from institutional engineering, election observation and civil society support to the promotion of certain economic and security frameworks. While the existing body of literature on 'democracy promotion' is indeed vast, an in-depth study of what 'democracy promoters' *actually do* when they promote democracy is still lacking. Instead of discussing the intentions of 'democracy promoters', their theoretical assumptions and supposedly universally valid models of democratisation, this book will first and foremost discuss what US and European 'democracy promoters' *actually do* when they promote democracy.

As 'democracy promotion' is arguably one of the defining features of global liberalism, this book will provide a critical discussion of the liberal project at large and of the seeming moral hierarchies between interveners and those intervened upon that inform the latter. The case of Jordan constitutes an extremely interesting example for a deconstruction of such liberal worldviews. Jordan is thus one of the main recipients worldwide of US and European foreign assistance in general and of 'democracy promotion' programmes in particular.[1] In 2018, only Israel and Egypt were projected to receive more US foreign aid than Jordan, a country with a population of only about 10 million people: $40 million out of the envisaged total of $1 billion in US assistance were assigned to programmes related to democracy, human rights and governance, which makes the 'democracy promotion' portfolio of the United States Agency for International Development (USAID) in Jordan one of the biggest worldwide, in absolute terms but especially relative to population figures.[2] On the European side, the EU's bilateral assistance to Jordan was scheduled to be around €90 million per year in 2014–2017, with a budget of approximately €22.5 million dedicated to activities aimed at reinforcing political reform and promoting democracy.[3] On top of this comes additional assistance from individual EU member states.

For a number of reasons, a study of US and European 'democracy promotion' programmes in the country is also both relevant and insightful beyond merely questions concerning 'democracy promotion' and Jordanian politics. In particular, it is the extent to which the teleological and deeply functionalist narrative of US and European 'democracy promoters' – according to which processes of democratisation, economic liberalisation, economic prosperity, a pro-Western foreign policy and stability are all mutually reinforcing – is also embraced by the Jordanian regime itself that makes Jordan such an interesting and fascinating case study. In this regard, select Western officials have described the country as, for instance, a 'model for the region in democracy, human rights and economic reforms on the one hand, and political development and the socio-economic transformation on the other',[4] or have more concisely simply stated that 'Jordan is on the right track'.[5]

Also, the case of Jordan (see Figure 1.1) provides a great example of a regime that – unlike Syria under Assad, Libya under Gaddafi, Iraq under Saddam and Egypt under Nasser – does not attempt to develop any

---

[1] See, among others, Khakee, A. et al., 'A long-lasting controversy: Western democracy promotion in Jordan', Mediterranean Academy of Diplomatic Studies and Al Urdun Al Jadid Research Center (UJRC), Malta and Amman, 2009, p. 5.

[2] US Government, Map of Foreign Assistance Worldwide, available at: www .foreignassistance.gov/explore.

[3] The figures are based on my own calculations related to the information provided in European External Action Service (EEAS) and European Commission (EC), *Programming of the European Neighbourhood Instrument (ENI) – 2014–2020 – Single Support Framework for EU Support to Jordan (2014–2017)*, https://ec.europa.eu/neighbour hood-enlargement/sites/near/files/single_support_framework_2014-2020.pdf, p. 9.

[4] US Ambassador in Amman, Edward Gnehm, paraphrased in: 'Jordan a model for the region – US ambassador', *Jordan Times*, 7 January 2004.

[5] EU Ambassador to Jordan, Patrick Renault, quoted in: Hazaimeh, H., 'Jordan makes tangible progress in reports – EU', *Jordan Times*, 13 May 2010.

distinct ideology, but instead openly embraces liberal democracy and free markets as political goals. In its near absence of counter-hegemonic ideological discourses, Jordanian politics can be seen as exemplary for the supposed gradual universalisation of liberal democratic forms of governance. As such, this book provides valuable insight to scholars with an interest in what precisely greater US and European policy presence in the Global South means. A study of US and European 'democracy promotion' in Jordan is also likely to tell us more about whether liberal democracy can indeed be promoted, and is likely to allow for a better understanding of power, rule, the politics of intervention and the creation of moral authority in the Middle East in general. Of central importance for the assumed exemplary role of Jordan in the region and for the alleged positive effects of external 'democracy promotion' interventions is the narrative of Jordan as a gradually reforming, liberalising and modernising state, as one where the king is 'ahead of the streets' (as a prominent member of the Jordanian regime put it in late 2013 at a non-public meeting) or as one where the liberal democratic dream indeed appears to be realisable.

Much research on Jordan reproduces deeply problematic notions of Jordanian society as fundamentally traditional and/or only gradually modernising. Such analyses tend to have a very clear idea of who acts upon whom, of the people, social practices and forms of behaviour in Jordan that are to be considered 'modern' as opposed to 'traditional', and of the developmental path on which Jordan supposedly finds itself. The troublesome tradition-modernity binary inherent to such approaches comes in different disguises, some of which I will briefly outline here.

Perhaps the most prominent theme in research on the Jordanian state is its artificiality.[6] Scholars regularly invoke 'the famous stroke of Churchill's pen'[7] that drew the country's borders; the fact that Transjordan's first designated ruler, Abdullah, came from the *ḥijāz* in present-day Saudi-Arabia; and the relative unattractiveness and remoteness of a territory that Wilson dismissively called a 'patch of desert'.[8] While these points and descriptions are indeed either true or at least somewhat understandable, the problem lies in the way in which they are often overemphasised. This has occurred to such an extent that a

---

[6] See for instance Krämer, G., 'Good counsel to the king: the Islamist opposition in Saudi Arabia, Jordan, and Morocco', in: Kostiner, J. (ed.), *Middle East Monarchies: The Challenge of Modernity* (Boulder: Lynne Rienner, 2000), pp. 257–288.

[7] Shlaim, A., *Lion of Jordan: The Life of King Hussein in War and Peace* (London: Allen Lane, 2007), p. 19.

[8] Wilson, M.C., *King Abdullah, Britain and the Making of Jordan* (New York: Cambridge University Press, 1987), p. 102.

considerable amount of research on Jordan appears to be more about the British colonial rulers and the Hashemite ruling family than actually about Jordanians themselves.[9]

As demonstrated by Tell, such an account of Jordanian history and politics fails to adequately explain the origins and, as such, also the resilience of monarchy in Jordan.[10] While Abdullah and the British indeed quite literally had to produce Jordanian national identity, this process also involved the construction of local Bedouins 'as the carriers of Jordan's true and authentic culture and traditions'.[11] Given that 'the tribe and the nation-state [thereby became] mutually dependent on each other',[12] as Massad remarks, it is clear that a simplistic understanding of Jordanian tribes – as, for instance, inherently traditional – fails to do justice to a much more complex reality.

Likewise, while Israeli claims about Jordan as Palestinians' 'alternative homeland' are a topic of heated debate in Jordanian politics,[13] an understanding of the latter as fundamentally shaped by a clear separation between East Bank Jordanians as passive supporters of the regime and West Bank Jordanians as agents of transformation is overly simplistic and misleading.[14] As a result of discrimination against Palestinian-Jordanians, in particular following the Jordanian civil war in 1970–1971, a number of scholars have noted a 'public sector/private sector divide that closely followed intercommunal lines'.[15]

But while public employment has indeed become a matter of patronage primarily distributed to East Bank Jordanians,[16] the social reality is marked by much more diverse, overlapping and changing forms of identification and mobilisation. Urban-rural tensions, rapidly growing income disparities and widespread feelings of estrangement with clientelist

---

[9] For similar critiques see Robins, P., *A History of Jordan* (Cambridge: Cambridge University Press, 2004), p. 4, and Tell, T.M., *The Social and Economic Origins of Monarchy in Jordan* (New York: Palgrave Macmillan, 2013), pp. 3 and 22.

[10] See Tell, *The Social and Economic Origins of Monarchy in Jordan*.

[11] Massad, J.A., *Colonial Effects: The Making of National Identity in Jordan* (New York: Columbia University Press, 2001), p. 71.

[12] Massad, *Colonial Effects*, p. 74.

[13] In 2019, the United Nations Relief and Works Agency (UNRWA) estimated the number of registered Palestinian refugees in Jordan at more than 2 million. See UNRWA, *Where We Work*, available at: www.unrwa.org/where-we-work/jordan. Most Palestinian refugees in Jordan have Jordanian citizenship.

[14] See for instance Tell, who strongly criticises such accounts. Tell, *The Social and Economic Origins of Monarchy in Jordan*, p. 22.

[15] Brand, L.A., 'Palestinians and Jordanians: a crisis of identity', *Journal of Palestine Studies*, Vol. 24, No. 4, Summer 1995, p. 53. See also Robins, A History of Jordan, p. 3.

[16] By 1986, half of the entire Jordanian labour force was working for the state. Brynen, R., 'Economic crisis and post-rentier democratization in the Arab world: the case of Jordan', *Canadian Journal of Political Science*, Vol. 25, No. 1, March 1992, p. 81.

politics among Jordanian youth at large are thus at least as important as the widely referenced East Banker-West Banker divide.[17]

As Jordan's external debt rapidly increased between 1980 and 1987, the country was forced to ask the International Monetary Fund (IMF) for debt rescheduling agreements and an associated economic stabilisation programme. This included the removal of a number of subsidies, which quickly led to heavy rioting and demonstrations. The 'Hashemite Compact' – the exchange of loyalty for economic security – suddenly appeared to be caught in a process of gradual disintegration.[18] Fully aware of the volatile situation, King Hussein tried to appease widespread feelings of disaffection by initiating a process of political liberalisation. It is at this particular point in Jordan's history that many contemporary descriptions of Jordanian politics by both the Jordanian regime and Western researchers and officials set in,[19] and the foundations for the popular narrative of an exceptional Jordanian reform-mindedness were laid. While most recent research on Jordanian politics is decidedly critical of such an understanding,[20] variations of the Jordanian reform narrative continue to inform analyses of contemporary Jordanian politics.

For instance, while Ryan provides a very detailed account of Jordanian politics in *Jordan and the Arab Uprisings* and pointedly remarks that

---

[17] For a discussion of the deep tensions in Jordan over national identity see Schwedler, J., 'Cop rock: protest, identity, and dancing riot police in Jordan', *Social Movement Studies*, Vol. 4, No. 2, September 2005, pp. 155–175. See also Ryan, C.R., *Jordan and the Arab Uprisings: Regime Survival and Politics beyond the State* (New York: Columbia University Press, 2018), chapter V, and Lynch, M., *State Interests and Public Spheres: The International Politics of Jordan's Identity* (New York: Columbia University Press, 1999).

[18] The term 'Hashemite Compact' is also used by Tell in *The Social and Economic Origins of Monarchy in Jordan*, pp. 12–13.

[19] See for instance Knowles, W., *Jordan since 1989: A Study in Political Economy* (London: I. B. Tauris, 2005), p. 210.

[20] See for instance Schwedler, 'The political geography of protest in neoliberal Jordan', *Middle East Critique*, Vol. 21, No. 3, 2012, pp. 259–270; Yom, S. and Al-Khatib, W., 'The politics of youth policymaking in Jordan', in: *POMEPS Studies, No. 31, Social Policy in the Middle East and North Africa* (Washington, D, October 2018), pp. 41–45, available at: https://pomeps.org/2018/08/02/the-politics-of-youth-policymaking-in-jordan/; Valbjørn, M., 'The 2013 parliamentary elections in Jordan: three stories and some general lessons', *Mediterranean Politics*, Vol. 18, No. 2, 2013, pp. 311–317; Albrecht, H., and Schlumberger, O., '"Waiting for Godot": regime change without democratization in the Middle East', *International Political Science Review*, Vol. 25, No. 4, October 2004, pp. 371–392; Bank, A. and Sunik, A., 'Parliamentary elections in Jordan, January 2013', *Electoral Studies*, Vol. 34, 2014, pp. 376–379; Valbjørn, M. and Bank, A., 'Examining the "post" in post-democratization: the future of Middle Eastern political rule through lenses of the past', *Middle East Critique*, Vol. 19, No. 3, 2010, pp. 183–200; and Martínez, J.C., 'Jordan's self-fulfilling prophecy: the production of feeble political parties and the perceived perils of democracy', *British Journal of Middle Eastern Studies*, Vol. 44, No. 3, 2017, pp. 356–372.

'regimes change in order to stay the same',[21] in more policy-oriented publications he speaks of political liberalisation in Jordan as an 'unfinished journey'[22] that began in 1989 and supposedly continues into the present. Despite Ryan's apt assessment that the word 'reform' may by now have lost most of its meaning for many Jordanians,[23] his use of such terminology importantly gives the rather teleological impression that Jordan is indeed caught in an ongoing process, or in what he has elsewhere called a 'continuing transition'.[24] Knowles even prematurely described 1989 as the start of a genuine process of democratisation.[25] While King Hussein did announce the end of martial law, order the first parliamentary elections since 1967 and end the ban on political parties that had been effective since 1957, this did certainly not amount to the start of a genuine democratic transition.[26]

Just as this political opening significantly boosted King Hussein's popularity, so did his opposition to the US-led military intervention in Kuwait and Iraq in 1991. Eager to regain the trust of the US after the Gulf war and to once again benefit from US foreign aid payments, King Hussein quickly shifted his foreign policy alignment and began to strongly support the US-sponsored Arab-Israeli peace process. Domestically, this strengthened the Muslim Brotherhood, which staunchly opposed the king's policy together with a number of other political parties. Above all else, the conclusion of peace with Israel, which had domestically only been made possible by a slide back into repression,[27] was part of a major foreign policy reorientation that made the US and Israel the new external guarantors of the Hashemite regime's survival.[28]

When Jordan implemented the second IMF economic adjustment programme in 1996 and again reduced public subsidies for basic foodstuffs, Jordanians once more responded with widespread riots. Unlike in 1989, however, the regime now adopted a policy of forceful repression and political de-liberalisation, thereby showing that the alleged democratic process initiated in 1989 was nothing but part of a constant

[21] Ryan, *Jordan and the Arab Uprisings*, p. 8.
[22] Ryan, C.R., 'Jordan's unfinished journey: parliamentary elections and the state of reform', *Project on Middle East Democracy (POMED)*, Policy Brief, March 2013.
[23] Ryan, *Jordan and the Arab Uprisings*, p. 145.
[24] Ryan, C.R., *Jordan in Transition: From Hussein to Abdullah* (London: Lynne Rienner Publishers, 2002), chapter 6.
[25] Knowles, *Jordan since 1989*, p. 210.
[26] Lust-Okar, E.M., 'The decline of Jordanian political parties: myth or reality?', *International Journal of Middle East Studies*, Vol. 33, No. 4, 2001, pp. 545–569.
[27] Bouillon, M., 'Walking the tightrope: Jordanian foreign policy from the Gulf crisis to the peace process and beyond', in: Joffé, G. (ed.), *Jordan in Transition: 1990–2000* (London: Hurst & Co., 2002), p. 13.
[28] Shlaim, *Lion of Jordan*, p. 554.

'oscillation between political liberalization and deliberalization'[29] under the larger goal of authoritarian stability and regime maintenance. In addition to the economic distress that a growing number of Jordanians had to withstand, the initial promises of a 'warm peace' and its alleged positive effects on Jordanian state and society were more and more openly counteracted by an increasingly aggressive Israeli foreign policy. As the Jordanian anti-normalisation movement gained greater popularity, King Hussein adopted a more and more authoritarian stance against his domestic critics.

King Abdullah II's succession to the throne in 1999 marked another break in Jordanian politics, as he – unlike his father – put a much stronger emphasis on economic liberalisation and privatisation, and wholeheartedly endorsed a neoliberal discourse of reform and modernity. The new king had undertaken most of his education in the US and England, briefly served in the British Army and, up until 1999, was probably only known to a wider Western audience due to his supporting role in a *Star Trek* episode. His (at least initially) less-than-perfect command of Standard Arabic, his Western education and his marriage to Queen Rania, who is of Palestinian origin, prompted some scepticism and made his interaction with East Bank Jordanian tribal leaders in particular much less cordial than that enjoyed by his late father. At the same time, however, Abdullah's prior position as Commander of the Jordanian Special Forces ensured the strong backing of the military. His enthusiasm for rapid economic liberalisation was quickly manifested in Jordan's accession to the World Trade Organization (WTO) in 1999 and in the signing of free trade agreements with the USA in 2000, and the EU in 2001, thereby further consolidating the image of Jordan as a 'forward-looking nation',[30] as remarked in a USAID document.[31]

Following the suspension of parliament in 2001, King Abdullah II governed until 2003 through more than one hundred 'temporary' laws, which – once parliament was reinstated – were retroactively ratified in their totality, thereby providing a good illustration of the role of the Jordanian parliament. Rather than a strong and independent legislative body, the latter plays an instrumental role as safety valve, as it helps the regime to 'shift responsibility for citizens' standard of living ... away from the Palace, thereby insulating the Palace from popular discontent with

---

[29] Albrecht and Schlumberger, 'Waiting for Godot', p. 385.

[30] USAID, *Strategic Statement Jordan 2007–2011*, p. 29, available at: http://pdf.usaid.gov/pdf_docs/Pdacn487.pdf.

[31] See also Bank, André and Schlumberger, Oliver, 'Jordan: between regime survival and economic reform', in: Perthes, V. (ed.), *Arab Elites: Negotiating the Politics of Change* (Boulder: Lynne Rienner, 2004), pp. 35–60.

neo-liberal economic reforms'.[32] The primary role of the government and its agencies is thus to offer a seemingly democratic and representative façade, rather than to function as a truly sovereign executive. Since King Abdullah II's accession to the throne, Jordanian governments last around nineteen months on average before they are dissolved by royal decree. Real power, in terms of appointing positions, defining strategic plans and controlling policymaking, lies primarily with the Royal Court and the influential General Intelligence Directorate (GID).[33] One EU diplomat based in Amman candidly remarked in this regard that 2.5 power centres exist in the country: the GID, the Royal Court and only then, and to a much lesser extent, the government. While she corrected herself after a moment and stated that perhaps it is rather 2¼, in a separate interview a Western 'democracy promoter' insisted on adding the US Embassy as most powerful actor, even before the GID and the Royal Court.[34]

The many top-down reform campaigns that King Abdullah II initiated in addition to his efforts at economic liberalisation not only failed to address the just-mentioned powerful role of the military, which effectively operates outside of any civilian control, and to curtail the far-reaching prerogatives of the king, but were not followed up by meaningful efforts to actually implement the lofty goals that had been agreed upon. The importance of the 'Jordan First' campaign in 2002, the 'National Agenda' in 2006 and the 'We are all Jordan' initiative in 2006 thus primarily lies in the construction of an impression of reform and in the reinforcement of Jordanian national identity. The importance of this façade of reform can scarcely be overemphasised, as it is what allows the regime to postpone confronting otherwise irreconcilable demands for equal representation and democracy, on the one hand, and for protection of Jordanian national identity *vis-à-vis* the perceived threat of a Palestinian 'takeover' on the other. Once the image of Jordan as 'reforming', 'liberalising' and/or 'democratising' is established, the deeply authoritarian nature of political power structures in the country can easily be downplayed and the scene is set for US and European 'democracy promoters' to further 'modernise' and 'reform' the country and support an allegedly already ongoing process.

The 'National Agenda' is particularly insightful in this regard. A royally appointed steering committee developed it in 2005 as a master plan for

---

[32] Greenwood, S., 'Jordan's "new bargain": the political economy of regime security', *Middle East Journal*, Vol. 57, No. 2, Spring 2003, p. 257.

[33] Moore, P., 'A political-economy history of Jordan's intelligence directorate', unpublished article, 2018, p. 1.

[34] Interviews with Isabella, an EU diplomat based in Jordan, Amman, 13 March 2013, and Paul, a 'democracy promoter' working in Jordan, Amman, 15 January 2013.

reform in Jordan. Attempting to provide guidelines for Jordan's development up until 2016, it draws an image of a country that is on a 'trajectory path'[35] paved with 'historic milestone[s]'[36] and 'transformation phases'.[37] Despite clearly formulated objectives of political reform, by the time of writing in 2018, neither the envisaged establishment of parties as 'one of the cornerstones in the political development process' nor '[t]he election of a politically representative parliament'[38] have been realised. Finally, the initiative, which included the assurance that it is 'by no means the end of the road, but the beginning of increased reforms',[39] much more likely signifies precisely that: the absence of real reform hidden behind a façade of constant readiness for it. In one important aspect, however, the 'National Agenda' achieved its objective, as both the US and the EU accepted it as starting point for their own efforts at 'democracy promotion', thereby both seemingly validating and subscribing to the regime's questionable reform narrative.[40]

More than ten years into King Abdullah II's rule, the conventional power bases of the regime began to criticise the latter on a thus far unprecedented scale. In May 2010 the powerful National Committee of Military Veterans publicly accused the regime of trying to solve the Palestinian question at the expense of East Bank Jordanians, and in February 2011 a number of tribal figures went as far as to directly criticise the royal family itself – in particular Queen Rania – for corruption and nepotism.[41] In light of the popular uprisings in Tunisia and Egypt, the size of protests in Jordan quickly grew when a diverse group of Islamists, leftists and unionists began protesting against price hikes, corruption and unemployment, and demanded the resignation of Prime Minister Samir Rifaʾi.

---

[35] National Agenda Steering Committee, *National Agenda: The Jordan We Strive for 2006–2015* (Amman: National Agenda Steering Committee, 2005), p. 4, available at: www.nationalagenda.jo/Portals/0/EnglishBooklet.pdf.

[36] National Agenda Steering Committee, *National Agenda*, p. 3.

[37] National Agenda Steering Committee, *National Agenda*, pp. 7–8.

[38] National Agenda Steering Committee, *National Agenda*, p. 14.

[39] National Agenda Steering Committee, *National Agenda*, p. 10.

[40] For the EU see ENPI, *Strategy Paper 2007–2013 & National Indicative Programme 2007–2010 – Jordan*, p. 13, available at: https://ec.europa.eu/europeaid/sites/devco/files/csp-nip-jordan-2007-2013_en.pdf. For the US see USAID, *Strategic Statement Jordan 2007–2011*, p. 1.

[41] National Committee of Military Veterans, 'A message from the National Committee for Retired Army Personnel', published in National Committee of Retired Army Personnel, 'Statement on defending state, identity against Israel's 'alternative homeland' – retired army', *Ammonnews*, 5 March 2010; Habib, R., 'Jordan tribes break taboo by targeting queen', *Ma'an News Agency*, 9 February 2011, available at: www.maannews.com/Content.aspx?id=358567.

Perhaps the most critical phenomenon of the protests was the rise of the so-called Ḥirāk (Arabic for 'movement') – a coalition of various East Bank tribal youth activist groups – which vigorously demanded restrictions on the king's absolutist powers. Unlike many other protestors, the Ḥirāk 'shied away from the anti-Palestinian xenophobia that flavoured the complaints of tribal shaykhs and other East Bank conservatives' and did not simply 'aim to extract economic payoffs from the palace',[42] as shown by Yom. Highlighting both the precarious situation of Palestinian-Jordanian citizens, as well as the importance of East Bank Jordanian identity discourses in Jordanian politics, the Ḥirāk 'deliberately chose to represent themselves as being purely East Banker'[43] – despite Palestinian-Jordanian participation – in order to thereby avoid accusations of disloyalty.[44]

Under increasing popular pressure, the king quickly replaced Samir Rifa'i and established a National Dialogue Committee (NDC) in March 2011 and a royal committee to review the constitution in April 2011, based on whose recommendations a number of constitutional amendments were implemented. The most important of these included the establishment of a Constitutional Court and an Independent Election Commission (IEC), as well as the adoption of a new political party and electoral law. Despite limiting the king's ability to postpone elections indefinitely, his far-reaching prerogatives were not curtailed and public demands for a constitutional monarchy remained unanswered.

In November 2012 the protests reached another climax when Prime Minister Abdullah Ensour – the fifth prime minister since the beginning of the protests in 2011 – announced the implementation of further IMF-demanded fuel and gas price hikes. The ensuing protests were notable for being the first during which a significant number of protestors not only demanded the reform, but also the fall, of the regime. Despite violent clashes throughout the country and the very limited nature of the reforms implemented thus far, both the US and the EU repeatedly voiced their support for what is regularly described as 'King Abdullah II's roadmap for reform'.[45] In January 2013 Jordan held – under the new electoral law and organised by the newly established IEC – its first parliamentary elections since the beginning of the Arab uprisings. While described by King

[42] Yom, S.L., 'Tribal politics in contemporary Jordan: the case of the hirak movement', *The Middle East Journal*, Vol. 68, No. 2, Spring 2014, pp. 229–230.

[43] Karmel, E.J., 'How revolutionary was Jordan's Hirak? what the incognito participation of Palestinian-Jordanians in Hirak tells us about the movements', *Identity Center*, Amman, June 2014, p. 5, available at: http://identity-center.org/sites/default/files/How%20Revolutionary%20Was%20Jordan%27s%20Hirak__0.pdf.

[44] For a detailed analysis of Ḥirāk see Ryan, *Jordan and the Arab Uprisings*, chapter IV.

[45] Toner, M.C. (Deputy Spokesperson, US DoS), 'Daily Press Briefing', Washington, DC, 15 November 2012.

Abdullah II as a 'move from the Jordanian Spring to the Jordanian Summer, a season of work and harvest',[46] gerrymandering and the structurally conditioned functioning of parliament as a service provider rather than an independent legislative power ensured that the elections once again led to a staunchly pro-regime parliament, with the king simply reappointing Ensour as prime minister.

It is against this backdrop that a high-ranking member of the Jordanian regime repeated the mantra of the exceptional Jordanian 'reform-mindedness' in front of Western researchers and policymakers at a non-public meeting in late 2013. Responding to a question about political reform in Jordan, he thus remarked in perhaps the most characteristic way possible that in Jordan, 'the word *reform* is not a strange word'. In light of the oscillation between political liberalisation and de-liberalisation that has been a characteristic of the Jordanian polity for almost thirty years, however, the primary function of this exceptional Jordanian familiarity with 'reform' appears to be that of protecting the stability of the authoritarian regime. In the words of Albrecht and Schlumberger, it is thus perhaps most pertinent to describe democratisation in Jordan by comparing it to Samuel Beckett's *Waiting for Godot*, where the main character just never shows up.[47]

In order to maintain the image of Jordan as a 'model for the region in democracy, human rights and economic reforms', and to protect the notion of Western liberal democracy as both morally superior and universally applicable, it is of fundamental importance to accept the image of an exceptional Jordanian reform-mindedness that relentlessly brings the country closer to the desired ideal. It is in this context that both USAID's description of Jordan as 'a principal voice for moderation, peace and reform in the Middle East … [and] as an oasis of stability and a model for progress in the region'[48] needs to be seen, as well as the EU's statement that 'Jordan's key strategic importance … lies in its commitment to reforms, openness to political development … and willingness to cooperate with the EU in promoting reform in the region'.[49]

The assumption that the Jordanian regime is both willing to reform and that Jordanian reform is indeed part of a wider process of gradual democratic transition is the direct precondition for external efforts at

---

[46] King Abdullah II, 'To the Jordanian people RE: elections' success', Royal Hashemite Court, Amman, letter translated from Arabic, 29 January 2013, available at: https://kingabdullah.jo/en/letters/letter-jordanian-people-elections.

[47] Albrecht and Schlumberger, 'Waiting for Godot'.

[48] USAID, *Strategic Statement Jordan 2007–2011*, p. 1.

[49] ENPI, *Strategy Paper 2007–2013 & National Indicative Programme 2007–2010 – Jordan*, p. 16.

'democracy promotion'. Drawing on the work of Heydemann, however, I argue that political reform in Jordan constitutes part of a wider strategy aimed at the maintenance and/or upgrading of the authoritarian regime.[50] As a consequence, I suggest that one also must question whether external efforts at 'democracy promotion' in the country, too, are perhaps only reconfiguring Jordanian authoritarianism, rather than challenging it.

Many of the Jordanian youth, politicians, officials and activists whom I interviewed in the course of my research were fundamentally sceptical of 'democracy promotion' programmes in the country and at times also doubted the relevance of an entire book focusing on them. One Jordanian economist only remarked that 'everybody realises that money and ... weapons are more important'.[51] But some 'democracy promoters' also questioned my choice of topic. The president of a well-known US 'democracy promotion' firm, for instance, found Jordan to be 'an unusual example in all kinds of ways'[52] for a book on 'democracy promotion'.

In light of the history of political (non-)reform in Jordan set out above, a study of Western 'democracy promotion' in the country amounts not only to questioning the regime's dubious reform narrative, but also to questioning a US and European politics of intervention that champions the Jordanian regime as an important 'anchor of stability' even as it continuously claims the moral high ground with assertions that it is helping to democratise it. The political sensitivity of the project of 'democracy promotion' in Jordan can scarcely be overstated.

Given that 'democracy promotion' interventions never occur in a vacuum, but always in a very specific political context, an analysis of the interaction of US and European 'democracy promoters' with the political context of Jordan is likely to tell us more about the alleged moral superiority and universal applicability of Western liberal conceptions of democracy. As such, the present book will also explore the (re)production of Western liberal democratic self-understandings and seeming moral hierarchies that result from the ongoing binary juxtaposition of external interveners, who supposedly know what democracy means and how it can be implemented, versus intervened-upon 'locals', who are regularly only defined in contrast to the former.

---

[50] Heydemann, S., 'Upgrading authoritarianism in the Arab world', The Saban Center for Middle East Policy at the Brookings Institution Analysis Paper Number 13, October 2007, available at: www.brookings.edu/wp-content/uploads/2016/06/10arabworld.pdf.

[51] Interview with Sami, Jordanian economist, Amman, 13 September 2012.

[52] Interview with Jacob, President of a US 'democracy promotion' firm, Washington, DC, 22 May 2013.

Further, while Jordan may indeed be an 'unusual' case – in so far as, for instance, the repercussions of the Israeli-Palestinian conflict and the geopolitical importance of the country to 'the West' are concerned – I argue that this unusualness only has the effect of better illuminating how liberal world views interact with structures that do not neatly fit the desired liberal democratic ideal. The fundamental tension that exists between highly idealised notions of liberal democracy on the one hand and the ways in which these actually materialise on the other is a key feature of the liberal project itself and can be observed in different manifestations all over the world. The specificity and/or unusualness of the Jordanian political context does thus – contrary to what some political scientists may claim – very much lend this exploration of efforts at 'democracy promotion' in Jordan to generalisation beyond that country, as it is ultimately a mere reminder of the fact that the imagined liberal democratic ideal does simply not exist.

Given that Jordan is one of the key recipients of US and European 'democracy promotion' assistance worldwide, scholars interested in what greater US and European policy presence in other regions of the Global South is likely to entail will also benefit from this book. The concrete interventions that international 'democracy promoters' implement are thus frequently not at all specific to the case of Jordan, but part of a universally applied and free-floating body of knowledge that operates irrespective of specific contexts, and which the very same people have often previously already applied in numerous other countries around the world.[53] Against this backdrop, I suggest that US and European 'democracy promotion' in Jordan needs to be understood as part of a much wider phenomenon of Western liberal attempts to export a supposedly universal and democratic model of governance, and to (re)construct conceptions of moral hierarchies.

The main research question that this book investigates concerns what US and European 'democracy promoters' in Jordan *actually do* when they promote democracy. I particularly focus on the unforeseen and contradictory consequences of US and European 'democracy promotion' in Jordan, on its self-perpetuating tendencies and on the usefulness of 'democracy promotion' as a rationale for a politics of control and intervention. On a more general level, this book is about the construction, the interaction and the effects of moral authority and power in the Middle East. Finally, just as 'money and weapons' facilitate external control over

---

[53] My reasoning here is informed by Ferguson, J., *The Anti-Politics Machine: 'Development,' Depoliticization, and Bureaucratic Power in Lesotho* (Minneapolis: University of Minnesota Press, 1994), pp. 257–259.

the Jordanian state and society, I suggest that so too do US and European attempts at 'democracy promotion'.[54] As I attempt to demonstrate, they smooth and ease the effects of 'money and weapons' and make a politics of control and intervention all the more effective, by reinforcing it with conceptions of moral superiority.

---

[54] An in-depth exploration of this argument – although only with examples of countries outside the Arab world – is provided by William Robinson in *Promoting Polyarchy: Globalization, US Intervention, and Hegemony* (Cambridge: Cambridge University Press, 1996).

Acknowledgements

In the past eight years of researching, writing, travelling and revising I had the fortune to meet a number of extremely generous and supportive people, without whom I would not have been able to complete this book.

First of all, I want to thank my PhD supervisors for their continuous support, and for having put me in a situation in which I often did not grasp the difficulties experienced by some other PhD students. I am deeply grateful to Charles Tripp for his confidence in me, his constructive criticism and his impressive ability to be both an academic source of inspiration and to always remain approachable and apply just the right mix of firm intervention and good-humoured support. I cannot emphasise enough how valuable his regular feedback was. I am also deeply indebted to my second supervisor, Laleh Khalili, who read much more of my thesis than most second supervisors, and whose enthusiasm has been a continuous source of inspiration. I am also very grateful to Matthew Nelson, for his detailed and helpful feedback on an earlier version of parts of Chapter 6. At SOAS, I benefited hugely from the discussions and workshops with fellow PhD students in the Politics Department, and would especially like to thank Jamil Mouawad, Sanaa Alimia, James Sunday and Hannes Baumann for their advice and support.

Since I started revising my PhD with the goal of turning it into this book, I have benefited greatly from the help and support of Nicola Pratt and Jamie Allinson, who gave me very valuable comments and helped me further clarify my research question. Anna Leander, Ziad Abu-Rish, Patrick Neveling, André Bank and Marc Lynch also offered helpful feedback on earlier versions of different chapters. Pete Moore and Christopher Parker commented on the entire manuscript and provided invaluable feedback and support. I am also grateful to Ursula Schröder and the participants at the 2016 workshop on 'Decentering International Interventions' in Berlin, to Ahmed Morsy and all the participants at the 2016 APSA-MENA workshop in Beirut, as well as to Philippe Aldrin and the participants at the 2018 'Faire de la politique extérieure sans en avoir l'air' workshop in Aix-en-Provence.

I would like to thank Andreas Mehler for all his support and confidence in me. The University of Freiburg and the Arnold Bergstraesser Institute (ABI) have provided me with an invaluable and inspiring institutional home over the past few years and I am deeply grateful to all my colleagues for their help and constructive criticism. I want to thank Lewis Turner, Christian von Lübke, Gregor Dobler and Clemens Jürgenmeyer for their feedback on earlier versions of parts of this book, as well as Benedikt Kamski for boosting my morale at regular table tennis matches. Finally, I very much enjoyed and benefited from the lively discussions with the participants at my 'US and European interventions in the name of democracy' seminars.

I am particularly grateful to the scholars who inspired me to pursue an academic path, and who have supported me since the beginning of my studies at the Oriental Institute at the University of Leipzig, particularly Eckehard Schulz, Monem Jumaili and Jörg Gertel. It was Stefanie Brinkmann's enthusiasm that confirmed my choice of studies.

During my field research in Jordan I benefited greatly from discussions with and the support of Katharina Lenner, Sylvie Janssens, Pascal Debruyne, Malika Bouziane, Ayoub Namour, Dana Dodeen, Hiba Mohammed and Yves Mirman. I am thankful also to Mylène Tisserant for her help with certain aspects of my research. My first weeks in Jordan, and my follow-up research trip, were made much easier by the great hospitality of Barbara Porter and her team at the American Center for Oriental Research (ACOR), and of Carol Palmer and her team at the Council for British Research in the Levant (CBRL). The hospitality and warmth of Alice and Abu Hatem – not to forget the occasional dish of wonderful Jordanian *manṣaf* – also helped me through difficult times and made the Jordanian winter much more bearable.

Special thanks go to Riad Al-Khoury, who has been a great source of support. I also want to express my gratitude to Khalid Kalaldeh. The regular meetings with Stevens Tucker were extremely helpful and while we might not always agree on 'democracy promotion', I learned a lot from our conversations and very much value all the support. A number of other contacts were also extremely helpful and generous with their time and resources, but can unfortunately not be named here.

I want to thank all my interviewees for having taken the time to meet me, and for having been willing to at times also share sensitive information. I am deeply grateful for their patience in explaining to me their work, Jordanian politics and various matters related to 'democracy promotion'. Ultimately, it is thanks to them that I was able to collect the information upon which this book is based. All these contributions notwithstanding, all remaining errors are of course mine alone.

I would like to thank the Friedrich Ebert Foundation (FES) and the German Academic Exchange Service (DAAD) for awarding me doctoral scholarships that together covered the entire period of my research. Without this generous financial support, I would without doubt have been unable to write the thesis on which this book is based. My research trip to Washington, DC was made possible through a Santander Mobility Award, for which I am also deeply grateful. Finally, I want to thank Cambridge University Press and in particular Maria Marsh, Natasha Whelan and Atifa Jiwa for their patience and help in getting this book published.

Most importantly, I would like to thank my parents, Uta and Martin Schütze, for their financial and emotional support, as well as my brothers, Sebastian and Florian, for a great time together in Jordan. Finally, I want to thank the wonderful Delphine Weil-Accardo for her love and support, as well as our son Félix for helping me to put 'democracy promotion' into perspective.

Note on Transliteration

Throughout the book I rely on the American Library Association – Library of Congress (ALA-LC) guidelines for romanisation of Arabic. To facilitate readability, however, I use the most common English spelling for personal and well-known place names (for example, Amman and King Abdullah II).

Abbreviations and Acronyms

ACC	Anti-Corruption Commission
ACED	Aqaba Community and Economic Development programme
ACILS	American Center for International Labor Solidarity
ACPD	Amman Center for Peace and Development
ACT	Aqaba Container Terminal
ADC	Aqaba Development Corporation
AED	Academy for Educational Development
AICI	American International Contractors Inc.
AIIE	Aqaba International Industrial Estate
ARA	Aqaba Regional Authority
ARD	Associates in Rural Development
ASEZ	Aqaba Special Economic Zone
ASEZA	Aqaba Special Economic Zone Authority
ATASP	Aqaba Technical Assistance Support Project
AZEM	Aqaba Zone Economic Mobilization programme
CEPPS	Consortium for Elections and Political Processes
CIPE	Center for International Private Enterprise
CPF	Crown Prince Foundation
CRS	Congressional Research Service
CSO	civil society organisation
CSP	civil society programme
CSS	Center for Strategic Studies
D/G	democracy and governance
DfID	Department for International Development
DoD	US Department of Defense
DONGO	donor-oriented NGO
DoS	US Department of State
EAT	election assessment team
ECC	Economic Consultative Council
EEAS	European External Action Service
EED	European Endowment for Democracy

EIDHR	European Instrument for Democracy and Human Rights
ENPI	European Neighbourhood and Partnership Instrument
EODS	EU Election Observation and Democratic Support project
EOM	electoral observation mission
ESF	Economic Support Funds
EU JDID	EU Support to Jordanian Democratic Institutions & Development
FES	Friedrich Ebert Foundation
FFF	Foundation for the Future
FHI 360	Family Health International 360
FMF	foreign military financing
FNS	Friedrich Naumann Foundation
FTA	free trade agreement
GID	General Intelligence Directorate
GJU	German Jordanian University
GoJ	Government of Jordan
GONGO	governmental NGO
HKJ	Hashemite Kingdom of Jordan
HSS	Hanns Seidel Foundation
IAF	Islamic Action Front
ICNL	International Center for Not-for-Profit Law
IDEA	Institute for Democracy and Electoral Assistance
IEC	Independent Election Commission
IFES	International Foundation for Electoral Systems
IRI	International Republican Institute
IYF	International Youth Foundation
JAF	Jordanian Armed Forces
JD	Jordanian *Dinar*
JIPTC	Jordan International Police Training Center
JMC	Joint Military Commission
KADDB	King Abdullah Design and Development Bureau
KAFD	King Abdullah II Fund for Development
KAS	Konrad Adenauer Foundation
KASOTC	King Abdullah II Special Operations Training Center
MENA	Middle East and North Africa
MoD	Jordanian Ministry of Defence
MoFA	Jordanian Ministry of Foreign Affairs
MoI	Jordanian Ministry of Interior
MoJ	Jordanian Ministry of Justice
MoMA	Jordanian Ministry of Municipal Affairs

MoPD	Jordanian Ministry of Political Development
MoPPA	Jordanian Ministry of Political and Parliamentary Affairs
MoPIC	Jordanian Ministry of Planning and International Cooperation
MoSD	Jordanian Ministry of Social Development
MOUT	military operations on urban terrain
MSI	Management Systems International
NCHR	National Centre for Human Rights
NDC	National Dialogue Committee
NDI	National Democratic Institute
NED	National Endowment for Democracy
NSA	non-state actor
OSF	Open Society Foundations
PFLP	Popular Front for the Liberation of Palestine
PLO	Palestine Liberation Organisation
PSD	Public Security Directorate
PSP	private sector participation
RONGO	royal NGO
RSS	Royal Scientific Society
SEZ	special economic zone
SNTV	single non-transferable vote
SOFEX	Special Operations Forces Exhibition and Conference
SPRING	Support to Partnership, Reform and Inclusive Growth programme
TSG	The Services Group
UNDP	United Nations Development Programme
UNRWA	United Nations Relief and Works Agency for Palestine Refugees in the Near East
USAID	United States Agency for International Development
QIZ	Qualifying Industrial Zone
WINEP	Washington Institute for Near East Policy

1 'Democracy Promotion' and Moral Authority

The Construction of Moral Authority

While this book focuses on US and European policy in Jordan, it also provides an illustration of what exactly greater US and European policy presence in the Global South means. As one of the biggest recipients of US and European foreign aid worldwide, Jordan represents in this regard not just a case study, but a state of the art. This book discusses what external 'democracy promoters' in Jordan *actually do* when they promote democracy. Since 1989 Jordan has been widely praised as a 'liberalising' and 'reforming' monarchy that is in the process of slow but gradual democratisation. This book will attempt to question such descriptions and, more importantly, will argue that external efforts at 'democracy promotion' in fact only reinforce Jordanian authoritarianism.

The dominant approaches to the study of 'democracy promotion' suffer from a number of deficiencies. The work of Carothers, De Gramont and Bush, for instance, features a narrow focus on developing policy recommendations and largely ignores more fundamental questions.[1] While much more critical, the work of Robinson, Gills, Rocamora and Wilson is marked by a structuralism that downplays the role of individual agency or dominant discourses in shaping and (re)producing the effects of 'democracy promotion'.[2] Finally, Guilhot's focus on the background of Western 'democracy promoters'

---

[1] See among others Carothers, T., *Aiding Democracy Abroad: The Learning Curve* (Washington, DC: Carnegie Endowment for International Peace, 1999); Carothers, T. and De Gramont, D., *Development Aid Confronts Politics: The Almost Revolution* (Washington, DC: Carnegie Endowment for International Peace, 2013); and Bush, S.S., *The Taming of Democracy Assistance: Why Democracy Promotion Does Not Confront Dictators* (Cambridge: Cambridge University Press, 2015).

[2] See, among others, Robinson, W.I., 'Globalization, the world system, and "democracy promotion" in U.S. foreign policy', *Theory and Society*, Vol. 25, No. 5, October 1996, pp. 615–65; Robinson, William I., *Promoting Polyarchy: Globalization, US Intervention, and Hegemony* (Cambridge: Cambridge University Press, 1996); Gills, B., Rocamora, J. and Wilson, R. (eds.), *Low Intensity Democracy: Political Power in the New World Order* (London: Pluto Press, 1993).

and Hobson and Kurki's focus on the conceptual assumptions of the latter is another area of concern. While they provide excellent studies of the aforementioned topics, the reader learns little about 'democracy promotion's' empirical reality.[3] Also, much research on the topic, such as Carapico's *Political Aid and Arab Activism*, views the project of 'democracy promotion' as consisting of only those activities that US and European donors explicitly subsume under the category of 'democracy promotion' in their funding reports.[4] Such an approach runs the risk of excluding some of the most important aspects of the 'democracy promotion' project. These include the particular notions of political economy and security that underlie Western interventions aimed at 'democracy promotion'.

This book attempts to answer the following key questions: Why has Jordanian authoritarianism been so remarkably stable despite extensive US and European efforts at 'democracy promotion'? What kind of power is (re)produced as seemingly universal narratives of democracy engage with the political context of Jordan? What explains the continuous growth of US and European 'democracy promotion' portfolios, considering the absence of any meaningful political liberalisation? And, finally, the main overarching research question, what exactly do US and European 'democracy promoters' do when they work on 'democracy promotion' programmes in Jordan?

In trying to address these questions, this book discusses 'democracy promotion' through a focus on practice. Instead of assessing whether 'democracy promotion' in Jordan does indeed work, or how it could be improved, this book investigates the often unintended and contradictory side effects that spring from 'democracy promotion's' underlying functionalist, teleological and universal assumptions as 'democracy promoters' engage with the specific political context of Jordan. The intention is to demonstrate how the interaction of universal narratives of democracy with the political context of Jordan leads to a (re)production of imagined

---

[3] While Guilhot's study has a very strong empirical foundation, it focuses almost entirely on the institutional background of 'democracy promotion' and on the social history of individual 'democracy promoters'. Guilhot, N., *The Democracy Makers: Human Rights and International Order* (New York: Columbia University Press, 2005). Hobson and Kurki provide a discussion of the conceptual politics of 'democracy promotion'. Hobson, C. and Kurki, M. (eds.), *The Conceptual Politics of Democracy Promotion* (Abingdon: Routledge, 2012).

[4] This is the case in most studies on the topic. While providing a fascinating in-depth study of attempts at 'democracy promotion' throughout the Middle East, Carapico does not discuss the notions of political economy and security that underlie them. Instead, she focuses on the fields of law, electoral representation, women's rights and civil society promotion. Carapico, S., *Political Aid and Arab Activism: Democracy Promotion, Justice, and Representation* (New York: Cambridge University Press, 2014).

moral hierarchies that then serve as an efficient rationale for a politics of control and intervention. The central argument of this book is that US and European 'democracy promotion' in Jordan in fact only reinforces Jordanian authoritarianism, that it confirms desired Western self-understandings as 'modern' and 'democratic' *vis-à-vis* 'the Jordanian non-democratic other' and that it serves as an efficient rationale for a politics of domination. I thus suggest that Jordanian authoritarianism is so stable not despite, but in part directly because of attempts at 'democracy promotion'.

While it was only after the end of the Cold War that the idea of 'democracy promotion' became 'a generic framework for the foreign policies of all Western countries',[5] its origins both in terms of practice and ideology date back much further. As shown by Smith, the idea of 'democracy promotion' first gained some prominence during the Philippine-American war between 1899 and 1902 and the subsequent US occupation:

It was a way of governing this possession on which both imperialists and anti-imperialists could agree. Imperialists could thereby tout the superiority of the Anglo-Saxon race, while anti-imperialists could reassure themselves that the ideals of self-government would not be endangered ... The result was important for the future of American foreign policy for the simple reason that American power now had a mission that justified its exercise ... now the United States had a moral purpose to its imperialism and could rest more easily.[6]

Yet the idea of 'democracy promotion' only became institutionalised in US politics after authoritarian regimes supported by the US and former European colonial powers – such as Iran under the Shah – came under increasing popular pressure in the late 1970s, and after the democratic transitions in Spain and Portugal among others.[7] The gradual 'replacement of coercive means of social control with consensual ones',[8] as described by Robinson, eventually reached its climax in the post-Cold War era, of which 'democracy promotion' was to become 'one of the defining characteristics',[9] as remarked by Hobson and Kurki.

Against the backdrop of a seeming affirmation of liberal market democracy as a morally superior and universally applicable mode of governance,

[5] Schmitter, P.C. and Brouwer, I., 'Conceptualizing, researching and evaluating democracy promotion and protection', *European University Institute (EUI)*, Florence, working paper no. 99/9, 1999, chapter III.2.
[6] Smith, T., *America's Mission: The United States and the Worldwide Struggle for Democracy in the Twentieth Century* (Princeton: Princeton University Press, 1994), p. 43.
[7] Robinson, *Promoting Polyarchy*, pp. 15–16.   [8] Robinson, *Promoting Polyarchy*, p. 16.
[9] Hobson, C. and Kurki, M., 'Introduction: the conceptual politics of democracy promotion', in: Hobson, C. and Kurki, M. (eds.), *The Conceptual Politics of Democracy Promotion* (Abingdon: Routledge, 2012), p. 1.

the notion of 'democracy promotion' is based on a staunchly teleological understanding of human history. According to Mitchell, the description of the latter as universal *telos* and 'genetic destiny' can be viewed as giving '[c]ontemporary political arrangements … a degree of inevitability'.[10] Attempts at 'democracy promotion' are thus deemed to aid a given country in progressing along a supposedly irreversible trajectory, and in reproducing clearly definable conditions, all of which have been derived from mystified narratives of past processes of democratisation and modernisation in 'the West'.[11] In claiming to have identified what progress and democracy mean, 'democracy promotion' and its ideological background in modernisation theory and neoconservative thought consequently feature the same kind of totalitarian character that Horkheimer and Adorno have identified in enlightenment thought.[12]

While, as Žižek remarks, it 'is easy to make fun of Fukuyama's notion of the End of History', it is important to note that 'the dominant ethos today *is* "Fukuyamaian": liberal-democratic capitalism is accepted as the finally found formula of the best possible society'.[13] In order to maintain its seeming moral authority, this 'imperialism of the universal',[14] as it is pointedly called by Bourdieu, tends to ignore 'the contextual': first, in order to open up the discursive space and the practical distance that enables and calls for the universally deployable 'democracy promotion' expert; second, in order to enable sense making of a context of contingency and fluidity; and third, in order to maintain the semblance of a universally existing and applicable moral truth. These points can be considered foundational requirements for the very idea of 'democracy promotion' itself.

---

[10] Mitchell, T., *Rule of Experts: Egypt, Techno-Politics, Modernity* (Berkeley: University of California Press, 2002), p. 179.

[11] For a discussion of the centrality of social democracy instead of liberal democracy in the consolidation of democratic rule in Europe after the Second World War, see Berman, S., 'The past and future of social democracy and the consequences for democracy promotion', in: Hobson, C. and Kurki, M. (eds.), *The Conceptual Politics of Democracy Promotion* (Abingdon: Routledge, 2012), pp. 68–84. For a discussion of the role that conflict and power-sharing arrangements, and not ideological commitment, played in democratic transitions, see Salamé, G. (ed.), *Democracy without Democrats? The Renewal of Politics in the Muslim World* (London: I.B. Tauris, 1994) and Kienle, E., 'Democracy promotion and the renewal of authoritarian rule', in: Schlumberger, (ed.), *Debating Arab Authoritarianism: Dynamics and Durability in Nondemocratic Regimes* (Stanford: Stanford University Press, 2007), pp. 231–249.

[12] Horkheimer, M., Adorno, T.W. and Noerr, G.S. (eds.), *Dialectic of Enlightenment: Philosophical Fragments*, tr. Jephcott, E. (Stanford: Stanford University Press, 2002), pp. 3–4.

[13] Žižek, S., *In Defense of Lost Causes* (London: Verso, 2008), p. 421.

[14] Bourdieu, P., *Acts of Resistance: Against the Tyranny of the Market*, tr. Nice, R. (New York: The New Press, 1998), p. 19.

In regard to the centrality of the claim of moral authority, German philosopher and political theorist Carl Schmitt succinctly argued in a 1927 critique of liberal democracy that '[t]he concept of humanity is an especially useful ideological instrument of imperialist expansion, and in its ethical-humanitarian form it is a specific vehicle of economic imperialism'.[15] In trying to critique a universal notion of morality, however, one can also quickly end up adopting overly relativistic viewpoints that question the existence of *any* morality. Grappling with this issue, Hopgood suggests that a 'kind of residual moral truth'[16] can be found in human rights reporting for instance. Hopgood notes that this truth 'clearly resonates fully only with a particular audience, one largely, although far from exclusively, rooted in the idealism of the West and its often sentimental, uncritical, unreflective, and contradictory attachment to notions of innocence, enlightenment, and moral progress'.[17]

All this is to say that even if theoretically some kind of objectively superior ideal form of democracy existed as humanity's moral peak, it would necessarily be so abstract that in the process of contingent human interpretation and contextual application it would immediately lose its universal applicability and objectivity, thereby eliminating any basis for the possible existence of an absolute moral superiority.[18] Since the construction of moral authority therefore relies on the absence of context, as also illustrated by Hopgood,[19] the on-the-ground processes of promoting and attempting to contextualise a certain idea of democracy as morally superior immediately compromise the idealism that underlies Western liberal world views.

The staunch belief in the possibility of contextualising a 'higher-order impartiality'[20] through Western 'democracy promotion' thus fundamentally ignores the contingency of human agency and the impact of contextual factors. The aspiration or pretence to implement moral authority consequently leads to a dangerously self-confirming line of argument, in which discourses 'produce self-fulfilling and self-sealing systems of action

---

[15] Schmitt, C., *The Concept of the Political*, tr. Schwab, G. (London: University of Chicago Press, 1996), p. 54.

[16] Hopgood, S., *Keepers of the Flame: Understanding Amnesty International* (London: Cornell University Press, 2006), p. 5; also see pp. 205–207.

[17] Hopgood, *Keepers of the Flame*, p. 207. Also see Mouffe, C., 'Democracy in a multipolar world', *Millennium: Journal of International Studies*, Vol. 37, No. 3, 2009, p. 557.

[18] Hopgood adds the important reservation that in 'the moment this recognition [that there is a form of moral truth] is cast into words, interpretation and mobilization, the triggering of the will begins, and then we are fully in the world of social construction'. Hopgood, *Keepers of the Flame*, p. 215; see also p. 207.

[19] Hopgood, *Keepers of the Flame*, p. 206.

[20] Nagel, T., 'Moral conflict and political legitimacy', in: Raz, J. (ed.), *Authority* (Oxford: Blackwell, 1990), p. 301.

and justification'.[21] Any outcome of 'democracy promotion' is then used 'by democracy promoters to urge the northern industrialized democracies to take a more proactive role in fostering democracy throughout the world',[22] as remarked by Schraeder. The presentation of democracy as functionally superior for the achievement of various often contradictory ends, such as stability, economic development, equality, security and peace – under the overarching argument of a higher morality – thus ultimately serves, in Mouffe's words, the establishment of 'order in a context of contingency'.[23]

The alleged moral superiority of a universally applicable model of democracy can only be maintained if the latter can be protected from the very contextual factors that 'democracy promotion' necessarily engages with when it is translated into projects on the ground. In short, the project of 'democracy promotion' needs to be presented as being *beyond politics*. If 'democracy promotion' is understood along these lines, contextual factors do not hold any major importance, as democracy has then already unequivocally been established as the universally superior mode of governance that acts upon the contextual, rather than the other way round. It is precisely the ignoring of some of the most fundamental questions about democracy, democracy's meaning, the various forms that democracy can take and the problematic relations it entails in specific contexts *vis-à-vis* other values that gives the project of 'democracy promotion' as carried out by the US and by European states its moral authority and vigour and makes it such a useful and effective tool for a politics of control and domination. It is by subordinating 'the contextual' to 'the universal' and 'the political' to 'the technical' that the 'order' to which Mouffe refers in the quotation above can be achieved and that the required distance is created, making 'the expert' a spokesperson of democracy in Jordan.[24]

What Democracy?

Democracy is widely referred to as what Gallie called an essentially contested concept.[25] This means that any conceptualisation of

[21] Wilson, Z., *Wishful Thinking, Wilful Blindness and Artful Amnesia: The UN and the Promotion of Good Governance, Democracy and Human Rights in Africa* (Halifax: Dalhousie University, PhD thesis, 2004), p. 28.

[22] Schraeder, P.J., 'The state of the art in international democracy promotion: results of a joint European-North American research network', *Democratization*, Vol. 10, No. 2, Summer 2003, p. 30.

[23] Mouffe, 'Democracy in a multipolar world', p. 549.

[24] See Mitchell, *Rule of Experts*.

[25] Gallie, W.B., 'Essentially contested concepts', *Proceedings of the Aristotelian Society, New Series*, Vol. 56, 1955–1956, pp. 183–187.

democracy is always a reflection of very specific contexts and particular ideological and normative approaches, and that no single definition can ever be described as the only valid one.[26] As demonstrated by among others Robinson, Gills, Rocamora and Wilson, however, US and European 'democracy promotion' is more accurately described as the promotion of polyarchy, liberal democracy or low-intensity democracy.[27] While this distinct model of democracy is at times also described, in direct reference to its conceptual founding fathers, as the Schumpeterian-Dahlian model, I mostly adopt the term 'procedural democracy', as it emphasises well its strong focus on democratic procedures. While all these terms are effectively used to describe the same phenomenon, they emphasise different aspects of it, including rule by a relatively small group of elected officials, mass participation channelled through elections, isolation of political rights from socio-economic rights and a strong focus on democratic institutions and procedures such as elections.

As Robinson puts it, the key function of this procedural definition of democracy lies in its departure from totalitarian singularities and its attempt to resolve 'the intrinsically contradictory nature of democratic thought under capitalism, in which one side stresses the sanctity of private property, and therefore legitimizes social and economic inequalities . . ., while the other side stresses popular sovereignty and human equality'.[28] The inherent tension that persists – albeit to a lesser degree – in understandings of procedural democracy too is thus addressed by an *ex ante* definitional disregard for democracy's relevance to socio-economic matters and by a simultaneous conceptual narrowing down of democracy's meaning to procedural questions alone.[29] The widely asserted universal moral superiority of Western liberal democratic values is consequently, as argued by Mouffe, not 'the manifestation of a deeper objectivity that would be exterior to the practices that brought it into being'[30] but the direct result of conscious ideological attempts at constructing democracy

---

[26] See Kurki, M., 'Democracy and conceptual contestability: reconsidering conceptions of democracy in democracy promotion', *International Studies Review*, Vol. 12, No. 3, 2010, p. 371.

[27] Robinson describes US 'democracy promotion' as the promotion of polyarchy. Robinson, 'Globalization, the world system, and "democracy promotion" in U.S. foreign policy', pp. 623–624. Gills, Rocamora and Wilson use the term 'low intensity democracy'. Gills, Rocamora and Wilson, *Low Intensity Democracy*.

[28] Robinson, *Promoting Polyarchy*, p. 52.

[29] See also Ayers, A.J., 'Demystifying democratisation: the global constitution of (neo)liberal polities in Africa', *Third World Quarterly*, Vol. 27, No. 2, 2006, pp. 321–338.

[30] Mouffe, 'Democracy in a multipolar world', p. 549.

as a means of social control that does not automatically challenge social difference, including socio-economic inequalities.[31]

I argue that it is in this context that proclamations of liberal democracies as 'the only truly and fully modern societies'[32] must be understood. According to Huntington, debate about the precise form and meaning of democracy was over by the 1970s, as 'Schumpeter had won'.[33] Further debate was deemed undesirable as, Huntington declared, '[f]uzzy norms do not yield useful analysis',[34] cannot be resolved into numbers and hence remain an illusion. To paraphrase Horkheimer and Adorno, the man of science/man of modernity now knew what democracy was and how it could be achieved, to the extent that he considered himself capable of making and promoting it.[35] The process of maintaining the illusory nature of other models of democracy was further aided by the emergence of democratisation as a distinct field of study. As demonstrated by Kurki, most so-called 'transitologists', such as Schmitter, Karl, Burnell and Whitehead, do indeed claim to view democracy as an essentially contested concept, but in the end nevertheless return to certain procedural elements as minimum default positions.[36] Elliott importantly reminds us in this regard that 'promoting democracy as a contested concept would imply that we can no longer think of Western countries like the UK as perfect and uncontested models of how democracy should be done'.[37]

The conceptual de-contestation of democracy was thus the key enabling factor for the global 'democracy promotion' project. The research published in 1989 by Diamond, Linz and Lipset – funded through the very first grant of the National Endowment for Democracy (NED)[38] – is a good illustration of the conceptual dominance of procedural democracy in both 'democracy promotion' research and practice. In their understanding of democracy, Diamond et al. thus speak of 'a political system, separate and apart from the economic and social system ... Indeed, a distinctive aspect of our approach is to insist that issues of so-called economic and social democracy be separated from the

---

[31] Robinson, 'Globalization, the world system, and "democracy promotion" in U.S. foreign policy', pp. 626–627.
[32] Diamond, L., and Plattner, M.F., 'Introduction', in: Diamond and Plattner (eds.), *The Global Resurgence of Democracy* (Baltimore: Johns Hopkins University Press, 1996), p. ix.
[33] Huntington, S.P., *The Third Wave: Democratization in the Late Twentieth Century* (Norman: University of Oklahoma, 1993), p. 6.
[34] Huntington, *The Third Wave*, p. 9.
[35] Horkheimer and Adorno, *Dialectic of Enlightenment*, pp. 4, 6.
[36] Kurki, 'Democracy and conceptual contestability', pp. 369–375.
[37] Elliott, C., *Democracy Promotion as Foreign Policy: Temporal Othering in International Relations* (New York: Routledge, 2017), p. 32.
[38] Guilhot, *The Democracy Makers*, p. 91.

question of governmental structure'.[39] In a more recent publication, Diamond asserts without reservation that '[t]he goal for every country should be a political system that combines democracy on the one hand with freedom, the rule of law, and good government on the other – in other words, *liberal democracy*'.[40]

In light of statements such as this, Müllerson characterised Diamond as 'either playing God or at least sounding like a secular messiah'.[41] Comparable to other religions, this 'secular religion'[42] – as Smith describes US 'democracy promotion' in general – has a very similar tendency to construct a self-contained and self-confirming system that fundamentally fails to grasp a reality that is much more diverse than imagined. The problem is thus proceduralism's denial of the fact that what may be seen as 'democratic' by some may be viewed as utterly 'undemocratic' by others.[43] Specific manifestations of moral values, such as equality for instance, in the concrete consequently 'always entail, as their very condition of possibility, some form of inequality'.[44]

Just as the alleged moral superiority of procedural democracy is ideologically constructed, so is the so-called 'unity of goodness' embraced by some advocates of 'democracy promotion'. This is perhaps most apparent in the work of Huntington. As Schmitter points out,[45] in his more recent work, Huntington changed his mind, turning away from viewing political order as the main concern[46] to arguing 'that democracy is good in itself and that . . . it has positive consequences for individual freedom, domestic stability, international peace, and the United States of America'.[47]

---

[39] Diamond, L., Linz, J. and Lipset, S.M., *Democracy in Developing Countries: Latin America, Volume 4* (Boulder: Lynne Rienner, 1989), p. xvi.

[40] Diamond, L., 'Universal democracy?' *Policy Review*, No. 119, 2003, p. 81; emphasis original. Emphasis in subsequent quotations is in the original text unless otherwise indicated.

[41] Müllerson, R., *Democracy: A Destiny of Humankind? A Qualified, Contingent and Contextual Case for Democracy Promotion* (New York: Nova Science Publishers, 2009), p. 11.

[42] Smith, T., 'From "fortunate vagueness" to "democratic globalism": American democracy promotion as imperialism', in: Hobson, C. and Kurki, M. (eds.), *The Conceptual Politics of Democracy Promotion* (Abingdon: Routledge, 2012), p. 201.

[43] See Mouffe, 'Democracy in a multipolar world', p. 550.

[44] Mouffe, *The Democratic Paradox* (London: Verso, 2009), p. 39.

[45] Schmitter, P.C., 'Review: democracy's third wave – *The Third Wave. Democratization in the Late Twentieth Century* by Samuel P. Huntington', *The Review of Politics*, Vol. 55, No. 2, Spring 1993, pp. 348–351.

[46] In his earlier work Huntington still wrote rather pejoratively that a 'pleasant conjuncture of blessings led Americans to believe in the unity of goodness: to assume that all good things go together and that the achievement of one desirable social goal aids in the achievement of others'. Huntington, S.P., *Political Order in Changing Societies* (London: Yale University Press, 1968), p. 5.

[47] Huntington, *The Third Wave*, p. xv.

Similar to other scholars, Huntington thus came to draw a direct line from democracy to security and other values, all of which may, depending on the context, be anything but mutually reinforcing. Despite their initial argument in favour of an analytical separation of politics and economics and their view of democratic values as independent from the socio-economic sphere, Diamond et al. in the very same book already quoted also insisted that democracy is reinforced by capitalist and free markets.[48] Above all, what this indicates is that any conceptualisation of democracy is a deeply political project full of implicit ideological assumptions and biases. While democracy was first isolated from all socio-economic matters, scholars now effectively constructed a link between procedural democracy, free market economies and pro-Western security arrangements. The most important effect of this embrace of a 'unity of goodness', however, was the resulting possibility of reframing US and Western foreign policies at large as part of 'democracy promotion'. By taming democracy and depriving it of its emancipatory potential – as illustrated by Abrahamsen among others[49] – the initial conceptual de-contestation of democracy had thus paved the way for the ensuing use of 'democracy promotion' as an overarching moral rationale.

In order not to construct the same self-sealing system criticised above, in this book the meaning of democracy is largely considered to be contingent upon context and interpretation. Democracy can consequently not be an outcome, but always remains a process or, as Almond states, is in a continuous 'state of becoming'.[50] Based on such an understanding, a universally valid democratic ideal end goal cannot be neatly defined or achieved, as neutral definitions or constructions of democracy do not exist in practice.[51] This brings up the question of what democracy actually means in Jordan. While I deliberately refrain from clearly defining the latter, my critique of narrow procedural understandings and my insistence on also discussing the notions of political economy and security that underlie attempts to promote procedural democracy implicitly mean that I argue in favour of an understanding of democracy that goes beyond ideals of individual freedom and participation to also encompass ideals of social equality.

---

[48] Diamond, Linz and Lipset, *Democracy in Developing Countries*, pp. 44–47.
[49] Abrahamsen, R., *Disciplining Democracy: Development Discourse and Good Governance in Africa* (London: Zed Books, 2000), p. 67.
[50] Almond, G.A., quoted in: Diamond, L., 'Introduction: political culture and democracy', in: Diamond, L. (ed.), *Political Culture and Democracy in Developing Countries* (Boulder: Lynne Rienner, 1993), p. 4.
[51] Abrahamsen, *Disciplining Democracy*, p. 67.

In this regard, I draw on, among others, the work of Abdel Rahman, Dana and Farsakh, who have explored the interlinkages between external attempts at 'democracy promotion', neoliberalism and processes of authoritarian reinforcement in the cases of Egypt and Palestine.[52] Taking my cue from the just-mentioned Abdel Rahman, who criticises the lack of empirically grounded and theoretically informed research on 'democracy promotion', what this book wants to offer first and foremost is an investigation of what the promoted understandings of (procedural) democracy (and the latter's implicit economy- and security-related assumptions) actually come to mean and entail in practice.[53]

Studying 'Democracy Promotion'

Despite the prominence of 'democracy promotion' as a rationale for Western foreign policies, theorisation of the topic has until recently remained rather scarce, with most of the existing literature coming from policymakers, whose open advocacy for 'democracy promotion' over-shadows scientific analyses.[54] In his 1999 book *Aiding Democracy Abroad*, for instance, Carothers only devotes a mere six-page 'Interlude for Skeptics' to addressing more fundamental questions going beyond the technical policy level.[55] As criticised by Alford, Carothers entirely ignores questions about the meaning of democracy, the motivation for 'democracy promotion', the logic of the models employed, difficulties of measurement and ethical challenges.[56] While Carothers recognises the inconsistencies of US 'democracy promotion', he simply renders them irrelevant for further research by stating that 'all major areas of U.S. foreign policy . . . are inconsistent in important ways'.[57]

Although Carothers pointedly critiques 'the missing link of power' in 'democracy promotion' and accuses 'democracy promoters' of treating

---

[52] Abdel Rahman, M., 'The politics of 'uncivil' society in Egypt', *Review of African Political Economy*, Vol. 29, No. 91, March 2002; Dana, T. 'The structural transformation of Palestinian civil society: key paradigm shifts', *Middle East Critique*, Vol. 24, No. 2, 2015; and Farsakh, L., 'Democracy promotion in Palestine: aid and the "de-democratization" of the West Bank and Gaza', Birzeit University, 2012, available at: http://rosaluxemburg .ps/wp-content/uploads/2015/03/Leila-Farsakh.pdf.

[53] See also Wolff, J. and Wurm, I., 'Towards a theory of external democracy promotion: a proposal for theoretical classification', *Security Dialogue*, Vol. 42, No. 1, 2011, pp. 77–78.

[54] It is impossible to mention all the authors who adopt a policy perspective. Thomas Carothers is, however, by far the most prominent. Carothers, *Aiding Democracy Abroad*.

[55] Carothers, *Aiding Democracy Abroad*, pp. 59–64.

[56] Alford, W.P., 'Review: exporting "the pursuit of happiness"', *Harvard Law Review*, Vol. 113, No. 7, 2000, p. 1694.

[57] Carothers, *Aiding Democracy Abroad*, p. 61.

political change 'in a pseudoscientific manner as a clinical process to be guided by manuals, technical seminars, and flowcharts',[58] he adopts the very same pseudoscientific approach. In his latest book, *Development Aid Confronts Politics: The Almost Revolution*, with De Gramont, Carothers thus suggests that the 'almost revolution' can eventually become a complete one, if only aid providers continue, among other things, to make 'increasing use of analytic tools'.[59] Just like the practitioners they criticise, the authors also invoke a technocratic process narrative and fundamentally ignore questions about the contested and context-dependent meanings of democracy. The same dynamic can be observed in Bush's analysis of US 'democracy promotion' in Jordan and Tunisia. While arguing convincingly that many 'democracy promotion' programmes do not confront dictators due to implementing organisations' focus on measurable and regime-compatible programmes, Bush concludes her study by suggesting that once the funding structure of democracy assistance is reformed, 'democracy promoters' can be 'set free' and 'succeed at their stated missions of advancing democracy around the world'.[60] The underlying desire of Bush, Carothers and De Gramont to improve 'democracy promotion' and to avoid more fundamental questions comes close to what Guilhot pointedly criticised in the work of O'Donnell, Schmitter and Whitehead as an attempt at raising 'to the level of theory the practical commitment in favour of democracy'.[61]

While Carothers and De Gramont write that 'it is hard not to slap one's forehead at the obviousness'[62] of the need to take into account political dynamics, it is similarly hard not to do so when reading the authors' critique, in light of their own adherence to a strangely apolitical and narrow understanding of politics. Besides remarking that 'the democratic governance orthodoxy ... is a credo rooted in empirical truth', they thus also explain that the latter is morally and practically superior since it is 'powerfully attractive' to simply export one's own form of governance, and because other models do not provide 'easily applicable policy recommendations'.[63] But even if this were not empirically 'true', it would not matter, as 'in any case, axiomatic approaches to public policy [such as "democracy promotion"] can survive a lack of empirical

---

[58] Carothers, *Aiding Democracy Abroad*, pp. 101–102.
[59] Carothers and De Gramont, *Development Aid Confronts Politics*, pp. 262–263.
[60] Bush, *The Taming of Democracy Assistance*, pp. 211, 232.
[61] Guilhot, *The Democracy Makers*, p. 138.
[62] Carothers and De Gramont, *Development Aid Confronts Politics*, p. 186.
[63] Carothers and De Gramont, *Development Aid Confronts Politics*, pp. 219–220.

validation for many years, or even indefinitely, if they are intuitively appealing or politically useful'.[64]

If 'democracy promotion' is apparently intuitively appealing regardless of empirical validation, it remains fundamentally unclear when it should ever not be undertaken. While much less overtly policy-oriented, Bush's analysis is permeated by the same apolitical and de-contextualised notions which only barely conceal the deeply ideological nature of the project at hand. Bush thus not only fails adequately to discuss the local political dynamics with which external interventions aimed at 'democracy promotion' necessarily engage, but also adopts a highly technocratic and ultimately illogical understanding of 'democracy promotion' as constituting an external 'attempt . . . to transform the domestic political practices and institutions of other countries while generally still preserving those states' sovereignty'.[65]

In the kind of policy-oriented literature analysed here, 'political' is only that which the authors want it to be. As Carothers and De Gramont provide a number of policy recommendations they thus confusingly insist that while these 'are all about politics, yet . . . [t]hey do not point to specific political goals'.[66] The 'political' cannot be made to disappear by limiting politics to procedural questions, however. Despite initially emphasising that they are not pursuing specific political goals, the authors nevertheless describe their work as *political in methods*' and claim that '*the central result of being more political in methods is not zealotry about ideological goals but greater realism about what aid can achieve and how it can do so.*'[67] Being political is thus effectively understood as the avoidance of any more substantive questions. In an excellent illustration of Li's *The Will to Improve* and Ferguson's *The Anti-Politics Machine*,[68] Carothers and De Gramont conclude that 'as long as donors continue to spend tens of billions of dollars a year in assistance, it remains crucial to try to improve aid practice'.[69]

Just as 'democracy promoters' view Jordan as a country full of opportunities for democratisation, with any upcoming challenges only further highlighting the urgency of the project at hand, Bush, Carothers and De Gramont adopt a similar perspective that takes a desired end goal (the

---

[64] Carothers and De Gramont, *Development Aid Confronts Politics*, p. 220.
[65] Bush, *The Taming of Democracy Assistance*, p. 211.
[66] Carothers and De Gramont, *Development Aid Confronts Politics*, p. 161.
[67] Carothers and De Gramont, *Development Aid Confronts Politics*, pp. 161–162.
[68] Li, T., *The Will to Improve: Governmentality, Development, and the Practice of Politics* (London: Duke University Press, 2007); Ferguson, J., *The Anti-Politics Machine: "Development," Depoliticization, and Bureaucratic Power in Lesotho* (Minneapolis: University of Minnesota Press, 1994).
[69] Carothers and De Gramont, *Development Aid Confronts Politics*, p. 277.

universal applicability of proceduralist conceptualisations of democracy) as implicit starting point, subsequently setting out to interpret almost any development they encounter as constituent, and evidence, of the allegedly inevitable process of liberal democracy's gradual universalisation. Finally, the significance of such technocratic analyses then lies much less in illustrating the reality of 'democracy promotion' than in reiterating its foundational assumptions and in this way (re)producing the impression that 'we' indeed know what democracy is and that it can thus also be promoted.[70]

Opposed to the technocratic literature briefly analysed here in the examples of Carothers, De Gramont and Bush, one can detect a number of critical approaches. These all share a strong critique of an implicit normativity in Western attempts at understanding sociopolitical developments in the Arab world, such as that raised by Cavatorta and Durac, and very powerfully by Anderson.[71] Advocates of what may be called a pluralist approach criticise the conceptual dominance of the liberal democratic model in much of the research on 'democracy promotion' and its actual practice. Kurki, for instance, demonstrates that many authors only pay lip service to the essentially contested nature of democracy's meaning. Further, a number of critical scholars have in recent years made important contributions to the study of 'democracy promotion' by responding to what Kurki describes as a need for pluralisation and contextualisation.[72] Sadiki's study of the contested nature and different meanings of democracy in the Arab Middle East can be named in this regard, as well as Guilhot's work on the institutionalisation of 'democracy promotion', the social history of networks of 'democracy promoters' and the social construction of 'democracy promotion' as a process of domination.[73] While such approaches are less concerned with the actual implementation level of specific 'democracy promotion' projects, they provide important insight into processes of subject formation. Exploring 'democracy promotion' as a form of foreign policy, Elliott argues that British 'democracy promotion' in Pakistan is ultimately about controlling the line of separation between 'modern', 'democratic' and 'developed' selves and 'foreign' and 'barbarian'

---

[70] The argument made here is similar to that of Mitchell in regard to USAID reports on capitalist development in Egypt. See Mitchell, *Rule of Experts*, p. 267.

[71] See, for instance, Cavatorta, F. and Durac, V., *Civil Society and Democratization in the Arab World: The Dynamics of Activism* (Abingdon: Routledge, 2011). See also Anderson, L., 'Searching where the light shines: studying democratization in the Middle East', *Annual Review of Political Science*, Vol. 9, 2006, pp. 189–214.

[72] Kurki, 'Democracy and conceptual contestability', pp. 376–379.

[73] Sadiki, L., *The Search for Arab Democracy: Discourses and Counter-Discourses* (London: Hurst Publishers, 2004); Guilhot, *The Democracy Makers*.

others.[74] Challand discusses the ways in which external civil society support in Palestine ignores the diverse forms of existing social organisation, thereby providing a good illustration of how the conceptual dominance of narrow liberal understandings of democracy is maintained and further entrenched in practice.[75]

Pursuing an approach of contextualising the grand narrative of 'democracy promotion' by illustrating its multiple effects on the project level, Carapico argues that 'Democracy promotion can be both a mode of empowerment and a modality of power'.[76] Unlike many other scholars, she demonstrates great familiarity also with the implementation level of 'democracy promotion' interventions, particularly focusing on the fields of rule of law, elections, women's empowerment and civil society in Egypt, Jordan, Morocco, Yemen, Lebanon, Tunisia, Algeria, Palestine and Iraq. Also emphasising the importance of contextual factors, Kienle is somewhat more pessimistic than Carapico, suggesting that '[t]he only conclusion that can safely be drawn is that standard recipes for democracy engineering contribute to the reconfiguration of authoritarian rule rather than to democratization'.[77] Brownlee provides a good illustration of this point in his study of US-Egyptian relations, pointedly entitled *Democracy Prevention*.[78] However, rather than discussing 'democracy promotion' interventions and their contradictory effects, he traces the evolution of bilateral relations between the US and Egypt and as such focuses primarily on economic and security arrangements.

Perhaps the most ardent criticism levelled at 'democracy promotion' comes from scholars who pursue a critical political economy approach, and from so-called neo-Gramscian writers. Robinson, for example, in his seminal book *Promoting Polyarchy*, describes the reorientation of US foreign policy from support for authoritarianism to the promotion of polyarchy as 'a political exigency of macro-economic restructuring on a world scale'.[79] While Robinson also argues for the need to overcome the hegemony of procedural democracy, his analysis is somewhat contradictory in as much as it leaves little space for the very possibility of such

---

[74] Elliott, *Democracy Promotion as Foreign Policy*. See also Schuetze, B., 'Marketing parliament: the constitutive effects of external attempts at parliamentary strengthening in Jordan', *Cooperation and Conflict*, Vol. 53, No. 2, 2018, pp. 237–258.

[75] Challand, B., *Palestinian Civil Society: Foreign Donors and the Power to Promote and Exclude* (London: Routledge, 2009).

[76] Carapico, *Political Aid and Arab Activism*, p. 200.

[77] Kienle, 'Democracy promotion and the renewal of authoritarian rule', p. 247.

[78] Brownlee, J., *Democracy Prevention: The Politics of the U.S.-Egyptian Alliance* (Cambridge: Cambridge University Press, 2012).

[79] Robinson, *Promoting Polyarchy*, p. 31. Another important example of a neo-Gramscian approach to the study of democracy and 'democracy promotion' is Gills, Rocamora and Wilson, *Low Intensity Democracy*.

a challenge. Where Guilhot and Robinson both view 'democracy promotion' as an imperial project of domination, for instance, the former does so based on a constructivist exploration of the processes by which individual actors in the 'democracy promotion' establishment came to embrace a model of procedural democracy, and the latter based on a much less agency-focused approach that privileges above all else structural features of the capitalist world economy as analytical categories. Along similar lines, Chandler argues that 'democracy promotion' is not to be understood as a process with a clear end, but rather as a permanent state of tutelage.[80]

To scholars who adopt a critical political economy approach, the gradual embrace of procedural democracy as the only 'real' form of democracy constitutes part of a larger imperial project of a transnational elite aimed at pre-empting more radical social change and at preserving social order in a context of neoliberal restructuring.[81] Much of the strength of such analyses comes from their refusal to accept the conceptual separation of the political and the economic spheres that is promoted by advocates of procedural democracy. Robinson thus insists forcefully that the promotion of polyarchy and neoliberalism needs to be analysed as one 'singular process in US foreign policy' and suggests that we should speak of the promotion of *'capitalist polyarchy'*.[82] Along the same line, Hassan finds that contemporary efforts at 'democracy promotion' largely view capitalism 'as the heart of democracy'.[83] Just as the above-mentioned Dana and Farsakh emphasise that any discussion of 'democracy promotion' interventions in Palestine needs to be situated within a wider critique of neoliberalism, Selim argues that democratisation processes in Egypt are heavily shaped by the way in which the country was integrated into global capitalism.[84] Farsakh makes the important point that by fostering individual relations with authority and the state,[85] rather than associational ones, neoliberal 'democracy promotion' in Palestine ultimately only weakens political engagement. Markakis situates his study of US 'democracy promotion' interventions in Egypt,

---

[80] Chandler, D., 'Back to the future? The limits of neo-Wilsonian ideals of exporting democracy', *Review of International Studies*, Vol. 32, No. 3, July 2006, p. 482.

[81] Robinson, *Promoting Polyarchy*, pp. 318–319. See also Hanieh, A., "Democracy promotion' and neo-liberalism in the Middle East', *State of Nature*, Vol. 3, Spring 2006, available at: http://links.org.au/node/224.

[82] Robinson, *Promoting Polyarchy*, pp. 55–56.

[83] Hassan, O., *Constructing America's Freedom Agenda for the Middle East: Democracy and domination* (London: Routledge, 2013), p. 64.

[84] Selim, G. M., *The International Dimensions of Democratization in Egypt: The Limits of Externally Induced Change* (London: Springer, 2015).

[85] Farsakh, 'Democracy promotion in Palestine', p. 2.

Iraq and Kuwait within Robinson's argument about a gradual shift away from coercive means of social control to social control via the imposition of elite-based democracies. However, he primarily discusses 'democracy promotion' through the lens of bilateral relations and provides little insight into the praxis-level implementation of 'democracy promotion'.[86]

Finally, it is possible to discern two key dividing lines in the study of 'democracy promotion' at large: one between approaches that view 'democracy promotion' as only that which donors understand as such versus approaches that tie in underlying economic and security-related assumptions, and a second between approaches that focus on 'democracy promotion' as a theme of bilateral relations versus approaches that explore the micropolitics of 'democracy promotion' – both on the project level and in terms of emerging political subjectivities. While a number of critical scholars have provided initial starting points for the critical study of the ways in which the micropolitics of 'democracy promotion' may actually reinforce authoritarian rule,[87] a systematic exploration of this dynamic that also takes into account underlying economic and security-related assumptions is still missing from the literature.

This book combines a practice-oriented approach, as applied by Carapico, with a focus on both material and ideational factors. In doing so, *Promoting Democracy, Reinforcing Authoritarianism* investigates the ways in which dominant ideas shape and (re)produce 'democracy promotion' as a process of domination. The intention here is to avoid a presentation of 'democracy promotion' as a structurally conditioned means of social control that now simply unfolds in a mechanical way.[88] By paying close attention to the social construction of processes of domination, this study is also able to explore the impact of 'democracy promotion' on political subjectivities and processes of identity formation. It is thus suggested that the contradictory effects of 'democracy promotion's' encounter with complex local dynamics play an important role in reinforcing desired self-understandings as 'liberal' and 'democratic' *vis-à-vis* the imagined 'Jordanian non-democratic other'. Questioning Western 'democracy promotion' in Jordan thus not only amounts to questioning its impact on Jordanian state and society, but also to questioning the often idealised Western liberal self-understandings that lie at the heart of the project of 'democracy promotion' itself.

---

[86] Markakis, D., *US Democracy Promotion in the Middle East: The Pursuit of Hegemony* (London: Routledge, 2016).

[87] See also Snider, Erin A., 'US democracy aid and the authoritarian state: evidence from Egypt and Morocco', *International Studies Quarterly*, Vol. 62, No. 4, 2018, pp. 795–808.

[88] Guilhot makes a similar critique of so-called neo-Gramscian approaches. See Guilhot, *The Democracy Makers*, pp. 16–17.

Also, a focus on ideational factors demonstrates that instead of being perpetuated by the structural conditions of the capitalist world economy, 'democracy promotion' is actually in many ways reproduced as a process of domination by its often unintended consequences, and by the very processes of resistance that it elicits.[89] Overall, the close attention that this book pays to the practical level of implementation is intended to provide a deep empirical grounding to an analysis of 'democracy promotion' as a practice and discourse that justifies a policy of control and domination. Further, one of the intentions of this book is to address the shortage of critical research on the topic that is both empirically grounded and theoretically informed.

As 'democracy promotion' constitutes an overall guideline for Western foreign policies, it needs to be interpreted as both the promotion of procedural democracy and the promotion of neoliberal restructuring, as suggested by the critical political economy approaches discussed earlier. By also analysing the understandings of political economy and of security that underlie US and European attempts at 'democracy promotion' in Jordan, this study refuses to analytically accept the separation of politics and economics, on which advocates of procedural democracy like Diamond et al. based their narrow understanding of democratic values as independent from the socio-economic sphere. My central assumption in this regard is that a narrow confinement of the discussion to the promotion of procedural democracy fails to acknowledge that the hegemonic position of procedural democracy in Western attempts at 'democracy promotion' is not at all external to the project of 'democracy promotion', but instead part and parcel of it.[90]

'Democracy promotion' in Jordan is then a field of practice that is constitutive of 'liberal' and 'democratic' subjectivities, as well as reinforcing of deeply authoritarian power structures and an external politics of control and domination. Two of my key concerns are thus the ongoing discursive (re)construction of 'democracy promotion' as a seeming moral obligation, and its often contradictory interaction with the authoritarian

---

[89] Ferguson provides a good illustration of this dynamic in regard to the reproduction of 'development' interventions. See Ferguson, *The Anti-Politics Machine*, pp. 12–13.

[90] The hegemony of procedural, liberal and/or polyarchic definitions of democracy in US and European 'democracy promotion' is illustrated by a wide range of scholars and, in the context of Jordan, is also confirmed by the empirical findings of this research. While Bridoux and Kurki suggest that ideological differences exist between US and EU efforts at 'democracy promotion', they themselves demonstrate that such differences are mostly limited to a somewhat less aggressive embrace of liberal values by the EU. See Bridoux, J. and Kurki, 'Cosmetic agreements and the cracks beneath: ideological convergences and divergences in US and EU democracy promotion in civil society', *Cambridge Review of International Affairs*, Vol. 28, No. 1, 2015, pp. 1–20.

structures and practices in place in the country. The latter point means that this book inquires much less into the 'success' or 'failure' of 'democracy promotion' than into its unintended side effects. Or, in the words of Ferguson, 'what is most important about a "development" project is not so much what it fails to do but what it does do'.[91] What is the actual impact of 'democracy promotion' on the ground? How precisely is Jordanian authoritarianism reinforced? How does 'democracy promotion' help in the (re)production of desired self-understandings as 'democratic' and 'modern'? And how do the promoted modes of procedural democracy interact with the economic and security configurations that are claimed to be mutually reinforcing of democratic values? Ultimately, my interest is in the kind of power that 'democracy promotion' interventions (re)produce. Does 'democracy promotion' enable local processes of democratisation to take root, or does it – in an unintended manner from the perspective of individual 'democracy promoters', and arguably in a more intentional one from the perspective of Western diplomats and officials – reinforce and perpetuate precisely those conditions and hierarchies of power that it initially set out to overcome?

Enabling 'Democracy Promotion' Interventions

The primacy of procedural democracy, the exclusion of socio-economic rights, the discourse of universal applicability and moral authority, and the protection of the 'unity of goodness' all fundamentally depend on interrelated processes of depoliticisation, de-contextualisation and technocratisation. One of the central arguments of this book is that US and European 'democracy promotion' in Jordan largely operates independently of the Jordanian political context in which it takes place. As a general framework for Western foreign policies, 'democracy promotion' has become the lens through which politics – in this case Jordanian – is made sense of, rather than the other way around. 'Democracy promotion' operates like a bubble that all involved parties contrive to maintain, but that ultimately only floats above Jordan,[92] and contributes to what one Jordanian economist pointedly called 'Potemkin villages'[93] of democratic appearance or procedure. Despite its invocation of a teleological notion of history with liberal democracy as humanity's climax, 'democracy promotion' needs to be viewed as a constant process in motion, rather than as

---

[91] Ferguson, *The Anti-Politics Machine*, p. 254.
[92] See also Chandrasekaran's discussion of US attempts to build democracy in Iraq. See Chandrasekaran, R., *Imperial Life in the Emerald City: Inside Baghdad's Green Zone* (London: Bloomsbury Publishing, 2006).
[93] Interview with Sami, Jordanian economist, Amman, 13 September 2012.

the result of a single conscious policy decision. As a direct consequence, 'democracy promotion' may tell us more about the 'democracy promoters' and their desired self-understandings than about the country in which it operates.[94]

As 'democracy promotion' is only intelligible within an analytical framework of gradual democratisation and reform, it is of utmost importance for it to maintain clear and universally valid ideas about the meaning of the desired democratic end goal and about the processes of democratisation that are deemed to lead there. A prominent assessment of US 'democracy promotion' published in 2007 by Finkel et al. found, for instance, that $10 million of US democracy and governance funding led to an average improvement of a country's freedom house ranking of 0.26 points.[95] Given this quantitatively proven impact of US efforts at 'democracy promotion', the local level of implementation can conveniently be ignored, and it seems to become irrelevant that in the case of Jordan an overall allocation of around $100 million in democracy and governance funds between 2011 and 2014 alone has not contributed any improvement of political freedom in the country. Instead, Jordan's so-called freedom rating remained consistently low at 5.5 ('not free') throughout the entire indicated time frame.[96]

The discursive supremacy of universal ideas of democracy and democratisation and their utter disconnection from the level of local politics not only implies the relegation of everything specifically Jordanian to a position of lesser relevance, but also requires the idealisation of past processes of democratisation in 'the West' and the deeply functionalist and technocratic transferral of the deduced democratisation mould onto Jordan. It is in this process of juxtaposing the allegedly universally applicable procedural democratic ideal to Jordanian politics that, first, the supposed moral inferiority of the latter and 'democracy promotion's' own purported moral authority are discursively confirmed; and, second, that the seeming need for a universally deployable and knowledgeable democracy expert arises. Just as the heavy focus on 'the process' that Jordan is deemed to be caught in provides legitimacy to the Jordanian regime's questionable reform narrative and creates a seeming need for external expertise about how this process can be accelerated, it also

---

[94] The deeply normative foundations of American political science are demonstrated by Oren among others. See Oren, I., *Our Enemies and US: America's Rivalries and the Making of Political Science* (New York: Cornell University Press, 2013).

[95] Finkel, S.E. et al., 'The effects of U.S. foreign assistance on democracy building, 1990–2003', *World Politics*, Vol. 59, No. 3, April 2007, p. 424.

[96] Freedom House, *Freedom in the World – Jordan*, available at: https://freedomhouse.org/report/freedom-world/2015/jordan#.Vceu3PlR2uI.

further reinforces existing power structures and the imagined moral hierarchies that constitute the foundational basis of 'democracy promotion'.

In order to implement the supposedly universal narrative of democracy in the specific context of Jordan, both democracy and Jordanian politics need to be rendered technical.[97] This entails an understanding of Jordanian authoritarianism as being largely due to factors that are manageable by the external 'democracy expert'. Structural issues beyond the control of 'democracy promoters', which would only call into question the overall narrative of procedural democracy's universal applicability, must therefore be ignored and/or downplayed. Among other things, this explains why most of the 'democracy promoters' interviewed construct their work as bound in space and time by the national borders of contemporary Jordan.

A recurrent theme among 'democracy promoters' is thus an analytical separation of their work and foreign policy, perhaps best illustrated in one 'democracy promoter's' remark that 'I'm not here to do foreign policy. I'm here to help Jordan ... develop its democratic institutions'.[98] This analytical separation is of major importance, as it enables both a sceptical distance towards Western foreign policies *vis-à-vis* the Arab world, and a great deal of idealism and passion about the job of 'democracy promotion' itself. The former is very much needed, in light of the rather negative image that most Jordanians have of the US in particular. The importance of this separation and of ignoring all matters related to the Israeli-Palestinian conflict, among other things, is illustrated by a 2006 poll of the Amman-based Center for Strategic Studies (CSS), according to which 11 per cent of the respondents viewed a lack of US political will as the greatest barrier to democracy in Jordan, while 7.8 per cent considered it to be fear of the so-called alternative homeland.[99]

Once such structural factors are discursively swept out of the way and judged to be irrelevant to the overall project of 'democracy promotion' in Jordan, the ground is prepared for a variety of seemingly technical, but deeply ideological, interventions. In the words of Mouffe, however, the political 'cannot be made to disappear by simply denying and wishing it away'.[100] This book therefore also investigates the notions of political economy and security that underlie US and European attempts at

---

[97] See Ferguson, *The Anti-Politics Machine*; Li, *The Will to Improve*.

[98] Interview with Robert, a 'democracy promoter' working in Jordan, Amman, 24 September 2012.

[99] CSS, *Democracy in Jordan – 2006 [ad-Dimuqrātiyah fi-l-Urdun – 2006]* (Amman: CSS – University of Jordan, 2006), p. 9. The other main factors named included regional instability (17.6 per cent), spread of corruption and favouritism (12.7 per cent) and continuation of the Israeli-Palestinian conflict (9.4 per cent).

[100] Mouffe, 'Democracy in a multipolar world', p. 550.

'democracy promotion' in Jordan and that are widely argued to be rein-forcing of the promotion of procedural democracy – for instance by referring to the earlier discussed 'unity of goodness'. To give contempor-ary procedural democracy a degree of inevitability, socio-economic ques-tions must first be evacuated from conceptualisations of democracy, only to be reintroduced again later.

The end of the Cold War provided a convenient opportunity for the construction of democracy and capitalism as mutually reinforcing and for the ignoring of the fundamental contradictions between the reality of neoliberal ideals of free markets and free trade on the one side, and demo-cratic ideals of equality on the other. According to what came to be called the 'Washington Consensus', electoral democracy, open markets, and free trade had not only been proven to be ultimately superior paradigms of governance, but were also to be 'seen as complementary and as going hand-in-hand'.[101] As remarked by Amin, democratisation was thus 'considered the necessary and natural product of submission to the rationality of the worldwide market. A simple dual equation [was] deduced from this logic: capitalism=democracy, democracy=capitalism.'[102] The expansion of market rationales as governing principles for the political and social spheres, too, could thereby be framed as mutually reinforcing of the promotion of democracy. In reality, this only 'prepared the ground for profoundly anti-democratic political ideas and practices to take root',[103] as noted by Brown among others, since authentic degrees of democratisation (that is, the filling of democratic procedures with socio-economic rights) became increasingly marginalised in favour of techno-cratic issues related to questions of efficiency and the interaction of forces of supply and demand.

Another major enabling factor for the pursuit of 'democracy promo-tion' interventions in countries in which 'the West' has traditionally favoured the support of authoritarian regimes is the securitisation of Kant's democratic peace proposition, according to which democracies rarely, or even never, go to war with one another.[104] Critiques of the

---

[101] See for instance Wiarda, Howard J., *Cracks in the Consensus: Debating the Democracy Agenda in U.S. Foreign Policy* (Washington, DC: Center for Strategic and International Studies (CSIS), 1997), esp. p. 16.

[102] Amin, S., 'The issue of democracy in the contemporary third world', in: Gills, Barry, Rocamora, Joel and Wilson, Richard (eds.), *Low Intensity Democracy: Political Power in the New World Order* (London: Pluto Press, 1993), p. 59.

[103] Brown, W., 'American nightmare: neoliberalism, neoconservatism, and de-democratization', *Political Theory*, Vol. 34, No. 6, December 2006, p. 702.

[104] Kant, I., *Perpetual Peace*, tr. Smith, C.M. (London: George Allen & Unwin, 1795/1917). For the concept of securitisation, see Buzan, B., Wæver, O. and de Wilde, J., *Security: A New Framework for Analysis* (London: Lynne Rienner, 1998).

hypothesis argue that the democratic peace is only a liberal peace,[105] and that processes of democratisation, as opposed to the potential end result, are highly prone to violence.[106] Ideas of democracy and security can thus of course be highly contradictory.[107] Another problem concerns the many different definitions of war, peace and democracy, which offer proponents of the democratic peace ways to *ex ante* exclude cases that would otherwise contradict their argument.[108] Despite these critiques, numerous scholars and policymakers today consider the hypothesis that democracies are more peaceful almost to be a scientific law. This led to the initial empowering potential of the hypothesis being turned upside down, as non-democratic states were now 'indirectly blamed for war'[109] and constructed as a threat. As Western liberal states were seen as having achieved the democratic peace, the project of democratisation was effectively externalised.[110] Violence between democratic and non-democratic states could thus be portrayed as normal and conveniently be blamed on the latter.[111]

As democracy had thereby become an issue of security, realist and neoconservative scholars were also able to embrace the 'democracy promotion' project. Heydemann importantly remarks in this regard that the objective was now the far 'more limited and entirely instrumental job of strengthening states to ensure their capacity to contain the extremist ideologies that now threaten the United States'.[112] For Fukuyama, it is only 'by securitizing nation building, with the limited aim of improving state capacity',[113] that US engagement with nation

---

[105] See for example Doyle, M.W., 'Kant, liberal legacies, and foreign affairs', in: Brown, M. E. et al. (eds.), *Debating the Democratic Peace* (London: MIT Press, 1997), pp. 3–57.

[106] See Mansfield, E.D. and Snyder, J., *Electing to Fight: Why Emerging Democracies Go to War* (Cambridge: MIT Press, 2005), p. 21.

[107] A prominent USAID-funded assessment of US 'democracy promotion' found that, in light of a US security priority, 'USAID DG [democracy and governance] is insignificant' in Afghanistan, Colombia, Egypt, Iraq, Turkey, Pakistan and also Jordan. Finkel, S. E. et al., *Deepening Our Understanding of the Effects of US Foreign Assistance on Democracy Building – Final Report* (USAID, Vanderbilt University, University of Pittsburgh, Latin American Public Opinion Project and Hertie School of Governance Berlin, 28 January 2008), p. 47.

[108] Spiro, D.E., 'The liberal peace: and yet it squirms', in: Brown, Michael E. et al. (eds.), *Debating the Democratic Peace* (London: MIT Press, 1997), pp. 351–354.

[109] Büger, C. and Villumsen, T., 'Beyond the gap: relevance, fields of practice and the securitizing consequences of (democratic peace) research', *Journal of International Relations and Development*, Vol. 10, No. 4, 2007, p. 433.

[110] Rupert, M., 'Democracy, peace: what's not to love?', in: Barkawi, T. and Laffey, M. (eds.), *Democracy, Liberalism, and War* (London: Lynne Rienner, 2001), p. 154.

[111] Büger and Villumsen, 'Beyond the gap', p. 433.

[112] Heydemann, S., 'In the shadow of democracy: review article', *Middle East Journal*, Vol. 60, No. 1, Winter 2006, p. 156.

[113] Heydemann, 'In the shadow of democracy', p. 156.

building and 'democracy promotion' became acceptable. Such an understanding not only views 'democracy promotion' interventions through a purely instrumental and strategic lens under the larger paradigm of stability and security, but also, importantly, based on the securitised democratic peace hypothesis, allows for the discursive framing of Western security support to the Jordanian regime as an important act of capacity building for a state that is allegedly in the process of democratising.

As the Jordanian political context is ignored or relegated to a secondary role relative to the procedural democratic ideal type, all the expertise required by individual 'democracy promoters' is of a deeply technocratic and seemingly universal nature. Since processes of democratisation are deemed to follow a universally valid model, prior experience in a country that has recently democratised is considered much more important than, say, knowledge of Arabic. The best example of this dynamic is the American National Democratic Institute (NDI) office in Amman. In 2013 its director was from Kosovo, the head of the youth programme and the election observation coordinator from Serbia and the head of the parliamentary programme from Lithuania.[114]

The underlying assumption of those who appointed these 'democracy promoters' clearly seems to be that processes of democratisation in Jordan occur, or do not occur, for the same reasons as in Eastern Europe. It is the international 'democracy promoter' who engages with and makes sense of Jordan, instead of the specificities of Jordanian politics shaping the views and projects of the Western officials who work in the country. Right from the outset, Jordan is thus seen as a passive recipient of a universally applicable mould, which only shows agency when following the externally prescribed narrative. Besides the many NDI employees from Eastern Europe, other 'democracy promoters' working in Jordan include experts on the former Soviet Union, Latin America and Africa. For practically all of the external 'democracy promoters' working in Jordan, the country is just another on a long list of countries of deployment, which include Afghanistan, Iraq, Kosovo, Bahrain, Ethiopia, East Timor, Mexico, Guatemala, Bolivia, the Philippines, etc. This global background of 'democracy promoters' working in Jordan is already a first indicator that the projects implemented in the country are not in any way

---

[114] This inherent comparison of contemporary Jordan to Eastern Europe after the end of the Cold War is also a recurrent feature of King Abdullah II's public discourse. See King Abdullah II, 'Each playing our part in a new democracy', Royal Hashemite Court, Amman, third discussion paper, 2 March 2013.

unique or country-specific, but merely variations of a universally applied model.

The universal and technical nature of the capacity-building interventions and awareness training implemented in Jordan implies that it is no longer the Jordanian regime or deeper structural issues specific to the case of Jordan that are problematised as primary barriers to processes of democratisation, but instead an alleged lack of knowledge and capacity among Jordanians themselves. The absence of democratic forms of governance in Jordan is thereby successfully transformed into a problem of capacity, awareness and implementation that could exist in the very same form in any other country, and that can now be managed and addressed.[115] The fundamental unwillingness or inability to take Jordanian authoritarianism seriously in and of itself – arguably a central feature of 'democracy promotion' interventions in general – then leads to a situation in which the Jordanian regime is mistakenly viewed as an agent of democratisation and Jordanians at large as 'not yet ready' for democracy. This not only has the effect of reproducing Jordanian authoritarianism under a democratic image, it also leads to the perpetuation of highly Orientalist notions that very effectively maintain the seeming need for constant foreign intervention. In this context Sabaratnam has called for a repoliticisation of 'assumptions of "difference"',[116] as these constitute the conceptual foundation for intervention.

The above-mentioned self-perpetuating dynamic also functions very well in the face of practical failure, as failure only serves to vindicate the alleged superiority of procedural democracy, and to discursively confirm Jordanian politics as marked by important shortcomings that still need to be addressed. Similarly, political de-liberalisations also only highlight the urgency of the project at hand and present no serious problem for the reproduction of 'democracy promotion' as a powerful process of domination. Ultimately, the central requirement for this perpetuation is the acceptance of procedural democracy as morally superior, the associated portrayal of Jordan as continuously progressing towards the desired ideal model and an understanding of 'democracy promoters' as well-intentioned and much-needed external experts and supporters of this assumed process.

---

[115] See Heydemann, 'In the shadow of democracy', p. 150.

[116] Sabaratnam, Meera, 'Avatars of Eurocentrism in the critique of the liberal peace', *Security Dialogue*, Vol. 44, No. 3, 2013, p. 260. See also Pascucci, E., 'The local labour building the international community: precarious work within humanitarian spaces', *Environment and Planning A: Economy and Space*, Vol. 51, No. 3, 2018.

'Democracy Promoters' in Jordan

Unlike Egypt or the United Arab Emirates, where offices of Western 'democracy promotion' institutions were raided and shut down in 2011 and 2012, Jordan is by and large a welcoming environment for US and European 'democracy promoters' – to the extent that it is perhaps the Arab country with the strongest in-country presence of such institutions. The two most important funding sources for 'democracy promotion' activities in the country are USAID and the EU, which again contract a number of Western non-profit quasi-governmental organisations and/or for-profit democracy contractors for the task of implementing projects on the ground. These latter are almost always carried out in conjunction with or via a local Jordanian NGO, ministry or other official entity. Jordan's absolute and per capita levels of foreign aid in general, and of 'democracy promotion' funds, are among the highest worldwide.

During my fieldwork, Jordan received a guaranteed annual funding level of $360 million in economic support funds (ESF) and $300 million in foreign military financing (FMF) from the US alone. Fifty-three per cent of the ESFs were provided as cash transfer assistance, for which the Jordanian government had to meet mutually agreed benchmarks.[117] The remaining ESFs are spent on USAID programmes in the country, the democracy and governance portfolio having received $25.42 million in 2013. As I approached the end of my fieldwork, the level of US funding had further increased to a guaranteed overall level of $1 billion per year and an envisaged democracy and governance portfolio of $47 million for 2016.[118]

The key US institutions engaged in 'democracy promotion' are the Department of State (DoS); the quasi-governmental NED, which receives an annual allocation from the US Congress; and USAID. In Jordan, US efforts at 'democracy promotion' are almost exclusively funded via USAID. The NED, which operates no country offices, provides direct grants to civil society organisations and allocates the remainder of its budget – in 2013, around 55 per cent – to its traditional four core grantees. These are the NDI, the International Republican Institute (IRI), the American Center for International Labor Solidarity (ACILS) and the Center for International Private Enterprise (CIPE). While all four organisations are active in Jordan, the IRI and in particular the NDI

---

[117] Sharp, J.M. 'Jordan: background and U.S. relations', CRS, Washington, DC, 1 April 2013, p. 10.
[118] US Government, Map of foreign assistance worldwide, available at: www .foreignassistance.gov/explore.

operate their own offices in Amman and stand out as major actors in the field of 'democracy promotion' in the country.

The NED, and in particular the NDI and IRI, were directly modelled on the German political party foundations, and were established under Ronald Reagan in 1983 by a group of neoconservatives as new institutional vehicles for the hitherto covert provision of political aid by the CIA to foreign political groups allied to the US. The NED, which has operated since its founding in 1983 under the same president, Carl Gershman, essentially works on the assumption 'that governmental money, if filtered through enough layers of bureaucracy, becomes "private" funding'.[119] Even though the NDI's and IRI's activities in Jordan are primarily funded through USAID, and not the NED, the latter still plays an important role as a powerful medium for the convergence of academic research on and global funding of 'democracy promotion'. The pseudo-academic and non-peer-reviewed *Journal of Democracy* is operated by the NED's Washington, DC office.

In light of strong scepticism, if not outright rejection, of US funding by various Jordanian civil society organisations and political activists, the NDI, which is loosely affiliated with the American Democratic Party, has in private conversations with different interviewees been referred to as a somewhat more acceptable donor and partner organisation than the IRI, which is affiliated with the Republican Party. In part as a consequence of this difference in perception, the NDI's Jordan office is considerably bigger than the IRI's and arguably constitutes the most prominent 'democracy promotion' actor in the country. In 2013 it had a total of fifty-seven full-time employees and, according to one employee, was running on an annual budget of $14 million. The central position of the NDI's Jordan office to the organisation at large was emphasised by the board of directors – chaired by former US Secretary of State Madeleine Albright – having convened in Amman for its 2013 NDI board meeting.

Another important US 'democracy promotion' organisation present in Amman is the International Foundation for Electoral Systems (IFES). Under a cooperative agreement (Consortium for Elections and Political Processes (CEPPS)) supervised by USAID, the IFES, NDI and IRI implement USAID's political processes strengthening programme in the country. The non-profit organisations are complemented by, among others, an office of Freedom House and the presence of Family Health International 360 (FHI 360), which – until widespread allegations of fraud regarding its activities in Pakistan and Afghanistan – used to be

---

[119] Conry, B., 'Loose cannon: the National Endowment for Democracy', *Cato Institute*, Washington, DC, Foreign Policy Briefing No. 27, 8 November 1993.

known as the Academy for Educational Development (AED). AED/FHI 360 is implementing USAID's civil society programme in Jordan.

The list of US for-profit organisations that were active in the field of 'democracy promotion' in Jordan while I was conducting my research includes, among others, the management company Tetra Tech DPK, which implements USAID's Rule of Law programme. Besides DPK consulting, Tetra Tech acquired the development consulting firm Associates in Rural Development (ARD) in 2007. As the names of some of the organisations now active in 'democracy promotion' indicate, many originated in the sphere of development aid and were gradually – in light of its growing financial attractiveness – also drawn into the field of 'democracy promotion'. Other for-profit consultancy firms active in 'democracy promotion' in Jordan include Democracy International Inc. and Management Systems International (MSI).

The overarching framework for EU-Jordanian relations is the 2002 Association Agreement. The most important funding mechanisms based on this are the European Neighbourhood and Partnership Instrument (ENPI) (2007–2013) and its successor, the European Neighbourhood Instrument (ENI) (2014–2020). EU bilateral assistance for Jordan was worth around €90 million per year between 2014 and 2017, including approximately €22.5 million for activities aimed at 'reinforcing the rule of law for enhanced accountability and equity in public service delivery'.[120] In contrast to USAID, which openly uses the term 'democracy and govern-ance' for its 'democracy promotion' activities, the EU tends to put such activities into a more technocratic developmental aid framework, with 'the consolidation of deep democracy'[121] only appearing as a specific objective under the overall objective of promoting the rule of law. While official EU documents are thus, as described by Kienle, 'less boisterous and more discreet',[122] an official of the European External Action Service (EEAS) nevertheless insisted that '"democracy promotion" is our pillar in the cooperation with Jordan.'[123]

In light of the wide range of EU funding tools, the figures need to be treated with some caution, as neat breakdowns of the totality of EU foreign assistance to Jordan and a clear identification of the 'democracy promotion' activities are hard to come by. Besides the traditional

---

[120] These figures are estimations based on the information provided in EEAS and European Commission (EC), *Programming of the European Neighbourhood Instrument (ENI) – 2014–2020 – Single Support Framework for EU support to Jordan (2014–2017)*, available at: https://ec.europa.eu/neighbourhood-enlargement/sites/near/files/single_support_fra mework_2014-2020.pdf, p. 9.

[121] EEAS and EC, *Programming of the European Neighbourhood Instrument*, p. 10.

[122] Kienle, 'Democracy promotion and the renewal of authoritarian rule', p. 236.

[123] Interview with Davide, EEAS official, Brussels, 10 March 2015.

financing of projects that are then implemented by a European 'democracy promotion' institution, the key funding mechanisms of the EU include budget support and twinning projects that bring together officials from an EU member state and a public institution of the beneficiary country. As part of the EU's response to the Arab uprisings, the EU established the so-called SPRING programme (Support to Partnership, Reform and Inclusive Growth) under the ENPI. While Jordan was initially to benefit from an additional €70 million, only a first tranche of €40 million was transferred via a Good Governance and Development Contract (GGDC). This form of direct budget support, which demonstrates full confidence in the recipient and is only very rarely used, was not further pursued however, as Jordan did not carry out the desired democratic reforms.[124]

Besides the above-mentioned bilateral aid instruments, a number of thematic funding tools are also available to Jordan. These include the European Instrument for Democracy and Human Rights (EIDHR), to which Jordanian NGOs can apply for direct support. While EIDHR funding, unlike that provided by the ENPI or the ENI, requires no formal consent from the Jordanian government, the latter circumvents this clause by demanding by force of Jordanian law that every Jordanian NGO seek the Council of Ministers' prior approval for any foreign funding. Finally, the European Endowment for Democracy (EED), which was established upon Polish initiative in 2012 and directly modelled on the American NED, is also active in Jordan, but by 2016 had extended only two rather small grants to Jordanian media organisations.

Alongside the EU's efforts at 'democracy promotion' in Jordan, which are administered by the local office of the EU delegation, a number of European countries provide additional bilateral assistance to Jordan, and offer somewhat limited 'democracy promotion' funding via their embassies. Particularly noteworthy on the European side are the German political party foundations, four of which operate an office in Amman. The two main ones, respectively affiliated to the German conservative and labour parties, are the Konrad Adenauer Foundation (KAS) and the Friedrich Ebert Foundation (FES). Just like the American NDI and IRI, the KAS and FES are also funded by annual allocations from the German state and may be seen as quasi-governmental organisations. During my research period, the Jordan office of the KAS was implementing an EU-funded programme to encourage political party activism. The

---

[124] A contributing factor to the EU's decision to withhold the second tranche was the effective end to a Jordanian moratorium on the use of capital punishment in late 2014, when eleven convicted murderers were hanged.

German political party institutions operate on a significantly smaller budget than their American counterparts; have a somewhat stronger focus on research than on outreach projects; and put more emphasis on operating through, or in conjunction with their respective local partner organisations.

Like USAID, the EU also relies on for-profit companies for some of its programmes. In 2014, for instance, the Madrid-based consultancy company Eptisa, in association with the German GFA Consulting Group and the Jordanian NGO Partners Jordan was awarded an EU-funded civil society and parliamentary support programme. While, in contrast to USAID, the EU does not rely on the same clear subdivision of its 'democracy promotion' activities in the four spheres of political processes, civil society, rule of law and governance, many EU- and USAID-funded programmes effectively address the same areas. The EU-funded Eptisa programme is thus equivalent to a USAID-funded parliamentary training programme implemented by the NDI, and to another funded by the British Foreign Office and the Department for International Development (DfID), which is implemented by the Westminster Foundation for Democracy. Also, in the sphere of political party training, both the IRI and the KAS implement programmes that are funded by the USAID and the EU, respectively. Furthermore, the Amman office of the United Nations Development Programme (UNDP) is implementing a very similar electoral assistance programme to that of USAID (implemented by the IFES), on behalf of the EU. Finally, also in terms of civil society support, USAID and the EU often fund the same organisations.

The key differences between US and European 'democracy promotion' activities in Jordan lie thus much less in their respective programmatic focuses than in their visibility, in the available funding, in the degree of acceptance by the Jordanian public at large and in the operationalisation and framing of interventions. Finally, a common problem of both US and European 'democracy promoters' in Jordan is actually spending all the funds available, as confirmed by a number of 'democracy promoters'. This is just another reminder of the fact that external attempts at 'democracy promotion' in Jordan more often operate independently of popular demands and/or political dynamics in the country rather than responding to them.

The legal basis on which the organisations mentioned so far operate is rather heterogeneous. The NDI and IRI run under the umbrella of USAID Jordan and are not registered separately in the country despite operating distinct offices outside of the US Embassy. The German FES is not registered as a distinct entity in Jordan, but instead operates as an official partner organisation of the Jordanian Royal Scientific Society (RSS). The German KAS, however, is registered with the Jordanian Ministry of Social Development (MoSD).

This list of 'democracy promotion' actors in Jordan is not exhaustive. In light of increasing funding levels, and as many organisations actively attempt to keep their programmes out of the public spotlight, it is practically impossible to build a complete list. Two other organisations should nevertheless be mentioned briefly – the Foundation for the Future (FFF) and the private Open Society Foundations (OSF), founded by the Hungarian-American businessman George Soros. During my field research period, the latter did not implement any major programmes that aimed directly at 'democracy promotion' and the former primarily used its office in Amman for programmes in other countries in the region. The FFF ceased its operations in October 2014.

Methodology, Sources and Chapter Outline

I rely on a mixed methods approach that includes intensive field research, a large number of qualitative interviews, participatory observation and analysis of various primary sources. My approach is interdisciplinary and combines ethnographic observation, an anthropological concern with the contested meanings and diverse impacts of global dynamics on the micro level and a somewhat traditional political science interest in the creation of power.

The sources used for this book include various reports and publications produced by US and European institutions active in Jordan; speeches and reports published by the Jordanian government and the Royal Hashemite Court, Jordanian and international newspapers; US Embassy cables published by the whistle-blower website WikiLeaks; and secondary literature on Jordanian politics, democracy and 'democracy promotion', 'developmental aid' and the politics of intervention, as well as authoritarian neoliberalism, critical security studies and militarism. Further, I conducted approximately 160 semi-structured qualitative interviews during my field research stays in Jordan from September 2012 to March 2013, and again in January and February 2015, as well as in Washington, DC in May and June 2013, and in Brussels in March 2015. I conducted interviews with US and European 'democracy promoters', diplomats, researchers and businessmen, as well as with Jordanian government representatives, public officials, researchers, businessmen, politicians, political activists, NGO employees and students. Most interviews lasted between one and three hours. The interviews were based on a list of prepared questions. I recorded most, except of course when interviewees preferred me not to do so.

While most interviews were conducted in English, a small number were also held in German and Arabic. When quoting from interviews originally conducted in German or Arabic, I have translated statements into English. In order to protect the anonymity of the interviewee, the translation of a source is not indicated. The vast majority of interviewees preferred to be anonymous. For the reader's benefit, I gave each interviewee a pseudonym, which generally attempts to reflect the interviewee's gender and country of origin. Some interviewees allowed their identification. When their real names did not add anything to my argument, however, I anonymised them too, but they may indeed be identifiable by the informed reader. Besides using pseudonyms, I also provide a brief job description for each interviewee ('democracy promoter', Western diplomat,[125] NGO employee, etc.). I use the term 'democracy promoter' for all persons working for one of the institutions discussed above and actively engaged in activities aimed at the promotion of democracy. As suggested by the title of this book, I view the term as deeply problematic, which is why I only use it in inverted commas. In addition to the interviews, I attended a number of public and non-public events, including electoral debates, conferences, workshops and training sessions. I also gained access to a number of confidential documents.

This book explores the nature and effect of US and European 'democracy promotion' in Jordan through a focus on practice. It does not, importantly, claim or attempt to provide a comprehensive picture of all 'democracy promotion' interventions in Jordan, but instead strives to present an in-depth discussion of different ideas for and practices of 'democracy promotion' in the country, and their effects. Based on the above critique of some of the literature, this research identifies three interrelated approaches to, and/or narratives of, 'democracy promotion'. The first is the notion of social and institutional engineering, which is essentially the idea of promoting procedural democracy (chapters 2, 3 and 4). The second is the political economy narrative (Chapter 5). The third is the idea that Jordan needs to be made 'secure' via external military

---

[125] I am fully aware of the many different meanings that the term 'the West' or 'Western' can come to convey, and of its questionable analytical usefulness. I nevertheless occasionally characterise 'democracy promoters' and/or 'democracy promotion' organisations as such, in order to avoid the tiresome and repetitive use of 'US and European', and in order to better protect the anonymity of interviewees, particularly Americans, who often wanted to be identified as 'Western democracy promoter'. For a more in-depth reflection on the use of the term 'the West' or 'Western' in a study of 'democracy promotion', see Carapico, *Political Aid and Arab Activism*, pp. 21–22.

and security collaboration, in order to become 'ready for democracy' (Chapter 6).

Chapter 2 begins with an investigation of attempts at institutional engineering. By demonstrating the primacy of 'the procedural' in over-arching US and European policy documents, as well as in discourses of 'democracy promoters', I argue that the underlying structural power dynamics of Jordanian authoritarianism are fundamentally ignored. The Jordanian regime is in important ways portrayed as a mere result of a lack of capacity among Jordanians at large and at times is even viewed as an agent of democratisation. Based on an in-depth analysis of an IRI-organised political party training event, the chapter contends that attempts at 'democracy promotion' strengthen authoritarian stability in the country, as they directly accept, depend on and reinforce the Jordanian regime's questionable reform narrative.

Chapter 3 analyses US and European efforts at electoral support and observation with the concrete example of Jordan's 2013 parliamentary elections. I argue that international 'democracy promoters' fundamentally fail to take seriously the potential durability of authoritarian modes of governance. Instead of an example of gradual procedural progress, as suggested by international electoral observers, I suggest that Jordanian elections primarily function as a means of what Heydemann aptly calls 'authoritarian upgrading'.[126] Among other areas, the chapter also pays particular attention to the role of researchers-cum-electoral observers in the reproduction of a narrative of Jordan as gradually 'reforming' and 'liberalising'. As the very possibility for authoritarian stability is thereby analytically ignored, the latter is effectively reinforced.

The discussion of US and European attempts at social and institutional engineering in Jordan is complemented in Chapter 4 by an investigation of civil society support and youth education. The chapter not only shows how such efforts subordinate Jordanian politics to an often idealised narrative of universally valid processes of democratisation, but also demonstrates that attempts at 'democracy promotion' tell us more about the 'democracy promoters' themselves and their desired self-understandings than about the context in which they operate. Despite its regular disregard of local political dynamics and related practical 'fail-ures', 'democracy promotion' is thus shown to function in a highly self-perpetuating manner. In particular, the chapter looks at an NDI programme aimed at youth education and participation, which the

---

[126] Heydemann, S., 'Upgrading authoritarianism in the Arab world', The Saban Center for Middle East Policy at the Brookings Institution Analysis Paper Number 13, October 2007, available at: www.brookings.edu/wp-content/uploads/2016/06/10arabworld.pdf.

organisation itself considers to be one of its largest and most successful programmes in the region.[127]

Building on the initial three chapters, which implicitly demonstrate that 'democracy promoters' approach their work through an assumed market logic, with political parties and state institutions as supposed forces of supply and civil society actors as forces of demand, Chapter 5 provides a more in-depth analysis of the notions of political economy that underlie the 'democracy promotion' project. The chapter shows that 'democracy promoters' widely view the promotion of procedural democracy as mutually reinforcing of the promotion of neoliberalism. Against this backdrop, the chapter analyses processes of neoliberal restructuring in Aqaba, which are directly supported by USAID under the assumption that they also help to enable eventual processes of democratisation. I argue that such efforts at neoliberal 'democracy promotion' are part and parcel of a wider strategy aimed at the consolidation of class power. Instead of enabling future processes of democratisation, such projects are demonstrated to only further deprive procedural democracy of its already strongly diluted emancipatory potential, as socio-economic inequalities are radically exacerbated.

Chapter 6 speaks to the wider literature on how ideas, conceptions and practices of democracy and security are thought to interrelate. It seeks to critique both the 'unity of goodness' that Huntington came to endorse in *The Third Wave*[128] and instrumentalist arguments in favour of 'democracy promotion' and based on a securitised democratic peace hypothesis, as for instance found in the work of Fukuyama.[129] While showing the widespread belief in the democratic peace among individual 'democracy promoters', the chapter illustrates how this falls prey to processes of militarisation with highly controversial effects on security, state and society in Jordan. It begins by discussing the ways in which 'democracy promoters' view their own work and security support to the Jordanian regime as mutually reinforcing. After providing a brief overview of the role of Jordanian security services, the chapter presents an in-depth analysis of US security support to Jordan via the example of US funding for a special operations training centre just outside Amman. At the core of the chapter lies an investigation of the controversial processes of militarisation and commercialisation that accompany such US security support, and that

---

[127] Political party training, electoral support and youth activities – which I discuss in chapters 2, 3 and 4 – are described by Bush as 'not regime-compatible' categories of 'democracy promotion'. I strongly disagree with such a classification. Bush, *The Taming of Democracy Assistance*, p. 57.

[128] Huntington, *The Third Wave*, p. xv. Also see Schmitter, 'Democracy's third wave'.

[129] See Heydemann, 'In the shadow of democracy', p. 156.

both drastically reduce the chances of the Jordanian security sector ever being put under popular control and reproduce deeply Orientalist images of Jordan as continuously requiring external aid and intervention in order for abstract notions of democracy, economic growth and security to be realised. Chapter 6 is in part based on an article previously published with *Security Dialogue*.[130]

Besides summarising the key findings of the book, Chapter 7 also discusses the current crisis of liberal politics and 'democracy promotion'. Against the backdrop of the global rise of populist politics, the chapter questions whether clear lines of separation can be drawn between imperial coercion, liberal intervention and growing populism. Ultimately, it suggests that just as imperial coercion and 'democracy promotion' are part of the same politics of control and domination, liberal interventionism and the various forms of structural violence associated with it have also played a major role in strengthening precisely those populist dynamics that now put the 'democracy promotion' project under increasing pressure.

---

[130] Schuetze, B., 'Simulating, marketing, and playing war: US-Jordanian military collaboration and the politics of commercial security', *Security Dialogue*, Vol. 48, No. 5, 2017, pp. 431–450.

2 Who's Afraid of Politics?

'In Jordan, Implementation Is Always the Real Challenge'

The Jordanian regime and US and European officials almost appear to be in competition when it comes to emphasising the importance and inevitability of incremental procedural change in Jordan's political development. This mutual insistence on an image of Jordan as caught in an irresistible process of democratisation both seemingly reconfirms the need to provide external support to further strengthen this process and reinforces the Jordanian regime's narrative of itself as democratising force.

On the Jordanian side, this reform discourse is of instrumental importance for the simulation of constant ongoing change. According to the king, '[r]eform is not merely a question of changes to laws and regulations. It requires an evolution in how citizens, civil servants and the representatives entrusted to make decisions on behalf of citizens operate and interact within the current system'.[1] In a 2013 discussion paper, King Abdullah II further stated that democratic progress in general and in the concrete case of 'transition to parliamentary government will deepen as parliamentary and political parties' work matures over coming parliamentary cycles', adding that 'political maturity comes from experience, guided by the will of the people through the ballot box'.[2]

According to the king's approach, which owes much to modernisation theory, if Jordanians simply participate long enough in proper democratic procedures, they will surely mature so that Jordan will eventually be able to reach the next of several 'transformation phases',[3] as stated in Jordan's

---

[1] King Abdullah II, 'Making our democratic system work for all Jordanians', Royal Hashemite Court, Amman, second discussion paper, 16 January 2013, available at: https:// kingabdullah.jo/en/discussion-papers/making-our-democratic-system-work-all-jordanians.

[2] King Abdullah II, 'Each playing our part in a new democracy', Royal Hashemite Court, Amman, third discussion paper, 2 March 2013, available at: https://kingabdullah.jo/en/ discussion-papers/each-playing-our-part-new-democracy.

[3] National Agenda Steering Committee, *National Agenda: The Jordan We Strive For, 2006–2015* (Amman: National Agenda Steering Committee, 2005), pp. 7–8, available at: www.nationalagenda.jo/Portals/0/EnglishBooklet.pdf.

National Agenda. The image given is one of constant progress along a clearly defined and generally agreed-upon 'trajectory path', which is seen as paved with 'historic milestone[s]'.[4] Importantly, Jordan's transition to democracy now appears primarily to depend on Jordanians themselves, on a maturing political culture and on the correct political procedures, while the need to change the substance of specific laws or regulations is relegated to a position of lesser importance. Since Jordan's 'firm political development path is now well underway',[5] all that seems to be required from external actors, such as the US and the EU, is mere support in the implementation of this already established process.

The Jordan Strategy Paper 2007–2013 of the European Neighbourhood and Partnership Instrument (ENPI) directly subscribes to this narrative, as it concludes that '[w]hile Jordan is willing to undertake reforms, there are difficulties implementing them'.[6] The curious indifference to anything beyond the procedural level is also apparent in remarks such as, '[i]n the Jordanian context ... implementation remains always the real challenge'.[7] Jordanians are thus implicitly described as weak at 'getting things done' and as requiring well-intended aid from abroad. Also, the observation is remarkable in its similarity to Fukuyama's notion of the end of history,[8] as it seems to suggest that in Jordanian politics and society, potential disagreements either present no challenge at all, or at least no 'real' one. The statement further seems to imply the rather dubious idea that there is no need for ideological debate, as either 'the end point of mankind's ideological evolution'[9] has been reached or the space for such ideological debate is certainly not deemed to be Jordan.

Along very similar lines, United States Agency for International Development (USAID) reports also appear to view Jordan as caught in an ongoing process that is slowly but irresistibly unfolding. In light of the seeming agreement on Jordan's 'trajectory path', the remaining problems and challenges then appear to be merely procedural. According to the USAID Jordan Country Development Cooperation Strategy 2013–2017,

---

[4] National Agenda Steering Committee, *National Agenda*, pp. 3–4.
[5] King Abdullah II, 'Goals, achievements and conventions: pillars for deepening our democratic transition', Royal Hashemite Court, Amman, fifth discussion paper, 13 September 2014, available at: https://kingabdullah.jo/en/discussion-papers/goals-achievements-and-conventions-pillars-deepening-our-democratic-transition.
[6] ENPI, *Jordan: Strategy Paper 2007–2013 & National Indicative Programme 2007–2010*, p. 11, available at: https://ec.europa.eu/europeaid/sites/devco/files/nip-jordan-2011-2013_en.pdf.
[7] ENPI, *Jordan*, p. 13.
[8] Fukuyama, F., 'The end of history?', *The National Interest*, Vol. 16, Summer 1989, pp. 3–18.
[9] Fukuyama, 'The end of history?'

for instance, the real problem is that 'implementation of reforms is still weak'.[10] The task at hand consequently seems to present itself as that of building local capacity to improve the ongoing process of Jordanian reforms and of enabling a faster 'take-off' through technical support for key Jordanian state institutions. Reiterating its strong agreement with the substance of Jordanian reform initiatives and concluding that insufficient democratisation in the country is ultimately due to problems of implementation, USAID Jordan finds that '[t]he 2005 National Agenda, a blueprint for extensive political and economic reform, would place Jordan firmly on a track towards democratization if fully implemented'.[11]

While most 'democracy promoters' working in Jordan have their doubts about how genuine the Jordanian regime's will to democratise really is, they still overwhelmingly subscribe to the procedural narrative outlined above. Discussing Jordanian efforts to fight corruption, one technical expert funded by the EU and working at a Jordanian government institution, for instance, explained that 'there are quite good laws here. They only need to be implemented'.[12] Similarly, another EU-funded expert based in a Jordanian ministry explained that 'Jordan is on the right path. [It] always has been ... The vision is there. Implementing it is hard'.[13]

In this chapter I discuss US and European efforts at institutional engineering, which aim at assisting the implementation of said vision. I do so through the example of capacity-building programmes for Jordanian state institutions and political party training programmes. The chapter is built around the central theoretical claim that 'democracy promotion' efforts at institutional engineering in Jordan are guided by a primacy of the procedural and a relative indifference to the substantive. Building on this, I argue that 'democracy promotion' functions as a highly self-perpetuating system of understanding Jordanian politics. Finally, I aim to demonstrate that rather than weakening authoritarianism, external efforts at institutional engineering in fact directly reinforce authoritarian stability in Jordan.

The genius of understanding procedures, institutions and capacity as lying at the heart of democracy is the premise that, as stated by Carapico, processes of democratisation thereby seem to 'evolve from bureaucratic-authoritarian conditions via expert consultation rather than by popular

---

[10] USAID, *Jordan Country Development Cooperation Strategy 2013–2017*, p. 17, available at: www.usaid.gov/jordan/documents/cdcs.

[11] USAID, *Democracy and Governance – Overview*, 28 February 2011, available at: http://jordan.usaid.gov/printme.aspx?webUrl=/en/OurWork/ProgramAr.

[12] Interview with Niklas, EU-funded technical expert, Amman, 19 March 2013.

[13] Interview with Charlotte, EU-funded technical expert, Amman, 28 January 2013.

mobilization'.[14] In thus making democratisation appear to be a 'matter of technique, of procedure, of program design and implementation',[15] as stated by Heydemann, the focus on the procedural not only seemingly reconfirms the need for the technical knowledge and expertise of 'democracy promoters', but importantly also reconfirms the Jordanian regime's own narrative of democratisation being more about capacity, procedures and institutions than about redistribution of power. In light of the extent to which international perceptions of the legitimacy of the Jordanian regime are linked to the latter appearing as an 'important stabilising and modernising influence'[16] and a 'principal voice for moderation, peace and reform in the Middle East',[17] as respectively stated in central EU and US documents, I argue that the strong procedural focus of 'democracy promotion' directly reinforces the perceived legitimacy of Jordanian authoritarianism.[18]

The highly selective focus on procedural weaknesses, shortcomings and absences, which automatically come to the fore when the conceptually narrow Western liberal democratic mould is pressed onto Jordanian politics, is shown to turn all those parts of Jordanian politics that cannot be made to fit 'democracy promotion's' functionalist conceptions into seeming abnormalities and deformations of the norm. The important effect of this is that what is problematised is no longer the peculiar power structures of Jordanian authoritarianism, but increasingly the 'nature' of Jordanians themselves. Once the causes for Jordanian authoritarianism are constructed as intimately linked to Jordanians' alleged lack of understanding of, and experience with democracy, perceptions of moral superiority are seemingly confirmed and expertise with supposedly universal international standards and best practices is discursively rendered more relevant than that of the specific political context of Jordan.[19]

Conceptual closures such as the narrowing down of democracy to its procedural variants are, as shown by Mitchell, Ferguson and Li, among

---

[14] Carapico, S., *Political Aid and Arab Activism: Democracy Promotion, Justice, and Representation* (New York: Cambridge University Press, 2014), p. 11.

[15] Heydemann, S., 'In the shadow of democracy: review article', *Middle East Journal*, Vol. 60, No. 1, Winter 2006, p. 150.

[16] ENPI, *Jordan*, p. 6.

[17] USAID, *USAID/Jordan Country Strategy 2010–2014* (Washington, DC, March 2010), p. 6.

[18] See also Lust-Okar, E., *Structuring Conflict in the Arab World: Incumbents, Opponents, and Institutions* (Cambridge: Cambridge University Press, 2005).

[19] See, among others, Chandler, D., 'Back to the future? The limits of neo-Wilsonian ideals of exporting democracy', *Review of International Studies*, Vol. 32, No. 3, July 2006, pp. 475–494.

others, a very characteristic feature of expert discourses.[20] These may, as argued by Ferguson in *The Anti-Politics Machine*, 'very effectively squash political challenges to the system ... by insistently reposing political questions ... as technical "problems"',[21] thereby excelling at the reproduction of existing power structures, only now in the name of 'development' or, in the case of this study, in the name of 'democracy'.

Overall, I aim to demonstrate that the regular practical failure of 'democracy promotion' is largely irrelevant to its continuous functioning. In light of this, I will pay particular attention to the different modes of institutional reproduction and their self-perpetuating tendencies. 'Democracy promotion' is finally shown to constitute a highly self-confirming system through which Jordanian politics and society are viewed, explained and kept in place.

Given the sheer size and number of US and European efforts at institutional engineering in Jordan, the approach in this chapter is necessarily selective.[22] The reasoning behind my focus on capacity-building and party training is twofold. Firstly, these sectors constitute some of the biggest fields of intervention for 'democracy promoters' in Jordan, with a number of US and European institutions engaged in them. Secondly, strong state institutions and active parties are widely assumed to be at the very core of functioning democracies.

Ultimately, my interest is in the kind of power that institutional engineering interventions (re)produce. I suggest that rather than responding to decisive Jordanian capacity needs, US and European efforts at institutional engineering in Jordan reinforce precisely those conditions that seemingly called for and justified external intervention to begin with. The effect is thus the perpetuation of exactly those hierarchies of power that the project of 'democracy promotion' initially set out to overcome.

'Pissing in the Wind'

On a regular basis, USAID commissions assessments of its Democracy and Governance (D/G) portfolio in Jordan, which aim at both evaluating ongoing and suggesting future interventions. The report of concern here

---

[20] Ferguson, J., *The Anti-Politics Machine: 'Development,' Depoliticization, and Bureaucratic Power in Lesotho* (Minneapolis: University of Minnesota Press, 1994); Li, T.M., *The Will to Improve: Governmentality, Development, and the Practice of Politics* (London: Duke University Press, 2007; Mitchell, T., *Rule of Experts: Egypt, Techno-Politics, Modernity* (Berkeley: University of California Press, 2002).

[21] Ferguson, *The Anti-Politics Machine*, p. 270.

[22] There are probably only a few Jordanian state institutions that are not in one way or another the direct target of US and/or European efforts at capacity-building and institutional engineering.

was developed in 2003 by Professor of Government Guilain Denoeux on behalf of the Washington, DC-based development consulting firm Management Systems International (MSI).[23]

Denoeux also authored a 2011 report that has, however, not been made publicly available. The 2003 report is remarkable in that it is – at least in part – a rare example of a break with the primacy of the procedural mentioned above. It both openly discusses a number of substantive problems and challenges the otherwise dominant process narrative. Despite this, the primacy of the procedural quickly reasserted its power, as the USAID Jordan D/G unit deliberately ignored the vast majority of the report's recommendations. While these were not binding in any way, the extent to which they were ignored is remarkable and indicative of 'democracy promotion's' dependence on a narrative of constant procedural progress. The report and its reception at USAID Jordan thus provide us with an excellent example for the kind of knowledge that has no place in 'democracy promotion' and that can and indeed must be ignored in order to ensure 'democracy promotion's' continuous functioning.[24]

As the report challenges the underlying narrative of the previously quoted US and EU documents, it finds that neither the Jordanian government nor the donor community actually has a significant interest in supporting genuine processes of democratisation in the country. It thus remarks that many of the Jordanians interviewed 'saw the donor community as basically complicit in a mode of government that gives the population only a subordinate and marginal role in decision-making . . . [and that treats it] as an obstacle, not as a partner'. Discussing the programmatic implications of the findings, the report states that 'the Jordanian public already yearns for greater opportunities to participate in the political process, and there is consequently little need to stimulate demands for democracy'. In direct contrast to previously discussed analyses that see Jordan's prospects for democratisation as primarily related to political culture, capacity and procedures, the assessment finds that in Jordan, the 'prospects for democratization are mostly a function of the extent of political will to reform within the governing elite'.[25]

---

[23] Denoeux, G. (MSI), Wilcox, O. (USAID) and Zawaneh, Z. (MSI), *Jordan Democracy and Governance Assessment* (USAID Center for Democracy and Governance and USAID/Jordan, August 2003), available at: http://pdf.usaid.gov/pdf_docs/pnadd348.pdf.

[24] See Li, *The Will to Improve*, esp. pp. 10–12, for a discussion of the project of rendering contentious issues technical, as well as for the role of closure in expert discourses.

[25] Denoeux, Wilcox and Zawaneh, *Jordan Democracy and Governance Assessment*, pp. 40–43.

The USAID Jordan D/G unit received the 2003 MSI assessment without a great deal of enthusiasm, as it did the 2011 report authored by Denoeux and which is marked by similar concerns. When looking at the programmes run by the USAID Jordan D/G portfolio at the time of this research, one can quickly note that the unit not only adopted a highly critical stance on the report's recommendations, but effectively went as far as to ignore them almost entirely. As stated by one 'democracy promoter' working in Jordan, 'the minute you begin to be a practitioner, you have to suspend [your] disbelief about some of the larger structures'.[26] In line with this perceived necessity to ignore certain knowledge when working as a practitioner, the D/G unit effectively decided to bury the MSI report.

Despite all recommendations pointing to the infeasibility of, and lack of need for, a rule of law programme, the USAID Jordan D/G unit wanted exactly the kind of 'prohibitively expensive USAID program'[27] that Denoeux et al. had explicitly warned against in 2003. The desired programme eventually became reality when the USAID Jordan D/G unit contracted Tetra Tech DPK for a $25 million, 2008–2013 rule of law programme, which included among other things the automation of all seventy-four courts in Jordan. While the programme officially aimed at '[e]mpowering judicial independence',[28] it remains unclear how it intended to achieve this goal in the absence of any significant legal change. The programme thus explicitly set out to address an issue about which the MSI report had stated that there is 'little, if anything, that the Mission can do'[29] about. Further, the D/G unit also contracted the American Bar Association for an $8.7 million legal education programme in 2004–2014. The unit thus once again implemented a programme that the MSI's 2003 assessment had explicitly recommended not be done, since, '[g]iven the absence of clear political will', it would 'yield, at best, only limited returns'.[30]

In light of this, a Washington, DC-based senior political advisor and former high-ranking USAID employee who had also been involved in the 2011 MSI report, remarked that: 'We were more sceptical of all these programmes than the [USAID Jordan] mission. Our report was not – I think – well received. [The USAID Jordan D/G officer] wanted a Rule of

---

[26] Interview with Michael, 'democracy promoter' working in Jordan, Amman, 24 February 2013.

[27] Denoeux, Wilcox and Zawaneh, *Jordan Democracy and Governance Assessment*, p. 46.

[28] USAID Jordan, 'Rule of Law Program', USAID Jordan, Democracy & Governance Sector – Project Profile, April 2012.

[29] Denoeux, Wilcox and Zawaneh, *Jordan Democracy and Governance Assessment*, p. 47.

[30] Denoeux, Wilcox and Zawaneh, *Jordan Democracy and Governance Assessment*, p. 47.

Law Programme no matter what. So … he created the Rule of Law Programme'.[31] Whether such a programme was really necessary and/or helpful was simply irrelevant. It is further worth remarking that the 2003 report had additionally recommended that 'civil society should not represent a primary focus of, or a stand-alone program within, the Mission's D/G portfolio'.[32] Again, the USAID Jordan D/G unit strongly desired to have such a stand-alone programme. Consequently, it also implemented one in direct opposition to the advice received, when it contracted Academy for Educational Development (AED) for an $18 million civil society programme in 2008–2013.

Aimed 'at cultivating a strong and vibrant civil society',[33] the programme set out to pursue precisely the kind of demand-driven approach that Denoeux et al. had deemed to be both unnecessary and unproductive in Jordan, as 'the Jordanian public already yearn[ed] for greater opportunities to participate in the political process'.[34] Besides noting that the report's recommendations were almost entirely ignored, it is also worth noting that Denoeux analysed Jordanian politics based on a highly questionable logic of the market, which I will criticise in more depth later in this chapter, as well as in Chapter 5.

Instead of being an exception, the tendency to ignore external advice and to effectively do that which had been recommended against appears as a recurrent theme in US attempts at 'democracy promotion' in Jordan. As I demonstrate in Chapter 4, the USAID Jordan D/G unit, through the National Democratic Institute (NDI), at the time of the research also carried out a civic education programme, thereby effectively aiming to 'alter the "outlook" of Jordanians … by seeking to make them more "civic-minded"'[35] – another activity that the MSI report had explicitly advised against.

A former high-ranking USAID employee who also co-authored MSI's 2011 report, openly admitted the following:

> Even if it [US 'democracy promotion' in Jordan] isn't counterproductive, it might be just not very useful and a waste of money … there are vested interests in continuing these programmes … the D/G officer in Jordan … that's how he makes a living. So, if you go there and you say: '… I don't think you're doing very much here and I think we should cut this down', what do you think [he] is

---

[31] Interview with Jim, senior political advisor and former high-ranking USAID employee, Washington, DC, 11 June 2013.

[32] Denoeux, Wilcox and Zawaneh, *Jordan Democracy and Governance Assessment*, p. 45.

[33] USAID Jordan, 'Civil Society Program', USAID Jordan, Democracy & Governance Sector – Project Profile, April 2012.

[34] Denoeux, Wilcox and Zawaneh, *Jordan Democracy and Governance Assessment*, p. 42.

[35] Denoeux, Wilcox and Zawaneh, *Jordan Democracy and Governance Assessment*, p. 44.

going to say? 'Sure. When do you want me to leave?' He's going to say, 'No. No. No. There's always hope. There's always whatever'. So, you've got people whose liveli-hood is being made this way and I don't mean to be too cynical about it, but that's one reason. The other is ... some people argue – I'm not one of them – 'there's always room. You should always keep trying ...'. There are some times when you should just ... take the money and give it back to the taxpayers is one possibility, but of course we'd never do that ... There's a very colourful American aphorism, 'pissing in the wind'. Well ... If you piss in the wind what do you think is going to happen?[36]

Beyond these institutional desires for reproduction, however, I suggest that 'democracy promotion' also directly reinforces authoritarian stability and perceptions of authoritarian legitimacy by endorsing, among other things, a view of the Jordanian regime as an agent of democratisation.[37]

'Not a Rational Decision'

[One] can try to identify contributing factors, but then we are confused when these institutions don't function as planned ... I'm struck by how much institutional functioning is dependent on situational culture ... We'd like to believe that, sort of, everybody can move in the same direction.[38]

If Jordan's prospects for democratisation are mostly a function of the extent of political will to reform within the governing elite, what is there left to do for external 'democracy promoters'? If there is little need to stimulate demands for democracy among Jordanians, then who still requires external 'expert' knowledge about international standards and best practices? And, finally, if the existing formally democratic procedures and mechanisms – Jordan's parliament, its political parties and elections – are not just marked by problems of implementation, but are instead seriously and substantially flawed, who still needs external 'democracy promoters'' expertise in how such procedures should be functioning in an ideal world?

As a reshaping of the USAID Jordan D/G portfolio according to the MSI report's recommendations 'would have reduced the total budget fairly substantially',[39] the assessment was effectively only used to tick a box. Both the 2003 and 2011 reports were read by no more than

---

[36] Interview with Jim, senior political advisor and former high-ranking USAID employee, Washington, DC, 11 June 2013.

[37] See, for instance, the article by the former IRI MENA Regional Director, Owen Kirby, 'Want democracy? Get a king', *The Middle East Quarterly*, December 2000, pp. 3–12.

[38] Interview with Michael, 'democracy promoter' working in Jordan, Amman, 21 November 2012.

[39] Interview with Jim, senior political advisor, former high-ranking USAID employee and co-author of the MSI 2011 report, Washington, DC, 11 June 2013.

a handful of people within USAID, among whom it elicited significant feelings of discomfort. While the 2011 report eventually also reached the head of USAID Jordan, as well as the US Ambassador to Jordan, both decided to do nothing about it. The handling of the MSI report by USAID Jordan staff is in this way reminiscent of Ferguson's observation in *The Anti-Politics Machine* that an 'academic analysis is of no use to a "development" agency unless it provides a place for the agency to plug itself in, unless it provides a charter for the sort of intervention that the agency is set up to do'.

The MSI report was 'unhelpful' for US 'democracy promoters' in Jordan and thus banished, as it failed to do 'what academic discourse inevitably fails to do'; it must make Jordan out to be an enormously promising candidate for the only sort of intervention that a 'democracy promotion' agency is capable of launching: the apolitical, technical capacity-building and institutional support intervention. Just as Ferguson remarked in regard to the 'development' intervention, the 'democracy promotion' intervention 'is a highly standardized operation'.[40] Interventions all over the world consist of very similar activities (support for state institutions, party training, parliamentary strengthening, electoral observation, NGO support, civic education, judicial training, etc.) that regularly tell us more about the 'democracy promoters' themselves and about their prior professional experiences than responding to the actual needs of the targeted society.

In the eyes of the USAID Jordan D/G unit, Denoeux et al. had simply found the wrong problems. After all, as one interviewee working in the field of 'democracy promotion' in Jordan anonymously confirmed, 'Jordan is a big market. We don't want to lose it'. The 'democracy promotion' activities that were eventually selected thus once again seemingly reconfirmed the common narrative about Jordan as continuously democratising and as a stable and modern partner in the region. In doing so they importantly redirect attention and blame for authoritarian practices away from the regime and instead towards the Jordanian population and society at large. The direct allocation of 'democracy promotion' funds to the Jordanian regime is instrumental in reinforcing the latter's perceived legitimacy as agent of democratisation. By endorsing the narrative of the procedural, 'democracy promotion' effectively helps in the construction of a stage upon which participating Jordanians can then perform acts of obedience to the king, thereby only further reinforcing authoritarian stability.

---

[40] For the past three quotations see Ferguson, *The Anti-Politics Machine*, p. 69.

Instead of Jordanian politics informing the nature of 'democracy promotion' activities, 'democracy promotion' and its reliance on the procedural has become the lens through which sense is being made of Jordanian politics. Any advice pointing to the unfeasibility or even counter-productive nature of certain interventions must be disregarded, in order to maintain the illusion that democratic change will only come through the identified institutional and procedural channels. While the regular commissioning of democracy and governance assessments points to what Mitchell describes as development discourse's wish 'to present itself as a detached centre of rationality and intelligence',[41] the actual handling of such assessments reveals the simulated nature of this rationality.

As admitted by 'democracy promoter' Michael, 'we're fiddling at the margin, because we don't want to think about change too much. We're happy Jordan is stable ... We want to have the fig leaf about Jordan becoming more democratic'. Michael added that 'Jordan is an atypical programme ... It's not a rational decision ... We need a programme because we need to have something visible'.[42] Just as US efforts at 'democracy promotion' in Jordan are shielded by a façade of rationality that evolves around, among other things, expert assessments which are then largely ignored, as well as around the staunch belief in the inevitability of processes of democratisation, EU efforts at institutional engineering are similarly characterised by a strong focus on the technical, a strangely apolitical view of Jordanian state institutions and by a strong underlying belief in the narrative of procedural change. Particularly interesting is the EU delegation's technical support contract with the Jordanian Ministry of Political Development (MoPD), signed under the EU's 2005–2012 Support to Human Rights and Good Governance Programme. It not only included €545,000 in technical assistance extended to the MoPD in the form of staff training, etc., but also grants to six Jordanian civil society organisations (CSOs), totalling €1 million, which were delivered through the ministry. Based on the intention to empower the latter by 'strengthening the MoPD's capacity in defining and managing donor funded projects and ... in improving political dialogue with civil societies',[43] as well as Jordanian NGOs, the programme's

---

[41] Mitchell, *Rule of Experts*, p. 242.

[42] Interview with Michael, 'democracy promoter' working in Jordan, Washington, DC, 20 June 2013.

[43] MoPIC and EU Programme Administration Office (PAO), *Support to Human Rights and Good Governance Programme – Draft Final Report – Narrative and Financial (June 2005– May 2012)*, 2013, p. 5.

draft final report finds that through the scheme, the MoPD 'gained credibility with the CSO'.[44]

This is a rather confusing assertion, however, as the NGOs selected by the MoPD and, by extension, by the government were precisely those less critical NGOs with whom the Ministry hardly needed to gain any further credibility, and those that had already long been the beneficiaries of EU efforts at capacity building. An EU diplomat based in Jordan admitted that upon her arrival she realised that 'we finance always the same organisations'.[45] As she named those that had been selected by the MoPD as beneficiaries of the EU grants she had to laugh, since more critical organisations had from the beginning refused to even apply, due to the scheme's administration by the Jordanian government. The EU-MoPD scheme is a good illustration of the flawed assumption of 'democracy promoters' that such programmes can indeed help build a political will to strengthen independent and critical CSOs where such a will simply does not exist.

The extent to which the reliance on a procedural narrative serves to continuously postpone the desired democratic change to a distant future becomes apparent in the following statement by a Jordanian Ministry of Planning and International Cooperation (MoPIC) official:

Sometimes our international partners want us to ... involve these institutions [CSOs] in certain issues, while we tell them that it's not possible. They cannot do it. I need them to develop to a certain extent where I can rely on their representation of society – their real representation of society – until they gain enough credibility and impartiality to be a real partner ... Until we reach this point, there's a process of improvements, of capacity building, of empowerment, of providing best international practices. There's a set of, a long list of requirements for civil society to develop to an extent where they can be reliable ... I'm not criticising them. It's a process. In Europe and in the US, it took hundreds of years for civil society to develop ... but still in Jordan we have not reached this point.[46]

Some of the NGOs involved in the EU-MoPD scheme had difficulty correctly accounting for their expenses. As a consequence, and further adding to the already strong scepticism on the Jordanian side about the general idea of state-run projects aimed at strengthening civil society, the EU demanded that MoPIC, as Jordan's focal point for all foreign assistance, now needed to ensure the back-payment of such unaccounted-for expenses.

---

[44] MoPIC and EU PAO, *Support to Human Rights and Good Governance Programme*, p. 6.
[45] Interview with Olivia, EU diplomat based in Jordan, Amman, 9 December 2012.
[46] Interview with Ahmad, MoPIC official, Amman, 11 October 2012.

Asked about the EU programme, Sandra, an American 'democracy promoter', responded as follows:

I certainly hope they never do this kind of project again, because it ... puts the NGOs under the supervision of a ministry who manages them ... It causes a lot of concern ... for the life of me, I don't understand why these projects continue to resurface year after year after year. When building an independent civil society, the last thing you need to be doing is to be giving the government money to build them![47]

The EU-MoPD programme fundamentally relied on the assumption that the Jordanian government was indeed seriously interested in a meaningful redistribution of power. The EU thus seemed to view Jordanian government institutions as purely technical implementing partners. The Jordanian side, however, endorsed a very similar view of international donors, albeit arguably with a different objective in mind. The previously quoted MoPIC official thus stated that donors such as the US and the EU

don't intervene in the substance ... But they support the supporting tools, like the commission [the Independent Election Commission], like the political parties, like empowering women, like encouraging youth to participate ... They do support political reforms, but ... not when it comes to substance.[48]

According to him, the definition of benchmarks for the receipt of US and EU budget support also exclusively related to 'the credibility of the process'.[49] Both US and EU officials thus confirmed that the applied benchmarks only relate to procedural issues, such as the provision of sufficient financial resources to the Independent Election Commission (IEC), or similar, but never to substantive problems such as electoral or political party law, as, unlike the many other interventions, this would constitute 'interference'[50] in Jordanian affairs, as one 'democracy promoter' put it. In their efforts at institutional engineering the US and the EU thus both fundamentally rely on the assumed sincerity of Jordanian reform initiatives like the National Agenda, viewing the latter as 'a blueprint for extensive political and economic reform'[51] and as 'fully in line with the Action Plan'.[52] Politics and the very possibility that the Jordanian regime's actions might not constitute only simple extensions of its publicly expressed intentions then seem to be inherently ignored and replaced by a never-ending simulation of ongoing processes of democratisation.

---

[47] Interview with Sandra, US 'democracy promoter' working on programmes in Jordan, Washington, DC, 19 June 2013.
[48] Interview with Ahmad, MoPIC official, Amman, 11 October 2012.
[49] Interview with Ahmad, MoPIC official, Amman, 11 October 2012.
[50] Interview with Adam, 'democracy promoter' working in Jordan, Amman, 14 October 2012.
[51] USAID, *Democracy and Governance – Overview*.   [52] ENPI, *Jordan*, p. 3.

Any concerns extending beyond the procedural thereby appear to have become entirely removed from the equation.

An undated EU document entitled *Action Fiche for Jordan – Democratic Governance* provides us with a good illustration of the tendency to see a world full of opportunities and signs of success, no matter what. In it, the authors claim, for instance, that the 2009 'dissolution of Parliament creates an opportunity for broader participation in dialogue concerning the nature and structure of democracy in Jordan'.[53] While it is true that the Jordanian parliament is extremely unpopular, interpreting its dissolution by royal decree as the creation of an opportunity for broader participation comes down to claiming that no matter what happens and/or what 'democracy promoters' do, 'democracy promotion' interventions are always deemed to be both justified and necessary.

But how do the embrace of the procedural narrative and the above self-perpetuating dynamics play out in practice? Discussing external attempts at political party training, I argue that such efforts directly reinforce authoritarian stability in Jordan by seemingly reconfirming Jordanians' lack of political awareness and democratic mentality. The result is an increasingly self-confirming politics of intervention and control.

Creating the Right Kind of Problem

> You [teach] people how to eat with knife and [fork], ... you seem very nice, but at the end the food is *mansaf*[54] ... You learn [democracy] by practice, like – if you want to ... learn to swim you go to the water. You can't learn swimming staying in the bed ... You should go to the water ... I know there's much, very much money – very very much was spent in the last ten years [by] many associations ... but in the end, you can't learn democracy. You can't practice![55]

On US television King Abdullah II stated in late 2012 that 'what we want to achieve is, left, right and centre, two to five political parties as quickly as possible. That sounds very simple, but getting there is going to be the challenge'.[56] Apart from the Islamic Action Front (IAF), political parties play practically no role in Jordanian politics. Parliamentary politics mostly revolves around shifting personality-based alliances and many of the

---

[53] EU Delegation in Jordan, *Action Fiche for Jordan – Democratic Governance*.
[54] *Mansaf*, the Jordanian national dish, is traditionally eaten with one's hands.
[55] Interview with a former Minister of Political Development, Amman, 21 November 2012.
[56] King Abdullah II, *The Daily Show* with Jon Stewart, 25 September 2012. Also, see Kifah and Jennifer (pseudonyms), 'Jon Stewart's theater of the absurd', *Jadaliyya*, 2 October 2012.

parties that do exist either struggle to develop a coherent programme or never really seemed to be interested in having one. According to a poll from 2012, 62 per cent of Jordanians do not trust political parties at all and 75 per cent are not even aware of any political party in the country, other than the IAF.[57] Seen from the procedural narrative discussed above, the state of political parties in Jordan appears as just another manifestation of the supposedly still underdeveloped and premodern nature of Jordanian politics. The USAID *Jordan Country Development Cooperation Strategy 2013–2017* accordingly found that in Jordan 'the traditional tribal system still overshadows the party system'.[58] In short, Jordan is condescendingly presented as a society characterised by personality and tribal-based modes of governance, which has not yet arrived at modernity.[59]

In stark contrast to such descriptions, the weakness of Jordan's political parties is actually the result of, among other things, a thirty-six-year ban on political parties (1957–1992) and an electoral law that strongly encourages voting patterns based on personal, family and tribal affiliations. Despite their legalisation in 1992 and repeated public statements by King Abdullah II that stronger political parties are a necessity, numerous restrictive regulations and practices are still in force today, effectively ensuring that many Jordanians remain highly sceptical and afraid of party politics. One among many examples are patronage systems like royal *makramah* scholarships, which require recipients to pledge that they will not affiliate with any political party.[60]

The most important cause for the weakness of Jordanian political party life is the highly restrictive nature of the Jordanian constitution in general and of the political party and electoral law in particular. The Jordanian parliament thus functions largely as a service provider rather than as

---

[57] IRI and Middle East Marketing and Research Consultants (MEMRC), 'National priorities, governance and political reform in Jordan', *National Public Opinion Poll No. 9*, 17–20 July 2012, pp. 23–24, available at: www.iri.org/sites/default/files/2012%20Septe mber%2024%20Survey%20of%20Jordanian%20Public%20Opinion,%20July%2017–20,%202012.pdf.

[58] USAID, *Jordan Country Development Cooperation Strategy 2013–2017*, p. 8.

[59] For a powerful critique of such accounts see Tell, T.M., *The Social and Economic Origins of Monarchy in Jordan* (New York: Palgrave Macmillan, 2013), pp. 5–25.

[60] Dhabaḥtūnā [Arabic for 'you slaughtered us'; a national campaign for student rights], *Fourth Annual Report of the National Campaign for Student Rights [Dhabaḥtūnā, at-taqrīr as-sanawīy ar-rābi' li-l-ḥamlah al-waṭanīyah min ajl ḥuqūq aṭ-ṭalabah]*, 5 February 2012. Original in Arabic, translated by the author. An employee of the royal *makramah* office at the University of Jordan estimated the number of recipients at this university at 12 per cent (interviewed in Amman, 24 January 2013). A founding member of the Dhabaḥtūnā initiative estimated the number of military scholarship holders at 20 per cent and that of royal court scholarship holders at 5 per cent (interviewed in Amman, 21 February 2013).

a strong and independent legislative body and the Jordanian electoral law up until 2016 was based on the single non-transferable vote (SNTV) system.[61] Together, SNTV and the limited powers of parliament ensured the continued dominance of voting patterns based on personal, family and tribal affiliations. Despite the abolition of the controversial SNTV system in 2016, numerous other factors ensure the ongoing weakness of Jordan's political parties. Parties are thus highly unlikely to be able to implement any form of political programme through parliament, as laws also need to be ratified by the king, as well as requiring the consent of the senate, which is appointed by the king. Due to parliament's weak legislative position, most voters opt for a candidate with whom they have family and/or tribal connections, in order to at least facilitate the later return of practical favours. Given the structurally conditioned weakness of the Jordanian parliament and in light of its primary function as an institution that facilitates the provision of state services and resources, it is no wonder that for most Jordanians, the act of voting for a party candidate is much less a sign of progress or modernity than simply irrational.

It is possible then to conclude at this point that the weakness of contemporary Jordanian political parties is the result of both historical developments and of the absence of a clear political will to abolish forms of ongoing discrimination. A recent study of political parties in Jordan finds that

Since 1989, . . . the state has successfully used party politics and reform to not only provide Jordan with a democratic image, but also to serve as a eudemonic legitimacy provider in lieu of its former reliance on neo-patrimonial links in a rentier system. No longer able to directly disseminate patronage to ensure the continued support of its key constituencies, . . . the state now uses elections to indirectly provide benefits to its pillars of support. As a result, and despite the fact that new political parties have proliferated and are able to operate relatively freely, electoral victories (and the material perks that follow with them) continue to be served to state loyalists, and political parties maintain their marginal importance.[62]

While many 'democracy promoters' in Jordan recognise the importance of the historical and structural factors analysed above, the inherent problem of doing so is that it makes the project of strengthening political parties appear to be dependent on factors that 'democracy promoters' are

---

[61] The 2012 election law saw the introduction of a parallel system, according to which twenty-seven seats are reserved for political parties and lists, which are then allocated through proportional representation, while the remaining 123 seats are reserved exclusively for independent candidates, thereby largely keeping the SNTV system intact.

[62] Identity Center, *Map of the Political Parties and Movements in Jordan* (Amman: Netherlands Institute for Multiparty Democracy and Embassy of the Kingdom of the Netherlands, 2013–2014), p. 23.

either unable or unwilling to influence. As there would ultimately be no need for 'democracy promotion' interventions if the weakness of political parties were entirely due to structural factors beyond the influence of 'democracy promoters', a competing explanation for the weakness of Jordanian political parties has gained prevalence among 'democracy promoters' working in Jordan – one that predominantly centres on the mentality and supposedly lacking political awareness of Jordanians themselves.

As many 'democracy promoters' resort to varying degrees to culturalist accounts that shift the blame for the weakness of political parties to Jordanians themselves, one can detect a convergence of the discourses of 'democracy promoters' to the patronising discourse of the king. According to this latter, as already quoted, reform in Jordan is less a question of changes to laws and regulations than one of citizens needing to evolve in how they operate and interact.[63] Presenting political party training as 'the right solution' thus depends directly on a relative disregard for the analysed structural limitations, as well as on a diagnosis of Jordanians as not yet having the correct mentality, as still being stuck in a traditional mindset and not yet understanding the concept of political parties. 'Democracy promotion' therefore needs to first create the correct 'problem', before it can present its universally applied tools and 'solutions' as relevant also in Jordan. It needs to establish and invent 'the Jordanian' as somebody who lacks political understanding, experience and knowledge, before it can then set out to train and educate him.[64]

Accordingly, an EU diplomat based in Jordan downplayed the importance of structural factors by instead identifying a need for a 'change of mentality'. She further elaborated that for Jordanians it is 'difficult to understand to vote for somebody they don't know' and that consequently one has to 'train and make citizens understand what a party is'.[65] Providing a further illustration of the prevalence of deeply culturalist approaches that problematise Jordanians themselves instead of Jordanian authoritarianism, another Western diplomat was genuinely distressed as she remarked that

even people [who have] a degree, a Master, a PhD, whatever, from abroad, [who] know the system – they will . . . vote for their relative. They will vote for the person of their group [instead of for a candidate running on a party platform]. It's really their mentality.[66]

---

[63] King Abdullah II, 'Making our democratic system work for all Jordanians'.
[64] See Ferguson, The Anti-Politics Machine, pp. 67–73.
[65] All three quotations from interview with Olivia, EU diplomat based in Jordan, Amman, 9 September 2012.
[66] Interview with Sofia, Western diplomat based in Jordan, Amman, 8 October 2012.

The image that emerges from such statements is one in which the Jordanian population is primarily characterised in terms of what it lacks; it does not exhibit the necessary mentality and it does not show an adequate understanding of the value of political parties. As 'democracy promoters' ignore and/or understate the importance of structural factors and instead problematise the 'nature' of Jordanians, they misunderstand local political dynamics and the underlying reasons for Jordanians' see-mingly backward and anti-modern behaviour. Many 'democracy promo-ters' thus fail to understand that the act of voting for a tribal candidate does not necessarily clash with conceptualisations of rationality and that, rather than constituting evidence of a lack of political awareness, not voting for political party candidates and not joining political parties may actually point to Jordanians' excellent grasp of the relevance of their vote, the power of parliament and the role of political parties.

In the following I argue that the relative disregard of authoritarian structures and the concomitant focus on Jordanians' culture, mentality and capacity are highly reinforcing of narratives that construct Jordanians as 'not yet ready for democracy'. I show that rather than contributing to meaningful processes of democratisation, this leads to a perpetuation of 'democracy promotion' interventions, which then continuously proble-matise Jordanians instead of challenging the very structures of Jordanian authoritarianism. Ironically, the more flawed and counterproductive the promoted processes and institutions appear, as many Jordanians are aware of the absence of democratic substance in them, the more powerful and convincing the procedural narrative and the supposed necessity of having 'to alter the "outlook" of Jordanians'[67] – as the MSI report described what it explicitly advised against – seems to become for 'democ-racy promoters'.

'Political Reform Is a Third Priority'

> You may develop a series of people in worthless parties, who later go on and do interesting things.[68]

In Jordan, the most ardent proponent of a strongly functionalist imagin-ary – such as the one suggesting that to become democratic, a country requires a similar political party spectrum to those of established Western democracies – is not the 'democracy promotion' establishment, but King Abdullah II himself. As the four German political foundations with offices

---

[67] Denoeux, Wilcox and Zawaneh, *Jordan Democracy and Governance Assessment*, p. 44.
[68] Interview with Michael, 'democracy promoter' working in Jordan, Amman, 24 January 2013.

in Amman – the Friedrich Ebert Foundation (FES), Konrad Adenauer Foundation (KAS), Hanns Seidel Foundation (HSS) and Friedrich Naumann Foundation (FNS) – are affiliated to the German labour party, conservative parties and liberal party, respectively, the king simply asked whether they could assist in the establishment of a similar party spectrum in Jordan. While the German foundations at the time politely rejected his request for cooperation, pointing to the need for parties to emerge organically from within Jordanian society, at the time of this research at least two distinct political party training programmes were being implemented – one by the KAS and another by the American International Republican Institute (IRI). Drawing on the work of Martínez, among others, I suggest that the monarchy and external 'democracy promoters' both rely heavily on narratives that emphasise party weakness and that thereby 'make Jordan appear as simply not ready for parliamentary democracy'.[69]

As the KAS programme was just about to start as I was finishing my field research, in the following I will focus primarily, but not exclusively, on the IRI programme for political party training. This was part of USAID's $9.9 million *Political Process Strengthening Program* 2010–2013, which the IRI was implementing with its American partner organisation, the NDI. Apart from various training sessions, in October 2012 the IRI and USAID, together with the Jordanian MoPD, held Jordan's first ever political parties fair, organised at the Sports City Complex in Amman. The underlying idea of the fair was to connect Jordanian youth to political parties and, in anticipation of the upcoming parliamentary elections in January 2013, to strengthen political parties and encourage Jordanian youth to become more politically active. USAID, the IRI and the MoPD had invited all Jordanian parties to the event, while the NDI had invited a large number of Jordanian youth, whom it had been training through a number of courses at Jordanian universities, some of which I discuss in more depth in Chapter 4.

In its 2013 final electoral observation mission report, the IRI itself interestingly found that 'political parties can truly develop only when the elected chamber they are running for has real authority'.[70] Similarly aware of the fundamental structural limitations for Jordanian political parties, 'democracy promoter' Robert admitted that 'it's a problematic environment for political parties … party work is handicapped by an

---

[69] Martínez, J.C., 'Jordan's self-fulfilling prophecy: the production of feeble political parties and the perceived perils of democracy', *British Journal of Middle Eastern Studies*, Vol. 44, No. 3, 2017, p. 358.
[70] IRI, *Jordan Parliamentary Elections January 23, 2013, Final Report*, 2013, p. 9.

election law that is not particularly evolving towards engagement or involving parties'. He continued:

they did redo the political party law. And it's not a bad law ... But the thing is, if you don't give parties anything to shoot for in the elections system then what's your political party law going to do for you? ... So they're moving, but it's herky-jerky. But democracy building is always like this. Where has it ever been smooth? ... It's just complicated. There are vested interests.[71]

As Robert continued, explaining the purpose of the political parties fair, one notes that, despite realising the inherently constrained environment for political parties, he eventually ends up framing the problem not in the language of political structures, but in that of deficient capacity and political culture. The weakness of Jordanian political parties thus no longer appears to be due to a restrictive political party and electoral law, but as increasingly due to Jordanians' lack of political knowledge. Robert carried on as follows:

We're going to do a workshop. We're going to do a youth fair. We'll invite 4,000 politically active youth from around the country and we're going to set up the political parties with booths, like at a common trade fair ... [We] train the political parties to market themselves, to have brochures, to try and hook these youths in with their message and get these youths to work as volunteers. That's a huge project ... We're going to give parties poll results and say, 'Look at these poll results and think about these poll results when you create your national list message. Talk about issues that people think are important to them. Just don't talk blablabla! Have a good message on the national level'. We're going to train parliamentary candidates in the campaign schools: two-day campaign schools, how to run a good campaign, how to interact with media, how to have a communication strategy – radio, newspaper, TV. What are you going to do? How are you going to get your message out? How are you going to target your audience? ... it's very ... capacity building. And you know, after the election we'll probably do a whole new programme to support the parties between elections depending on whether they got into parliament or got out of parliament. If you're out of parliament, you have to see if these people keep their promises in parliament. You have to be active. You have to make statements.[72]

Apart from the slow turning of structural and substantive issues into procedural ones related to a perceived lack of capacity and a supposed inability to talk about issues that 'are important', what is of particular interest here is Robert's framing of his work within the market logic of

[71] Interview with Robert, 'democracy promoter' working in Jordan, Amman, 24 September 2012.
[72] Interview with Robert, 'democracy promoter' working in Jordan, Amman, 24 September 2012.

supply and demand,[73] and his conviction that no matter how successful the current programme is, there is always a need for a follow-up programme. Just as the previously discussed EU capacity-building programme viewed Jordanian ministries as technical implementing partners, Robert, in his description of the political parties fair, similarly assumed that if parties were adequately trained and provided with detailed information about what Jordanians want, then surely they would eventually become more important.

Before discussing the parties fair in more depth, a few more comments are needed on the language of supply and demand that Robert used in his description of the fair. This market logic is indeed not only found in individual statements such as Robert's, but seems to lie at the very foundation of USAID efforts at 'democracy promotion'. While the IRI trains political parties, seen as the forces of supply, the NDI trains Jordanian students and youth, who are viewed as the forces of demand. At the core of USAID efforts at 'democracy promotion' one can thus discern a staunch belief in the benefits of an imagined equilibrium of the market. Once the question of political parties' weakness is depoliticised by seeing it as the result of a hitherto deficient interplay between supply and demand, the issue ceases to be a question of power and control and becomes a problem of management. As remarked by Mitchell, the reliance on the image of 'the market' is an efficient means to ignore deeply political questions about the distribution of power, as it 'reduces ... interrelated but very unequal concentrations of power into nominally equivalent buyers and sellers, and represents the inequality between them as the market's equilibrium'.[74]

Once the weakness of political parties is analysed through the lens of 'the market', the task of strengthening them effectively becomes a technical matter of improving marketing skills, providing poll results, etc. While many Jordanian political parties do not have clear programmes and consequently should hardly be understood as political parties in the conventional sense, the market logic allows 'democracy promoters' to detach this need of many parties to create their 'product' from the structures of Jordanian authoritarianism. Instead, it suddenly appears as a consequence of an interaction between the forces of supply and demand that has thus far been inadequate. Providing parties with poll results and encouraging them to adapt their 'product' according to 'what the poll says

---

[73] See also Schuetze, B., 'Marketing parliament: the constitutive effects of external attempts at parliamentary strengthening in Jordan', *Cooperation and Conflict*, Vol. 53, No. 2, 2018, pp. 237–258.

[74] Mitchell, *Rule of Experts*, p. 227.

people are interested [in]'[75] thus seemingly becomes an important step on the path of improving the efficiency of the market. While many Jordanians are highly critical of 'supermarket'-like parties that simply deliver whatever is demanded of them, for many 'democracy promoters' it seems only logical that telling parties in a clear and transparent way what 'the people want' is an important tool to make the latter more attractive.

A 2012 IRI-commissioned poll set out to do this and asked Jordanians whether economic reform, political reform or fighting corruption was most important to them. A large majority, 57 per cent, named fighting corruption as their first priority, followed by economic reform at 29 per cent and political reform a distant third at 12 per cent.[76] This seems to provide evidence for highly questionable claims that economics and politics can be separated and that Jordanians are unhappy with widespread corruption and the weak economy, but not with Jordan's political system.

While the reliability of polls that ask the population of an authoritarian and repressive state about the importance of political reform is somewhat questionable, the way in which such polls are subsequently used is particularly disturbing. Discussing similar opinion polls, one 'democracy promoter' remarked:

What do the people want? Let's look at [the] political poll . . . Political reform is way down here. Corruption is up here and economic development. Let's be honest. It's a minority that is on the streets. OK. We've got to be realists here. It doesn't mean . . . that things are going well here. It just means that political reform is . . . a third priority.[77]

As the poll clearly establishes 'what the people want', it seems only logical to also encourage parties to act accordingly:

We say to the parties, 'OK. Talk about what the people, talk about what the poll says people are interested [in]. Talk about your economic development policies. What are you going to do about unemployment? And don't just say something stupid . . . what kind of intelligent words are you going to say about corruption? And, finally, if you talk about political reform, talk about it third'.[78]

In short, 'democracy promoters' used the opinion polls discussed here in order to encourage political party representatives in a repressive and

[75] Interview with Robert, 'democracy promoter' working in Jordan, Amman, 24 September 2012.
[76] IRI and MEMRC, 'National priorities, governance and political reform in Jordan', p. 16.
[77] Interview with Robert, 'democracy promoter' working in Jordan, Amman, 24 September 2012.
[78] Interview with Robert, 'democracy promoter' working in Jordan, Amman, 24 September 2012.

authoritarian state to focus on the development of economic policies and strategies for fighting corruption, but to refrain from any debate about the political system itself.

Marketing Political Parties

By the entrance to the conference hall at the Sports City Complex, a big poster heralded the IRI, MoPD and USAID-organised event as Jordan's 'first political parties fair'. The poster further asked the participants in giant letters in Jordanian Arabic whether they were 'afraid of politics',[79] a sketch of a rather worried looking face complementing the question (see Figure 2.1). In contrast to the above-quoted MSI report, which explicitly remarked that 'visible US involvement in democracy-promotion activities in Jordan would be unwise',[80] the poster advertising the event featured the logos of USAID and IRI, and representatives of the latter also gave introductory speeches at the event.

As the organisers viewed themselves as neutral facilitators of democratisation processes, they had invited all of the then twenty-three officially licensed political parties, of which only thirteen accepted, however. Those parties that were better known to the wider public seemed more likely to reject the invitation than those that were rather unknown: out of the seven best-known parties, only two were willing to present themselves at the fair, while five of the seven least-known responded positively to the invitation.[81] The prominent role of USAID and IRI in the organisation of the event seems to have played a direct role in preventing more Jordanian parties from participating. Just as all leftist parties had declined the invitation, Jordan's most prominent political party, the IAF, had also done so. A high-ranking member only stated that 'we refused the invitation ... because it was backed by USAID'.[82] This inability to reach some of the more important Jordanian parties and the concomitant interaction with those of only marginal importance has important effects that I will elaborate on below. As 'the process' is the discursive framework

---

[79] Poster at the entrance of the political parties fair in Hussein Youth City, Amman, 20 October 2012, translated by the author (original Arabic: *awwal multaqā li-l-aḥzāb as-siyāsiyah* and *btkhāf min as-siyāsah?*).

[80] Denoeux, Wilcox and Zawaneh, *Jordan Democracy and Governance Assessment*, p. 57.

[81] See IRI and MEMRC, 'National priorities, governance and political reform in Jordan', p. 24. The parties that attended the event were (in order of popularity according to the above-quoted poll): National Current, the Islamic Centrist Party, the Jordanian Unified Front Party, the National Jordanian Party, the Jordanian National Youth Party, the Justice and Development Party, the Welfare Party, the Risālah Party, the Duʿāʾ Party, the Justice and Reform Party, the Freedom and Equality Party, the Jordan Reform Party and Jordan National Union.

[82] Interview with Fadi, high-ranking member of the IAF, Amman, 10 October 2012.

شو بتعرف عن الأحزاب السياسية؟
شو برامجهم؟
ليش مهم يكون عنّا أحزاب؟

وزارة التنمية السياسية

بالتعاون مع

المعهد الجمهوري الدولي
الممول من الوكالة الامريكية للتنمية الدولية USAID

تدعوكم لحضور

أول ملتقى للأحزاب السياسية

في قاعة عمّان بمدينة الحسين للشباب يوم السبت ٢٠١٢/١٠/٢٠
من الساعة ١٠ صباحاً للساعة ٥ مساءً

رح يكون في سكتشات بتخبرنا أكثر عن الأحزاب وكمان بتقدر تسأل أي سؤال بيخطر ببالك للأحزاب المشاركة

ما تنسى يوم السبت ٢٠١٢/١٠/٢٠ بأي وقت بين الساعة ١٠ الصبح للساعة ٥ المسا

بنستناك انت واصحابك ... وعلى فكرة الكل معزوم ...

للإستفسار : ٧٧٦٦٥٤،٥٧٠

المعهد الجمهوري الدولي   الوكالة الامريكية للتنمية الدولية   وزارة التنمية السياسية

Figure 2.1 Leaflet handed out at a political parties fair organised by USAID, IRI and MoPD on 20 October 2012, in Amman. A poster version was installed at the entrance of the venue. © USAID / Jordan.

through which Jordanian politics is analysed, all those who refuse to participate in it and who doubt its sincerity are effectively ignored. Criticising the parties that decided not to attend the event, one participant at the fair only noted that, 'as they didn't come, they don't want to work for Jordan'.

As US 'democracy promotion' is only able to interact with a narrow part of the Jordanian party spectrum, it (re-)produces in its activities a distorted image of Jordanian politics that seemingly justifies precisely those kinds of interventions that so fundamentally fail to grasp the true reasons for the relative weakness of contemporary Jordanian political parties. As more popular and meaningful parties mostly boycott training and outreach events organised in particular by US 'democracy promoters', and as many of those parties that are willing to interact with 'democracy promoters' do indeed seem to suffer from a lack of capacity, the culturalist and capacity-focused discourses of the latter reveal their self-confirming tendencies. The perception that further training and capacity building is needed in order to overcome Jordanian authoritarianism is thereby both powerfully perpetuated and simultaneously shows its inherent futility.

During one of the sessions at the fair the representatives introduced their respective parties to the audience. While most only had the time for a few sentences, the representative of the National Current (at-Tayyār al-Waṭaniy), a party formed by Abdul Hadi al-Majali, a staunch conservative and former minister, was allowed several minutes to present his party without interruption. One 'democracy promoter' who had been involved in the planning of the fair later described this as one of the very few shortcomings of the event, which he otherwise saw as a success. While the difference in time given to party representatives was certainly worthy of critique, other non-procedural matters such as the absence of the IAF and leftist parties, all of whom questioned the sincerity of the organisers' intention to promote democracy in the country to begin with, were arguably of much greater importance. Also, some students were quick to point out that one of their peers, who apparently had been at Jordan University since 2000, was, as 'everybody knows', 'working for the intelligence services within the university'. One girl elaborated, explaining that besides participating in the NDI's democracy education courses for Jordanian youth, the presumed employee of the Jordanian intelligence service is 'always there when we have problems'. Finally, the identity of the organisers, the absence of some of the more serious political parties and the presumed presence of the secret service – which was probably one of the reasons why many of the parties present displayed large photos of King Abdullah II on their booths (see Figure 2.2) – all contributed to

Figure 2.2 Booth of the Welfare Party (Hizb al-Rifāh) at the political parties fair, Amman, 20 October 2012. Photo by the author.

seriously compromising the credibility of the event and clearly illustrate that there are indeed pretty good reasons for Jordanian political activists to 'be afraid of politics'.

During the speeches given by the party representatives, several individuals in the audience intervened with short poems praising the king, to which the audience responded with applause and repeated calls of 'Long live the king!' (*ya'īsh al-malik!*). Thereafter, the youth and university students present had the opportunity to meet the party representatives at booths set up in the entrance hall, where the latter also distributed party leaflets and programmes. In the afternoon the event continued with role play sessions prepared by participants in NDI's 'I participate' (*anā ushārik*) courses, as well as a panel discussion by political party representatives, which was very poorly attended by the invited youth, as most seemed not particularly keen on engaging with the political parties present. As the party representatives debated inside, most of the youth were thus chatting outside and taking photos of each other under the posters advertising the event.

In one of the role play sessions presented by NDI's students, a woman complained to her husband about their son, as he wanted to join a party. In the ensuing conversation the son mentioned the NDI programme, but his father continued to talk about tribes and ultimately asked him in a rather confused manner whether he wanted to join all the parties. A student watching the sketch succinctly described it as 'old versus new mentality'. While this is exactly the kind of condescending modernisation theory-inspired interpretation desired by the regime,[83] which wants to present itself as a democratising and modernising force, it would be fundamentally wrong to assume that institutions and procedures such as parties and elections constitute in and of themselves any meaningful threat to Jordanian authoritarianism.[84] One participant in the panel discussion criticised the parties present for being like 'supermarkets'; that is, for not having a clear programme but simply offering anything that people might be interested in. Illustrating the efficiency of the Jordanian regime's strategy of publicly calling for party activism (and thereby boosting its legitimacy as a supposedly democratising force), while at the same time maintaining a firm hold over parties, another participant bitterly remarked that 'the guy who fought me because I am a party activist [when political parties were still forbidden] has now created a party'.

After one of the sketches, suddenly the song 'Our high flag' (yā bayraqunā al-ʿālī) began to play on the PA system, and several participants quickly started dancing along. Many of the youth present then began to sing:

> Our high flag Abdullah II
> Our high flag
> We are your swords my homeland
> . . . you are very dear and your people loves you
> . . . Abdullah you are the people's king
> The one who protects the Hashemite nation
> . . . we are the youth generation who are proud of our king
> . . . and our dignity stems from yours
> And the knight is one of us and we are proud . . .[85]

Watching the participants – according to the organisers, all politically interested youth – dance and sing, praising King Abdullah II, Farah,

---

[83] See also Tell, *The Social and Economic Origins of Monarchy in Jordan*, pp. 5–25.

[84] See Schwedler, J., 'The political geography of protest in neoliberal Jordan', *Middle East Critique*, Vol. 21, No. 3, p. 261.

[85] Al-Lawziyīn, 'Yā bayraqunā al-ʿālī' ('Our high flag'). Translated from Arabic by the author based on an anonymous online translation available at: www.allthelyrics.com/forum/showthread.php?t=115600.

a student attending the fair, remarked only that 'there will never be political development in Jordan, because people don't separate between the king and the state'. When after a later role play session some participants again began to dance to a song praising the Hashemite ruling family, she added that

the king is very safe ... Seeing this – they take the elite of students and they are like that! ... His Majesty is right in saying it is too early to go to constitutional monarchy if political activists just clap and support the king in a stupid way.[86]

Instead of contributing to processes of democratisation, the event organised by the MoPD, USAID and IRI thus seems to have effectively become an opportunity for people to perform their obedience to the king.

The Vicious Circle of 'Democracy Promotion'

Despite its good intentions, the parties fair elicited consequences and dynamics that were precisely the opposite of what the organisers had hoped to achieve. Instead of becoming more interested in political parties, Farah, the above-quoted student, concluded that the king is right to say that his people are not yet 'ready for democracy'. Similarly, instead of increasing the pressure on the regime by, for instance, empowering those oppositional forces that suffer most from regime oppression, the fair was largely a showcase event for regime supporters. The central intention behind the event, which Washington, DC-based IRI official Richard described as trying to 'provide ... venues that allow for diverse perspectives to be heard', was destined to failure from the beginning. While it was true, as remarked by Richard, that 'in no way did IRI attempt to exclude any party', practically all oppositional parties fundamentally refused to accept a US organisation as a neutral facilitator of processes of democratisation and consequently refused the invitation. In light of what Richard described as the intention behind the fair, it was then rather ironic that he insisted on viewing it as a success. In noting that the event showed 'that there is a constituency in Jordan that is very much supportive of the palace and the king',[87] he himself acknowledged that the fair had done anything but provide a venue 'for diverse perspectives to be heard'. While it is true that a considerable number of Jordanians are strongly supportive of King Abdullah II, the provision of a stage for pro-regime forces to celebrate

---

[86] Interview with Farah, Jordanian student, Amman, 20 October 2012.
[87] The last three quotations come from an interview with Richard, IRI official, Washington, DC, 23 May 2013.

the king certainly contradicts the intention of 'democracy promoters' to empower alternative political forces.

The organisers' insistence that the fair had been a success becomes somewhat more comprehensible as one realises that the fair did indeed succeed in maintaining and confirming the narrative of the procedural. Throughout the event, USAID and IRI representatives once again felt vindicated in their belief that Jordanians still require a lot of training, capacity building and awareness-raising before the country can ever become democratic. The example of the political parties fair thus well illustrates the extent to which US 'democracy promotion' perpetuates rather than challenges existing power structures. As practically all issues are rendered matters of procedural concern, 'democracy promoters' may further feel reassured that it is not their inability and/or unwillingness to deal with substantive challenges that contributes to preventing 'democracy promotion' from having the desired impact, but instead others' incomplete participation in the process. Particularly interesting was the reaction of a former high-level US Department of State (DoS) employee upon hearing my description of the event. While her comments need to be read with some indulgence as she had previously not heard about the fair, it is above all her view of 'democracy promotion' as a panacea that makes it worthwhile to quote her at some length here. Commenting on my observations, she suggested that

other students may have walked out of that event saying, 'These political parties are all corrupt bottom-feeders. They're all just in it to get what they can get from the regime. Screw them all. I'm going to join the leftist parties with my friends'. Right. You don't know what the effect is on the ... intended audience. That's what I'm saying. Now, I don't want to excuse it and I'm not trying to say that this was a valuable exercise because it sounds just like a hilarious disaster.

She continued, admitting that

they have to tell you it's a success, because it's taxpayer money and they have to spend it well ... But sometimes it's an event that is so patently useless ... or counterproductive that it reveals to the broader audience what's wrong with their own system ... that it reveals to people what are their needs. Maybe one of the people who was there, who had joined one of these royalist parties, because he thought he could work in the system ... was so disgusted by what he ended up involved in that he's now working with some friends very quietly to start another party ... Sometimes, if a society is at a tipping point where there has been a long record of failed reform or rhetoric that wasn't followed up by reality, part of the dynamic of that top-down-process losing credibility is events like this ... This event is another chipping away at the credibility of the top-down process. And so over time you can't have too many fairs like that before they become a joke. And then at some point the Minister of Political Development says: 'Oh my god. We can't do it this way. This has no credibility. We have to try something else'.[88]

'Democracy promotion' is thus always portrayed as good. It is productive either because it directly encourages people to engage politically and push for reform or because it is actually so counterproductive that it indirectly encourages people to engage and push for reform. What matters is that external intervention and input is always required, as without it Jordanians would lack either the capacity to be 'true democrats' or the ability to realise 'what's wrong with their own system'. This logic knows neither underlying substantive contradictions, nor alternative dynamics that might bring into question the very existence of an assumed trajectory towards democracy, but instead only knows the language of relentless procedural progress.

It is remarkable how this logic pervades discourses and practices of 'democracy promotion' in Jordan and how it succeeds in drawing in even those who are otherwise sceptical of the usefulness of interventions in such spheres as political party training. While critical of the IRI programme, the director of one Jordanian NGO eventually helped the German foundation KAS to develop a rival political party training programme. Despite being very aware of the multiple structural barriers faced by political parties and political activists, he also subscribed to the procedural narrative, emphasising that he supported 'every single attempt to increase participation'.[89] While the Berlin headquarters of the KAS, which holds in high esteem the prestige associated with EU-funded programmes, had strongly encouraged the initial application, the new director of the Amman office, who was appointed just after the application had been submitted, was initially rather sceptical of the potential of efforts at political party training in the country. That the KAS Jordan office was eventually awarded the €500,000 programme was in no small measure aided by the fact that its application had been the one and only response to the EU's call for applications.

Reflecting the scepticism towards US and European party training efforts that can to some extent also be found among individual Western 'democracy promoters' themselves, one such 'democracy promoter' exclaimed: 'How naïve can people ... be to believe that one can achieve something there [i.e. in political party training]?!' Fully aware of the fact that it is not particularly interesting for anybody to join political parties

---

[88] Interview with Mary, former high-ranking US DoS official, Washington, DC, 18 June 2013.
[89] Interview with Said, director of a Jordanian NGO, Amman, 22 January 2013.

considering their weak position in a similarly weak parliament, among other factors, he concluded that 'perhaps one doesn't believe it, but just thinks that one has to do something'.[90]

This chapter has explored the ways in which 'democracy promotion' efforts that aim at institutional engineering directly help the Jordanian regime to portray the country as undergoing a continuous process of democratisation. It has demonstrated that while attempts at capacity building and political party training are extremely effective at maintaining the illusion of an ongoing process, they fundamentally ignore underlying structures of power. Instead of contributing to meaningful processes of democratisation, I have argued that the procedural openings provided by the Jordanian regime and tapped into by external 'democracy promoters' need, first and foremost, to be seen as constant affirmations of the procedural narrative, and as enabling the construction of a façade of democracy – 'Potemkin villages',[91] as one interviewee put it. As 'democracy promotion' efforts aimed at institutional engineering increase the legitimacy of the supposedly liberalising Jordanian regime and elicit contradictory and sometimes even self-defeating consequences, they actually strengthen authoritarian stability in the country. The narrow portrayal of democracy in its procedural variant further allows for the emergence of the universally deployable and knowledgeable 'democracy promotion' expert. It is also of central importance for the conception of a trajectory towards democracy, which again plays a crucial role in the reproduction of the moral hierarchy that lies at the core of 'democracy promotion'.

The primacy of the procedural, then, constitutes the very link that connects the interests of external 'democracy promoters' on the one side and Jordanian authoritarianism on the other, binding them together in a strange relationship of mutual dependence. External 'democracy promoters' have an inherent interest in describing Jordan as being on a trajectory towards democracy, as the seeming existence of such a process reconfirms conceptions of Western moral superiority, as well as the founding narrative of 'democracy promotion' itself. For the Jordanian regime, the insistence on democracy as a process and the maintenance of an ongoing demand for the technical expertise of 'democracy promoters' in turn serves the crucial purpose of shifting blame for authoritarianism onto Jordanians. In their respective reliance on the procedural narrative, both sides thus effectively reproduce that which makes the other appear legitimate, while real democratisation, whose

---

[90] Interview with Paul, 'democracy promoter' working in Jordan, Amman, 15 January 2013.

[91] Interview with Sami, Jordanian economist, Amman, 13 September 2012.

realisation still requires a great deal of training, education and capacity building, is postponed to a distant future.

It was not, therefore, due to some normative superiority that Schumpeter and his understanding of procedural democracy 'won'[92] the battle over democracy's meaning, as argued by Huntington. Much more relevant was a very concrete interest in conceptual closure shared by both external powers, such as the US and the EU, and authoritarian regimes like the Jordanian authorities. In this regard, one can detect among 'democracy promoters' what one may call the functionality of the dysfunctional: Jordan is constructed as sufficiently dysfunctional – 'unelected monarchs are a thing of the past'[93] – for it to require external interventions, and as adequately functional – 'having a democratiser from above ... is a good model'[94] – that it does not bring into question the overarching narrative of the procedural. As I have argued, taking authoritarianism seriously in and of itself, however, fundamentally means to do the latter.

---

[92] Huntington, *The Third Wave*, p. 6.

[93] Interview with Robert, 'democracy promoter' working in Jordan, Amman, 24 September 2012.

[94] Interview with Adam, 'democracy promoter' working in Jordan, Amman, 14 October 2012.

3   Supporting, Mobilising for and Ignoring Jordanian Elections

'Moral Claims' and Jordan's 2013 Elections

> The most important thing to come out of these elections isn't really . . . the individuals sitting in parliament for the next term, but rather the establishment of the IEC as a credible body to organise future elections in Jordan.[1]

The run-up to and the immediate aftermath of the 2013 parliamentary elections were marked by a very similar disregard for the actual structures of power that govern Jordanian politics to that which has been discussed in regard to efforts at political party training in Chapter 2.[2] The decisive topic within the struggle to dominate interpretation between the political forces boycotting the 2013 elections – most prominently the IAF and various leftist groups[3] – and those managing, participating in and observing them, was the question of the relevance of the post-2011 reforms of the electoral framework (the establishment of the Independent Election Commission (IEC), introduction of twenty-seven national list seats, use of preprinted ballots, assigning voters to specific polling centres, legal recognition of national and international observers, etc.). As I argue in this section, the heavy focus of international 'democracy promoters' and electoral observers on assessing technical and legal aspects of the elections' correct management by the IEC directly encouraged the sidelining of questions about the distribution of power. The conduct of well-administered elections for a largely impotent parliament based on a highly discriminatory electoral law thereby effectively became an alleged sign of democratic progress.

---

[1] Interview with Daniel, international electoral advisor, Amman, 8 December 2012.

[2] Volpi and Cavatorta, among others, discuss the tendency to laud electoral competitions 'without questioning where real power actually lies'. Volpi, F. and Cavatorta, F., 'Introduction: forgetting democratization? Recasting power and authority in a plural Muslim world', in: Volpi, F. and Cavatorta, F. (eds.), *Democratization in the Muslim World: Changing Patterns of Power and Authority* (Abingdon: Routledge, 2007), p. 6.

[3] Other political forces that boycotted the 2013 parliamentary elections included the Communist Party, the Jordanian Popular Democratic Unity Party, the National Front for Reform, as well as large parts of the al-Ḥirāk popular movements.

Opposition groups largely viewed the above-mentioned amendments as merely cosmetic in nature, with the head of the Islamic Action Front (IAF), Hamzah Mansour, calling the elections 'a theatrical gimmick meant to maintain the government's strong grip on power'.[4] However, according to UNDP Jordan – the implementing partner of an EU-financed $5.3 million electoral assistance programme – the May 2012 establishment of the IEC constituted a 'milestone in the political reform process'.[5] Despite the IEC replacing the Ministry of Interior (MoI) in supervising the elections and despite its head, former Foreign Minister Abdalillah al-Khateeb, being widely respected for his integrity, important questions nevertheless remained. Among other issues, the IEC had only been established a mere nine months before the elections. Also, the IEC's supposed financial and administrative independence could be seriously questioned, as its board of commissioners is appointed by royal decree and most of its staff are on short-term contracts or seconded from the MoI.[6]

Besides the EU-financed technical support project, the United States Agency for International Development (USAID) was, during my research period, financing a similar elections administration programme, worth $4 million and implemented by the International Foundation for Electoral Systems (IFES). Both projects focused heavily on training and capacity development for the newly established IEC and almost seemed to attribute more importance to the IEC itself than to the elections, as also illustrated in the introductory quotation of a long-time international electoral advisor above. This heavy focus on procedures and institutions is closely connected to widely acknowledged irregularities in previous parliamentary elections.[7] Also, it is based on the belief that the technical improvement of procedures will help further the desired process of democratisation, irrespective of the limited powers of parliament, the strong rural bias in the delimitation of electoral districts and the discrimination against political parties inherent to the electoral law.

---

[4] Hamzah Mansour, head of the IAF, quoted in: *Democracy Digest*, 'Jordan's Islamists step up anti-election campaign', 16 January 2013, available at: www.thenational.ae/world/me na/jordanian-islamists-step-up-anti-election-threats-1.467561.

[5] UNDP Jordan, 'Electoral assistance in Jordan: a project funded by the European Union and implemented by UNDP', *Brief/Background*, available at: www.jo.undp.org/content/ jordan/en/home/operations/projects/d.

[6] See Jordan Independent Electoral Commission Law No. 11, 2012.

[7] While the former head of the GID, Muhammad Raqqad, openly acknowledged falsifying the 2007 elections, the 2010 elections saw the controversial use of virtual subdistricts that did not correspond to any geographic area and, among others, allowed for several winning candidates to receive fewer votes than losing candidates in the same district. See NDI, *Final International Election Observation Report on the Jordanian Parliamentary Elections, November 9, 2010*, 2011, p. 35.

'Democracy promoter' Michael defended this procedural focus as follows: 'When you're working on mechanics and you put in place a mechanical process with integrity, it has some impact ... With a structurally distorted system it is necessary, but not sufficient. But necessary – it's a first step'.[8] Such a view, however, ignores the fact that a manipulation of the electoral process itself was not even needed in order to still obtain a largely powerless and unrepresentative parliament as its outcome. An important role in this regard was played by the single non-transferable vote (SNTV) system (also in multiple-seat constituencies) introduced in 1993 (and abolished in 2016) and the highly discriminatory electoral district delimitation.

An International IDEA handbook describes the challenge that the SNTV system represents for political parties:

> In, for example, a four-member district, a candidate with just over 20 per cent of the vote is guaranteed election. A party with 50 per cent of the vote could thus expect to win two seats in a four-member district. If each candidate polls 25 per cent, this will happen. If, however, one candidate polls 40 per cent and the other 10 per cent, the second candidate may not be elected. If the party puts up three candidates, the danger of 'vote-splitting' makes it even less likely that the party will win two seats.[9]

The SNTV system thereby gives a strong advantage to independent candidates over those organised in strong political parties. An experienced European electoral observer described the SNTV system, which by 2005 was only being used for elections in Afghanistan, the Pitcairn Islands, Vanuatu and Jordan,[10] as follows:

> It's a very evil system ... It has awful consequences. And we can see it in Afghanistan ... it has the effect of undermining the building of political parties and undermining the capacity of the parliament to function properly ... SNTV is probably the worst and the most manipulative electoral system that exists.[11]

While the eventual abolition of the controversial system in 2016 led to a marginally stronger party representation – in 2016, nine parties won thirty out of 130 seats overall, compared to twenty-two parties winning twenty-seven out of 150 seats in 2013 – the fundamental problem of parliament's extremely weak legislative power and its resultant

---

[8] Interview with Michael, 'democracy promoter' working in Jordan, Amman, 12 December 2012.
[9] IDEA, *Electoral System Design: The New International IDEA Handbook* (Stockholm: International IDEA Handbook Series, 2005), p. 113.
[10] IDEA, *Electoral System Design*, p. 33.
[11] Interview with Pascal, European electoral observer, Brussels, 9 March 2015.

functioning as a patronage provider remains. Consequently, the abolition of the SNTV system can hardly be seen as a major turning point.

Another central problem of Jordan's electoral system is the highly discriminatory distribution of seats per constituency. While this is effectively an anti-urban bias, in light of the country's population distribution, it simultaneously amounts to one against Palestinian-Jordanians, who live predominantly in urban centres such as Amman, az-Zarqā' and Irbid. In the 2013 elections, the 6,733 registered voters in the Ma'an 2 constituency were thus able to elect one MP while the same result required 48,701 registered voters in the Irbid 7 constituency.[12] The structures of power in Jordan are thus fundamentally designed in such a way that elections described by the EU election observation mission (EOM) as 'transparent and credible'[13] still lead to a staunchly conservative pro-regime parliament. The severe distortions in the electoral law and the district delimitation ultimately predetermine the electoral outcome to such an extent that US and European technical support for the electoral process – despite regular assurances about supporting 'a democratic process, not an outcome'[14] – effectively constitutes direct assistance in the reproduction of Jordanian authoritarianism, only now in the name of democracy.[15]

Apart from the establishment of the IEC, the other major novelty in the 2013 elections was the introduction of a mixed electoral system, according to which twenty-seven of the total of 150 seats were reserved for a newly introduced national list, to be allocated through proportional representation. The remainder continued to be allocated based on the SNTV system. While the Jordanian regime described the introduction of the national list as an important starting point for the emergence of stronger political parties, competition for the national list seats was opened to any group of at least nine individuals, which resulted in a total of sixty-one lists running for the twenty-seven seats. Only a few of these lists were actually linked to political parties, however, the majority being non-partisan regional coalitions of individuals and groups largely unknown in the political arena (see Figure 3.1). The portion of national list seats (18 per cent of all seats in parliament) also fell far short of the demands of

---

[12] European Union (EU) Election Observation Mission, *Final Report: Parliamentary Elections 2013*, 2013, p. 4.

[13] EU Election Observation Mission, *Final Report: Parliamentary Elections 2013*, p. 3.

[14] Interview with Oliver, Western diplomat based in Jordan, Amman, 29 January 2013.

[15] Schwedler makes the important point that 'there is no zero-sum game between democracy and authoritarianism' and that authoritarian regimes such as the Jordanian have selectively adopted liberal democratic practices. Schwedler, J., 'The political geography of protest in neoliberal Jordan', *Middle East Critique*, Vol. 21, No. 3, 2012, p. 260.

Figure 3.1 Car of a Duʿāʾ (Democratic Arab Islamic Movement) bloc supporter. Amman, January 2013. Photo by the author.

opposition groups, which had not only asked for 50 per cent of all seats to be allocated via proportional representation through the national list but, perhaps somewhat more importantly, had also demanded parliamentary control over the formation of government, direct election of the upper house and the abolition of the king's right to dissolve parliament.

Despite the limited nature of the reforms surrounding the electoral environment, US and European 'democracy promoters' widely interpreted the introduction of the national list as an important precedent. In the run-up to the elections an international electoral advisor based in Amman argued that

if a list gets 30 per cent they will perhaps only get nine seats ... but they will be able to claim that they have 30 per cent support. [This is a] new dimension ... They won't be able to win a majority or significant plurality, but [a] moral claim.[16]

---

[16] Interview with Tim, international electoral advisor, Amman, 4 December 2012.

Besides the establishment of the IEC and the introduction of the national list, King Abdullah II also announced that the 2013 elections would be the start of a 'transition to parliamentary government',[17] adding the procedural caveat that '[i]nternational experience suggests this will require several parliamentary cycles to develop and mature [as] [t]he key driver of the timeline is our success in developing national political parties'.[18] While the constitutional provisions regarding the king's right to appoint both prime minister and ministers remained unchanged,[19] King Abdullah II publicly pledged that following the 2013 elections the designation of both would occur 'based on consultation with the majority coalition of parliamentary blocs'.[20]

Providing a good overview of some of the reforms of the electoral framework, as well as outlining the role of international 'democracy promoters', a Ministry of Planning and International Cooperation (MoPIC) official explained the following:

Our roadmap for political reforms is pretty clear for the time being. We have parliamentary elections soon ... Then we are supposed to move to parliamentary government ... We have a new political parties law, a new public gatherings law. We have established the Constitutional Court. We have established the Independent Electoral Commission to supervise elections as compared to a previous position where the government used to supervise elections with the MoI. This is a major breakthrough in our political history ... The role of donors including the EU and the US government through USAID is to support this ... roadmap.[21]

The Logic of Authoritarian Elections and 'the Nature of Jordanians'

Like the previously analysed efforts at capacity building and political party training, electoral support and observation activities also rely on the assumption that technical support promotes processes of democratisation. As a supposed cornerstone of democracy, elections are widely seen as perhaps the most necessary procedure required in a democratic transition. While I do not intend to question the importance of popular elections for ideals of democracy per se, I argue that the normative bias of

---

[17] King Abdullah II, 'Making our democratic system work for all Jordanians', Royal Hashemite Court, Amman, second discussion paper, 16 January 2013, available at: https://kingabdul lah.jo/en/discussion-papers/making-our-democratic-system-work-all-jordanians.
[18] King Abdullah II, 'Making our democratic system work for all Jordanians'.
[19] Constitution of the Hashemite Kingdom of Jordan, Article 35.
[20] King Abdullah II, 'Making our democratic system work for all Jordanians'.
[21] Interview with Ahmad, MoPIC official, Amman, 11 October 2012.

'democracy promoters' and electoral observers in favour of democracy has seriously constrained their analytical frameworks and their understandings of regimes widely described under the banner of semi-authoritarianism, hybrid regimes, electoral authoritarianism, liberalised autocracies, etc.[22] This has occurred to such an extent that the possibility that elections under authoritarianism might be guided by fundamentally illiberal logics, and that democratic procedures might only facilitate an upgrading of authoritarianism, is regularly ignored, as authoritarianism itself is both normatively and analytically viewed as a mere deformation of a desired universal democratic ideal, rather than as a potentially stable regime type in and of itself.[23]

Discussing democracy and authoritarianism, Przeworski argued in 1991 that steps in political liberalisation are 'inherently unstable'.[24] This implies a view of the above-mentioned 'authoritarianism with adjectives' not as potentially stable distinct forms of governance, but instead as mere interim stages of a country's imagined gradual path to democracy. This idea is critiqued by Lust-Okar, among others, who contends that 'political liberalization is not inherently unstable'[25] and that authoritarian rulers may actually use certain democratic procedures with the effect of strengthening authoritarian rule. Along similar lines, Cavatorta suggests that while authoritarian and democratic types of governance may indeed be converging – as Fukuyama and other proponents of a liberal democratic teleology argue – 'they are not converging where Fukuyama expected',[26] but are instead both moving 'towards liberal authoritarianism'.[27]

If, however, one accepts the proposition that such liberal-authoritarian modes of governance may in and of themselves constitute a distinct '*type* of political system',[28] as argued by Brumberg, instead of just an inherently volatile intermediate stage, one also must acknowledge that elections and electoral observation missions (EOMs) in such political systems may

---

[22] See, for instance, Brumberg, who uses the term 'liberalised autocracy'. Brumberg, D., 'Democratization in the Arab world? The trap of liberalized autocracy', *Journal of Democracy*, Vol. 13, No. 4, October 2002, pp.56–68.

[23] For the notion of authoritarian upgrading see Heydemann, S., 'Upgrading authoritarianism in the Arab world', The Saban Center for Middle East Policy at the Brookings Institution, Analysis Paper Number 13, October 2007, available at: www.brookings.edu /wp-content/uploads/2016/06/10arabworld.pdf.

[24] Przeworski, A., *Democracy and the Market: Political and Economic Reforms in Eastern Europe and Latin America* (Cambridge: Cambridge University Press, 1991), p. 58.

[25] Lust-Okar, *Structuring Conflict in the Arab World*, p. 4.

[26] Cavatorta, F., 'The convergence of governance: upgrading authoritarianism in the Arab world and downgrading democracy elsewhere?', *Middle East Critique*, Vol. 19, No. 3, Fall 2010, p. 227.

[27] Cavatorta, 'The convergence of governance', p. 219.

[28] Brumberg, 'Democratization in the Arab world?', p. 56.

unfold according to fundamentally different logics and meanings than in established liberal democracies. As demonstrated by a number of researchers, elections under authoritarianism may thus actually reinforce authoritarian structures of power instead of contributing to a democratic transition. Lust-Okar convincingly shows that Jordanian parliamentary elections are more about patronage than about policy and ultimately tend to strengthen the staunchly pro-regime nature of Jordan's parliament.[29] Brown discusses the degree of legitimisation that the conduct of elections widely entails – either by frustrating would-be opponents or by convincing external elites of a supposedly existing democratic reform process.[30] And Carapico emphasises that elections under authoritarianism often look more 'like natives performing democracy for election tourists'[31] than like the meaningful arenas for democratic competition over popular representation and control of the leading positions in the state that 'democracy promoters' aim to establish.

The central characteristic that such descriptions share is a focus on the ways in which different actors view elections from very different perspectives and accordingly construct and attach a multiplicity of meanings to their performance. Instead of labelling elections with a universally valid generic function, the above scholars pay close attention to what Wedeen describes as context-dependent 'processes of meaning-construction'.[32] Following such an approach, in this chapter I pay particular attention to the ways in which 'democracy promoters' and international electoral observers invest Jordanian elections with seeming democratic meaning. I demonstrate that the latter is regularly at odds with the signification that such elections hold for most Jordanians. Further, I offer the concrete example of Jordan's 2013 parliamentary elections – the country's first post-'Arab Spring' elections – and suggest that they constitute a powerful space of convergence for procedural narratives of the Jordanian regime, the international 'democracy promotion' industry and academic researchers, who by ignoring the possibility for authoritarian stability ultimately only reinforce it.

The deep-seated normative refusal to see elections under authoritarianism as anything other than a more or less credible step towards liberal

---

[29] Lust-Okar, 'Elections under authoritarianism: preliminary lessons from Jordan', *Democratization*, Vol.13, No. 3, June 2006, pp. 456–471.

[30] Brown, N.J., 'Dictatorship and democracy through the prism of Arab elections', in Brown, N.J. (ed.), *The Dynamics of Democratization: Dictatorship, Development, and Diffusion* (Baltimore: The Johns Hopkins University Press, 2011), pp. 49–50.

[31] Carapico, S., *Political Aid and Arab Activism: Democracy Promotion, Justice, and Representation* (New York: Cambridge University Press, 2014), p. 70.

[32] Wedeen, L., 'Conceptualizing culture: possibilities for political science', *The American Political Science Review*, Vol. 96, No. 4, December 2002, p. 717.

democracy has important effects for Western countries engaged in 'democracy promotion'. By invoking the procedural narrative, conceptions of a moral hierarchy are thus seemingly reconfirmed. Also, the relentless pressuring of liberal authoritarian modes and practices of governance – including elections under authoritarianism – into a teleological mould of inevitable democratic transformation is of instrumental importance in convincing Western and Arab publics of the claim that, irrespective of Western political, economic and military support for local authoritarianism, 'democracy promotion' activities and the regular conduct of elections assist in the eventual realisation of gradual democratic transformation.

Instead of practically challenging some of the structural conditions that reinforce Jordanian authoritarianism, international 'democracy promotion' and electoral observation activities are primarily concerned with making Jordanian authoritarianism appear to be a temporary phenomenon that can and will eventually be overcome. As long as the reasons for and the practices of Jordanian authoritarianism remain so severely misunderstood, any attempt at challenging it is condemned to fail. As democracy constitutes what Anderson called a 'sentimental favourite'[33] of Western social scientists, the mixing of research and advocacy is particularly detrimental in this regard, as it leads to the continuous championing of the procedural narrative already discussed in Chapter 2.

Election observation and assistance is perhaps the most prominent part of 'democracy promotion'. In the *Handbook for European Union Election Observation* the EU Commissioner for External Relations and Neighbourhood Policy accordingly describes it as 'a vital component of European Union activities to promote democracy, human rights and the rule of law worldwide'.[34] At the heart of such efforts at electoral observation and assistance one may note an inherent tension between the will to further a democratic process through supposedly technocratic and apolitical means on the one side and the realisation that such a process is itself a very political matter in any country deemed to transition from authoritarianism to democracy on the other. Attempting to ignore or downplay this political dimension, a number of international guidelines emphasise the alleged neutrality and objectivity of election observation. The *UN*

---

[33] Anderson, 'Democracy in the Arab world: a critique of the political culture approach', in: Brynen, R., Korany, B. and Noble, P. (eds.), *Political Liberalization and Democratization in the Arab World* (Boulder: Lynne Rienner, 1995), p. 77.

[34] Benita Ferrero-Waldner (EU Commissioner for External Relations and Neighbourhood Policy) in: European Commission (EC), *Handbook for European Union Election Observation* (Brussels: European Commission, 2009), preface.

Declaration of Principles for International Election Observation, for instance, finds that it

> is process oriented, not concerned with any particular electoral result, and is concerned with results only to the degree that they are reported honestly and accurately in a transparent and timely manner.[35]

However, it is important to realise that, in so far as election observation 'seek[s] to make a positive contribution to the process, ... [without] interfer[ing] in the way in which an election is conducted',[36] as stated in the EU handbook, a decision to observe a given election is always also already a judgement that said democratic process actually exists and that it is to a certain extent authentic. This is unequivocally recognised in an *EU Election Assistance and Observation* communication from 2000, which finds that '[a]n observation exercise normally provides some degree of legitimisation'.[37] The central problem of international election observation then is that the presupposition of an ongoing democratic process directly requires a narrow view of elections as the unambiguous component of a slow and gradual democratic transition. In its heavy focus on 'the procedural' and a teleological understanding of human history with democracy as its alleged peak, international election observation then fails to realise that, in the context of authoritarianism, the rationale underlying the conduct of elections may not at all be one of inevitable democratic transition.

As I show in this chapter, the current relevance of parliamentary elections in Jordan lies above all in their potential to serve as a means for authoritarian upgrading.[38] Western actors such as the EU, however, widely adhere to staunchly functionalist readings that fundamentally ignore such alternative meanings of elections. One EU document thus remarks that no matter where they are held, elections 'are part of a slow and gradual development towards democracy'.[39] Similar difficulties in separating desired normative visions from a much more diverse reality can be found in reports of the American National Democratic Institute (NDI). While the NDI calls upon local '[a]uthorities ... [to] realize that

---

[35] UN, *Declaration of Principles for International Election Observation* (New York: United Nations, October 2005), p. 3. The declaration is endorsed by over twenty 'democracy promotion' agencies and multilateral institutions, including the Carter Centre, the EC, IFES, IDEA, IRI and NDI.
[36] EC, *Handbook for European Union Election Observation*, p. 7.
[37] Commission of the European Communities, *Communication from the Commission on EU Election Assistance and Observation*, COM(2000) 191 final (Brussels: European Commission, April 2000), p. 17.
[38] See Heydemann, 'Upgrading authoritarianism in the Arab world'.
[39] Commission of the European Communities, *Communication from the Commission on EU Election Assistance and Observation*, p. 7.

elections are more than technical matters',[40] it appears to view elections through a narrow technical lens that does not allow for the possibility that they could function as anything else than as a means for democracy. In a guide for democratic elections, the NDI thus states that 'elections provide the definitive means for the population to exercise its right to periodically rebalance the distribution of political power'.[41]

In stark contrast to such functionalist and one-dimensional interpretations, Lust-Okar has argued that, in the case of Jordan, while involving 'a significant amount of competition', elections under authoritarianism are much more about patronage and 'gaining access to the state'[42] than about policy and/or contesting the leading positions in the state. Given the Jordanian parliament's highly limited legislative power and its role as patronage provider, she notes a strong inclination among Jordanian voters to choose pro-regime candidates, who have guaranteed access to state resources, over opposition candidates, thereby further reinforcing the existing pro-regime bias of the Jordanian parliament and authoritarian stability at large. In light of the above, Lust-Okar suggests that the role of electoral observers in changing the balance of power is regularly overestimated and that rather, 'the logic of authoritarian elections should lead us to question the value of pressing for, and applauding, the introduction of elections in authoritarian regimes'[43] to begin with.

This failure to fully understand the alternative, illiberal logic of elections ultimately has the effect of turning electoral assistance and observation missions into a contributing factor for authoritarian stability, instead of one for democratic transition. Overall, what is at stake here is the popular understanding of countries such as Jordan as 'liberalising autocracies' caught in a supposedly inexorable process of democratisation, which is viewed as only intermittently halted due to either momentarily being caught in a 'trap', and/or due to authoritarian 'survival strategies'.[44] In contrast to such interpretations, I want to suggest here that the study of authoritarian elections requires a view of the latter as a component of

---

[40] Merloe, P., *Promoting Legal Frameworks for Democratic Elections: An NDI Guide for Developing Election Laws and Law Commentaries* (Washington, DC: National Democratic Institute (NDI), 2008), p. 23.

[41] Merloe, *Promoting Legal Frameworks for Democratic Elections*, p. 37.

[42] Lust-Okar, 'Elections under authoritarianism', pp. 459–460.

[43] Lust-Okar, 'Elections under authoritarianism', p. 468.

[44] Critical of 'survival strategy' narratives, Brumberg argues that so-called liberalised autocracies need to be viewed as a distinct type of political system, rather than as a mere interim stage on the way to democracy. While I strongly agree with his critique, I am sceptical of the usefulness of the notion of a 'trap of liberalised autocracy', as it appears to maintain the assumption that authoritarianism is somewhat of a deviation of the 'natural' order. See Brumberg, 'Democratization in the Arab world?', p. 56.

a distinct political system that is authoritarian first and foremost, rather than being caught in any linear model of democratisation.

The technical language of election observation and assistance missions directly helps to uphold a process discourse and an image of democratic transition. In Jordan, it is rather difficult, if not entirely impossible, to corroborate such an image with any observable meaningful redistribution of political power. Further, the interpretation of elections under authoritarianism, not within a framework of patronage and regime stability, but within one of democratic transition also provides an opportunity for the continuous reinforcement of highly culturalist arguments that problematise the imagined Jordanian herself more than authoritarian power structures and the illiberal logics underlying Jordanian parliamentary elections.

A high-ranking member of the 2013 EU EOM in Jordan emphasised that 'we are a technical mission and we see things from a technical point strictly'.[45] Along very similar lines, a high-level employee of a Washington, DC-based American 'democracy promotion' organisation active in Jordan said that

One of the great things about [our organisation] especially is neutrality . . . the fact that [we do] things so neutrally makes a huge difference I think in the reception that we get . . . the technical information provided is always going to be useful I think.[46]

Upon closer investigation, however, the opposite appears much more pertinent, as the 'technical information provided' constitutes an important degree of legitimisation for the democratic transition narrative of the Jordanian regime. The insistence on a highly normative understanding of elections, and the associated inability to view them as the opportunity for the strengthening of patronage networks that they represent to most Jordanian voters, goes hand in hand with an important misinterpretation of what are widely deemed to be indicators of democratic legitimacy. Many electoral observers thus saw the relatively high numbers of voters registering for and participating in Jordan's 2013 elections as a sign of Jordanians' trust in the regime's reform narrative, instead of proof of the functioning of Jordanian elections as 'an arena of patronage distribution'.[47] Similarly, the relative calm – in comparison, for instance, to Tunisia, Egypt and Syria – that characterised Jordanian politics in the period preceding and following the 2013 elections was misread by some as a general feature of Jordanians at large, rather than as evidence for the

---

[45] Interview with Katerina, European electoral observer, Amman, 30 January 2013.
[46] Interview with Maryam, 'democracy promoter', Washington, DC, 10 June 2013.
[47] Lust-Okar, 'Elections under authoritarianism', p. 460.

successful functioning of Jordanian elections – only not in the way that 'democracy promoters' intend.

'Democracy promoters' and electoral observers tend then to ignore the possibility that Jordanian parliamentary elections might be primarily shaped neither by the presence, nor by the lack, of those liberal democratic logics desired, but instead by a fundamentally different alternative logic revolving around patronage opportunities. The American 'democracy promoter' quoted above also remarked that

Jordanians by nature are not the kind of people who are going to take to the streets ... The problem I think is that in the Middle East when people run for elections, they're not running around ... topics. They don't have platforms. And just getting people to even think ... about ... the people that they're electing having platforms is an entirely new concept ... in the Middle East people don't really think in terms of issues.[48]

The inability to acknowledge that elections in Jordan might function according to a fundamentally different logic than the one desired by 'democracy promoters' thus directly contributed to a deeply problematic interpretation of Jordan's 2013 elections as popular confirmation of the regime and/or as an indication of Jordanians' alleged backwardness and premodern nature.

Electoral Observation, or How to Endorse the Regime

While previous elections in Jordan, such as in 2010, had already been observed to some extent by international organisations, the 2013 parliamentary elections were the first to see full cooperation between the Jordanian authorities and international electoral observers.[49] Responding to a Jordanian invitation, an EU exploratory mission had recommended in late 2012 that the EU should not just send an election experts mission (EEM), or an election assessment team (EAT), but instead a fully fledged EOM. As remarked by a member of the EU's exploratory mission, given the larger context of the Arab uprisings,

it was always going to be an EOM ... It was the first [EOM in Jordan], but it was a very important election ... This was within the wider context of the Arab Spring. There had been an election reform ... – very limited – yes. That's true. But there

---

[48] Interview with Maryam, 'democracy promoter', Washington, DC, 10 June 2013. See also Schuetze, B., 'Marketing parliament: the constitutive effects of external attempts at parliamentary strengthening in Jordan', *Cooperation and Conflict*, Vol. 53, No. 2, 2018, pp. 237–258.

[49] For a discussion of why election monitoring became an international norm see Hyde, S. D, *The Pseudo-Democrat's Dilemma: Why Election Observation Became an International Norm* (Ithaca: Cornell University Press, 2011).

had been some development ... [in] particular, the creation of the election commission [IEC], which we thought deserved support. And they did a very good job ... even though they [the board of commissioners of the IEC] were all nominated ... by the king.[50]

While the EU had a strong interest in facilitating a procedurally acceptable election, the US also wanted to maintain the image of slow, procedural, evolutionary change. Maryam, a high-ranking American 'democracy promoter', put it as follows:

The US in Jordan was very interested in making these elections happen and [in] mak[ing] these elections happen credibly, because they didn't want there to be the same type of thing that's happening in the Arab Spring all over ... Jordan is extremely important to US security interests ... Democracy promotion in Jordan is extremely important to the security situation. And I think that's part of why the US government has been really actively involved in how these elections went ... part of the reason the US was putting such an emphasis on it was because – hopefully [it was] not just for appearances – they do want this incremental change that comes without the entire country overthrowing a leader that is in the US's security interests to keep; but at the same time, to start moving towards democracy, even if it's in a more incremental fashion than in Tunisia.[51]

As explained in Chapter 2, the maintenance of the procedural narrative was the overarching concern for both US and EU 'democracy promoters' and electoral observers in Jordan. While the fact that Jordan's electoral framework did not require any further manipulation in order to nevertheless reproduce a staunchly pro-regime parliament was not lost on US or EU electoral observers, both could celebrate the successful conduct of procedurally largely correct and transparent elections as supposed proof that the country was indeed gradually transitioning to democracy. As stated by a high-ranking member of the 2013 EU EOM in Jordan, 'the important thing is to see that the process was in accordance to the law and in accordance to the international commitments of the country'.[52]

Besides supporting the conduct of the 2013 parliamentary elections through the aforementioned USAID and EU-financed technical support projects for the IEC, and alongside EOMs carried out by NDI, IRI and the EU, the US and the EU also gave considerable support to three domestic election observation teams.[53] The eighty EU observers, a delegation of members of the European parliament, fifty NDI observers

---

[50] Interview with Pascal, European electoral observer, Brussels, 9 March 2015.
[51] Interview with Maryam, 'democracy promoter', Washington, DC, 10 June 2013.
[52] Interview with Katerina, European electoral observer, Amman, 30 January 2013.
[53] Apart from the NDI, IRI and the EU, the Arab League and the Organisation of Islamic Cooperation also conducted EOMs of the 2013 parliamentary elections. The Carter Center carried out a somewhat smaller study mission.

and around fifteen IRI observers were thus complemented by another 7,300 domestic observers, more than 60 per cent of whom were deployed by one of the three national EOM teams (the RASED coalition led by the Al-Hayat Center, the Integrity coalition led by the Identity Center, and the National Team led by the National Centre for Human Rights (NCHR)), all of which were again funded by, among others, the EU and the NDI. In their pre-election assessments both the NDI and the IRI openly acknowledged the fundamental limitations of Jordan's upcoming parliamentary elections discussed above. The IRI stated that 'recent changes to the electoral framework offer limited progress and despite some positive change are a missed opportunity for greater reform', adding that 'fundamental challenges to political reform have not been addressed'. That said, it nevertheless found that both the establishment of the IEC and the introduction of national lists 'should make a positive impact'.[54]

Particularly interesting is the NDI's pre-election assessment. After remarking that the 'NDI recognizes that it is only the Jordanian people that can determine the credibility of their elections'[55] – a statement that, if genuine, would hardly have to be made – the report goes into quite some detail in outlining precisely how the credibility of the Jordanian elections should be determined. Among other things, the NDI assessment criticised the absence of a legal framework for the king's vision of parliamentary government and explained that even if a group won 50 per cent of the national vote it would only receive less than 10 per cent of all seats in parliament. Further, it convincingly argued that the way the national list had been implemented actually incentivised the creation of tribal lists instead of encouraging the creation of parties. Finally, the NDI concluded that '[n]evertheless, the national lists represent an important, if limited, innovation'.[56] Justifying its technical support for an election administered under a strongly discriminatory electoral law, the NDI assessment proceeded by quoting an anonymous political analyst:

It is important to get the rules right and to encourage people to exercise the voting franchise, even in a flawed system. Then, next time, they will be poised to take advantage of a better law, should it appear.[57]

---

[54] For all three quotations see IRI, *Pre-Election Assessment Statement*, 3 December 2012, p. 1.

[55] NDI, *Pre-Election Assessment Delegation Statement Regarding Jordan's 2013 Legislative Elections*, 19 November 2012, p. 1.

[56] NDI, *Pre-Election Assessment Delegation Statement Regarding Jordan's 2013 Legislative Elections*, p. 3.

[57] Unnamed political analyst, quoted in NDI, *Pre-Election Assessment Delegation Statement Regarding Jordan's 2013 Legislative Elections*, p. 3.

The absence of equal participatory opportunities and representation is thus accepted, as long as the rules and processes within the 'flawed system' are technically 'right'. The possibility that such processes increasingly lose credibility as substantive democratisation remains but a distant, imagined 'next time, should it appear', is fundamentally ignored. Just one paragraph later, the NDI itself conveniently deconstructs the importance of 'getting the rules right', as it finds that, unlike in Jordan,

[e]lections held elsewhere in the region, including Tunisia and Egypt, demonstrate that citizens can have confidence in an expedited, even imperfect, process when they believe that the intent of officials is to administer a process that allows voters free expression and when election results are seen to reflect the will of the people.[58]

Besides technically supporting and observing the electoral process, electoral observers and 'democracy promoters' also took very concrete steps in order to shore up its credibility. The EU and the NDI co-financed the printing of leaflets that directly encouraged Jordanians to register for and participate in the elections. One such leaflet (see Figure 3.2), produced with the support of the EU and the Jordanian Al-Hayat Center, which was also leading the national RASED EOM, featured the slogan, 'Participation is the optimal way for change – participate ... truly'.[59]

Despite the many remaining shortcomings of the electoral law and the boycott of the elections by a significant part of the Jordanian political spectrum, 'democracy promoters' both heavily invested in the electoral process itself and actively participated in a campaign that had no other goal apart from ensuring the highest possible registration of voters and turnout on election day. Even though none of the demands of the opposition had been addressed seriously, the US and the EU desperately held on to their belief in the neutrality of the electoral process and in participation as 'a good in itself',[60] as asserted by one EU official.

As the EU, NDI and IRI participated in the mobilisation of voters for an election of which many Jordanians remained highly critical, the partisan nature of their work became clearly apparent. International electoral analyst Mike was deeply sceptical of such parallel attempts by Western institutions and local civil society organisations to both mobilise voters and conduct allegedly impartial electoral observation. He described this as 'a balancing act that can not in any way be achieved in a way that abides by the [UN]

---

[58] NDI, *Pre-Election Assessment Delegation Statement Regarding Jordan's 2013 Legislative Elections*, p. 4.

[59] The original slogan in Arabic translated by the author: 'al-mushārakah hiya as-sabīl al-amthal li-t-taghyīr – shārik ṣaḥ'.

[60] Interview with Pascal, European electoral observer, Brussels, 9 March 2015.

Figure 3.2 Voter mobilisation leaflet funded and produced by the EU and the Al-Hayat Center. Such leaflets were distributed in the run-up to Jordan's parliamentary elections on 23 January 2013. The slogan reads: 'Participation is the optimal way for change – participate . . . truly', and below 'Election day – your constitutional right'. © EU Delegation Office.

principles'.[61] As 'democracy promoters', electoral observers and the Jordanian regime all had substantial stakes in the electoral process, they shared a similar concern about protecting its credibility.

Instead of analysing the parliamentary election and the extent to which it was democratic in light of the election's (in)ability to affect domestic power structures, as suggested in the study mission report of the Carter Center,[62] for whom the above-quoted Lust had worked as local political analyst, most international electoral observers and 'democracy promoters' simply accepted the king's portrayal of the elections as a 'litmus test'[63] for the regime's reform narrative, with election turnout as

[61] Interview with Mike, international electoral analyst, Amman, 31 January 2013.
[62] Carter Center, *Study Mission Report on Jordan's 2013 Parliamentary Elections*, 14 February 2013, p. 1.
[63] King Abdullah II, paraphrased *Jordan Times*, 'Parliamentary elections the defining moment in Jordan Spring – king', 8 August 2012, available at: https://kingabdullah.jo/e n/news/parliamentary-elections-defining-moment-jordan-spring-king.

supposed key indicator. Washington, DC-based IRI official Richard explained:

> We can give commentary on the mechanics of the process ... but in terms of ... the acceptance of the process and the acceptance of the results, Jordanians are ultimately the people that are going to decide how real the reform process is ... And the best measure for it ... is voter turnout in this election versus previously.[64]

In its final report the IRI simply echoed the king's wording and described the elections as 'largely a referendum on the king's efforts toward reform'.[65] The fundamental problem of such an understanding is that it wrongly assumes the percentage of registered and participating voters to be an indicator for popular satisfaction with the king and the regime. As argued by Lust-Okar, elections and election campaigns in Jordan are much less about ideology and political programmes – or indeed about making any kind of larger political statement – than about patronage opportunities.[66] As the Jordanian parliament largely functions as a services parliament, as shown by Clark,[67] it is likely that a considerable number of Jordanians registered for and participated in the elections in the hope of obtaining benefits in return for their votes and/ or due to family and/or tribal bonds they hoped to strengthen, rather than due to their general consent with the regime. In the case of many Palestinian-Jordanians, one may further add rumours that failure to register might lead to a withdrawal of national identity cards.[68] A simple equation of registration for and participation in the elections with popular endorsement of the regime is highly misleading.

This is nevertheless precisely the way in which many 'democracy promoters' understood the elections. A day before the official end of the registration period in October 2012, Adam, a 'democracy promoter' based in Amman, explained that

> People are satisfied: 2.2 million registered for voting even though they don't know whom to vote for.[69] This is significant! This is an endorsement of the regime and shows that security is important.[70]

---

[64] Interview with Richard, IRI official, Washington, DC, 23 May 2013.

[65] IRI, *Jordan Parliamentary Elections January 23, 2013, Final Report*, 2013, p. 10.

[66] Lust-Okar, 'Elections under authoritarianism', pp. 456–471.

[67] Clark, J., 'Questioning power, mobilization, and strategies of the Islamist opposition: how strong is the Muslim Brotherhood in Jordan?', in: Albrecht, H. (ed.), *Contentious Politics in the Middle East: Political Opposition under Authoritarianism* (Gainesville: University Press of Florida, 2010), p. 126.

[68] Carter Center, *Study Mission Report on Jordan's 2013 Parliamentary Elections*, p. 16.

[69] At the end of the registration phase, which was extended twice, 71 per cent of eligible voters had registered.

[70] Interview with Adam, 'democracy promoter' working in Jordan, Amman, 14 October 2012.

From the initial desire to view the electoral process as a sign of democratic progress via an interpretation of the election as confirmation of the regime's reform efforts, Adam now acknowledged that the external relevance of the 2013 electoral process lay in demonstrating that Jordanians not only endorsed the regime's reform narrative, but the regime as a whole. Or, as pointedly stated by Abu-Rish,

the discussion on politics in Jordan has shifted from debating the efficacy of elections as a form of political practice to a celebration of the conducting of elections as a sign of progress. The actual rules regulating the elections, or the distribution of power within state institutions – most notably, between the palace and the parliament – is of secondary relevance in such discussions.[71]

For Adam, as long as they had registered and would participate in the elections, it did not matter that many Jordanians did not know most of the lists and parties that were about to run for parliament. The remaining shortcomings of the electoral law, the severely limited power of parliament and the improbability of any of the parties running on the national list actually securing a meaningful 'moral claim', not to speak of a transition to parliamentary government, were all topics of only minor importance for Adam, as long as the process of democratisation could be portrayed as ongoing. In light of this embrace of the procedural narrative by external observers and 'democracy promoters', and given the general disregard for the actual power dynamics underlying the elections, Abu-Rish convincingly argues that the 2013 parliamentary elections should be understood as a display of 'the success of authoritarianism in Jordan'[72] rather than demonstrating a sign of democratic progress.

Prime Minister Abdullah Ensour provided a great example of the disregard for non-procedural issues and the portrayal of the process as an end goal in itself. Shortly before the elections, he thus warned in the *Jordan Times* that

if people do not head to the polls, then the Western media will say that the opposition groups that called for boycotting the elections succeeded and they should rule ... Therefore, everyone should vote regardless of their disagreements and reservations regarding the Elections Law [or else contribute to] conveying the wrong message about Jordan.[73]

---

[71] Abu-Rish, Z., 'Romancing the throne: *The New York Times* and the endorsement of authoritarianism in Jordan', *Jadaliyya*, 3 February 2013.

[72] Abu-Rish, 'Romancing the throne'.

[73] Prime Minister Abdullah Ensour, quoted in Husseini, Rana, 'Ensour encourages women to participate in elections', *Jordan Times*, 6 January 2013, available at: www.vista.sahafi.jo /art.php?id=dc9ba71cd69485a8eaccfc8d29b47a000fa011b0.

Further, Ensour called upon opposition groups to work towards changing the elections law from within the very parliament that was determined by it. Similarly, in the first of a series of discussion papers, in December 2012 King Abdullah II drew a direct line from what he called 'practices of good democratic citizenship'[74] to participation in the upcoming elections.

As demonstrated, international electoral observers and 'democracy promoters' directly helped the Jordanian regime both technically and discursively in portraying participation in what was widely acknowledged to be a 'flawed system' as a meaningful and important act of democratic citizenship. Despite hanging on to the narrative of slow procedural democratic change, some electoral observers admitted to the fundamental improbability of such change actually materialising. The IRI's final report, for instance, quotes its observer team for the southern city of Ma'an: 'There is low optimism that anything can change through the ballot. The IEC is doing a good job, and the processes are different, but the outcome won't necessarily be better'.[75]

'Progress in Small Steps'?

Ensour's fear that low turnout might encourage Western media to conclude that opposition groups should rule proved unfounded. In light of an official turnout of 57 per cent of registered voters, the international media widely celebrated the elections as an 'important first step in rebuilding trust',[76] as a success in a test 'that many doubted [Jordan] could pass',[77] or as sign of 'Progress in Small Steps',[78] as a *New York Times* article suggested. Despite the fact that the actual turnout, in terms of eligible voters, amounted to only 40 per cent, or even only 36 per cent depending

---

[74] King Abdullah II, 'Our journey to forge our path towards democracy', Royal Hashemite Court, Amman, first discussion paper, 29 December 2012, available at: https://kingab dullah.jo/en/discussion-papers/our-journey-forge-our-path-towards-democracy.

[75] IRI observer team in Ma'an, quoted in IRI, *Jordan Parliamentary Elections January 23, 2013, Final Report*, p. 37.

[76] Atalla, M., 'Silver lining of the Jordanian elections', *Open Democracy*, 28 January 2013, available at: www.opendemocracy.net/en/silver-lining-of-jordanian-elections/.

[77] Kuttab, D., 'Islamists boycott fails in Jordan's elections', *Huffington Post*, 24 January 2013, available at: www.huffpost.com/entry/post_b_2539174?guccounter=1&guce_ referrer=aHR0cHM6Ly93d3cuZ29vZ2xlLmZyLw&guce_referrer_sig=AQAAADVGq Sr2NfbPDMA9iTd_MWgXnLyodinVsTqez8fvXbeE4dNcAzbtT644iPGyIrlgYghat CLWI9nwALbKi_GWpwmPHorYZSnrZL-gyK4VncZN03Lv5D5Ja2sj8EuCm NkdxHCMqh5yR1V9Q5NYhpwRXhj6fcGlCNZWyP0d51AUcGLc.

[78] Sweis, R.F., 'In Jordan, progress in small steps', *New York Times*, 30 January 2013, available at: www.nytimes.com/2013/01/31/world/middleeast/in-jordan-progress-in-small-steps.html.

on the number of eligible voters quoted,[79] the boycott by opposition groups was quickly dismissed as a failure and the IAF and the secular parties that had participated were described by one commentator as 'the biggest losers'[80] of the elections. A US Department of State (DoS) spokesperson agreed that the elections constituted 'an important step in the ongoing reform process', as well as a 'milestone'[81] that could be built upon. Other Western representatives made similar remarks.[82]

Unsurprisingly, the respective final reports of the EU, NDI and IRI EOMs all endorsed very similar narratives that typically both praised the procedural advances and noted the continued existence of various short-comings. The overall process that Jordan was believed to be pursuing was importantly diagnosed as both intact and ongoing. The EU's final report found that 'procedures were largely followed with minor proce-dural irregularities that did not impact on the integrity of the process'.[83] The NDI's final report remarked that the 'elections represent a marked technical advancement in procedures and administration', while also adding that '[n]evertheless, systemic distortions remain'.[84] The IRI's final report in turn declared the elections to have been 'a step forward for Jordan on its path towards a constitutional monarchy' despite then talking about 'another rubber-stamp parliament' and elections as 'a transactional event, where huge sums of money are wielded among impoverished citizens who want their piece of the pie'.[85] Both praise and critique were comfortably reconciled by invoking the notion of an irrevocable trajectory to democracy. The elections were thus deemed to have shown 'both the significant progress Jordan has made and the long road ahead'.[86]

What is particularly remarkable about the international media responses and the EOM reports is their relative disregard for the actual results of the elections in favour of a constant focus on the procedural. Mirroring the assessment of international electoral advisor Daniel quoted in the epigraph, one analyst stated that '[t]he parliament that has been elected is not what is exciting, what is exciting is the prospect of future

---

[79] This relates to the inclusion or exclusion of out-of-country voters and members of the military, who are legally not allowed to vote. See IRI, *Jordan Parliamentary Elections January 23, 2013, Final Report*, p. 22, footnote 20.

[80] Kuttab, 'Islamists boycott fails in Jordan's elections'.

[81] Nuland, V. (Spokesperson, US DoS), 'Daily press briefing', DoS, Washington, DC, 25 January 2013.

[82] See Hazaimeh, H., 'UK, US commend polls, pledge more support', *Jordan Times*, 26 January 2013.

[83] EU Election Observation Mission, *Final Report: Parliamentary Elections 2013*, p. 5.

[84] NDI, *Final Report on the Jordanian Parliamentary Elections, January 23, 2013*, 2013, p. 3.

[85] IRI, *Jordan Parliamentary Elections January 23, 2013, Final Report*, pp. 8, 9, 31.

[86] IRI, *Jordan Parliamentary Elections January 23, 2013, Final Report*, p. 8.

elections being run in the same fashion'.[87] The focus on what is perceived as a long-term procedural gain thereby once again seemingly allowed for the disregard of the deeply undemocratic nature of Jordanian politics at present. The key analytical problem of such interpretations is precisely this blending and merging of talk about 'progress', 'important steps' and 'milestones' with the implicit acknowledgement that the legislative process remains entirely regime-controlled and that at least 75 per cent of the new MPs are loyal to the regime.[88]

Also, such analyses point to what Abu-Rish, in a response to the above-quoted *New York Times* article, pointedly termed 'an important recalibration of the indicators of legitimacy among reporters and analysts alike'.[89] As conceptualisations of democracy are increasingly narrowed down to the technically well-administered implementation of procedures and simultaneously emptied of large parts of their emancipatory content, one may observe a strange reversal of roles and perceptions. While Jordan's authoritarian regime received widespread praise for its commitment to democracy both before and after the 2013 elections, various commentators dismissed as apathetic, lazy and indifferent those political forces that criticised the elections for merely reproducing authoritarian power under a democratic disguise.[90] Abu-Rish forcefully describes this sharp dismissal of alternative, non-procedural understandings of democracy as a recurrent strategy of liberal discourses which, by obfuscating the underlying structures of power, attempt to portray procedural democratic progress as both inevitable and without alternative.[91]

To the disappointment of international 'democracy promoters', the conduct of what were widely perceived as procedurally transparent and credible elections was quickly followed by a masterpiece of elite circulation and authoritarian upgrading. As sixty-one lists had competed for only twenty-seven national list seats, the Islamic Centrist Party (Wasaṭ

---

[87] Atalla, 'Silver lining of the Jordanian elections'.
[88] See, in particular, Abu-Rish, 'Romancing the throne'. For the figure of 75 per cent, see Valbjørn, M., 'The 2013 parliamentary elections in Jordan: three stories and some general lessons', *Mediterranean Politics*, Vol. 18, No. 2, 2013, p. 314. See also Fahim, K., 'Loyalists to dominate Jordan's new parliament', *New York Times*, 24 January 2013, available at: www.nytimes.com/2013/01/25/world/middleeast/jordan-elections-favor-government-loyalists.html?ref=world&_r=0.
[89] Abu-Rish, 'Romancing the throne'.
[90] See, for instance, Kuttab, who finds that 'in most cases, it is easy to blame the absence of participation in elections on apathy and laziness, rather than on a determined boycott'. Kuttab, 'Islamists boycott fails in Jordan's elections'. See also Heydemann, who argues that '[a]mong the broader public, however, it is apathy and indifference, rather than active opposition, which seem to capture the mood'. Heydemann, S., 'Breaking through Jordan's apathy barrier?' *United States Institute of Peace*, 22 January 2013.
[91] See Abu-Rish, Z., 'Jordan, liberalism, and the question of boycott', *Jadaliyya*, 9 November 2010.

al-Islāmī) had become the strongest party of Jordan's new parliament with a mere three seats. While it also gained fourteen seats at the district level – that is, via the traditional SNTV system – these only partly increased the strength of the party as a united bloc in parliament, as the success of these MPs owed at least as much to their individual reputations as to their party affiliation. Already the election of former Minister of Interior Saad Hayel Srour to the post of speaker of parliament showed both the limitations of the Islamic Centrist Party's power – its own candidate was defeated by Srour – and the parliament's strong pro-regime stance.

The appointment of Srour, a staunch conservative and regime supporter, had been preceded by the king's appointment of former Prime Minister Fayez Tarawneh, who is similarly viewed as a strong regime loyalist, to the influential position of Chief of Royal Court. As the twenty-seven national list seats were shared among twenty-two different lists and the cohesiveness of the blocs that had formed before the election for the speaker of parliament rapidly declined after it, the king's promised transition to parliamentary government proved somewhat difficult. Once Tarawneh had, on behalf of the king, concluded his consultations with the newly elected MPs, the king thus simply reappointed Ensour as prime minister. The new cabinet finally included not a single MP, providing further evidence of the minimal significance that both king and prime minister ascribe to the parliament, and leading one MP to conclude that the king's idea of parliamentary government had 'failed'.[92]

Who Won the Elections?

Considering the weakness of both political parties and parliament, one may wonder who benefited most of the 2013 parliamentary elections. Kuttab pointed to both the IEC and to local and international electoral observers,[93] and indeed, the IEC did gain a great deal of recognition from various stakeholders for its administration of the elections, and at first sight also seemed to have established itself as a 'credible body to organise future elections',[94] as international electoral advisor Daniel had hoped in late 2012. Several events in the months following the elections call for a more cautious interpretation, however. The apparent procedural gains quickly began to crumble when the widely respected head of the IEC resigned shortly after the elections and the king decided to leave the post vacant for almost a year. The management of Jordan's municipal

---

[92] Interview with a Jordanian MP, Amman, 19 January 2015.
[93] Kuttab, 'Islamists boycott fails in Jordan's elections'.
[94] Interview with Daniel, international electoral advisor, Amman, 8 December 2012.

elections in August 2013 by the Ministry of Municipal Affairs (MoMA) instead of the IEC,[95] which only played the role of monitoring the elections, further eroded the political weight of an institution that many international electoral advisors and observers had hailed as the most important achievement of the 2013 parliamentary elections. Rather than deciding simply not to conduct any training programmes, IFES now chose to train MoMA personnel instead of IEC staff – a decision that prompted one Jordanian political activist to describe IFES as a 'right-wing ... governmental party'.[96] International 'democracy promotion' agencies such as IFES not only provide technical support to Jordanian state institutions such as ministries and the IEC, however, but also find themselves in direct competition with the latter – for instance, when it comes to finding and hiring competent and qualified staff. For example, one former high-ranking and widely respected IEC employee was by early 2015 working as a new programme director for the American NDI.

When in April 2014 the king eventually appointed a new chairman and board of commissioners for the IEC, one Jordanian commentator described its new composition as an indicator that it was turning into just another 'governmental department'.[97] A few months later, in August 2014, the Jordanian parliament approved, upon royal initiative, two important constitutional amendments. While the first expanded the jurisdiction of the IEC to include the administration of municipal elections, the second amendment gave the king the exclusive authority to appoint both the chairman of the Joint Chiefs-of-Staff and the director of the General Intelligence Directorate (GID).[98] The latter amendment was widely interpreted as a deliberate attempt to secure the state against the consequences of a potential future handover of governmental power and thus as preparation for potential further procedural steps towards an eventual transition to parliamentary government, while simultaneously radically depleting the latter of its democratic substance. Although the initial establishment of the IEC and its conduct of the 2013 elections may indeed constitute a procedural success, the subsequent months and years demonstrated how easily such acts of limited political liberalisation can be reversed, halted and/or emptied of their democratic meaning.

---

[95] This became possible as the parliament had failed to amend the municipalities law in time. The latter still designated the MoMA as the entity responsible for the management of municipal elections, and not the IEC.

[96] Interview with Zaid, political activist, Amman, 15 January 2015.

[97] Kheitan, F., 'If only they had not realised the void' [*Laytahā lam taftun li-l-farāgh*], *Al-Ghad*, 27 April 2014. Originally in Arabic, translated by the author.

[98] While the king had thus far effectively also appointed the two positions, formally he still required an initial nomination by the prime minister, which is no longer necessary.

It may then be right, as suggested by Kuttab, that the most important winners of the 2013 parliamentary elections were indeed those who observed them, rather than parliament itself or the individuals who competed in and/or managed the elections – even if in a somewhat more mundane sense than imagined. Election observer Sebastian, for instance, explained – with a clear feeling of pride – that he gets 'jealous looks due to the many missions'[99] he has already been on. Another important factor that must not be ignored is that electoral observation is 'sort of fun',[100] as one 'democracy promoter' working in Jordan put it. Inclusion in an EOM may in some instances thus constitute a political favour and/or courtesy extended to high-level employees and political friends rather than a decision based on professional skills and experiences.

While the members of the EU EOM had largely been selected based on previous experience, attended training sessions and various technocratic skills – only the chief observer, a Member of the European Parliament, was an active politician – the composition of the NDI and IRI EOM teams pointed to a less technocratic and more overtly political approach in US electoral observation. The IRI team included a Czech senator, former members of the Canadian Parliament, a high-level employee of the Council on Foreign Relations, as well as a vice president at the investment bank J.P. Morgan and the former chief of staff to the Republican presidential candidate Mitt Romney. Among NDI's most prominent observers was former president of Bolivia Jorge Quiroga, as well as the chairman of the Nigerian Independent National Electoral Commission. In contrast to the EU EOM, inclusion in the NDI and IRI teams appears to have been heavily based on political seniority and personal connections. Professional knowledge of Jordanian politics and/or democratic procedures seems to have been decisive for consideration as electoral observer in some cases, and entirely irrelevant in others.

In some instances, individuals' roles in the internal politics of the organising institution appear to have been the overriding factor, as one may assume in regard to the consideration of a vice president at J.P. Morgan and a former chief of staff of a presidential candidate. While the European approach to electoral observation appears to some extent to be an extension of a perceived need for apolitical technical experts as facilitators of processes of democratisation, the US approach appears, first and foremost, to reflect a conceptualisation of democracy as universal value, hence justifying the inclusion of a former Bolivian president and

---

[99] Interview with Sebastian, international election observer, Amman, 21 January 2013.
[100] Interview with Michael, 'democracy promoter' working in Jordan, Amman, 24 January 2013.

a high-level Nigerian public servant. In total, the NDI EOM in Jordan included not only eleven observers from the Middle East and thirteen from the USA and Canada, but also nine from Eastern Europe, six from Western Europe, four from Latin America, three from sub-Saharan Africa, and observers from New Zealand, Indonesia and East Timor.

While individual electoral observers were surely among the beneficiaries of the elections in terms of professional and personal experience, the most important effects of the EU, NDI and IRI EOMs were the apparent confirmation of the alleged moral authority of international 'democracy promoters' in assessing elections worldwide, and the considerable boost that the EOM reports gave to procedural narratives. As the procedural narrative is replicated in academic work, as well as in policy and EOM reports, more fundamental questions tend to be ignored.

This can best be illustrated through another striking feature of the NDI and IRI EOM teams: the inclusion of established researchers and policymakers. The academic background of some of the electoral observers lends additional weight to the 'democracy promotion' narrative. Danya Greenfield, Deputy Director of the Rafik Hariri Center for the Middle East at the Atlantic Council in Washington, DC, and an NDI electoral observer in Jordan, wrote in a *Foreign Policy* article in January 2013 that 'Jordan's parliamentary election ... generated some optimism'. In the same breath, Greenfield admitted that this was not really related to any democratic substance, as '[t]he big questions had little to do with the appeal of specific political platforms or even the candidates themselves, but rather with process and turnout',[101] thereby once again ignoring that popular desire to benefit from patronage opportunities was much more likely the driving factor behind the 57 per cent turnout. In a policy brief written two months after the elections, Curtis Ryan, associate professor of political science and NDI electoral observer in Jordan, affirmed the king's narrative:

King Abdullah has described the 2013 elections as a milestone and Jordanian reform as a journey. That is a useful metaphor, because the positive aspects of the elections and the reforms so far can and should be appreciated, but must also be seen in each case as just another step in a longer process. Jordan, in short, isn't there yet.[102]

For other electoral observers, such as David Schenker, IRI observer, former Pentagon policy aide and current director of the Washington

---

[101] Greenfield, D., 'Optimism after Jordan's election', *Foreign Policy*, 25 January 2013, available at: https://foreignpolicy.com/2013/01/25/optimism-after-jordans-election/.
[102] Ryan, C.R., 'Jordan's unfinished journey: parliamentary elections and the state of reform', *Project on Middle East Democracy (POMED)*, Policy Brief, March 2013, p. 6.

Institute for Near East Policy's (WINEP) Program on Arab Politics, the question arises whether the key concern is actually a democratic transition at all, or rather the very opposite, ongoing regime security.[103]

The interaction between academic research on Jordan and the wider 'democracy promotion' industry indeed seems to have become so close that alternatives to the procedural dogma are increasingly ignored in the ensuing body of knowledge. The procedural narrative thus appears to be either endorsed as the defining principle for Jordanian politics or questioned in terms of its political desirability, but it is only rarely questioned in and of itself. In the few cases when it is not the theoretical foundation for research, but its subject, the feedback loop back to 'democracy promotion' appears to be closed to any non-procedural knowledge.

Steven Heydemann, for instance, vice president of the United States Institute of Peace, is highly sceptical of the chances, as well as of the alleged inevitability, of a Jordanian transition to democracy. In his academic work he strongly criticises technocratic understandings of democratisation, the notion of democracy as a universal value and much of the policy literature on 'democracy promotion' at large.[104] While Heydemann is thus known for his important work on the notion of authoritarian upgrading, which constitutes a major step in pushing the study of authoritarianism away from the view that it is a mere object of liberalism's incessant pressures, the IRI EOM, for which he worked as an electoral observer, fundamentally ignored the possibility of authoritarian upgrading and relied on a narrative of unremitting procedural progress. But even Heydemann's critique of the procedural narrative falls short in important aspects.

Although he acknowledges that in reaction to past efforts at 'democracy promotion', many regimes successfully responded with strategies of authoritarian upgrading, his conclusion that '[w]hat is needed ... is a second generation of democracy promotion policies: democracy promotion 2.0'[105] demonstrates well the fundamental difficulty of approaching the study of authoritarianism as more than just the study of a deviation from what is portrayed as the universal moral norm. The normative insistence on a liberal procedural narrative thus seriously obfuscates the possibility that authoritarian regimes such as the Jordanian might not actually exist 'despite the best efforts of the United States [and] its

---

[103] See, for instance, Schenker, D., 'Saving Jordan's King Abdullah must be a U.S. priority', *The Wall Street Journal*, 20 March 2013, available at: www.wsj.com/articles/SB10001424127887323829504578267951332697058.

[104] See, for instance, Heydemann, S., 'In the shadow of democracy: review article', *Middle East Journal*, Vol. 60, No. 1, Winter 2006, pp. 146–157.

[105] Heydemann, 'Upgrading authoritarianism in the Arab world', p. 32.

European Union partners',[106] as argued by Heydemann, but rather irrespective of them, or perhaps in part even because of these efforts. That is to say that in order to maintain the powerful narrative of Jordan as a country on the path to democracy, the Jordanian regime actually relies on US and European 'democracy promoters' playing the crucial role of 'experts' in processes of democratisation, who intermittently confirm that rather than being in a relatively stable state of authoritarianism, the desired transition to democracy is still alive and well.

This chapter has argued that in the case of Jordan's 2013 parliamentary elections, international electoral observation largely failed to take authoritarian modes of governance seriously in and of themselves, and instead viewed them as characteristic of what is deemed to be an intermittent stage on a country's path to democracy. In contrast to such a description, ongoing electoral discrimination against political parties and Palestinian-Jordanians, and the deliberate undermining of parliamentary power do not just constitute limited procedural shortcomings, but are rather fundamental traits of Jordanian authoritarianism that fulfil two important tasks. Firstly, they protect perceptions of Jordanian national identity against the perceived threat of a transformation of Jordan into an 'alternative homeland' for the Palestinians.[107] And secondly, in doing so and in discriminating against Palestinian-Jordanians, Jordanian authoritarianism powerfully perpetuates the image of Jordanians as 'not yet ready' for democracy, thereby setting the stage for permanent 'democracy promotion' interventions. Further, I have argued that the conduct of elections in Jordan has only helped the Jordanian regime in its objective of strengthening authoritarian rule. I have shown that the insistence of electoral observers and 'democracy promoters' on interpreting elections within a strict procedural framework not only ignores the ways in which Jordanian voters and politicians make meaning of elections, but also the sharp disconnect between claims of procedural progress on the one hand and the reality of authoritarian upgrading on the other.

Finally, if one were to accept the relative stability of Jordanian authoritarianism and the latter's existence as more than just a deformation of a universally valid democratic norm, one would also have to fundamentally question the need for and the possibility of international 'democracy promotion'. A narrow understanding of Jordanian authoritarianism as caught in a gradual process of democratic transformation importantly prevents this, and as a consequence renders Jordan the perfect candidate

---

[106] Heydemann, 'Upgrading authoritarianism in the Arab world', p. vii.
[107] See International Crisis Group, *Popular Protest in North Africa and the Middle East (IX): Dallying with Reform in a Divided Jordan* (Amman/Brussels: Middle East/North Africa Report No. 118, 12 March 2012).

for 'democracy promotion' interventions. The country thus effectively becomes a permanent playground for the continuous reassertion of Western feelings of moral superiority. Beyond the level of Jordanian domestic politics, the regular performance of elections in Jordan and the concomitant assessment of external experts that although procedural progress is visible, important shortcomings remain thus fulfil the important function of providing an outlet for Western moral idealist concerns, while simultaneously avoiding undermining realist complacency with the presumed geopolitical benefits of an authoritarian Jordan (see Chapter 6). The democratic process that Jordan is widely seen to be caught in then actually tells us more about desired and often idealised Western self-understandings than about the meaning of Jordanian parliamentary elections for Jordanians themselves. Pursuing this point in more depth in the following chapter, I will investigate further the ways in which external efforts at civil society support in Jordan exhibit such a dimension of Western-centrism.

4   The Jordanian Civil Society Market

When Batman Comes Knocking

Whatever you do to knock on the door of the system to open up is good ... So NDI, IRI, Batman, Robin Hood, whoever does that ... it doesn't really matter.[1]

You got me my objectives. You got me my overall problem. You got me even my activities. I mean – why don't you just ... implement it yourself ...? What's the civil society ... for?![2]

The Orient then seems to be, not an unlimited extension beyond the familiar European world, but rather a closed field, a theatrical stage affixed to Europe.[3]

This chapter is complementary to the previous two in so far as 'democracy promoters' regularly understand democracy in terms of a 'political market' – that is as a system of governance that is realised when a balance between the forces of supply, seen as the institutions of the state discussed by the previous two chapters, and those of demand, understood as civil society, is achieved.[4]

This chapter makes two interrelated theoretical claims. First, I argue that efforts at civil society support in Jordan tell us more about 'democracy promoters' themselves and about their desires to (re)confirm

---

[1] Interview with Omar, Jordanian employee of a USAID financed civil society support programme, Amman, 18 March 2013.
[2] Interview with Zaid, political activist, Amman, 17 October 2012.
[3] Said, E., *Orientalism* (New York: Vintage Books, 1978), p. 63.
[4] The USAID Jordan D/G portfolio appears to be directly grounded in a logic of supply and demand, as it funds the IRI to train political parties, understood as forces of supply, and the NDI to train Jordanian youth, understood as forces of demand. Due to the much smaller size of the IRI Jordan office, this logic is to some extent also replicated in the NDI programme, with parliamentary strengthening constituting the training for the assumed forces of supply. The USAID-commissioned 2003 MSI report also bases itself on such a market logic of supply and demand. See also Teti, A., 'Democracy without social justice: marginalization of social and economic rights in EU democracy assistance policy after the Arab uprisings', *Middle East Critique*, Vol. 24, No. 1, 2015, pp. 9–25, especially p. 17, and Guazzone, L. and Pioppi, D., *The Arab State and Neo-Liberal Globalization: The Restructuring of State Power in the Middle East* (Reading: Ithaca Press, 2012).

self-understandings as 'modern', 'liberal' and 'democratic' than they tell us about the state and development of Jordanian politics. Second, I claim that as a direct consequence of this Western-centrism, the continuous functioning of civil society support (understood as its perpetuation rather than the achievement of the desired objectives) depends on a disregard for the specific context in which it operates and on the associated ability to maintain the dominance of a narrative of 'the universal' over everything considered Jordanian.

The prominent role of civil society support in 'democracy promotion' in Jordan rests on a number of core premises: first, on the assumption that Jordanian civil society is weak; second, on a normative understanding of civil society as inherently pro-democratic; and, third, on the acceptance of the market logic according to which the supply of civil society funding will result in more demand for the promoted values. Together, these assumptions allow for the previously discussed shifting of blame for Jordanian authoritarianism away from the regime and instead towards a supposedly still inadequately organised and educated, and somewhat 'uncivil' Jordanian society (see Chapter 2). As I question these assumptions, I draw on, among others, the work of Abdel Rahman, Carapico, Dana and Farsakh.[5] Since efforts at supporting civil society shift the focus of attention to questions of political culture, the establishment of democratic institutions increasingly appears to depend on participation, advocacy and awareness, while these might actually be 'a *result* of habituation to these kinds of institutions'.[6] As Anderson remarks, this turning to '[p]olitical culture analysis can be very seductive, particularly to policy-makers looking for short, neat explanations of the complexities they face'.[7] Hamid pointedly notes that '[i]t was never quite explained how a democratic culture could emerge under dictatorship'.[8]

The observation that civil society research and programmes often focus on what is absent – for example, a lack of strong parties and a lack of

[5] Abdel Rahman, M., 'The politics of 'uncivil' society in Egypt', *Review of African Political Economy*, Vol. 29, No. 91, March 2002, pp. 21–35; Carapico, S., *Political Aid and Arab Activism: Democracy Promotion, Justice, and Representation* (New York: Cambridge University Press, 2014); Dana, T., 'The structural transformation of Palestinian civil society: key paradigm shifts', *Middle East Critique*, Vol. 24, No. 2, 2015, pp. 191–210; Farsakh, L., 'Democracy promotion in Palestine: aid and the "de-democratization" of the West Bank and Gaza', Birzeit University, 2012, pp. 1–25, available at: http://rosaluxem burg.ps/wp-content/uploads/2015/03/Leila-Farsakh.pdf.

[6] Anderson, L., 'Democracy in the Arab world: a critique of the political culture approach', in: Brynen, R., Korany, B. and Noble, P. (eds.), *Political Liberalization and Democratization in the Arab World* (Boulder: Lynne Rienner, 1995), p. 89.

[7] Anderson, 'Democracy in the Arab world', p. 90.

[8] Hamid, S., 'The struggle for Middle East democracy', *Cairo Review of Global Affairs*, Vol. 1, 2011, pp. 18–29.

vibrant civil societies – is nothing new. Albrecht and Schlumberger have criticised this Western-centrism by noting that in significant parts of the body of knowledge that deals with democracy in the Middle East, 'the main character just never shows up'.[9] On a similar note, Anderson suggests that the unfortunate preoccupation with that which is absent has led to many Middle East political scientists neglecting major political dynamics and forces in the region, as they were 'searching where the light shines'.[10] As I strongly agree with these criticisms, I suggest that besides the dimension of failure (failing to understand local politics and failing to 'deliver' the envisaged and hoped-for developments), the deeply ideological and productive dimension (reproducing 'Western' self-understandings and perceptions of moral superiority) deserves more attention. In this regard, I rely on Said's understanding of the Orient as 'not an unlimited extension beyond the familiar European world, but rather a closed field, a theatrical stage affixed to Europe'.[11] I argue that the main character in US and European 'democracy promotion' in Jordan is neither Jordan, nor democracy, nor even an imagined Jordanian democracy, but instead a Western self-understanding as 'democratic' *vis-à-vis* 'the Jordanian non-democratic other'.[12] I contend that the field of civil society support in Jordan then quite literally constitutes the kind of theatrical stage that Said spoke of, as it provides external civil society 'supporters' with an opportunity to re-enact their feeling of 'being modern'.[13]

The instrumental task of ignoring and/or abstracting Jordanian politics importantly enables the subsequent comparison and juxtaposition of it to idealised and romanticised narratives of past processes of democratisation in 'the West'. This act of disregard, abstraction and comparison is of crucial importance in the maintenance of the moral differential on which the idea of 'democracy promotion' so fundamentally relies. Counter to what a common understanding of 'democracy promotion' would suggest, it is therefore not the overcoming of differences that is central to its

---

[9] Albrecht, H. and Schlumberger, O., '"Waiting for Godot": regime change without democratization in the Middle East', *International Political Science Review*, Vol. 25, No. 4, October 2004, p. 371.

[10] Anderson, L., 'Searching where the light shines: studying democratization in the Middle East', *Annual Review of Political Science*, Vol. 9, 2006, pp. 189–214.

[11] Said, *Orientalism*, p. 63.

[12] See also Schuetze, B., 'Marketing parliament: the constitutive effects of external attempts at parliamentary strengthening in Jordan', *Cooperation and Conflict*, Vol. 53, No. 2, 2018, pp. 237–258.

[13] See Hann, who remarks that debates about civil society are closely linked to also the debate about modernity. Hann, C., 'Introduction – political society and civil anthropology', in: Hann, C. and Dunn, E. (eds.), *Civil Society: Challenging Western Models* (London: Routledge, 1996), p. 6.

functioning, but arguably to some extent the exact opposite – that is, their maintenance. As Jordanian politics is subjected to an idealised and seemingly universal model, many sociopolitical particularities are either ignored or assessed as mere variations of a morally superior norm. 'Democracy promotion's' reliance on a supposedly universally applicable mould then only accentuates even further the ways in which Jordanian politics appears to be essentially different. Sabaratnam has, in this regard, demonstrated the important role of deeply problematic 'assumptions of 'difference'[14] for the apparent justification of intervention. The reproduction of such impressions of essential difference has the effect of both making the task of 'democracy promotion' appear all the more urgent and reproducing images of 'the non-democratic other', in relation to which 'democratic' self-understandings become seemingly meaningful and significant.[15]

What is arguably most striking about the term 'civil society' is the lack of analytical clarity surrounding it, as well as its acceptance by both liberals and conservatives as something inherently positive.[16] Despite, or perhaps because of, its widespread use, the term has come under increasing scholarly critique for being 'analytically useless and obfuscating',[17] as argued by Petras, or for constituting 'a normative football, representing a bulwark of freedom and anti-totalitarianism to . . . [some] while signifying the spearhead of Western imperialism to [others]',[18] as argued by Bellin. In a more recent study, Durac and Cavatorta similarly deplore 'the "normativity" that is implicit in the use and application of the term', further adding that the mainstream liberal approach to civil society 'severely limits the analysis of the political reality of the Middle East and North Africa'.[19] Underlying such critical research is Bayart's observation that '[t]here is no teleological virtue in the notion of civil society'.[20] This implies that the effect of civil society support may differ depending on the political context in which it occurs. If one takes

[14] Sabaratnam, M., 'Avatars of Eurocentrism in the critique of the liberal peace', *Security Dialogue*, Vol. 44, No. 3, 2013, p. 260.

[15] See Oren, I., *Our Enemies and US: America's Rivalries and the Making of Political Science* (New York: Cornell University Press, 2013), p. 17.

[16] Kamat, S., 'NGOs and the new democracy: the false saviors of international development', *Harvard International Review*, Vol. 25, No. 1, Spring 2003, pp. 65–69.

[17] Petras, J., 'NGOs: in the service of imperialism', *Journal of Contemporary Asia*, Vol. 29, No. 4, 1999, p. 431.

[18] Bellin, E., 'Civil society: effective tool of analysis for Middle East politics?', *PS: Political Science and Politics*, Vol. 27, No. 3, September 1994, p. 509.

[19] Cavatorta, F. and Durac, V., *Civil Society and Democratization in the Arab World: The Dynamics of Activism* (Abingdon: Routledge, 2011), p. 2.

[20] Bayart, J.F., 'Civil society in Africa', in: Chabal, C. (ed.), *Political Domination in Africa: Reflections on the Limits of Power* (Cambridge: Cambridge University Press, 1986), p. 118.

this observation seriously, it becomes obvious that the assumed moral authority of civil society support, as well as its supposed universal applicability as a means of democratisation, can only be upheld as long as the specific political context in which it operates is either ignored or at least subordinated to a romanticised universal narrative.[21]

This section looks at who is actually supported 'to knock on the door of the system' – in the words of the Jordanian employee of a USAID-financed civil society support programme, quoted in the epigraph to this chapter – and whether this really helps in opening it. In his fourth discussion paper, published in 2013, King Abdullah II remarked that 'one of the key requirements for democratisation efforts is enhancing the role of civil society in monitoring and elevating the political performance of all institutions, by enrooting a democratic culture across society'.[22] The 2003 *Jordan Democracy and Governance Assessment* commissioned by USAID similarly flat out asserts that in Jordan, '[c]ivil society is weak and fragmented, particularly in terms of advocacy groups capable of articulating, defending, and pushing forward a reform agenda'.[23] In order to remedy this perceived shortcoming and despite the report's explicit warning that the 'structural weaknesses' of civil society in Jordan 'cannot easily be overcome through donor intervention',[24] USAID Jordan contracted the US firm Academy for Educational Development (AED) to run an $18 million civil society programme from 2008 to 2013.[25] Based on a view of civil society as a 'hallmark of a democratic society',[26] the programme aimed 'at cultivating a strong and vibrant civil society in Jordan'.[27] Jordanian authoritarianism is thus largely portrayed as the effect of Jordan's 'weak' civil society, whose members 'require ...

---

[21] See also Hopgood, S., *Keepers of the Flame: Understanding Amnesty International* (London: Cornell University Press, 2006), p. 5; see also p. 206.

[22] King Abdullah II, 'Towards democratic empowerment and "active citizenship"', Royal Hashemite Court, Amman, fourth discussion paper, 2 June 2013, available at: https://kingabdullah.jo/en/discussion-papers/towards-democratic-empowerment-and-active-citizenship.

[23] Denoeux, G. (MSI), Wilcox, O. (USAID) and Zawaneh, Z. (MSI), *Jordan Democracy and Governance Assessment*, USAID Center for Democracy and Governance and USAID/Jordan, August 2003, p. 11, available at: http://pdf.usaid.gov/pdf_docs/pnadd348.pdf.

[24] Denoeux, Wilcox and Zawaneh, *Jordan Democracy and Governance Assessment*, p. 44.

[25] Due to evidence of serious corporate misconduct at USAID-commissioned AED projects in Afghanistan and Pakistan AED transferred all of its programmes to the USAID contractor Family Health International (FHI), which eventually came to form FHI 360. The AED civil society programme in Jordan was thus concluded by FHI 360.

[26] USAID, *Democracy and Governance: A Conceptual Framework* (Washington, DC: Office of Democracy and Governance, USAID, technical publication series, November 1998), p. 15.

[27] USAID Jordan, 'Civil Society Program', USAID Jordan, Democracy & Governance Sector – Project Profile, April 2012.

a better understanding ... of the definition, purpose and importance of civil society'.[28]

The European Commission (EC) similarly views an empowered civil society as 'a crucial component of any democratic system and ... an asset in itself'.[29] Specifically discussing Jordan, in the record of a 2014 modification of its 2010 €10 million Support to Democratic Governance programme, the EC found that the 'key challenge is the weak and inconsistent role of the civil society to contribute actively to public policy development, monitoring and implementation'.[30] In light of this supposed weakness and considering the allegedly pro-democratic nature of civil society, the EU-commissioned *Mapping Study of Non-State Actors in Jordan* (2010) noted that '[c]onsiderable investment is required to strengthen the capacity of civil society to play a more effective role in all aspects of sustainable development'.[31] The report thus draws a direct causal link between insufficient financial investment, a supposedly weak civil society and Jordanian authoritarianism, thereby turning a deeply political issue into a matter of finances.

The picture that emerges is one of Jordanian civil society as weak and as not yet understanding, or fulfilling, the role that, according to US and EU 'democracy promoters', but also according to the Jordanian king, it is supposed to play. Jordanian state officials and external 'democracy promoters' thus widely describe Jordanian civil society as 'lack[ing] basic political and civic education'[32] and as requiring external aid, which is seen as trying to 'bring civil society to another level'.[33] Upon closer investigation, however, the assumption that Jordanian civil society is weak appears to be a direct result of a narrow definition of civil society as inherently liberal. Most of the 'democracy promotion' support is thus directed to but a small fragment of what constitutes Jordan's actually existing civil society. While at least 1,334 Jordanian organisations participated

---

[28] USAID Jordan, 'Civil Society Program'.

[29] EC, *Communication from the Commission to the European Parliament, the Council, the European Economic and Social Committee and the Committee of the Regions – The Roots of Democracy and Sustainable Development: Europe's Engagement with Civil Society in External Relations* (Brussels: European Commission, 12 September 2012), p. 3.

[30] EC, *Commission Implementing Decision of 11.6.2014 Modifying Decision C(2010) 7441 on the Annual Action Programme 2010 in Favour of the Kingdom of Jordan for the 'Support to Democratic Governance' Programme* (Brussels: European Commission, 11 June 2014), annex, p. 2.

[31] Williamson, W. and Hakki, H., *Mapping Study of Non-State Actors in Jordan* (The European Union's MED – Mediterranean Programme for the Hashemite Kingdom of Jordan, July 2010), p. 14.

[32] Interview with Adam, 'democracy promoter' working in Jordan, Amman, 14 October 2012.

[33] Interview with Pascal, European electoral observer, Brussels, 9 March 2015.

between 2008 and 2013 in a USAID-funded civil society support project and 135 Jordanian partners received US financial support,[34] most of the larger US and European civil society support grants in the field of democracy and governance are absorbed by a relatively small number of organisations.[35] The majority of Jordanian civil society has thus not benefited in any concrete sense from external civil society support,[36] as the latter effectively becomes an exercise in self-reference and a tool for the reinforcement of state social control.

Wiktorowicz and Yom argue that due to highly restrictive legal environments, the marked growth of associational activity only enabled the state to monitor collective action more efficiently.[37] Wiktorowicz concludes that in a context of 'political liberalization from above, civil society may act to reify regime power',[38] rather than empower independent social groups. Jordan's 2008 law of societies (no. 51) and its 2009 amendment (no. 22), for instance, require Jordanian societies to obtain approval from the Council of Ministers for any foreign funding.[39] Also, societies are prohibited by law from working towards 'political goals'.[40] Yet neither the law of societies nor the law on political parties provides a definition of the term 'political', leaving its interpretation to the government's discretion.

Due to the many restrictions in the law of societies, several organisations benefiting from US and European civil society support have registered as not-for-profit companies with the Ministry of Industry and Commerce, established two legal entities (as company and society) or

---

[34] FHI 360, *Jordan Civil Society Program – October 5, 2008–October 4, 2013: Final Report* (Washington, DC: FHI 360, submitted to USAID Jordan, 3 January 2014), p. 3.

[35] A 2010 study described Jordanian civil society as consisting of 5,703 organisations. Al Urdun Al Jadid Research Center, Civil Society Index – Analytical Country Report: Jordan 2010, *the Contemporary Jordanian Civil Society: Characteristics, Challenges and Tasks* (Amman: Civicus, Foundation for the Future and UNDP, 2010), p. 26. The FHI 360-administered and USAID-funded civil society programme, and to a lesser extent also the NDI, are the two key US donors/funding mechanisms. On the European side, the EU's European Instrument for Democracy and Human Rights (EIDHR) programme, the EU's bilateral support programme and, to a lesser extent, individual embassies and the German foundations are some of the central sources of funding.

[36] See Abu-Dalbouh, W., 'Jordan and the Euro-Mediterranean Partnership', in: Fernández, H.A. and Youngs, R. (eds.), *The Euro-Mediterranean Partnership: Assessing the First Decade* (Madrid: Real Instituto Elcano, FRIDE, 2005), p. 140.

[37] Wiktorowicz, Q., 'Civil society as social control: state power in Jordan', *Comparative Politics*, Vol. 33, No. 1, October 2000, pp. 43–61; Yom, S.L., 'Civil society and democratization in the Arab world', *Middle East Review of International Affairs*, Vol. 9, No. 4, December 2005, pp. 14–33.

[38] Wiktorowicz, 'Civil society as social control', p. 58.

[39] The first time approval was denied was in June 2012, regarding a project aimed at assisting migrant workers by the NGO Tamkeen.

[40] ICNL, Law of Societies (No. 51 of 2008) as Amended by Law No. 22 of 2009, unofficial translation by the ICNL, Article 3.A.1.

operate as for-profit companies and thus pay taxes but avoid the level of intervention that societies face. The bureaucratic leverage that the Jordanian state holds over recipients of US and European civil society aid thus renders toothless EU programmes such as the European Instrument for Democracy and Human Rights (EIDHR), whose grantees can officially be selected without the approval of the Jordanian government. Further, an employee of a USAID-funded civil society support programme criticised the technocratic approach of donors and the strength of royal and governmental NGOs (RONGOs and GONGOs), remarking that RONGOs 'send you a technically very good proposal. What do you do with it? ... USAID ... doesn't have a mechanism to exclude them'.[41]

One EU official defended support for RONGOs and GONGOs on selected topics, but noted that overall it is only helpful if more radical organisations are also supported:

It could work as part of a range of products – providing that we also can do work on civil society with organisations who have a more radical agenda ... But given that that part of the civil society support is not happening in Jordan ... if we don't have any input from independent civil society then I think any progress that we can expect is really very limited.[42]

While USAID implements its civil society support programme through the US firm Family Health International (FHI) 360, the EU delegation's 2012 media and civil society programme relied on the quasi-governmental National Center for Human Rights (NCHR) as main implementing partner, and its 2011 Support to Democratic Governance programme relied on the Jordanian Ministry of Political Development (MoPD) as contracting partner. The board of the NCHR, which was established by royal decree and previously headed by a former director of the General Intelligence Directorate, is entirely appointed by the king. The EU official quoted above, Toby, described the NCHR as follows:

I believe it is playing a role of defending whatever actions the government take, using almost arguments of sophistry, quite frankly ... If Burayzat [Head of the NCHR] was my lawyer at court, I'd sack him. So, frankly, I don't actually see what [is the] use of this organisation. I don't know if you're familiar with the Belgian expression a *bloempot* ... It's a flower pot that you set in the window and it looks nice. For me, the National Center for Human Rights is a *bloempot* ... I don't consider that it's playing a positive role in terms of improving the situation of

---

[41] Interview with Omar, Jordanian employee of a USAID financed civil society support programme, Amman, 18 March 2013.
[42] Interview with Toby, EU official, Brussels, 17 March 2015.

human rights in Jordan ... for me, this organisation is not one that ... we should have confidence in.[43]

Asked about the usefulness of turning the MoPD[44] or the quasi-governmental NCHR into a 'gate-keeper of funding for civil society',[45] EU official Toby agreed 'that there is something inimical about working through government organisations to defend, to build, independent civil society'.[46]

'There Is Always a Market'

Feeling compelled to choose between NGOs and Jordan's political parties, many activists and public intellectuals prefer the much more lucrative and politically safer NGO sector. Before joining the NGO world, the head of the Al-Quds Center had been active in a political party. Ironically, at the time of my field research he was working with the German Konrad Adenauer Foundation (KAS) on a €500,000 EU-funded programme that aimed at encouraging exactly the kind of political party activism that he himself had abandoned.

Several authors have pointed to the questionable and possibly counterproductive effects that arise when the arena of political debate and battles for democratisation shifts in this manner to the NGO world. Langohr, for instance, critiques what she calls the 'assumption of the leading opposition role in several liberalizing Arab regimes by advocacy nongovernmental organizations', arguing that this process actually 'decreases chances for democratization', since NGOs advocate for very specific groups and/or principles and are thus 'ill-equipped to mobilize a much broader set of constituencies around the larger goal of regime change'.[47] She further draws attention to many NGOs' dependence on foreign funding and in turn their independence from local constituencies.

Along similar lines, Jad critiques the process of NGO-isation of social movements and political opposition groups for transforming 'issues of collective concern ... into projects in isolation from the general context in which they are applied'.[48] It thus appears that civil society promotion may

---

[43] Interview with Toby, EU official, Brussels, 17 March 2015.
[44] See also the EU-MoPD programme discussed in Chapter 2.
[45] See also International Human Rights Network, *Human Rights NGO Capacity Building – Iraq: Next Steps Report* (Oldcastle, Ireland: IHRN, 2005), p. 9. Also see Carapico, *Political Aid and Arab Activism*, pp. 183–186.
[46] Interview with Toby, EU official, Brussels, 17 March 2015.
[47] Langohr, V., 'Too much civil society, too little politics: Egypt and liberalizing Arab regimes', *Comparative Politics*, Vol. 36, No. 2, January 2004, p. 182.
[48] Jad, I., 'NGOs: between buzzwords and social movements', *Development in Practice*, Vol. 17, No. 4/5, August 2007, p. 623.

actually 'foreclose prospects for unruly or take-to-the-streets revolutionary upheavals by entrusting democratization to paid Western consultants and their slick promotional advertisements',[49] as Carapico writes. Another forceful critique of NGOs' growing political role is provided by Petras, who conceives of NGO leaders as 'a kind of neo-compradore group that doesn't produce any useful commodity but does function to produce services for the donor countries'.[50] Viewing NGOs as facilitators of 'a new type of cultural and economic colonialism', Petras pointedly suggests that in order for NGOs to meaningfully challenge neoliberal and authoritarian structures, they should 'stop being NGOs and convert themselves into members of socio-political movements'.[51]

Jordan's 2013 parliamentary elections provided a good illustration of the prominent role that Jordanian civil society – or, better, a narrow group of select NGOs – came to assume *vis-à-vis* political parties. As the elections approached, it appeared as though the most vocal observer of the process was not the group of opposition parties that boycotted the elections, but the group of civil society organisations observing them (the NCHR, Identity Center and Al-Hayat Center) – all of which received considerable US and European financial support. One Jordanian analyst argued, for instance, that besides the regime, the real winner of the election was civil society and the RASED coalition in particular, led by the Al-Hayat Center, rather than the MPs and political parties that actually won seats in parliament.[52]

As indicated by the turning of (party) activists into project implementers and the associated fostering of a culture of dependence, as well as by the close ties between many externally supported NGOs and the Jordanian state apparatus, the supply of civil society funding from US and European donors regularly produces effects other than strengthening an independent Jordanian civil society. Just as the growing inflow of Iraq-linked funds to Jordanian NGOs during the Iraq war often led to NGOs redirecting their efforts away from Jordan,[53] the ongoing war in Syria contributes to a denationalisation of Jordanian civil society activism away

---

[49] Carapico, *Political Aid and Arab Activism*, p. 189.
[50] Petras, 'NGOs: in the service of imperialism', p. 430.
[51] Petras, 'NGOs: in the service of imperialism', pp. 434, 439.
[52] Kuttab, D., 'Islamists boycott fails in Jordan's elections', *Huffington Post*, 24 January 2013, available at: www.huffpost.com/entry/post_b_2539174?guccounter=1&guce_referrer=aHR0cHM6Ly93d3cuZ29vZ2xlLmZyLw&guce_referrer_sig=AQAAADVGqSr2NfbPDMA9iTd_MWgXnLyodinVsTqez8fvXbeE4dNcAzbt T644iPGyIrlgYghatCLWI9nwALbKi_GWpwmPHorYZSnrZL-gyK4VncZN 03Lv5D5Ja2sj8EuCmNkdxHCMqh5yR1V9Q5NYhpwRXhj6fcGlCNZWyP0d51 AUcGLc.
[53] Interview with Sandra, US 'democracy promoter' working on programmes in Jordan, Washington, DC, 22 May 2013.

from Jordanian politics in and of itself to the provision of support and aid for Syrian refugees. A Jordanian political activist working for a Jordanian NGO thus explained in early 2015 that any project proposal 'with Syrian refugees in will get funding'.[54]

Benefiting from major external support, some Jordanian civil society organisations have in recent years expanded significantly and denationalised their activities. The Al-Hayat Center, for instance, now also operates offices in Palestine and Morocco and has implemented training in Libya, Egypt, Lebanon, Tunisia, Sudan and Algeria among other places. The Identity Center has undergone a similar process of expansion and also operates an office in Iraq, with past projects also in Morocco and Sudan. A number of international organisations similarly use their offices in Jordan for programmes in other countries in the region. Until it ceased its activities in late 2014, the Foundation for the Future (FFF) was based in Jordan, from where it oversaw programmes across the whole Middle East, as well as in Pakistan, Afghanistan and Iran. The foundation, which operated through a partnership agreement with the Jordanian Ministry of Foreign Affairs (MoFA), was officially registered only in the US, however. As a direct consequence of its physical presence in Jordan, it took a rather hesitant stance on Jordanian politics and, similar to the Open Society Foundations (OSF), which during my research period had made a strategic decision not to work directly on political issues in Jordan, mostly refrained from implementing projects that could be perceived as critical.

Carapico speaks in this regard of competing attempts of national authorities to nationalise and closely regulate voluntary activism on the one side and, on the other, of activists and international organisations to denationalise it by applying for funding and registering abroad and by encouraging cross-border activism.[55] In the context of Jordan, these dynamics seem to conflate in the creation of islands of transnational civic activism that operate under close national control and simultaneously denationalise and deflect activism away from Jordan itself. While the supply of civil society funding in the cases discussed thus far had the effect of redirecting demand – that is, organisations' activities – away from Jordan, at other times the neoliberal assumption that '[t]here is always a market',[56] as a former US DoS official remarked, seemed to collapse entirely. This is particularly striking in the case of funding aimed

---

[54] Interview with Zaid, political activist, Amman, 15 January 2015.
[55] Carapico, *Political Aid and Arab Activism*, pp. 150–198.
[56] Interview with Mary, former high-ranking US DoS official, Washington, DC, 18 June 2013.

at enhancing civil society relations between Israel and Jordan. The EU's Partnership for Peace programme, for instance, has consistently failed to attract Jordanian NGOs, with practically all funding going to international organisations instead. The only notable exception is the Amman Center for Peace and Development (ACPD), which in 2012/2013 was awarded a grant under the EU's Partnership for Peace programme together with the Israeli S. Daniel Abraham Center for Strategic Dialogue and the Israeli office of the German KAS. Due to the political sensitivity of such projects, the ACPD has become a popular target for anti-normalisation activists and deliberately tries to keep a low public profile.

Calling the ACPD non-governmental is rather misleading, however, as it was established by former general and head of Jordanian Military Intelligence Mansour Abu Rashid in 1999 after he had been asked to do so, presumably by the royal court.[57] The history and internal structure of organisations such as the ACPD, NCHR and King Hussein Foundation – to name but a few – illustrate the difficulties of drawing a clear boundary between Jordanian civil society and the state. At the same time, however, it is also important to remind oneself that far from the romanticised notion of Western civil society as independent of the state, most of the US and European organisations that support and/or cooperate with the likes of the ACPD, NCHR and King Hussein Foundation find themselves in a similarly close relationship with the states in which they originated, as do their Jordanian counterparts. The German foundations and their American equivalents are thus all substantially state-funded, institutionally connected to the two countries' political establishments, as well as serving an important role as a somewhat less official extension of German and American foreign policy. As the boundary between state and civil society is blurred and as the Jordanian state apparatus has imposed various legal restrictions upon civil society, it becomes apparent that external programmes aimed at strengthening Jordanian civil society may actually lead to a strengthening of the state instead. In the following section I will discuss in more depth some of the conceptual considerations underlying US and European organisations' choice of local grantees. In doing so, I pay particular attention to the contrast between the values that are deemed to be promoted and the organisations that are, or are not, supported.

---

[57] See Jerusalem Summit 2004, Gen. (Ret.) Mansour Abu Rashid, available at: www .jerusalemsummit.org/eng/short.php?speaker=190&summit=31.

Transformational Technocrats and the 'Good' Jordanian Non-State Actor

According to most US and European 'democracy promoters' in Jordan, it is a matter of fact that the Jordanian civil society lacks advocacy skills, as well as democratic legitimacy. Helen, an American 'democracy promoter' with extensive experience in Jordan, remarked that Jordanian civil society was 'so bad at advocacy – it was atrocious – because civil society had always been thought of as service provision rather than advocacy'.[58] A EuropeAid official similarly invoked the supposed weakness of Jordanian civil society when explaining the absence of meaningful democratic reforms in the country:

> A society only changes if everybody in a society wants a society to change – or at least a big part … And I think … civil society organisations should look at themselves and ask themselves: 'Are we really representative of something or are we just talking for ourselves and for our limited group of people?'[59]

Instead of supporting those organisations that hold internal elections, that represent a significant part of Jordanian society, and/or that have a proven record in advocacy, both USAID and the EU demonstrate a clear preference for technocratic organisations that lack in most of the above qualities, but can be trained in these aspects. Further, as I discuss in more detail in the following, external organisations at times deliberately ignore existing Jordanian initiatives, preferring instead to set up their own programmes.

Searching for suitable subcontractors, and interested in what Petras calls 'social science intelligence',[60] external donors have engaged in a number of attempts to map Jordanian civil society. Some of the most notable such projects include the *Guide to Political Life in Jordan 2007–2011* published by the German Friedrich Ebert Foundation (FES) in cooperation with the Jordanian Phenix Center,[61] a complementary *Comprehensive Guide to Civil Society Organisations in Jordan 2010*, which provides a 480-page phone-book-like directory of Jordanian civil society,[62] a 2010 study conducted by the Jordanian Al Urdun Al Jadid Research Center entitled *The Contemporary Jordanian Civil Society: Characteristics, Challenges and*

---

[58] Interview with Helen, 'democracy promoter' with work experience in Jordan, Washington, DC, 30 May 2013.
[59] Interview with Emmanuel, EU official, Brussels, 16 March 2015.
[60] Petras, 'NGOs: in the service of imperialism', p. 432.
[61] FES, *Guide to Political Life in Jordan 2007–2011* (Amman: FES and Phenix Center, 2008).
[62] FES, Comprehensive Guide to Civil Society Organisations in Jordan 2010 (Amman: FES and Phenix Center, 2010).

Tasks,[63] as well as a 2010 EU-commissioned *Mapping Study of Non-State Actors in Jordan*.[64] Such reports are not particularly reliable, however,[65] since they all ignore informal organisations and, depending on their approach, include or exclude a number of other actors. While the FES and the EU studies exclude kinship and tribal associations, the Al Urdun Al Jadid study explicitly includes them. Similarly, the latter provides ample space for a discussion of the Islamic background of many Jordanian civil society actors, while the EU study completely ignores it.

Attempting to facilitate the selection of future grantees, the EU mapping study developed what it called '[c]riteria to define a "good" NSA [non-state actor] as a contracted partner for public policy dialogue'.[66] The criterion that particularly stands out next to 'responsive to constituency', 'democratic' and 'proactively on the side of the excluded' is 'transformational'. The 'objectively verifiable indicator' for 'transformational' is, according to the report, 'emphasis on changing selves as much as changing others' and 'evidence that they address root causes rather than symptoms of exclusion'.[67] While it is somewhat unclear how the former can be objectively verified (the report suggests participation in local decision-making and financial accounts), its choice as indicator illustrates well the typical liberal emphasis primarily on the individual as responsible unit. Once again, Jordanian authoritarianism thereby becomes less of a structural problem than one of political culture and supposedly inadequate values among individual Jordanians.

The truly 'good' Jordanian NSA accordingly presents itself as the liberally transformational technocratic one that focuses primarily on questions of political culture, rather than challenging underlying structures of exclusion. Besides GONGOs and RONGOs, the key beneficiaries of Western civil society support in the field of democracy and governance are thus a group of what the EU report terms 'development professional NGOs'. While the report provides a very positive assessment of Jordan's 'membership-based NGOs' (professional associations, trade unions, women's associations, etc.), and strongly commends their elected structures, experience of advocacy and ability to mobilise, such NGOs are practically ignored. This is particularly remarkable as the report itself states that some of the strongly supported 'development professional NGOs' 'lack feedback mechanisms to gain a mandate to speak on behalf of excluded groups', rely on a technocratic approach, depend on external

[63] Al Urdun Al Jadid Research Center, *Civil Society Index – Analytical Country Report*.
[64] Williamson and Hakki, *Mapping Study of Non-State Actors in Jordan*.
[65] See Carapico, *Political Aid and Arab Activism*, p. 166.
[66] Williamson and Hakki, *Mapping Study of Non-State Actors in Jordan*, p. 32.
[67] Williamson and Hakki, *Mapping Study of Non-State Actors in Jordan*, p. 32.

funding and may be 'motivated more by the opportunity for financial rewards . . . rather than working for the common good'.[68]

The key strength of professional associations – namely their deeply political approach, which is a direct extension of their willingness to advocate, that is, precisely what USAID and the EU supposedly seek to support – is in the eyes of Western donors also their greatest weakness. In short, even if an organisation is internally democratic, has a proven record in advocacy and speaks on behalf of a significant part of the Jordanian public, if it is 'transformational' in a political, rather than a technocratic sense, and is willing to challenge underlying power structures, rather than merely transform 'selves and others', the above criteria seem to become irrelevant. It is thus the willingness of the 'development professional NGOs' to be technocratic when it comes to structures of exclusion, and transformational when it comes to political culture, that makes them the perfect partners for US and European civil society funding.

It would be wrong to conceive of such mapping studies as attempts to substantially change the choice of grantees and/or the way in which these function. Rather, their role is that of maintaining an impression of ongoing procedural change. This façade is of instrumental help in ignoring the fact that those civil society actors which have a proven record in advocacy, which speak for large parts of the Jordanian public and which are internally democratic are mostly to be found outside of the narrow group of supported NGOs.

A high-ranking EU diplomat based in Amman openly explained that the EU programmes 'always finance the same organisations . . . because [the] EU has heavy procedures and they understand how to submit a proper project proposal – they are the only ones who know how', adding that a 'focus on youth [is] very difficult [as] many youth movements refuse to be supported'.[69] The ensuing 'major problem with absorption capacity in Jordan'[70] that several US and European 'democracy promoters' complain about then presents itself much less as a weakness of Jordanian civil society than as the direct result of the narrow liberal and technocratic bias with which US and European 'democracy promoters' approach Jordanian civil society. 'Democracy promoter' Michael

---

[68] Williamson and Hakki, *Mapping Study of Non-State Actors in Jordan*, pp. 24–26.

[69] Both quotations taken from interview with Olivia, EU diplomat based in Jordan, Amman, 9 December 2012.

[70] Interview with Toby, EU official, Brussels, 17 March 2015. 'Democracy promoter' Helen also explained that 'we had a difficult time spending our 25–30 million': interview with Helen, 'democracy promoter' with work experience in Jordan, Washington, DC, 30 May 2013.

admitted that there is a 'limited set of NGOs, parties, etc. one can work with ... The ones that are edgiest are the least likely to participate'.[71]

Besides the professional associations, one may further note tribal associations, Islamic NGOs, newly emerging social movements such as the Ḥirāk and a number of leftist groups among those Jordanian civil society actors that are effectively ignored by, and/or actively protect themselves against, US and European civil society programmes. The powerful effect of this mutual disregard is a constant perpetuation among US and European 'democracy promoters' of the notion that Jordanian civil society is weak. The Jordan Bar Association, for example, which is closely related to the anti-normalisation movement and the Islamic Action Front, has refused to be part of both the USAID-financed Enhancing Legal Education and Human Rights Programme (implemented by the American Bar Association) and the Rule of Law Programme (implemented by Tetra Tech DPK). In contrast to the widespread perception among many 'democracy promoters' that Jordanians are 'politically apathetic',[72] the EU-commissioned mapping study ironically described Jordan's professional associations as overly 'politicised'.[73]

The Western-centrism of many external analyses – the EU study, for instance, entirely ignores tribal association as a possible constituent of Jordan's civil society – also manifests itself in the ways in which 'democracy promoters' try to make sense of the persistence of those forms of social organisation that do not neatly fit the liberal mould. 'Democracy promoter' Helen was thus fully aware of the political importance of tribes in Jordan, but was nevertheless unable to see them in anything but 'Western' terms: 'Jordan has parties. They're called tribes'.[74] This phenomenon of either excluding and ignoring those forms of Jordanian social organisation that do not fit the desired image, or viewing them as deficient imitations of morally superior Western models, extends well beyond the question of tribes.

When the Ḥirāk emerged as organisers of countrywide anti-regime protests in 2011 and 2012, US and European 'democracy promoters' had major difficulties in making sense of the informal youth movements in and of themselves – not to mention the practically impossible tasks of mapping them and/or weaving them into a Western-funded net of 'civil

---

[71] Interview with Michael, 'democracy promoter' working in Jordan, Amman, 21 November 2012.
[72] Interview with Helen, 'democracy promoter' with work experience in Jordan, Washington, DC, 30 May 2013.
[73] Williamson and Hakki, *Mapping Study of Non-State Actors in Jordan*, p. 29.
[74] Interview with Helen, 'democracy promoter' with work experience in Jordan, Washington, DC, 30 May 2013.

society support' programmes. As one 'democracy promoter' remarked, the Ḥirāk were deliberately 'making themselves immune from assistance [*sic*]'.[75] While informality was arguably their most central feature, in their analyses of the Ḥirāk, many 'democracy promoters' used formal association and its assumed role in Western liberal democracies as the constant point of reference. For 'democracy promoter' Stefan, it was therefore clear that the Ḥirāk represented nothing but a prototype of political parties: 'That is [the] inevitable future. The Ḥirāk are going to become political parties'.[76]

Besides professional, tribal and informal associations, Jordan's Islamic organisations, which constitute the large majority of all Jordanian non-state actors, are also absent from US and European civil society programmes.[77] The EU-commissioned mapping study indeed treats them as if they did not exist at all and does not mention an Islamic NGO or note their mere existence even once. EU official Toby justified this exclusion of Islamic associations in EU civil society support by referring to the EU's promotion of gender equality as irreconcilable with their social conservatism.[78] At this point it once again becomes apparent that different understandings and/or values of democracy may at times be highly contradictory and that democracy acquires very different meanings in different contexts. EU official Toby admitted that

[i]f we were to have pure democracy … in Jordan then the country would probably be more reactionary [than] now, because almost the only forces which are pushing the agenda for women's rights forward are the Hashemite organisations [i.e. the royal NGOs].[79]

As external 'democracy promoters' pursue a narrow liberal agenda, more representative actors of Jordanian civil society are ignored and/or actively protect themselves against external support. Most US and European funding is thus targeted at the aforementioned GONGOs, RONGOs and professional development NGOs and is directed towards the support of specific groups (migrant workers, the disabled, youth, women, etc.) and particular principles (gender equality, entrepreneurship, the fight against racism, etc.) which, while highly commendable in and of themselves, are far too narrow for a wider opposition movement to

---

[75] Interview with Michael, 'democracy promoter' working in Jordan, Amman, 21 November 2012.

[76] Interview with Stefan, 'democracy promoter' working in Jordan, Amman, 29 January 2013.

[77] See Bicchi, F., 'Want funding? Don't mention Islam: EU democracy promotion in the Mediterranean', *CFSP Forum*, Vol. 4, No. 2, March 2006, pp. 10–12.

[78] Interview with Toby, EU official, Brussels, 17 March 2015.

[79] Interview with Toby, EU official, Brussels, 17 March 2015.

rally around and effectively challenge authoritarian rule. The primary effect of the programmes then appears to be social control and demobilisation rather than empowerment.[80] In order to better understand the extent to which 'democracy promoters' ignore locally grown 'transformational' groups that are 'willing and able to challenge existing power structures' in favour of technocratic NGOs and/or externally established initiatives, it is helpful to investigate in more depth the USAID youth programmes in the country.[81]

Anā Ushārik

The central intention of US- and European-funded youth support programmes in Jordan is not the collective empowerment of existing groups, but their disciplining and the channelling of collective discontent into more easily controllable and manageable forms. This is also the reason why most locally grown social movements 'made themselves immune' from such external attempts at youth support. The best illustration of this dynamic is arguably the National Democratic Institute (NDI) Jordan youth political participation programme, which was established in late 2011 apparently in direct response to the countrywide protests of that year and to rising fears among international donors of the possibility of revolutionary change. One 'democracy promoter' thus described the NDI programme's objectives as, among other things, providing 'civil society tools to fight for their causes without … going and torching places'.[82]

While the focus on stability and peaceful means of protest may at first sight appear to be laudable, the inherent problem of such analyses and programmes is their offhand depiction of Jordanian civil society as prone to violence, weak and practically non-existent and the related securitisation of Jordanian youth.[83] Also, the implicit association of processes of democratisation with peaceful evolutionary reform both idealises past

---

[80] See Wiktorowicz, who speaks of civil society institutions more as 'an instrument of state social control than a mechanism of collective empowerment'. Wiktorowicz, 'Civil society as social control', p. 43. Also see Jad, 'NGOs: between buzzwords and social movements', pp. 622–629 and Farsakh, 'Democracy promotion in Palestine', pp. 1–25.

[81] See also Schuetze, B., 'Misrepresenting the contextual and idealising the universal: how US efforts at democracy promotion bolster authoritarianism in Jordan', Arnold-Bergstraesser-Institut, working paper, No. 3, 2016, available at: https://www.arnold-bergstraesser.de/sites/default/files/field/pub-download/abi_working_paper_3_benjamin_schuetze_misrepresenting_the_contextual_and_idealising_the_universal_0.pdf.

[82] Interview with Stefan, 'democracy promoter' working in Jordan, Amman, 29 January 2013.

[83] See also Sukarieh, M. and Tannock, S., 'The global securitisation of youth', *Third World Quarterly*, Vol. 39, No. 5, 2018, pp. 854–870.

transitions to democracy elsewhere and ignores the centrality of street-level movements and violent conflict in these. Reflecting on past transitions in established democracies and the current popularity of civil society support, Kienle remarks that the 'inability of . . . civil societies to promote democracy is not surprising if one accepts that in established democracies they were not at the origin of democratization either'.[84] Kienle further contends that '[t]here is no empirical evidence that the dissemination of values and norms actually contributes to democratization'.[85] Instead, I suggest that 'democracy promotion' appears above all to be a means of reinforcing desired self-understandings as 'modern' and 'democratic'. Oren helpfully remarks in this regard that

identity, or self-understanding, is virtually vacuous unless placed in relation to an 'Other'; it is only by way of delineating contrasts and similarities to 'Them' that 'US' acquires a meaning . . . and because identity is a relational concept, the envisioning and re-visioning of 'America' necessarily involve the (re)envisioning of the outside world.[86]

Conceptualising 'democracy promotion' along these lines helps to better comprehend why it can sustain itself despite the regular disregard of the Jordanian politics within which it operates. Also, it helps to better understand the romanticisation of past processes of democratisation, as well as the overemphasis on liberal civil society, participation, education and peaceful advocacy *vis-à-vis* the violence and apathy in many Western civil societies and the role of conflict in past democratic transitions.[87]

Aksartova pointedly notes that following the fall of the Soviet Union, the 'idea of civil society helped to redefine what set the West apart from the rest of the world'.[88] In light of the above discussion and as also suggested by Wickham,[89] I argue that it is much more interesting to study civil society support by turning the civil society supporters themselves into the objects of inquiry, rather than those whom they allegedly support. This means challenging the all too common commitment to

---

[84] Kienle, E., 'Democracy promotion and the renewal of authoritarian rule', in: Schlumberger, Oliver (ed.), *Debating Arab Authoritarianism: Dynamics and Durability in Nondemocratic Regimes* (Stanford: Stanford University Press, 2007), p. 246.

[85] Kienle, 'Democracy promotion and the renewal of authoritarian rule', p. 239.

[86] Oren, *Our Enemies and US*, p. 17.

[87] See Tempest, C., 'Myths from Eastern Europe and the legend of the West', *Democratization*, Vol. 4, No. 1, 1997, pp.132–144, and Berman, S., 'Civil society and the collapse of the Weimar Republic', *World Politics*, Vol. 49, No. 3, April 1997, pp.401–429.

[88] Aksartova, S., 'Why NGOs? How American donors embraced civil society after the Cold War', *The International Journal of Not-for-Profit Law*, Vol. 8, No. 3, May 2006, p. 18. See also Carapico, *Political Aid and Arab Activism*, p. 155.

[89] See Wickham, C.R., 'Beyond democratization: political change in the Arab world', *PS: Political Science and Politics*, Vol. 27, No. 3, September 1994, p. 509.

conceiving the targets of civil society support, on the one hand, as passive receiving objects waiting to be studied and put in categories and, on the other, the implementers of such support as active subjects developing criteria for 'good' (and implicitly also 'bad') local civil society actors and respectively researching and aiding (or ignoring) these.

Some scholars, such as Yom, have convincingly argued that the 'political potency [of Arab civil society] is more a function of researchers' implicit prejudices when addressing the region's social landscape than a measure of empirical fact'.[90] Based on this observation, I will now – with the example of the NDI's youth political participation programme in Jordan – show in more detail how civil society support manifests itself in practice and what it does (and does not) tell us about Jordanian society and external 'democracy promoters'.

In December 2011, NDI Jordan established its youth political participation programme. According to the NDI, this is 'one of the largest and most successful NDI programmes in the Middle East'.[91] Under its umbrella, in 2012 the NDI officially launched the Anā Ushārik (Arabic for 'I participate') programme as its main activity, which was created after prior discussions with the deans of student affairs at a number of Jordanian universities. With the support of the royal court, an agreement was signed that allowed the NDI to run political participation and educational courses in Jordanian universities.[92] The NDI describes its extracurricular programme as follows:

> Through lessons and debates, youth openly discuss democratic practices and current events while learning about the principles of democracy, human rights, political parties and elections. Ana Usharek students are able to gain skills for conducting meaningful and respectful debates with their peers, helping them to become active citizens who participate in the political process.[93]

In late 2012, the NDI employed at least sixteen coordinators – all recent Jordanian university graduates – who were each allocated one of the eleven participating universities, where they were responsible for a total of eighty-five Anā Ushārik courses. In the summer 2012 semester alone the NDI thus trained 1,300 Jordanian students.[94] By late 2017 the

---

[90] Yom, 'Civil society and democratization in the Arab world', p. 21.
[91] NDI Jordan, promotional video, 30 October 2013, available at: www.youtube.com/watch?v=AIH_I-fCj6k.
[92] During my research period, participation in the Anā Ushārik course was one of the options for the community service requirement at the University of Jordan.
[93] NDI and USAID, 'Ana Usharek – Empowering youth at Jordanian universities to play an informed role in Jordan's political & decision-making processes', *Ana Usharek* 6, December 2014, p. 2.
[94] Interview with Ali, 'democracy promoter' working in Jordan, Amman, 30 September 2012.

programme had expanded substantially and, according to leading NDI staff, already involved over 24,000 students from twenty-eight universities and 330 schools.[95]

Both in the NDI staff administering the programme – many of whom are from Eastern Europe – and in the material used during training sessions, the NDI's Anā Ushārik programme appears to be attempting to reproduce what it considers to be the conditions and context that enabled the so-called colour revolutions in, among other places, Serbia in 2000, Georgia in 2003 and Ukraine in 2004. Perhaps one of the most central common themes in these was the use of strategies of civil disobedience and the prominent role of US-supported student and youth movements in bringing down socialist-leaning governments critical of the US. Following NATO bombardments in 1999, the Serbian student movement Otpor (Serbian for 'resistance') – a beneficiary of USAID, NED and IRI funds – played a central role in the overthrow of the authoritarian regime of Slobodan Milosevic. The Georgian youth movement Kmara (Georgian for 'enough') was subsequently modelled on the example of Otpor and received support from the US-based OSF among others, while the Ukrainian Pora (Ukrainian for 'it's time') had been trained by Otpor itself, and aided by Freedom House, among others.

One of the many fundamental differences between the transitions in Serbia, Georgia and Ukraine and the political situation in Jordan, however, is of course that the Jordanian regime is closely allied to the US and the opposition highly critical of it. This helps explain why the NDI's Anā Ushārik programme focuses primarily on education and participation, rather than on civil disobedience. Further, instead of supporting existing student and youth initiatives, as USAID had in Serbia, Georgia and Ukraine, NDI Jordan chose to establish its own initiative and ignored existing groups such as the Jordanian Ḥirāk movement, as well as politicised student movements such as Dhabaḥtūnā (Arabic for 'you slaughtered us'). The Dhabaḥtūnā initiative, established by a leading member of the Jordanian Democratic Popular Unity Party, which emerged out of the Popular Front for the Liberation of Palestine (PFLP), is Jordan's 'only [student] movement across universities and colleges'.[96] While Dhabaḥtūnā and the Ḥirāk movement do not hold US 'democracy promotion' activities in high esteem, they arguably represent the Jordanian organisational equivalents to Otpor, Kmara and Pora, in so far as the

---

[95] Leslie Campbell (MENA regional director of NDI), National Democratic Institute @NDI, *Twitter*, 7 November 2017, available at: https://twitter.com/NDI/status/927922558225272834.

[96] Al Urdun Al Jadid Research Center, *Civil Society Index – Analytical Country Report*, p. 65.

latter were also politicised movements closely affiliated to political parties.[97]

Given the fundamentally incomparable political contexts[98] – above all, in terms of the incumbent authoritarian regimes' foreign policy orientations and the very different regional environments – the effects of the NDI's Anā Ushārik programme are very different to those of Otpor, Kmara and Pora. Providing an indication of this disparity, one European 'democracy promoter' described his experiences with the Eastern European staff of NDI Jordan as follows:

These are all good people, no question . . . But when they talk it is obvious that the Jordanians don't give a shit. They're not interested whatsoever. They don't even understand what they're talking about. And they're only happy again when [name of a Jordanian civil society representative] begins to explain his view of the whole story for three hours . . . We're too far away from reality and our expectations are too high . . . Basically I would say that as a general rule they talk past each other.[99]

'Be Positive!'

The NDI's Anā Ushārik initiative is fundamentally based on the assumption that Jordanian youth are not adequately educated about democracy and that addressing this supposed shortcoming will help increase the country's chances for democratisation. This is in direct opposition to observations made in the USAID-commissioned democracy and governance assessment discussed in Chapter 2. As such, the programme directly replicates the discourse of the Jordanian king. Discussing the prospects of Jordanian democracy on US television, the latter patronisingly explained in late 2012 that 'we are so far at the start of this issue . . . How do we get the people to step into the position of power?'[100] Commenting on the king's remarks, 'democracy promoter' Stefan responded as follows:

I know a lot of people got offended when he said that Jordanians know nothing about dialogue and democracy and so on. But . . . not a lot of people know about . . . how the system works. Do a research in Germany and . . . you will be amazed how many people don't care or . . . don't know how exactly a law initiative

---

[97] Otpor later merged into the Serbian Democratic Party and Pora eventually established its own political party.

[98] Hamid juxtaposes the clear and unapologetic rhetoric of the West in Eastern Europe with that in the Arab world. Hamid, 'The struggle for Middle East democracy'. Carapico further mentions the tendency to ignore the role of NATO bombardments in toppling Milosevic, in order to portray the Serbian transition as a 'pacifist, native, civilian campaign'. Carapico, *Political Aid and Arab Activism*, p. 195.

[99] Interview with Paul, 'democracy promoter' working in Jordan, Amman, 18 January 2015. See also Schuetze, 'Marketing parliament'.

[100] King Abdullah II, *The Daily Show* with Jon Stewart, 25 September 2012.

becomes a law for example … So people can be really offended, but look at the [electoral] campaigns – they're really like nineteenth-century campaigns … Everybody is voting for very … narrow personal interests. So, when you look at that and you hear what [the] king says, he's not far from the truth.[101]

Besides his criticism of a lack of knowledge among the Jordanian public, what is particularly interesting in Stefan's remarks is his own acknowledgement that the very same lack of knowledge about democratic procedures can also be found in functioning democracies. This fundamentally brings into question the supposed centrality of education to processes of democratisation. 'Democracy promoter' Michael, who was familiar with the NDI programme, relied on very similar assumptions as Stefan and explained that while 'the intention is to use Anā Ushārik to change the system … this is a long-term project of building people who are more informed and interested in politics'.[102] During another meeting he added that the NDI is 'careful to not talk about domestic politics too much'[103] and instead consciously chose to focus on international standards and best practices. NDI employee Tareq confirmed this and explained that 'we present ourselves as an educational expertise think tank … [consulting with] the beneficiaries on what they actually need' – before then specifying that 'I think at this moment Jordan needs that kind of international expertise'.[104] He illustrated his argument by describing students, who participated in the programme and, according to him, 'became political advocates [from] very naughty students … [who were initially] just shouting and cursing each other … Why would somebody think that this is harmful?'[105]

Critics of the NDI programme took a very different stance on the relevance of participation and international standards and best practices for the advancement of processes of democratisation. Similar to the critique of efforts at political party training in Chapter 2, some political activists complained that encouraging participation and advocacy per se within a highly restricted political environment may, instead of widening political space, actually have the contrary effect of seemingly legitimising the regime's strategy of shifting blame for ongoing authoritarianism away

---

[101] Interview with Stefan, 'democracy promoter' working in Jordan, Amman, 29 January 2013.

[102] Interview with Michael, 'democracy promoter' working in Jordan, Amman, 24 January 2013.

[103] Interview with Michael, 'democracy promoter' working in Jordan, Amman, 25 March 2013.

[104] Both quotations are taken from an interview with Tareq, 'democracy promoter' working in Jordan, Amman, 15 January 2013.

[105] Interview with Tareq, 'democracy promoter' working in Jordan, Amman, 15 January 2013.

from itself and onto Jordanians. The NDI's Anā Ushārik programme indeed seems to understand democracy primarily as a matter of individual Jordanians' political culture. A 2012 newsletter published by the programme thus offers some 'Tips to be Democratic'.[106] (see Figure 4.1) These include the advice to '[l]isten to your family members very well and respect their points of view', to 'not cut in line' and, most of all, to '[b]e positive!'[107]

The very same dynamic of turning Jordanian authoritarianism into a matter of the supposedly inadequate political culture of Jordanians could also be noted in the thinking of 'democracy promoter' Stefan. As he explained that many of his Jordanian staff had not participated in the 2013 parliamentary elections, due to the marginal importance of parliament as a legislative body and the highly restrictive electoral law, he remarked that

I don't get angry, but I get disappointed ... the only way that the system will change is if there is pressure coming from people who want change ... my colleagues who don't want to vote – I asked them, 'OK, you have no one to vote for. Why didn't you create your own party? ... Why don't you start up a campaign to change the election system so you can put pressure on election commission? ... You know this is the twenty-first century. Don't give me that bullshit ... Nobody gives you democracy. You have to win it. You have to fight for it' ... whenever people complain they just ... want to sit ... and watch TV and want democracy to somehow give birth to itself.[108]

While this activist approach is understandable given Stefan's involvement in the democratisation of his own country of origin, it is highly questionable whether such an approach would lead to a similar outcome in Jordan. In direct contrast to the above comments, a 2003 USAID-commissioned democracy and governance assessment thus found that

Jordan's central problem from a D/G [democracy and governance] perspective is not insufficient demands for political participation ... [Instead, in Jordan] prospects for democratization are mostly a function of the extent of political will to reform within the governing elite.[109]

In light of the marginal effect of public participation on Jordanian decision-making, Jordanian political activist Zaid, who was at the time

---

[106] NDI and USAID, 'I participate – empowering youth at Jordanian universities to play an informed role in Jordan's political and decision-making processes program newsletter', *Ana Usharek* 1, June 2012, p. 2.

[107] NDI and USAID, 'I participate – empowering youth at Jordanian universities', p. 2.

[108] Interview with Stefan, 'democracy promoter' working in Jordan, Amman, 29 January 2013.

[109] Denoeux, Wilcox and Zawaneh, *Jordan Democracy and Governance Assessment*, pp. 42–43.

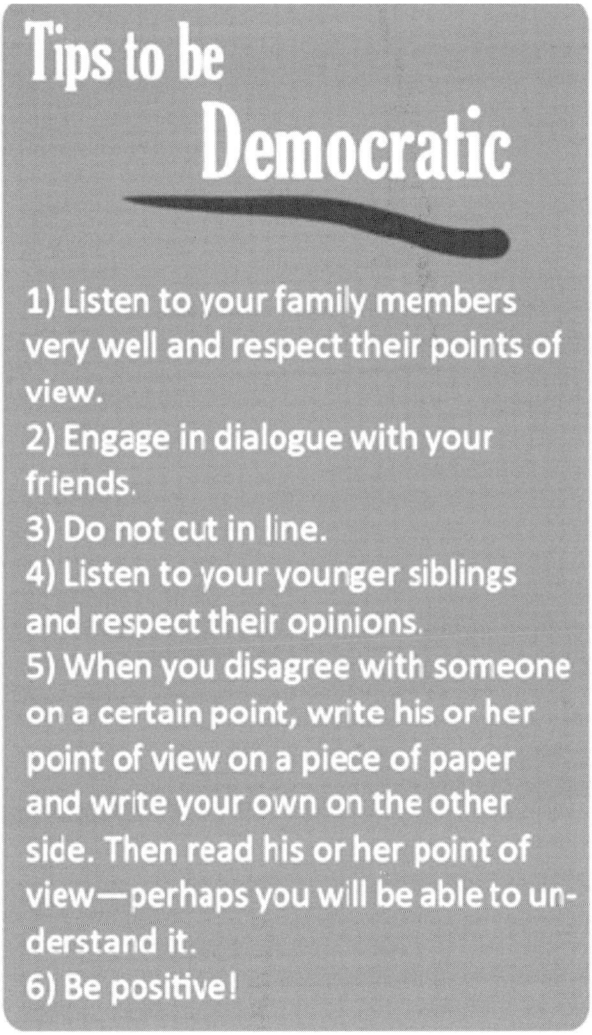

Tips to be Democratic

1) Listen to your family members very well and respect their points of view.
2) Engage in dialogue with your friends.
3) Do not cut in line.
4) Listen to your younger siblings and respect their opinions.
5) When you disagree with someone on a certain point, write his or her point of view on a piece of paper and write your own on the other side. Then read his or her point of view—perhaps you will be able to understand it.
6) Be positive!

Figure 4.1 'Tips to be Democratic'; info box in the 'I participate' newsletter. Anā Ushārik programme, NDI Jordan, 1st edition, June 2012, p. 2. © NDI Jordan.

also working for a Jordanian NGO, was highly critical of any efforts at merely encouraging more participation. He thus directly compared the NDI's Anā Ushārik programme to the work of the MoPD and argued that instead of 'giving [Jordanians] sessions about how important it is ... to participate in the general political life in Jordan or [to know] how to design an advocacy plan', the NDI should work towards increasing the political space for all Jordanians. Zaid then stated that

I feel like it's pointless to [say that] ... it just is what the king literally does [*sic*]. He goes on TV and says that students should be ... politically active inside universities. Political parties should be stronger ... And then you go to the university and see that it's restricted! OK – the guy just told us to do so! Well – it is restricted.[110]

The Anā Ushārik course evolves around five modules: democracy, human rights, elections and the role of political parties and media in democracy. One NDI employee succinctly described the five documents an 'executive summary of ... democracy ... mostly focusing on the international standards and best practices'.[111] The Arabic documents that the NDI prepared for its coordinators to use as guidelines in their courses present topics such as political freedoms and social rights, the processual character of democracy, key characteristics of democratic elections, different types of electoral system, human rights and international human rights treaties, the importance of political parties for democracy and the role that different media play in democracies. The documents do not, however, include a discussion of Jordanian politics, except in rather general terms, such as in a timeline of the supposed 'democratic development in Jordan 1921–2012'. Also, a copy of the Jordanian 2012 electoral law is provided, as well as a timeline of 'electoral development in Jordan', a selection of the international human rights treaties signed by Jordan, a brief overview over the main political camps in the country and central Jordanian legislation related to the role of media.[112]

While one 'democracy promoter' celebrated the programme as 'the first time that Jordanians can discuss politics on universities – that was like a no-go-area before',[113] many Jordanian political activists, but also NGO workers, remained highly critical of the NDI's activities. Noting the restrictive disciplinary procedures at Jordanian universities that

---

[110] Interview with Zaid, political activist, Amman, 18 January 2013.
[111] Interview with Ali, 'democracy promoter' working in Jordan, Amman, 30 September 2012.
[112] The five documents prepared by the NDI Anā Ushārik programme are in Arabic, undated and entitled as follows (translations by the author): 'Introduction to democracy' [*Madkhal ilā ad-dimuqrāṭīyah*], 'The electoral process' [*Al-'amalīyah al-intikhābīyah*], 'Human rights' [*Ḥuqūq al-insān'*], 'The role of political parties in the democratic process' [*Dawr al-aḥzāb as-siyāsīyah fī-l-'amalīyah ad-dimuqrātīyah*] and 'The role of media in the democratic process' [*Dawr al-i'lām fī-l-'amalīyah ad-dimuqrātīyah*].
[113] Interview with Stefan, 'democracy promoter' working in Jordan, Amman, 29 January 2013.

forbid 'the promotion of party activities or political and regional ideas on campus',[114] as well as the 'exercise of any activity of a political, sectarian or regional kind'[115] by student clubs, the NDI's special permission to engage in political education in universities was widely interpreted as unjustified preferential treatment for a foreign institution. One political activist explicitly complained that the 'NDI has offices in universities, but Jordanian political parties are not allowed to'.[116] Illustrating the point that many Jordanians do not see the NDI as in any way neutral or non-partisan, one NDI employee explained that part of the institute's work is to assure participants that it is not the CIA. Noor, a Jordanian employee of another Western organisation, further noted that due to the existing restrictions on political activism, those students who are critical of the regime and of the role of the US in the region are highly unlikely to participate in the NDI courses. She then ironically remarked: 'Democracy courses? I love this. It's a beautiful word. What's the outcome? ... Of course they are happy and they're in love with the project. But they will end up producing loyalists who are cheering for the king'.[117]

Other students appeared to be somewhat confused that the king and the NDI should encourage them to become politically active, while university and scholarship regulations explicitly punish political activism. Approximately 20 per cent of Jordanian students thus benefit from a scholarship from the Jordanian military (*makramat jaysh*),[118] which explicitly requires them to sign a pledge that they will not become politically active. The military scholarships and the associated pledges are one of the topics that the Dhabaḥtūnā initiative campaigns against. Jordanian NDI employee Tareq also noted that the army scholarships 'deactivate you politically even if you're not in

---

[114] Hashemite University, 'Student disciplinary procedures system, 2003' [*Niẓām ta'dīb aṭ-ṭalaba fī-l-jāmi'ah al-hāshimīyah – niẓām raqm 107 li-sanah 2003*], 3 n, available at: https://hu.edu.jo/Regulations/student/%D8%AF%D9%84%D9%8A%D9%84%20% D8%A7%D9%84%D8%B7%D8%A7%D9%84%D8%A8.htm. Original in Arabic, translated by the author.

[115] Hashemite University, 'Instructions for student societies in the Hashemite University' [*Ta'līmāt al-jam'īyāt al-'ilmīyah aṭ-ṭullābīyah fī-l-jāmi'ah al-hāshimīyah*], undated, chapter 1, point 5, available at: https://hu.edu.jo/Regulations/student/%D8%AF%D9 %84%D9%8A%D9%84%20%D8%A7%D9%84%D8%B7%D8%A7%D9%84%D8 %A8.htm. Original in Arabic, translated by the author.

[116] Interview with Zaid, political activist, Amman, 10 November 2012.

[117] Interview with Noor, Jordanian employee of a Western organisation, Amman, 2 December 2012.

[118] Dhabaḥtūnā, *Study on the politics of higher education and medical faculties – February 2013* [*Dirāsah ḥawl siyāsat at-ta'līm al-'ālī wa-l-kulliyāt aṭ-ṭibbīyah – shubbāṭ 2013*], p. 9, available at: www.thab7toona.org. Original in Arabic, translated by the author. Students whose parents are working in the Jordanian military can benefit from such scholarships. After their studies, only a minority of the scholarship recipients join the military.

[the] army', before adding that 'this pledge is ... being mentioned by our students in the sessions', and then remarking that 'it's been mentioned in the presence of the king several times but there was no actual action against it'.[119] 'Democracy promoter' Stefan concurred and explained that the biggest challenge is assuaging 'the fear of participants ... [as] some students register and then a few weeks later ask us to delete everything about them'.[120] Asked about the army scholarships, he only remarked that 'the one who gives you a grant specifies the conditions ... there are fifty-seven more important issues than that'.[121]

Questioned about barriers to democracy in Jordan and the lack of any real democratisation despite decades of 'reform processes' and programmes such as those of the NDI, NDI employee Ali replied:

> Maybe they're not taken seriously. I don't know ... There's nothing secret about this ... you're sitting in a room ... with a group of very smart young Jordanians and you can solve the biggest problem of Jordan – no matter what it is. But you step outside of this group and you feel that there's maybe a miscommunication, maybe there's a missing link. I don't know.[122]

Finding democratic solutions to even 'the biggest problem of Jordan' thus seems to rely, as implied by Ali, on the protective abstractness of classroom discussions that largely remain detached from the Jordanian political context and from all those messy aspects that cannot readily be made to fit the mould of international standards and best practices. Ali himself was quite aware of what he called 'a missing link' and of the fact that, once confronted with the reality outside the classroom, the limited effects of the NDI's efforts at 'democracy promotion' and youth education clearly became apparent.

'Welcome to the Republic of Ibar'

> [T]he seemingly objective concepts of political science mask normative visions of US. When political scientists debate abstract analytical concepts – including, prominently, the concept of democracy – they actually debate America's identity, and what it should be.[123]

---

[119] Interview with Tareq, 'democracy promoter' working in Jordan, Amman, 15 January 2013.
[120] Interview with Stefan, 'democracy promoter' working in Jordan, Amman, 27 March 2013.
[121] Interview with Stefan, 'democracy promoter' working in Jordan, Amman, 23 March 2013.
[122] Interview with Ali, 'democracy promoter' working in Jordan, Amman, 30 September 2012.
[123] Oren, *Our Enemies and US*, pp. 16–17.

In November 2012, the NDI launched a youth political leadership and advocacy programme called Anā Ushārik + as an accompaniment to its education and awareness programme Anā Ushārik.[124] As part of this new programme, the NDI decided to train 250 former Anā Ushārik participants in advocacy skills and, based on agreements with various Jordanian NGOs, provided the former with internship opportunities.[125] At the end of the course the participants would then put to use the experience and training provided by NDI's youth coordinators to create their own advocacy campaigns in small groups. While the initial Anā Ushārik programme is based on the assumption that more education will increase the chances of democratisation, the extension of the programme is explicitly based on the assumption that besides education, advocacy has a particularly central role to play.

One 'democracy promoter' accordingly explained that '[i]f you think about democracy in Germany or in the US – the core of it is people organising around whatever is their issue and doing something about it'. He further added that

[w]e want them to start being kind of constructive civil society actors, which means we want them to advocate for whatever they want to advocate ... But ideally I want to see a vibrant civil society where different groups advocate for different issues using democratic methods. That's what I want to see.[126]

Similar to many other 'democracy promoters', Stefan saw the importance of advocacy training in channelling public discontent into a peaceful and 'productive' path, as well as in creating public pressure on the Jordanian government to reform. Talking about Jordanian youth, he explained that

if the only tool they know is protests and street violence then I don't have high hopes for this country ... because sooner or later ... you're going to have a critical mass on the streets and that's it – new revolution, which is not always bad, but there are better ways to do this transition to democracy. And we think that the better way would be if the youth learned about democratic tools of influencing the public opinion. Sometimes it's really difficult to actually ... make them believe that ... these tools work. But what they don't know and what I know through my experience is that every government responds to public pressure. Every – even North Korean dictators can only go as far as the public opinion allows them to ... It works everywhere ... I often use the example of where I come from ... When you live in a dictatorship you tend to think these guys hear everything, they know

---

[124] The NDI also conducts regular youth forums, a summer and winter school of politics and national debate competitions. Former participants of the Anā Ushārik and Anā Ushārik + programmes also established the Anā Ushārik alumni club.

[125] By late 2014 the NDI's Anā Ushārik + programme had 900 participants.

[126] Interview with Stefan, 'democracy promoter' working in Jordan, Amman, 29 January 2013.

everything, they can arrest you every second, you know. But in reality – and that's what we learned after the regime was gone – they lived in constant fear.[127]

The above statement is marked by a staunch belief in the possibilities of gradual procedural change despite many of the participating youth expressing serious doubts concerning this. Another aspect that stands out is the strong conviction that advocacy as a tool for encouraging processes of democratisation 'works everywhere' and Stefan's reference in this regard to his own experience. While it goes without saying that the power of the Jordanian regime is limited and that public opinion clearly does play an important role, Stefan seemed to fundamentally ignore the possibility that the reasons for authoritarian stability in Jordan might differ from those for former authoritarian rule in his country of origin. For many Jordanians it is thus unclear how precisely advocacy, education and participation per se should help solve still today largely unresolved and politically sensitive questions about Jordanian national identity and citizenship.

The head of a Jordanian policy research NGO stressed in this regard the deeply political, rather than simply procedural, reasons for the lack of political reform: 'How can we talk about political reform in Jordan while we are hearing some of the Israeli politicians saying [to the] Palestinians: "If you would like to establish your independent state go to Jordan to establish it"? We couldn't!'[128] An experienced human rights activist and employee of a USAID-financed civil society support programme was similarly adamant in emphasising that the assumptions regarding advocacy as a means for democratisation are highly problematic when applied to Jordan.[129]

US and European 'democracy promoters' widely assume, however, that advocacy NGOs are the most important segment of every civil society. Presenting advocacy in itself – in contrast to advocacy for or against a specific political topic – as central to processes of democratisation importantly allows for the technocratisation of democracy, as training courses in advocacy skills are then much more concerned with seemingly apolitical areas than with Jordanian politics. The ensuing decontextualised 'democracy promotion' interventions should then be understood as an efficient means for the (re)confirmation of desired self-understandings, rather than as conscious responses to specific issues

---

[127] Interview with Stefan, 'democracy promoter' working in Jordan, Amman, 29 January 2013.

[128] Interview with Nasser, director of a Jordanian NGO, Amman, 9 February 2015.

[129] Interview with Omar, Jordanian employee of a USAID-financed civil society support programme, Amman, 18 March 2013.

pertaining to Jordanian politics. During my research period, NDI employees were planning Anā Ushārik + training courses in campaign organising, marketing skills, as well as in 'how to create a good message'. Moreover, the NDI office was considering inviting the best Anā Ushārik + participants to a summer school abroad. At the time, the NDI was considering Poland and Portugal as possible destinations – the reason for Poland presumably being its relatively recent democratisation in 1989 and the reason for Portugal being, as stated by one employee, that 'Portugal is the Middle East of Europe – in the most beautiful sense – [it is] relaxed and charming and ha[s] issues and refugees'. Although the 2014 Anā Ushārik + summer school was eventually held in Amman, it evolved around a simulation of the German political system with five groups of students each representing one of the five main political parties in Germany.[130]

Besides the highly Orientalist description of that which is deemed to be 'typically' Middle Eastern, Europe is implicitly presented in such statements as the example that potential Jordanian processes of democratisation should follow. Features of Jordanian politics and Orientalist conceptions of it are thus abstracted and decontextualised until they eventually appear as generic characteristics present also in other countries, where they however seem to be much less complicated and, most importantly, surmountable. Once the refugees are no longer Palestinian and the environment is no longer the real Middle East, but instead 'the Middle East of Europe', the dominance of universal narratives over the specificities of Jordanian politics powerfully reconfirms itself and processes of Jordanian democratisation seem realisable. As human history's supposed *telos* is thereby reasserted, so is the seeming necessity for 'democracy promoters' as facilitators of its correct unfolding.

The importance of rendering the specifically Jordanian political context less relevant, in order to make processes of democratisation appear more easily achievable could also be observed during a training event for the NDI's youth coordinators in March 2013, in the course of which the NDI youth coordinators present had to develop and discuss imaginary campaign plans. In order to 'practice in a safe environment' the participants were given a two-page document entitled 'Welcome to the Republic of Ibar'.[131] The document briefly outlined the central political, economic and social conditions of the imaginary model republic Ibar, against the background of which participants were asked to discuss their campaign

---

[130] NDI and USAID, 'Ana Usharek – empowering youth at Jordanian universities', *Ana Usharek* 6, p. 7.
[131] NDI Jordan, 'Welcome to the Republic of Ibar', document for training purposes, undated. The quotations in the following paragraphs all come from this document.

plans. Supposedly, the model of Ibar had initially been developed for NDI training sessions already held in Bahrain and was now to serve the same purpose in Jordan.

The state of Ibar only shares a few similarities with Jordan. The document characterises it as a 'democratic republic', which is 'divided almost equally in two camps – traditionalists and modernists' – with a corresponding division among Ibar's political parties. The document thus clearly encourages NDI's youth coordinators to reproduce modernisation theory's deeply problematic binary dichotomy of tradition vs modernity.[132] Politics in Ibar appears largely to be an extension of seemingly technical choices, such as whether to invest in the construction of new schools or rather in the modernisation of existing ones. Within this imaginary context the NDI youth coordinators were asked to play the roles of members of one of Ibar's two parties, of Ibar's teachers association, a youth business initiative and a fishermen's union.

While Ibar is portrayed as entirely fictitious and is supposed to serve the purpose of letting the NDI youth coordinators discuss issues related to democracy without getting bogged down in either local Jordanian politics or indeed in any undesired messy contextual politics, Ibar turns out to be not quite as imaginary, abstract and/or universal as presented. The very real and existing Ibar is thus closely related to the countries of origin of several senior NDI Jordan employees, as it turns out to be the name of a river that first flows through the home country of NDI Jordan's director (Kosovo), then reaches that of both the youth programme manager and the 2013 election observation coordinator (Serbia), before it flows into the West Morava close to the Serbian town of Kraljevo and eventually, for Bahraini and Jordanian youth, turns into the 'Republic of Ibar'.

Instead of discussing concrete issues of Jordanian politics, the participants in the session simulated democracy with an imaginary democratic state that the NDI 'democracy promoters' themselves call home. 'Democracy promotion' in Jordan thus appears more focused on the background and origin of the 'democracy promoters' themselves than on Jordan. Further, while 'democracy promoters' regularly attempt to present their work as something that 'works everywhere' and deliberately distance it from any specific political context – contemplating summer schools in either Poland or Portugal and asking Jordanian youth to simulate democracy with the example of Ibar – the centrality of 'the contextual' even in such attempts at decontextualisation always lurks just beneath the surface. The role of 'democracy promoters' in Jordan

---

[132] See also Tell, T.M., *The Social and Economic Origins of Monarchy in Jordan* (New York: Palgrave Macmillan, 2013), pp. 5–7.

then appears to be that of ensuring by means of abstraction, comparison and to some extent direct disregard, that the desired universal model always continues to dominate Jordanian politics.

In order to make Jordanian democracy appear achievable and to maintain its own supposed moral authority, 'democracy promotion' in Jordan inherently needs to downplay the relevance of 'the contextual'. All those aspects that cannot readily be made to fit the liberal democratic mould need to be ignored or at least abstracted and subsequently compared to the imagined liberal democratic ideal, so that the cultural, institutional and moral differential upon which the idea of 'democracy promotion' so fundamentally depends (re-)emerges. Ibar is therefore – as far as the description goes – neither marked by a protracted struggle over the precise meaning of its national identity nor affected by refugees, potentially hostile neighbouring states or a powerful secret service, all of which would only act as reminders that the power of advocacy to encourage processes of democratisation may be severely limited depending on the context.

If Jordan's political parties are regularly accused of being like supermarkets, then the NDI Anā Ushārik + programme represents the supermarket-isation of advocacy. The campaigns implemented by the Anā Ushārik + students thus cover the whole range of possible topics from campaigns that aimed at abolishing the SNTV system and increasing the number of national list seats to campaigns aimed at improving university services, applying the death penalty, ensuring justice to rape victims, curbing child begging, reintroducing military service, moving street vendors to designated markets, punishing the overloading of vehicles, stopping plans for a nuclear power plant and enforcing a law against smoking in public places.

The majority of the NDI's advocacy campaigns were thus on topics that are relatively marginal to understandings of democracy. The common feature that most campaigns shared was a focus on very specific principles and target groups, all of which are rather unlikely to lead to the kind of widespread popular support that is required to challenge authoritarian rule.[133] The key effect of advocacy campaigns that are as diverse as the ones listed above thus seems to be the formation and confirmation of 'modern', 'liberal' and 'democratic' self-understandings in the absence of an actual process of democratisation. Before discussing this point in more depth, I will briefly elaborate on the focus of many 'democracy promoters' on topics that remain relatively marginal to an actual redistribution of political power.

---

[133] Langohr, 'Too much civil society, too little politics', p. 200.

(Un)Intended Spillover Effects

Just as one Anā Ushārik + campaign advocated for the construction of ramps for disabled students at Jordanian universities, a focus on disability rights at the time also featured prominently in the USAID Jordan D/G portfolio. Besides a 2011–2013 $3.2 million project Integrating Disabled Persons within Jordanian Society, implemented by Mercy Corps, USAID's 2008–2013 $18 million Jordan Civil Society Program (CSP), implemented by FHI 360, also included a comprehensive disability rights programme. While these campaigns and programmes aimed at addressing very important topics, it is at least as important to realise that the advancement of disability rights does not in any way require a meaningful redistribution of power that would represent a challenge to Jordanian authoritarianism. 'Democracy promoter' Jennifer acknowledged this tendency to avoid politically more relevant topics, describing disability rights as 'a safe issue'.[134] Helen, who had previously worked as a 'democracy promoter' in Jordan, explained the strong focus on disability rights:

We discovered that . . . the organisations in civil society that were most willing to be advocates were . . . civil society organisations that worked on disabilities. They were willing to advocate and so we poured a ton of money in . . . because these were the people who were willing to go in and protest in front of the Ministry of the Interior around accessibility for voting . . . we weren't able to get a whole bunch of democracy NGOs to go out and do advocacy. We had people in wheelchairs. And it was the first time ever that there had been a protest in front of the Ministry of Interior and the minister of interior came out and spoke to protestors. And they actually resulted in the election law being much better for . . . persons with disabilities' access [sic]. So in Jordan it was one of those things where you had to find where the openings could be . . . Everybody thought I was a saint in Jordan because I worked with all these blind people and all these people in wheelchairs and it was entirely selfish . . . it was because they were the best advocates in the whole country. And if I wanted to teach advocacy, they were the best example I could find.[135]

While the USAID-supported TAKAFO[136] campaign by Jordanian disability rights activists successfully ensured better accessibility to polling stations for voters with disabilities during Jordan's 2010 parliamentary elections, the strong focus on disability rights advocacy as a means for wider democratisation clearly shows its limitations. Apart from better access for voters with disabilities, the 2010 elections are, as

---

[134] Skype interview with Jennifer, 'democracy promoter' working in Jordan, 17 February 2015.
[135] Interview with Helen, 'democracy promoter' with work experience in Jordan, Washington, DC, 30 May 2013.
[136] An acronym derived from the Arabic word for 'equity'.

noted by Helen, primarily known for widespread allegations of electoral fraud and for – together with the 2007 elections – arguably being some of the worst elections that Jordan ever had. The popular idea among 'democracy promoters' that, regardless of the issue at hand, any advocacy is better than none is regularly justified and explained by resorting to procedural narratives and to claims about supposed future spillover effects into more clearly political arenas. The seeming support for any advocacy comes with important caveats, however. Just as the widespread conviction about the dismal state of advocacy in Jordan ignores, as I have shown, the existing Jordanian civil society, it is also based on the highly questionable notion that advocacy should be naturally bound by the limits of the nation state in which it operates.

In March 2010 the US Embassy in Amman organised a meeting between US Vice President Biden, among others, and several Jordanian civil society activists, including a disability rights and a women's rights activist. During the meeting, the activists insisted on advocating for the rights of Palestinians living in Gaza, who were at the time suffering from the Israeli siege, and not for women's and disability rights. Helen, who was also present at the meeting, was deeply disappointed:

She [a Palestinian-Jordanian women's rights activist] only talked about the Palestinian [issue], which was a shame, because she had much more important things to talk about and I was personally offended that she chose to use ... [the meeting] as an opportunity not to talk about important things happening in Jordan ... There are plenty of things she could have talked about within the Jordanian context ... But to her the Palestinian thing was way more important.[137]

In such instances, when US support for advocacy does indeed contribute to the hoped-for spillover effects into more clearly political arenas, these appear to be fundamentally undesired. Helen thereby reduced widespread claims that any advocacy is better than none to absurdity, as she patronisingly assumed to know better what topics are really important for processes of democratisation in Jordan and even felt personally offended that Jordanian activists might disagree. Apart from this, the encouragement of advocacy by 'democracy promoters' in Jordan seems to either lead to campaigns on 'safe issues' like disability rights or to largely remain in the manageable abstractions of the Republic of Ibar.

If another example were needed of the questionable utility of civil society support, youth participation and advocacy per se as means for a redistribution of political power, the Jordanian royal court provided it in 2013 through the establishment of the Jordanian regime's own democracy

---

[137] Interview with Helen, 'democracy promoter' with work experience in Jordan, Washington, DC, 30 May 2013.

empowerment programme. Since 2013 the King Abdullah II Fund for Development (KAFD) has run the so-called Dimuqrāṭī (Arabic for 'democratic') initiative. Among other goals, and somewhat similar to the discussed USAID and NDI programmes, this initiative aims at '[p]romoting and developing the principles and values of democracy'[138] by means of dialogue and social entrepreneurship.[139] In early 2014 five participants and alumni from the NDI's Anā Ushārik + programme also won grants from the KAFD's Dimuqrāṭī initiative. The students, whom the NDI had provided with technical assistance on proposal writing, successfully secured grants worth between JD500 and JD5,000, with which they planned to organise campaigns and advocacy workshops on campus and communal violence, to establish a school newspaper and to develop a mobile phone application to raise youth awareness on Jordan's constitution.[140] While it is questionable how such projects help to challenge deeply authoritarian power dynamics, one effect of the NDI and KAFD programmes is clear: they help to produce a new generation of Jordanian 'civil society professionals' who are both knowledgeable in the formalities of obtaining foreign grants and prefer to view Jordanian authoritarianism as a matter of a supposedly inadequate political culture among Jordanians themselves over asking more fundamental questions regarding the distribution of power in the country.

Since the signing of a memorandum of understanding between USAID, the NDI and the Crown Prince Foundation (CPF) in August 2018, the Anā Ushārik programme is now even directly implemented by a so-called RONGO, raising further doubts about whether it empowers Jordanian youth, or rather – as I have suggested – authoritarian rule.[141]

'It's in Our DNA'

Finally, promotion of democracy, human rights and governance is a reflection of fundamental American values and identity.[142]

---

[138] King Abdullah II, Royal Hashemite Court, Initiatives – The Democracy Empowerment Programme, undated, available at: http://kingabdullah.jo/index.php/en_US/initiatives/view/id/107.html.

[139] See also Kreitmeyr, N., 'Neoliberal co-optation and authoritarian renewal: social entrepreneurship networks in Jordan and Morocco', *Globalizations*, Vol. 16, No. 3, 2019, pp. 289–303.

[140] NDI and USAID, 'Ana Usharek – empowering youth at Jordanian universities to play an informed role in Jordan's political & decision-making processes', *Ana Usharek* 5, April 2014, pp. 6–7.

[141] For a similar argument, see also Yom, S. and Al-Khatib, W., 'The politics of youth policymaking in Jordan', in: *POMEPS Studies, No. 31, Social Policy in the Middle East and North Africa* (Washington, DC, October 2018), p. 45.

[142] USAID, USAID Strategy on Democracy, Human Rights and Governance (Washington, DC: USAID, June 2013), p. 4.

The acts of juxtaposing the scepticism of Jordanian students about the power of advocacy to 'what I know through my experience', trying to find a similar but supposedly less complicated 'Middle East of Europe' that can serve as an example for Jordanian democratisation and asking students to simulate democracy with the example of an imaginary country linked to the home countries of several of NDI's Jordan staff, all share one characteristic: they appear to be more about the 'democracy promoters' themselves and about their own backgrounds than about Jordan. I thus argue that 'democracy promotion' in Jordan is less a project aimed at understanding and (re)shaping Jordanian politics in line with imagined universal democratic norms than one that provides Western 'democrats' with a stage upon which they can reconfirm their own 'liberal', 'modern' and 'democratic' self-understandings in contrast to the supposedly backward and undemocratic nature of Jordanians.[143]

'Democracy promotion' thus appears to be part of a self-serving ideology that simultaneously reproduces and claims to overcome an imagined moral differential. It is precisely because 'democracy promotion' is so much more about the 'democracy promoters' themselves than about the political context in which it operates that it is so resilient. The ensuing Western-centrism then provides a fertile environment for the flourishing of ignorance about local political dynamics and for Orientalist interpretations that view Jordan as an inherently dysfunctional negative image of 'our' desired self-understandings. One EU-funded technical expert based in a Jordanian ministry noted a fundamental difference between Jordanian and 'Western' culture since, in Jordan 'you do the deed to create the image [while] we would be more concerned about the substance'.[144] Another 'democracy promoter' had come to similar conclusions and was of the opinion that one of the key reasons for the lack of democratisation in Jordan was the scarcity of Jordanian partners

who are able to think in a European or Western way ... Of course, it would be helpful if I spoke Arabic fluently – no doubt. But I would still not know the language of the people here ... I always need a language professional. And I am not talking about the interpreter.[145]

Many 'democracy promoters' in Jordan are thus incapable of understanding Jordanian politics other than by comparing it to the supposed

---

[143] See Said, *Orientalism*, especially p. 63. For the same argument outlined here, but in the context of external attempts at parliamentary strengthening, see Schuetze, 'Marketing parliament'.

[144] Interview with Charlotte, EU-funded technical expert, Amman, 28 January 2013.

[145] Interview with Paul, 'democracy promoter' working in Jordan, Amman, 18 January 2015. See also Schuetze, 'Marketing parliament'.

Western ideal. By doing so, they necessarily render the former inferior, and in a seeming act of self-defence turn authoritarianism into a question of political culture. Their own failure to adequately grasp Jordanian politics thus very effectively perpetuates the assumption of the existence of a fundamental difference between 'the democratic self' and the 'Jordanian non-democratic other'. Several Jordanian political activists and/or NGO workers interviewed were indeed of the opinion that efforts at 'democracy promotion' are motivated by desired self-understandings as 'democratic' and 'liberal' among 'democracy promoters', and by the strong will to confirm these *vis-à-vis* the 'Jordanian non-democratic other', rather than by a genuine interest in understanding Jordanian politics and promoting Jordanian democracy. A Jordanian with extensive experience of working for US-funded programmes aimed at 'democracy promotion' simply concluded, 'we are like the PR agency for the [US] foreign policy'.[146]

This all points to the importance of understanding 'democracy promotion' as a field of practice that aids in the (re)constitution of 'modern', 'liberal' and 'democratic' self-understandings. This not only applies to US and European 'democracy promoters', but also to Jordanians who work for and/or participate in US and European-funded programmes. A Jordanian employee of the NDI explained, for example, that working for the NDI in Jordan gives one the 'feeling of doing something good for one's country'.[147] The website of the German Jordanian University (GJU) tellingly described the NDI's Anā Ushārik programme in 2012 as intending 'to empower its students and polish their personality'.[148] Similarly, in its colourful *Ana Usharek* newsletter, the NDI describes students who received their certificates at a 2014 graduation ceremony as 'celebrating their commitment to democracy in Jordan'.[149] A photo (see Figure 4.2) of participants proudly presenting their certificates in front of NDI and USAID banners complements the description.

---

[146] Interview with Lara, Jordanian employee of a US-funded 'democracy promotion' programme, Amman, 14 November 2012.

[147] Interview with Ali, 'democracy promoter' working in Jordan, Amman, 30 September 2012. Pascucci calls for more research 'on the political subjectivities that emerge as humanitarian aid increasingly becomes something people from the Global South provide to other people from and within the Global South.' Pascucci, E., 'The local labour building the international community: precarious work within humanitarian spaces', *Environment and Planning A: Economy and Space*, Vol. 51, No. 3, 2018, p. 15.

[148] GJU, Ana Usharek Initiative at GJU – Amman, 11 November 2012, available at: www.gju.edu.jo/page.aspx?type=n&lng=en&id=292.

[149] NDI and USAID, 'Ana Usharek – empowering youth at Jordanian universities', *Ana Usharek* 6, p. 4.

Figure 4.2 Photo of Anā Ushārik participants in the *Ana Usharek* newsletter. Below the photo is the following statement: '3,760 Jordanian students graduate in ceremonies celebrating their commitment to democracy in Jordan'. Anā Ushārik programme, NDI Jordan, edition 6, December 2014, p. 4. © NDI Jordan.

As the EU celebrated the international day of democracy in late 2017, and the launch of its new 'democracy promotion' programme, worth €17.6 million, it did so by organising a 'Score for Democracy' football cup (see Figure 4.3). Providing a fairly appropriate illustration of Jordan's 'democratic reform process', the Ministry of Political and Parliamentary Affairs (MoPPA) team won the cup against teams representing, among others, the IEC, the media, civil society, the EU, the House of Representatives and members of Jordan's women national team. The General Intelligence Directorate and the royal court did not participate. Democracy in Jordan thus increasingly appears to be a fancy US- and EU-sponsored event in which 'everyone is a winner',[150] as the EU twitter account was quick to proclaim, an event that is fun to participate in and/or evolves around individual self-promotion, personal development and CV enhancement. Just as participants in the EU-sponsored football cup can score goals for democracy, participants in the NDI's youth participation programme can graduate in it.

The motivations of many Western 'democracy promoters' frequently appear to be highly self-centred. Numerous 'democracy promoters' thus explained their choice of work in terms of a personal feeling of responsibility that at times appeared to be rooted in an almost religious sense of mission. The head of one US 'democracy promotion' firm and USAID implementer stated that '[w]e in more affluent countries have some kind

[150] EU-JDID, @EUJDID, *Twitter*, 16 September 2017, available at: https://twitter.com/EUJDID/status/909131685874331648.

Figure 4.3 Poster announcing the EU's 'Score for Democracy' football cup, held in Amman on 16 September 2017. © EU Delegation Office. Available at: https://twitter.com/ECESeu/status/908592115130748928.

of moral and ethical obligation to try to help people in other countries live better lives and we believe that democracy is something that's in their interests'.[151] It is precisely this role that 'democracy promotion' plays for the (re)confirmation of desired self-understandings as moral and ethical that helps to better grasp its power and effectiveness as rationale for Western foreign policies. While it may appear to be a weakness or short-coming to those trying to improve 'democracy promotion', this self-centeredness is arguably 'democracy promotion''s greatest strength, as it renders the project almost entirely independent of the context within which it operates.

As 'democracy promotion' is more about 'us' and about reaffirming 'our' desired self-understanding as 'democratic' *vis-à-vis* 'the non-democratic other', its often limited or contradictory impacts on the ground have so far not seriously diminished popular support for it or negatively impacted on Western governments' endorsement of it as a rationale for their respective foreign policies. In the words of one US DoS official,

[a] critique of democracy promotion in the US would not get anywhere. The majority of people would say, 'You have to go out and try' ... It's almost like we don't have a choice. It's almost like it's written in the US DNA.[152]

This certainly seemed to be the case for, among others, 'democracy promoter' Robert. At the end of one of our meetings, he said:

[151] Interview with Jacob, President of a US 'democracy promotion' firm, Washington, DC, 22 May 2013.
[152] Interview with John, US DoS official, Washington, DC, 18 June 2013.

We are building bridges ... Some call it politics; I call it a human process. That's what gets me up in the morning ... I feel fortunate that I am from a liberal country ... For me, it's all personal, not political.[153]

This chapter has explored US and European efforts at civil society support in Jordan. Given the restrictive Jordanian legal environment and the narrow focus on a largely unrepresentative group of NGOs in the selection of grantees, I have argued that civil society support reinforces Jordanian state social control rather than empowering independent social actors. I have demonstrated that the image of Jordanian civil society as weak is a direct result of a normative understanding of civil society as liberal, as a consequence of which large parts of Jordan's existing civil society are effectively ignored. Questioning the notion that civil society is an inherently pro-democratic force, the chapter further emphasises the Eastern European origins of select civil society support efforts in Jordan and highlighted the entrenchment of these efforts in idealised understandings of past processes of democratisation. I have demonstrated that efforts at civil society support and particular programmes aimed at youth education, participation and advocacy regularly ignore (Islamic NGOs, tribes, professional associations, the Dhabaḥtūnā initiative, etc.), depoliticise (advocacy for very specific groups and principles, such as disability rights), abstract (Ibar and the 'Middle East of Europe') and compare (contemplating a summer school in Poland or Portugal) Jordanian politics, rather than taking it seriously in and of itself.

I have further argued that civil society support in Jordan is more concerned with romanticised visions of 'the West' and desired self-understandings as 'modern' and 'democratic' than with Jordanian politics. While this absence of context serves the purpose of maintaining a semblance of universal moral authority, US and European 'democracy promoters' in Jordan also of course constitute, in order to gain political authority, a very concrete political actor. It is, however, precisely as a consequence of this – when 'democracy promoters' reinforce the Jordanian regime's claims about democratisation as more a matter of the education, participation and capacity of Jordanians than a redistribution of power, when 'democracy promoters' differentiate between 'good' and 'bad' Jordanian non-state actors, and when political activists view their work as similar to that of the MoPD – that many Jordanians perceive the moral authority of external attempts at 'democracy promotion' to be severely compromised. Finally, I have suggested

---

[153] Interview with Robert, 'democracy promoter' working in Jordan, Amman, 24 September 2012.

that even in the face of such a loss of its moral foundation, 'democracy promotion' proves immensely resilient as a rationale for Western foreign policies.

As 'democracy promotion' functions largely independently from the context in which it operates and is to a significant extent a matter of confirming desired self-understandings as 'modern' and 'democratic', it operates outside of the narrow constraints of political context and practical success or failure. Instead, it is situated in the realm of belief which, in the words of Durkheim, 'precedes proofs, which leads the mind to overlook the insufficiency of the logical reasons, and which thus prepares it for the proposition whose acceptance is desired'.[154]

---

[154] Durkheim, E., *The Elementary Forms of the Religious Life*, tr. Swain, J.W. (London: George Allen, 1915), p. 360.

5   Break on Through to the Other Side

Neoliberal 'Democracy Promotion'

> I view free trade as an important ally in what Ronald Reagan called 'a forward strategy for freedom.' The case for trade is not just monetary, but moral. Economic freedom creates habits of liberty. And habits of liberty create expectations of democracy.[1]

> Promoting polyarchy and promoting neo-liberal restructuring has become a singular process in US foreign policy.[2]

The previous chapters discussed US and European efforts at 'democracy promotion' in Jordan through a focus on institutional engineering, electoral observation and civil society support. I argued that 'democracy promotion' interventions are based on a procedural narrative of democracy which effectively helps to postpone any meaningful redistribution of power to a distant future, thus only reinforcing Jordanian authoritarianism. I suggested that to the extent that external efforts at 'democracy promotion' are premised on seemingly universal narratives of democratisation, they reveal more about desired Western self-understandings as 'liberal' and 'democratic' than they respond to issues of authoritarian state control in Jordan.

A recurrent theme in the previous chapters is the imposition of market logics in spheres commonly assumed to be relatively unrelated to the economic. This neoliberal conversion of 'every political or social problem into market terms',[3] as stated by Brown, could be seen in a predominant understanding among many 'democracy promoters' that Jordanian authoritarianism is related to a still inadequate interaction of the forces of supply (state institutions and parties) and demand (civil society), as

---

[1] Bush, G.W., 'A distinctly American internationalism', speech at the Ronald Reagan Presidential Library, Simi Valley, California, 19 November 1999.

[2] Robinson, W.I., *Promoting Polyarchy: Globalization, US Intervention, and Hegemony* (Cambridge: Cambridge University Press, 1996), p. 55.

[3] Brown, W., 'American nightmare: neoliberalism, neoconservatism, and de-democratization', *Political Theory*, Vol. 34, No. 6, December 2006, p. 704.

illustrated in the MSI report discussed in Chapter 2. One 'democracy promoter''s likening of political parties to participants in a trade fair, who – in order to be strengthened – only need to be supplied with detailed information about their customers' demands, and the underlying division of labour in USAID's 'democracy promotion' programmes (with the NDI training the assumed forces of demand and mostly the IRI those of supply) further illustrate 'democracy promotion''s embrace of a neoliberal rationality.

Building upon the previously analysed examples, I will in this chapter discuss in more depth the convergence of neoliberalism with efforts at 'democracy promotion'.[4] Similar to Robinson, Gills et al., Hanieh and Hassan, I view the promotion of procedural democracy and that of neo-liberal restructuring as two sides of the same coin, or as a 'singular process',[5] in Robinson's words. The following two points make such an understanding necessary. First, a significant number of politicians, such as US President George W. Bush (quoted above in the epigraph), but also other US and European representatives, as well as so-called democratisation scholars, view free trade and free markets as tools for democratisation.[6] Second, the promotion of procedural democracy, as discussed in the previous three chapters, rests on the assumption that democracy is first and foremost about process. While such a definition seems to resolve 'the intrinsically contradictory nature of democratic thought under capitalism',[7] it effectively does so by limiting democracy to simple questions of procedure, and by making socio-economic inequalities seemingly irrelevant to questions of democracy. As the analytical separation of democracy from socio-economic concerns constitutes a foundational requirement for the promotion of procedural democracy, any critical investigation of 'democracy promotion' must also question this conceptual restriction and investigate the notions of political economy that underlie contemporary attempts at 'democracy promotion'. While this chapter is thus to a large extent a discussion of the ways in which US and European 'democracy promoters' assist in the neoliberal restructuring of Jordan, this

---

[4] For a discussion of such attempts at promoting neoliberal procedural notions of democracy in Africa, see Ayers, A.J., 'Demystifying democratisation: the global constitution of (neo)liberal polities in Africa', *Third World Quarterly*, Vol. 27, No. 2, 2006, pp. 321–338.

[5] Robinson, *Promoting Polyarchy*, p. 55. See also Gills, B., Rocamora, J. and Wilson, R. (eds.), *Low Intensity Democracy: Political Power in the New World Order* (London: Pluto Press, 1993); Hanieh, A., '"Democracy promotion" and neo-liberalism in the Middle East', *State of Nature*, Vol. 3, Spring 2006, available at: http://links.org.au/node/224; Hassan, O., *Constructing America's Freedom Agenda for the Middle East: Democracy and Domination* (London: Routledge, 2013).

[6] See for instance Diamond, L., Linz, J. and Lipset, S.M., *Democracy in Developing Countries: Latin America, Volume 4* (Boulder: Lynne Rienner, 1989), pp. 44–47.

[7] Robinson, *Promoting Polyarchy*, p. 52.

is of crucial importance for a better illustration of the precise meaning that ideals of democracy come to hold in a context of neoliberalism.

One of the most well-known proponents of a causal link between economic growth and democracy is Lipset, who famously argued in 1959 that 'the more well-to-do a nation, the greater the chances that it will sustain democracy'.[8] Modernisation theory and its highly functionalist view of capitalism as an inherent source of economic growth and democratisation, was subsequently, as remarked by Hassan, institutionalised in US foreign and security policy, which 'has since embodied an explicit teleological link between economic growth and democratisation'.[9] The end of the Cold War and the alleged triumph of capitalism, free markets, neoliberalism and liberal democracy only further reinforced such deeply teleological understandings of human history, and led to what Achcar pointedly calls a 'neoliberal euphoria'.[10] This was perhaps most vividly expressed in Fukuyama's announcement of the 'end of history', the supposedly imminent 'universalization of Western liberal democracy', and the assumed concomitant 'growing "Common Marketization" of international relations'.[11]

This chapter is built around the central claim that 'democracy promotion' activities in Jordan directly build on and reinforce a marketisation of sociopolitical life. Just as USAID has since its establishment relied heavily on modernisation theory in general, and on Rostow's highly teleological argument that every society undergoes the same distinct stages of growth in particular,[12] the same deterministic approach can also be identified at the heart of contemporary USAID attempts at 'democracy promotion'. As quoted by Robinson, a USAID report from 1990 found that the promotion of procedural democracy 'is complementary to and supportive of the transition to market-oriented economies'.[13] Based on an in-depth investigation of 'democracy promotion' assistance in the neoliberal restructuring of Jordan, and of this restructuring's effects on Jordanian state and society, I critique such claims and argue that the emancipatory potential of procedural democracy in a context of neoliberalism is highly constrained, as the latter effectively constitutes an elite project aimed at

---

[8] Lipset, S.M., 'Some social requisites of democracy: economic development and political legitimacy', *The American Political Science Review*, Vol. 53, No. 1, March 1959, p. 75.

[9] Hassan, *Constructing America's Freedom Agenda for the Middle East*, p. 64.

[10] Achcar, G., *The People Want: A Radical Exploration of the Arab Uprising* (London: Saqi Books, 2013), p. 109.

[11] Fukuyama, F., 'The end of history?', *The National Interest*, Vol. 16, Summer 1989, pp. 3–18.

[12] Rostow, W.W., *The Stages of Economic Growth: A Non-Communist Manifesto* (New York: Cambridge University Press, 1960).

[13] USAID, quoted in: Robinson, *Promoting Polyarchy*, pp. 55–56.

the restoration of class power, as suggested by Harvey.[14] In particular, I intend to demonstrate that, contrary to neoliberalism's 'claim to an apparent neutrality and "objectivity" of analysis'[15] (according to Hanieh, a core feature of neoliberal ideology), the project of neoliberal 'democracy promotion' in Jordan needs to be understood as a fundamental part of a wider anti-democratic and imperial project targeted at the further marginalisation of the poor, and the normalisation of Arab-Israeli relations in the absence of a political settlement of the Israeli-Palestinian conflict. As 'democracy promotion' directly assists in the marketisation of human life, and in the removal of a country's economic decision-making from popular control, I concur with Hanieh in his understanding of 'democracy promotion' 'as one component of neo-liberal imperialism'.[16]

As in previous chapters, I will begin with a discussion of the ways in which US and European officials and 'democracy promoters' discursively link desired processes of democratisation to the specific strategy of interest in this chapter: the support and encouragement of free trade and free markets. In order to do so I provide a brief overview of the experience of the Qualifying Industrial Zone (QIZ) agreement and some of the effects of the free trade agreements (FTAs) signed by Jordan. This will be followed by an in-depth analysis of the neoliberal transition of Aqaba and USAID's role within it. I chose the city of Aqaba as a case study since the Aqaba Special Economic Zone (ASEZ) has come to be the most prominent of a range of projects that epitomise neoliberal reform in Jordan.[17] Also, USAID Jordan staff justify the absence of distinct USAID Jordan 'democracy promotion' efforts in Aqaba by referring to the assumed mutually reinforcing relation between neoliberalism and democracy. As capacity-building programmes in support of the Aqaba Special Economic Zone Authority (ASEZA) are deemed to have the desired effect of encouraging a gradual transition to democracy, distinct efforts at 'democracy promotion' are seen as unnecessary. Building on an exploration of the multiple ways in which neoliberal 'democracy

---

[14] Harvey, David, 'Neoliberalism as creative destruction', *Annals of the American Academy of Political and Social Science*, Vol. 610, NAFTA and Beyond: Alternative Perspectives in the Study of Global Trade and Development, March 2007, pp. 22–44.

[15] Hanieh, A., *Lineages of Revolt: Issues of Contemporary Capitalism in the Middle East* (Chicago: Haymarket Books, 2013), p. 15.

[16] Hanieh, *Lineages of Revolt*, especially pp. 34–36 and 64–66. See also Hanieh, '"Democracy promotion" and neo-liberalism in the Middle East'.

[17] See also Parker, C., 'Tunnel-bypasses and minarets of capitalism: Amman as neoliberal assemblage', *Political Geography*, Vol. 28, No. 2, 2009, pp. 110–120. For an anthropological study of special economic zones and their class relations, see Neveling, P., 'Export processing zones and global class formation', in: Carrier, J.G. and Kalb, D. (eds.), *Anthropologies of Class: Power, Practice and Inequality* (Cambridge: Cambridge University Press, 2015), pp. 164–182.

promotion' in Aqaba has only increased human vulnerabilities and further marginalised the poor, I demonstrate the ways in which exclusion and exploitation prepare the ground for neoliberal 'democracy promotion' to contribute to an imperial agenda of control and domination. The following sections are largely based on the study of various confidential and non-public documents authored and/or used by the USAID Aqaba support programmes.

FTAs, QIZs and Democracy

Only nine days after the terrorist attacks on 11 September 2001, US Trade Representative Zoellick publicly outlined what would soon become the rationale behind President Bush's 'Freedom Agenda'. In a *Washington Post* article, he explained:

Trade is about more than economic efficiency. It promotes the values at the heart of this protracted struggle ... In particular, Congress needs to complete action on the U.S. free trade agreement with Jordan, our first such commitment in the Arab world ... America's trade leadership can build a coalition of countries that cherish liberty in all its aspects. Open markets are vital for developing nations, many of them fragile democracies that rely on the international economy to overcome poverty and create opportunity ... The terrorists deliberately chose the World Trade towers as their target. While their blow toppled the towers, it cannot and will not shake the foundation of world trade and freedom.[18]

Two years later – the US-Jordan free trade agreement was successfully implemented in late 2001 – Zoellick gave another widely quoted speech at the World Economic Forum in Amman. Against the backdrop of what he called 'a proud past – when the Middle East was the vibrant core of global trade ... [and] the world's pre-eminent bazaar',[19] he repeated an earlier statement by President Bush. Dropping Bush's rather brief remark about the need for political reform and reconciliation,[20] Zoellick asserted that '[o]ld patterns of conflict in the Middle East can be broken ... if all concerned will let go of the bitterness, hatred, and violence, and get on with the serious work of economic development'.[21]

---

[18] Zoellick, R.B. (US Trade Representative), 'Countering terror with trade', *Washington Post*, 20 September 2001, available at: www.washingtonpost.com/archive/opinions/200 1/09/20/countering-terror-with-trade/aa1e3f27-f069-4b66-b752-8d141876d0b7/.

[19] Zoellick, R.B., 'Global trade and the Middle East: reawakening a vibrant past', remarks at the World Economic Forum, Amman, 23 June 2003.

[20] The original statement by Bush ends: 'the serious work of economic development, and political reform, and reconciliation'. Bush, G.W., 'The future of Iraq', speech at the American Enterprise Institute, Washington, DC, 26 February 2003.

[21] Zoellick, 'Global trade and the Middle East'.

As remarked by Moore, '[f]or many in Jordan and the Arab world, this statement sounds like: "Let go of your grievances about justice, human rights and double standards. Focus instead on making money"'.[22] Besides a supposed link between free trade, US leadership, economic growth and freedom, Bush and Zoellick also assumed mutually reinforcing effects of free trade on regional peace and stability. According to Wittes, Deputy Assistant Secretary of State for Near Eastern Affairs in 2009–2012, the

> idea is that free-market reforms can act as tools of democratization, because economic liberalization, and the economic growth it generates, will build an independent middle class that will then demand secure property rights, due process of law, and eventually political rights and freedoms from their governments.[23]

As the first country in the Arab world to sign a free trade agreement with the US, a member of the World Trade Organisation (WTO), an 'advanced status' partner of the EU and one of only two Arab countries to have signed a peace treaty with Israel, Jordan is something of a poster child for the 'unity of goodness' outlined here. This is alleged to include, among other things, free trade and free markets, regional peace, processes of democratisation and economic growth. In reality, these treaties and agreements largely failed to lead to an increase in high-value exports, knock-on effects on political liberalisation or a reduction in poverty and unemployment, but instead only deepened Jordan's economic dependence.

Since the onset of economic liberalisation in the early 1990s, neoliberal reforms in Jordan have regularly been linked to efforts to normalise the country's relations with Israel. Following the 1994 Israeli-Jordanian peace agreement, a series of economic summits was held with precisely this goal.[24] Further, in 1998 the German Konrad Adenauer Foundation (KAS) and the American Center for International Private Enterprise (CIPE) explored the possibilities of a future free trade agreement between Israel and Jordan.[25] According to the CIPE, such efforts at establishing free trade directly contribute to the promotion of

---

[22] Moore, P., 'The newest Jordan: free trade, peace and an ace in the hole', *Middle East Research and Information Project*, 26 June 2003.

[23] Wittes, T.C. and Yerkes, S.E ., 'What price freedom? Assessing the Bush administration's freedom agenda', The Saban Center for Middle East Policy at the Brookings Institution, Analysis Paper, No. 10, September 2006, p. 6.

[24] Hanieh, *Lineages of Revolt*, pp. 35–36.

[25] Baskin, G. and Al Qaq, Z. (eds.), *Israeli-Palestinian-Jordanian Trade: Present Issues, Future Possibilities* (Jerusalem: Israel/Palestine Center for Research and Information (IPCRI), Center for International Private Enterprise (CIPE) and Konrad Adenauer Foundation (KAS), April 1998).

democracy. The organisation, one of USAID's four core grantees, describes its mission as 'strengthening democracy around the globe through private enterprise and market-oriented reform'.[26] The clearest manifestation of the assumption that economic growth and development in Jordan require the normalisation of relations with Israel was, however, the establishment of thirteen QIZs in the country beginning in 1996. The QIZ agreement, which is effectively an amendment to the US-Israeli free trade agreement, laid the foundations for the 2001 US-Jordanian free trade agreement and the wider pursuit of an export-led growth strategy. It failed to produce any of the alleged knock-on effects on political liberalisation in Jordan, however.

Besides benefiting from duty- and quota-free access to the US, companies operating in a QIZ are also exempt from customs tariffs, income taxes and social security taxes, as long as at least 8 per cent (7 per cent for high-tech goods) of the value of the exported goods originates from Israeli businesses. While constituting a key component of neoliberal economic reform aimed at triggering industrial transformation in Jordan, and indeed successfully contributing to an impressive 57-fold increase of Jordanian exports to the US between 1996 and 2006,[27] the QIZs have 'not produced backward linkages to any significant extent',[28] as stated by Kardoosh. The zones thus rely overwhelmingly on foreign workers; in 2010 the QIZs employed around 8,000 Jordanian and 28,000 non-Jordanian workers.[29] Further, the zones primarily produce low-value items, such as textiles and garments, whose production does not lead to any major linkages with the local economy. In addition, by 2005 not a single purely Arab company was active in a QIZ.[30] Given the various tax exemptions and the predominance of foreign labour, Moore concluded that 'while (mostly foreign) QIZ investors, owners and managers may realize nice returns, the zones have backfired as contributors to productive development, employment growth or Israeli-Jordanian normalization'.[31]

Besides contributing to a substantial increase of foreign currency earnings and exports – in 2003 the QIZs accounted for 84 per cent of

[26] CIPE mission statement, available at: www.cipe.org.
[27] See US Census Bureau, 'Foreign trade, trade in goods with Jordan', available at: www.census.gov/foreign-trade/balance/c5110.html.
[28] Kardoosh, M.A., 'Qualifying Industrial Zones and sustainable development in Jordan', Jordan Centre for Public Policy Research and Dialogue, February 2005, p. 37.
[29] See figures 12 and 13 in FES and RSS, *The Future of Jordan's Qualified Industrial Zones (QIZs)*, Amman, 2013, pp. 12–13.
[30] Kardoosh, 'Qualifying Industrial Zones and sustainable development in Jordan', p. 27.
[31] Moore, 'The newest Jordan'.

Jordanian exports to the US[32] – and thereby improving Jordan's macro-economic performance, the zones have come under heavy fire for widespread physical abuse against their predominantly Southeast Asian workforce. The dismal working conditions indeed remain one of the main reasons for the low number of Jordanians willing to work in a QIZ.[33] Rather than encouraging sustainable economic development and political change, the effects of the QIZs were thus, as argued by Hanieh, 'to weld together Israeli and Arab capital in the joint exploitation of cheap labor, with exports aimed at the US market'.[34] The assumption that the zones would play a role in reinvigorating the peace process similarly failed to materialise.[35]

Finally, the initial boost of Jordanian exports to the US was short-lived. Once international textile and garment quotas were eliminated when the Multi-Fibre Arrangement expired in 2005, the low-value export-led growth strategy pursued by the QIZs fully revealed the unequal and uneven nature of Jordan's integration into global capitalism.[36] As highly competitive producers from China, India and Bangladesh could now access Western markets quota-free, they no longer depended on the once-unique competitive advantage of Jordanian QIZs, and quickly relocated their production away from Jordan.[37] Accordingly, Jordanian exports to the US dropped sharply after 2006 (from $1.4 billion in 2006 to $0.9 billion in 2009),[38] and Jordan eventually returned to its traditional trade imbalance (only between 2002 and 2008 did Jordan benefit from an overall surplus in trade with the US).

While Jordanian exports to the US have a consistently low value added, Jordanian exports to the EU remain limited by a lack of liberalisation of market access for Jordanian agricultural goods, and by continued subsidies for the EU's own agricultural production. Against this backdrop, Jordan's membership of the WTO and the signing of free trade agreements with the US and the EU primarily had the effect of boosting

---

[32] Bolle, M.J., Prados, A. and Sharp, J., *Qualifying Industrial Zones in Jordan: A Model for Promoting Peace and Development in the Middle East?*, CRS, Washington, DC, 26 January 2005, p. 4.

[33] See Institute for Global Labour and Human Rights, *Sexual Predators and Serial Rapists Run Wild at Wal-Mart Supplier in Jordan: Young Women Workers Raped, Tortured and Beaten at the Classic Factory* (Pittsburgh: Institute for Global Labour and Human Rights, June 2011).

[34] Hanieh, *Lineages of Revolt*, p. 36.

[35] FES and RSS, *The Future of Jordan's Qualified Industrial Zones*, p. 7.

[36] See Hanieh, *Lineages of Revolt*, p. 20, and Allinson, J., *The Struggle for the State in Jordan: The Social Origins of Alliances in the Middle East* (London: I.B. Tauris, 2016).

[37] FES and RSS, *The Future of Jordan's Qualified Industrial Zones*, p. 12.

[38] US Census Bureau, 'Foreign trade, trade in goods with Jordan'.

imports.[39] A direct consequence of becoming 'one of the most open economies in the region'[40] was thus an associated ever-increasing dependence on foreign capital inflows, in order to counter the growing trade imbalance and prevent a depletion of the Jordanian currency. Discussing economic liberalisation in the Middle East in general, Hanieh draws the following conclusions:

> With the region inserted into the world market on the basis of its cheap labor and a flexible, informalized workforce – fully subordinate to the needs of accumulation in the EU and the United States – neoliberal policies have acted to nurture the growth of large domestic capital and provided enormously profitable opportunities for foreign investors.[41]

Regarding the specific case of Jordan, a number of scholars have similarly come to question the assumptions underlying the US and EU approaches. While Gylfason et al. insist that the introduction of free trade and free markets in general, and the establishment of a deep and comprehensive free trade agreement in particular, constitute 'a crash course in modernising society', and 'a central element of a functioning market economy and ultimately of a functioning democracy',[42] El-Anis finds that the impacts of trade liberalisation on economic growth have been highly limited in Jordan.[43] Moore fundamentally questions the supposedly democratising effects of free trade and economic liberalisation, suggesting that 'if Jordan is any guide, the main effect has been to further concentrate political power'.[44] In another article, Moore and Schrank argue, with reference to the triangular trade between England, West Africa and British North America between the sixteenth and early nineteenth century, that 'the lessons of world history suggest that investors, entrepreneurs and firms capitalize upon foreign trade by exploiting, rather than transforming, their preexisting social and political institutions'.[45] They further contend that

---

[39] Busse, M. and Gröning, S., 'Assessing the impact of trade liberalization: the case of Jordan', *Journal of Economic Integration*, Vol. 27, No. 3, September 2012, p. 480.

[40] World Bank, *Hashemite Kingdom of Jordan Development Policy Review: Improving Institutions, Fiscal Policies and Structural Reforms for Greater Growth Resilience and Sustained Job Creation – Volume 1: Synthesis*, Poverty Reduction and Economic Management Department, Middle East and North Africa Region, 30 June 2012, p. 27.

[41] Hanieh, *Lineages of Revolt*, pp. 72–73.

[42] Gylfason, T., Martínez-Zarzoso, I. and Wijkman, P.M., 'Can free trade help convert the "Arab Spring" into permanent peace and democracy?' *Defence and Peace Economics*, Vol. 26, No. 3, 2015, p. 264.

[43] El-Anis, I., *Jordan and the United States: The Political Economy of Trade and Economic Reform in the Middle East* (London: I.B. Tauris, 2011), p. xvii.

[44] Moore, P.W., 'QIZs, FTAs, USAID and the MEFTA: a political economy of acronyms', *Middle East Report*, No. 234, Spring 2005, p. 19.

[45] Moore, P.W. and Schrank, A., 'Commerce and conflict: U.S. effort to counter terrorism with trade may backfire', *Middle East Policy*, Vol. X, No. 3, Fall 2003, p. 112.

'[w]hatever Washington's original goals and intentions, the QIZs and the FTA have clearly been incorporated into a home-grown Jordanian effort to ensure regime stability by expanding business access to exogenously funded, yet state-mediated, profits'.[46] As remarked by Moore, the failure of trade liberalisation to trigger any meaningful processes of political liberalisation thus primarily reminds us that caution 'is warranted in assuming uniform political roles for business regardless of context'.[47] Describing 'uneven and combined development as a process of contradictory universalisation', Allinson similarly warns against 'any notion of a homogenous capitalist modernity'.[48] The fact that 'military and security services were the only sector growing in structural adjustment',[49] as observed by Baylouny, is reminiscent of the strong linkages, not between neoliberalism and democratisation, but instead between neoliberalism and Jordanian authoritarianism, as demonstrated by Hanieh and Martínez among others.[50] This is also in line with more recent literature on authoritarian neoliberalism in general.[51]

Many 'democracy promoters', diplomats and policymakers, however, fundamentally insist on the supposed existence of mutually reinforcing linkages between a private sector-driven capitalist economy and processes of democratisation. The exploitative nature of economic liberalisation in Jordan is thus portrayed as a mere temporary side effect of a wider transitional process that will eventually lead to a system in which there are 'only winners'. As the neoliberal democratic dream always remains on the horizon, it only seems reasonable that the interim period leading up to its imagined realisation requires ongoing external interventions to balance out supposedly temporary negative socio-economic side effects. The narrative of neoliberal 'democracy promotion' in this regard serves a perpetual policy of intervention.

The following statement by a former high-ranking US DoS official clearly demonstrates the dynamics just described and deserves to be

---

[46] Moore and Schrank, 'Commerce and conflict', p. 117.

[47] Moore, P.W., *Doing Business in the Middle East: Politics and Economic Crisis in Jordan and Kuwait* (Cambridge: Cambridge University Press, 2004), p. 177.

[48] Allinson, *The Struggle for the State in Jordan*, p. 2.

[49] Baylouny, A.M., 'Militarizing welfare: neo-liberalism and Jordanian policy', *Middle East Journal*, Vol. 62, No. 2, Spring 2008, p. 301.

[50] Hanieh, *Lineages of Revolt*, pp. 64–66, and Martínez, J.C., 'Leavening neoliberalization's uneven pathways: bread, governance and political rationalities in the Hashemite Kingdom of Jordan', *Mediterranean Politics*, Vol. 22, No. 4, 2017, pp. 464–483.

[51] See Bruff, I., 'The rise of authoritarian neoliberalism', *Rethinking Marxism*, Vol. 26, No. 1, 2014, pp. 113–129 and Tansel, C.B. (ed.), *States of Discipline: Authoritarian Neoliberalism and the Contested Reproduction of Capitalist Order* (London: Rowman & Littlefield International, 2017).

quoted at some length. Fully aware of the risks associated with an economic transformation in Jordan, she explained that

when you need to shift the economic foundations of a society's model for
success from rentierism to something that's private sector-driven, that's
risky! There are adjustment costs involved in that. People lose. Segments of
society are losers when that happens, and they will resist ... But the only way
out is through. You have to get through that process to the other side, to
a system where there is opportunity for all to benefit. Now, you can also ease
those adjustment costs. So, if you're worried about East Bankers who are going
to lose as you invest more in private sector growth and reducing subsidies ...
[o]ne could envision for example a US assistance programme that ..., while
supporting what the Jordanians want to do on institutional reform, is also
supporting very targeted programmes designed to help those who will be
disadvantaged by market-oriented economic reforms ... So we don't only
help the Jordanians with their education system and we don't only help them
with water security and we don't only help them with institutional reform – we
also help them by basically – to put it crassly – paying off the losers. And that's
part of the necessary transition.[52]

In the following, I will discuss this 'necessary transition' in more depth
through the example of Aqaba. In doing so, I will pay close attention to
the role of local USAID programmes, and to the controversial effects of
Aqaba's neoliberal transition on popular accountability and representation, socio-economic rights and the public sector. Drawing on the work of
Robinson, I argue that the project of neoliberal 'democracy promotion'
simultaneously aims at the pre-emption of radical political change – by
advancing a narrow understanding of democracy that separates it from all
matters of socio-economic concern, as illustrated in the previous chapters – and at the further aggravation of socio-economic inequalities.[53] In
particular, I show how USAID actively embraces an analytical separation
of politics from economics, and supported a radical transfer of formerly
public assets into the private sphere. By fundamentally reducing the
role of the public sector, the neoliberal restructuring of the city is
shown to drastically narrow the space which could potentially be governed by democratic values. Finally, in a context of growing 'social
authoritarianism',[54] the promotion of procedural democracy becomes
fundamentally void of any emancipatory potential and effectively constitutes nothing more than a tool for legitimising socio-economic inequalities. An embrace of neoliberal restructuring as a supposed force of

---

[52] Interview with Mary, former high-ranking US DoS official, Washington, DC,
18 June 2013.
[53] Robinson, *Promoting Polyarchy*, pp. 318–319, 344.
[54] Robinson, *Promoting Polyarchy*, p. 376.

emancipation and empowerment is thus shown only to aggravate deeply authoritarian modes of governance.[55]

Aqaba's Neoliberal Transition: ASEZA and USAID

The ASEZ is widely understood as a cornerstone of Jordan's 'necessary transition' to neoliberalism. In the following I sketch some of the steps in this transition, as well as USAID's role within it. I do so in four parts; first I discuss the founding of ASEZA in 2001 and the abolition of municipal elections, then the transformation of Aqaba's land, property and state-owned enterprises to private ownership under the control of the Aqaba Development Corporation (ADC) in 2004. This is followed by an analysis of some of the sociopolitical effects and then by the final section, in which I place Aqaba's neoliberal transition in a wider perspective of attempts to consolidate class power. I argue that USAID played a central role in Aqaba's neoliberal transition and that, instead of encouraging processes of democratisation, this only led to the further entrenchment of authoritarian structures of power, the marginalisation of great parts of Aqaba's population and the empowerment of affluent international business elites.

King Abdullah II established the ASEZ in May 2001 as an 'investor nirvana'[56] that would supposedly 'turn sand into gold'[57] – the advertising slogan of the ASEZ – and help boost Jordan's exports, economic growth and employment. Directly modelled on UAE's Jabal Ali free zone, the ASEZ was developed based on a $1.2 million master plan completed in 1999 by the US company The Services Group (TSG), which had been contracted by the Aqaba Regional Authority (ARA) with the support of a World Bank loan.[58] Among the TSG report's recommendations were the creation of the ASEZA and the concomitant dissolution of the elected municipality of Aqaba.[59] Replacing both the ARA and the elected municipality, the newly created ASEZA put the approximately 90,000 people who at the time lived in the 375 square kilometres of the ASEZ under the

---

[55] The implementation of the so-called Jordan Compact is the latest manifestation of such dynamics. See Lenner, K. and Turner, L., 'Learning from the Jordan Compact', *Forced Migration Review*, No. 57, February 2018, pp. 48–51.

[56] Marks, D. (ed.), *Executive Jordan* (Amman: Gulf Media Consulting, 2007), p. 86.

[57] Aqaba Special Economic Zone Authority (ASEZA), advertisement, in Marks, *Executive Jordan*, pp. 4–5.

[58] Debruyne, P., *Spatial Rearticulations of Statehood: 'Jordan's Geographies of Power under Globalization'* (Ghent: Ghent University, PhD thesis, 2014), p. 169.

[59] See Kardoosh, M.A., 'The Aqaba Special Economic Zone, Jordan: a case study of governance', University of Bonn, Center for Development Research, 2005, p. 11.

direct control of a board of six commissioners, all of whom are appointed by the Jordanian cabinet.

With ASEZA executing independent command over governance, regulation and development, Aqaba effectively became an 'extra-territorial city' and, according to Alaime, 'the symbol of a forward-looking country that wants to play a role in the new global economy'.[60] Companies and investors operating in the ASEZ benefit from freedom from foreign equity restrictions on investments, full repatriation of profits and capital, the possibility of 100 per cent foreign ownership, duty-free import of all commercial products, a full exemption from social services tax, land and building taxes, and taxes on distributed dividends and profits, as well as from a 5 per cent flat income tax (which is 35 per cent in other parts of Jordan).[61] Further, the zone advertises itself as 'a low wage environment with flexible labour laws that allow for up to 70 percent of foreign workers for registered enterprises'.[62] Equipped with these incentives, the ASEZ seemed like an 'economic development engine',[63] as stated in a 2003 report by US engineering giant Bechtel, which would now only need to be 'kick-started'. With 75 per cent of ASEZA's revenues (accrued from the collection of income and sales taxes) set to flow back to the Jordanian central government, the zone was deemed to be a major source of revenue for the latter,[64] as well as a catalyst for wider economic growth premised on the neoliberal assumption of free markets and their supposed trickle-down effects.

A US Embassy cable from 2004 explicitly remarked that ASEZA officials 'subscribe to the "trickle-down theory" of economics, in that the initial benefits of the development plans are intended to benefit the wealthy, but eventually, tangible benefits will filter down to the lower rungs of society'.[65] As described by former ASEZA Chief Commissioner (2004–2007) and former Prime Minister Nader Dahabi, the economic reforms that led to the creation of the ASEZ were deliberately designed as a blueprint for later replication in the rest of the country:

The beauty of ASEZA is that this is a new governance model in Jordan, and they will emulate this model later on in the remainder of the country. We create a board

---

[60] Alaime, M., 'Aqaba an extra-territorial city', in Ababsa, M. (ed.), *Atlas of Jordan: History, Territories and Society* (Beirut: Presses de l'IFPO, 2013), p. 410.

[61] Kardoosh, 'The Aqaba Special Economic Zone, Jordan', p. 4; ASEZA, 'Investment incentives', available at: www.aqabazone.com/Pages/viewpage.aspx?pageID=56.

[62] Marks, *Executive Jordan*, p. 102.

[63] Bechtel, *Draft Business Plan for the Aqaba Development Company*, 31 August 2003, introduction, section 1, pp. 1–2.

[64] Aqaba Special Economic Zone (ASEZ) law for the year 2000, law no. 32, article 42.

[65] US Embassy Amman cable, 'Aqaba authorities confront social, regional challenges', 1 April 2004, *Wikileaks*, 04Amman2554.

of commissioners over a defined piece of land and g[i]ve them all the authority, so they may make decisions very quickly. ASEZA laws g[i]ve all authority in the area to the board of commissioners. The investor has a real one-stop shop ... This is the beauty. This is a new model for the public sector, very close to the private sector.[66]

While economic liberalisation is officially portrayed as going hand in hand with efforts at political liberalisation,[67] the example of the ASEZ demonstrates well the ease with which neoliberal reforms actually led to a reinforcement of authoritarian modes of governance. Former ASEZA Chief Commissioner Dahabi offers a striking illustration of such dynamics, as he describes the role of the local community in the ASEZ in a glossy corporate advertisement book entitled *Executive Jordan*:

The local community is integral to the future success of Aqaba. We replaced the local municipality; the board of commissioners is now the municipality. There are no elections, no municipality in ASEZA. A just dictatorship is better than a democracy. Treat people equally. The local community was deprived of their rights to elect their representatives. Instead, I appointed a consultative council from 18 leaders from the community to talk to them, men and women, hear their concerns – tell them what we are doing and receive their feedback.[68]

A US Embassy cable from 2008 offers a further example for the extent to which the advance of free market reforms in Jordan depended on authoritarian power relations, rather than on democracy. It summarises a conversation between US Embassy political officers and then ASEZA Deputy Chief Commissioner Bilal al-Bashir:

Dr. Bilal Al-Bashir ... conceded to poloffs [political officers] that the Special Economic Zone 'was not democratic,' but characterized this as an advantage. 'People (in Aqaba) are not interested in empowerment – they just want things done,' Bashir explained. He expressed concern that holding ASEZA electorally accountable might disrupt the development process in Aqaba and negatively affect the long-term vision for the Zone. He favorably compared the efficient model of ASEZA with other local governments in Jordan, which he called 'hamstrung' by the incidentals and trivialities of day-to-day politics. Bashir said the community was reaping the benefits of this foresight, pointing to Aqaba's exceptional GDP growth statistics.[69]

---

[66] Nader Dahabi (ASEZA Chief Commissioner 2004–2007), quoted in: Marks, *Executive Jordan*, p. 92.

[67] See, for instance, National Agenda Steering Committee, *National Agenda: The Jordan We Strive For, 2006–2015* (Amman: National Agenda Steering Committee, 2005), available at: www.nationalagenda.jo/Portals/0/EnglishBooklet.pdf, p. 3.

[68] Nader Dahabi, quoted in: Marks, *Executive Jordan*, p. 93.

[69] US Embassy Amman cable, 'Aqaba faces the challenges of growth', 14 August 2008, *Wikileaks*, 08Amman2383.

Before discussing the socio-economic effects of the ASEZ in more depth, the role of external actors in its establishment deserves some attention. While the Jordan-based 'democracy promoter' Michael was highly critical of ASEZA – describing it as 'perverse; it is one thing to create such zones, but another to take away local elections' – he insisted, 'You can't blame the donor community [for] the way ... they articulated the economic zones'.[70] This attempt to both downplay the role of the US and the EU in the establishment of ASEZA and analytically separate the underlying idea of neoliberalism from its real-life effects fundamentally ignores the facts. It was thus not despite its authoritarian nature that ASEZA attracted large-scale investments ($8 billion in investment pledges in its first seven years), but precisely because of its lack of democratic accountability, as remarked by al-Bashir himself above. Also, both the EU and USAID had played a central role in the establishment of ASEZA, as shown by Debruyne, and Peters and Moore, among others, who describe ASEZA as 'USAID's baby'.[71] Besides a €10 million 2002–2008 tourism promotion project by EuropeAid, it was in particular USAID that facilitated the founding of ASEZA. Former US Ambassador to Jordan David Hale acknowledged in a 2008 US Embassy cable that 'USAID was instrumental in the formation of ASEZA and current USAID projects are continuing to grow the human resources and planning capacity of ASEZA and the Aqaba Development Corporation (ADC)'.[72]

In line with Jordan's own effective outsourcing of the Aqaba region, USAID Jordan operated its support to the ASEZ in isolation from its other activities in the country. Due to the presence of distinct USAID Aqaba programmes in support of ASEZA – and assuming that these also had the desired effect of promoting democracy – the USAID Jordan democracy and governance portfolio deliberately excluded the Aqaba region from its 'democracy promotion' activities in the rest of the country.[73] USAID Jordan thus assumed democratisation, in the words of Amin, to be 'the necessary and natural product of submission to the

---

[70] Interview with Michael, 'democracy promoter' working in Jordan, Amman, 12 December 2012.

[71] Peters, A.M. and Moore, P.W., 'Beyond boom and bust: external rents, durable authoritarianism, and institutional adaptation in the Hashemite Kingdom of Jordan', *Studies in Comparative International Development*, Vol. 44, No. 3, 2009, p. 278. Also see Debruyne, *Spatial Rearticulations of Statehood*, especially pp. 169–180.

[72] US Embassy Amman cable, 'Aqaba development update', 3 April 2008, *Wikileaks*, 08Amman1000.

[73] Interview with Michael, 'democracy promoter' working in Jordan, Amman, 24 January 2013.

rationality of the worldwide market. A simple dual equation is deduced from this logic: capitalism = democracy, democracy = capitalism'.[74]

The first USAID programme in support of ASEZA was the $19 million Aqaba Technical Assistance Support Project (ATASP). It not only played a central role in the drafting of the ASEZ law, but also in ASEZA's handling of labour, tax and custom-related issues and in initial training and capacity building.[75] ATASP was followed by the Aqaba Zone Economic Mobilization (AZEM; the English transliteration of the Arabic word for 'strength') project in 2004, the Aqaba Community and Economic Development (ACED) programme in 2007 ($22.9 million) and ACED II in 2014.[76] ACED and ACED II were implemented by AECOM, a US provider of management support services and legal successor of the US firm TSG, which had developed the initial ASEZA master plan in 1999, and had been acquired by AECOM in 2008.

While these programmes included a so-called community development component, which I discuss later on, they relied on the very same market-centred approach that ASEZA itself also depended on. As I demonstrate throughout this chapter, USAID thereby directly assisted in the gradual transformation of socio-economic rights into matters of charity and cor-porate social responsibility.[77] When the AZEM project, which was imple-mented by the US consulting firm Nathan Associates, advised ASEZA to serve the community more in a 2004 *Aqaba Community Profile*, in doing so it nonchalantly described the latter as ASEZA's 'customer'.[78] Two years later, an AZEM presentation found that the USAID programme had successfully 'improved ASEZA's internal efficiency & made it customer focused'.[79] In the following sections I elaborate on what this customer focus really meant. Already, however, it becomes apparent that at the very core of USAID's activities in Aqaba lay a staunch belief in the need to deepen existing, and establish new, markets. Neoliberal 'democracy pro-motion' can then be seen to be preventing more radical democratic change in two complementary ways: first, by embracing a narrow proce-dural understanding of democracy that separates democratic values from

---

[74] Amin, S., 'The issue of democracy in the contemporary third world', in: Gills, Barry, Rocamora, Joel and Wilson, Richard (eds.), *Low Intensity Democracy: Political Power in the New World Order* (London: Pluto Press, 1993), p. 60.

[75] USAID Jordan, *United States Support for the City of Aqaba*, April 2004, p. 2.

[76] ATASP, AZEM, ACED and ACED II are officially part of the USAID Jordan economic development portfolio.

[77] See also Teti, A., 'Democracy without social justice: marginalization of social and economic rights in EU democracy assistance policy after the Arab uprisings', *Middle East Critique*, Vol. 24, No. 1, 2015, pp. 9–25.

[78] AZEM, USAID and Nathan Associates, *Aqaba Community Profile*, June 2004, p. 5.

[79] AZEM and USAID, *Overview of the AZEM Project*, PowerPoint presentation, 1 June 2006, slide 8.

questions of socio-economic equality; and second, by subordinating more and more aspects of socio-economic life to principles of private ownership and competition.[80]

'Insulating Development from Politics'

A central step in the analytical separation of politics from economics was the 2004 establishment of ADC. The creation of one entity responsible for regulation (ASEZA) and another for development and investment (ADC) had already been part of the initial plans for the ASEZ, and was supposed to help insulate development from politics. Following the elimination of all avenues of public participation in decision-making processes in 2001, the founding of the ADC as a private shareholding company equally owned by the Jordanian government and ASEZA represented another major advance in the neoliberal transition of the city. Practically all ownership of formerly public land, property and companies was now transferred from ASEZA to the publicly owned private company ADC. While still publicly owned, the eventual full privatisation of ADC was already the ultimate goal. In a confidential *Draft Business Plan for the Aqaba Development Company*, for which ASEZA had contracted the US corporation Bechtel, the latter answers the question, 'Why a Development Company?' by referring to *inter alia* the following points.[81]

First, Bechtel deemed the reliance on 'private sector driving principals and access to a wide pool of technical and financial expertise and resources through the "Strategic Partner"' – read Bechtel itself, or another private enterprise that would help run ADC; eventually the multinational company BearingPoint was contracted as manager of ADC's start-up operations – as necessary '[t]o accelerate the development of the ASEZ'.[82] Second, Bechtel described the introduction and maintenance of 'international best practices in the management of the ASEZ development program' as requiring 'private sector management'.[83] As the report remarks later on, this was to entail an overall '40 percent increase over the current ASEZA salary ranges to reflect a competitive premium for attracting suitable employees'.[84] Also, eleven out of nineteen executive positions were, according to Bechtel, to be sourced from outside

---

[80] See Amin, 'The issue of democracy in the contemporary third world', p. 63.

[81] The dynamics discussed here are reminiscent of those analysed in Ferguson, J., *The Anti-Politics Machine: 'Development,' Depoliticization, and Bureaucratic Power in Lesotho* (Minneapolis: University of Minnesota Press, 1994).

[82] Bechtel, *Draft Business Plan for the Aqaba Development Company*, executive summary, p. 2.

[83] Bechtel, *Draft Business Plan for the Aqaba Development Company*, executive summary, p. 2.

[84] Bechtel, *Draft Business Plan for the Aqaba Development Company*, management & staffing, section 9, p. 26.

of Jordan. The report refers in this regard to undisclosed studies which indicated that the required 'niche areas of expertise ... are not widely available in the HKJ [Hashemite Kingdom of Jordan]'.[85] Finally, the 'competitive premium' would require labour costs of JD5.6 million for seventy-eight full-time ADC staff.[86] According to Bechtel's suggestions, and assuming an average monthly income of JD150 among the population of Aqaba, the seventy-eight ADC employees would thus earn approximately as much as about one-fifteenth (about 3,100) of the 46,551 Jordanians who at that time constituted the total working population of the ASEZ.[87]

Third, Bechtel explained the need for ADC by remarking that '[t]he development company will help insulate development decisions from the political process, thereby allowing the decisions to be made for economic development reasons rather than political reasons'.[88] This insulation was only to operate in one direction, however, reducing government control over ADC and simultaneously increasing private sector control over public funds. ADC's entire initial working capital of JD23 million was thus provided by the Jordanian government, which again financed this public subsidy for a private company through a JD20 million cash transfer from USAID.[89] In light of a predicted ADC 'funding gap of approximately JD 150 million over the next five years'[90] – primarily as a result of major capital investments related to Aqaba port (the relocation of the commercial port alone cost $700 million) – Bechtel proposed that the Jordanian government provide these 'approximately JD 150 million (+/-30 per cent) in financial support to ADC'.[91] In case any future ADC funding gaps emerged there was no doubt how they would be

[85] Bechtel, *Draft Business Plan for the Aqaba Development Company*, management & staffing, section 9, p. 17.

[86] Bechtel, *Draft Business Plan for the Aqaba Development Company*, management & staffing, section 9, pp. 18, 19, 26. The report suggests that as the number of executives from abroad could again be reduced after three years – since by then cheaper local staff would have benefited sufficiently from 'on-the-job-training' – the total salary costs would eventually decline to about JD3.5 million.

[87] AZEM, USAID and Nathan Associates, *Aqaba Community Profile*, pp. 11, 13. The report finds that 48.5 per cent of the working population in the ASEZ earned between JD100 and JD199 per month.

[88] Bechtel, *Draft Business Plan for the Aqaba Development Company*, executive summary, p. 2. The report gives another four reasons, which I do not specifically name here.

[89] AZEM, USAID and Nathan Associates, *ASEZA and ADC: Building a New Partnership – A Concept Paper*, 14 October 2004, p. 4. The report does not explicitly mention the author. However it mentions twice that certain information was, or was not, made available to 'the AZEM team', thus suggesting that it was developed by the AZEM project.

[90] Bechtel, *Draft Business Plan for the Aqaba Development Company*, executive summary, p. 14.

[91] Bechtel, *Draft Business Plan for the Aqaba Development Company*, executive summary, p. 1.

closed: 'When a funding gap exists after other sources are exhausted, ADC will need Government support to bridge the gap in the form of a sovereign guarantee or direct funding'.[92]

According to the Bechtel draft business plan for ADC, once the public treasury completed the capital investments that were required to move the port to the south of Aqaba and make it profitable, ADC would be ready to be sold to private investors, in order to then 'grow into an efficient and profitable private-sector conglomerate, developing, investing, managing and operating major assets in the ASEZ'.[93] For the time being, the 100 per cent government ownership of ADC (50 per cent of shares worth JD11.5 million are owned by both the Jordanian government and ASEZA, with the latter holding an additional type B stock, which gives it strategic voting control)[94] constituted both a challenge and an advantage in Bechtel's eyes. While public influence on ADC needed to be curtailed as much as possible – through the above-mentioned private sector management principals, ADC's corporate governance provisions, a proposed appeals procedure and a management contract with a private sector management contractor (BearingPoint) – a welcome advantage of initial full public ownership was that it '[e]nables public funding, if necessary'.[95]

The central theme underlying both the Bechtel report and the subsequent establishment of ADC is a peculiar understanding of economic development entirely detached from politics and political influence. Bechtel in fact speaks of 'shielding'[96] operations that are required in this regard. In such an understanding of economics, human life only appears to be relevant to economic development to the extent to which it is able to function as customer or consumer. While Bechtel suggests the management of '*Lifetime Partnerships* with investors'[97] as a unique selling point to increase the appeal of ADC in the global market, it also proposes what it calls a 'people-versus-business division', which only naturally 'leads to the division of assets and revenue streams, development roles and responsibilities of key enablers'.[98] Practically all of the major assets and rights that

---

[92] Bechtel, *Draft Business Plan for the Aqaba Development Company*, ADC strategy, section 2, p. 2.

[93] Bechtel, *Draft Business Plan for the Aqaba Development Company*, ADC strategy, section 2, p. 1.

[94] AZEM, USAID and Nathan Associates, *ASEZA and ADC*, p. 4, footnote 1.

[95] Bechtel, *Draft Business Plan for the Aqaba Development Company*, ADC strategy, section 2, table 2-2, pp. 5–6.

[96] Bechtel, *Draft Business Plan for the Aqaba Development Company*, legal organization, section 8, p. 1.

[97] Bechtel, *Draft Business Plan for the Aqaba Development Company*, core capabilities, section 7, p. 9.

[98] Bechtel, *Draft Business Plan for the Aqaba Development Company*, executive summary, p. 7.

the Jordanian government had transferred to ASEZA in 2001 were thus now recommended to be transferred to ADC, which was to become responsible for all matters related to 'development'. The eventual transfer included Aqaba's airport, all land classified for industry, retail and tourism, as well as the port, which thus far had been under the control of the Aqaba Port Corporation (APC) – a public company that used to operate under the Jordanian Ministry of Transport. Up until its privatisation, the port had been the city's largest employer.

Throughout its report, Bechtel emphasised the importance of ADC not only acquiring ownership of the land of the port, but also securing 'the excess cashflow generated by the Port ... to be able to utilize this to become self sustaining'.[99] With an estimated annual profit margin of approximately JD25 million in 2004 and JD70 million in 2022, Bechtel considered the port simply too valuable to be left in public hands, and so it was to be transferred to ADC. According to Bechtel's own estimations, it would eventually account 'for more than 75 percent of the aggregate operating margin for ADC businesses'.[100] The revenues earned by the government of Jordan from ASEZA (JD12.7 million in 2005) are ultimately more than counterbalanced by the income foregone. ADC's effective net income in 2005, which would previously have gone to the government, thus constituted JD44 million.[101]

A non-public 2004 concept paper developed by the USAID AZEM project for the management of both ASEZA and ADC described the reasoning behind ADC's establishment:

Empiricists as well as theoreticians point out to the available evidence, which overwhelmingly indicates that the private sector is better suited to serve consumers [*sic*] needs. Competitive private business participation ensures the provision of better, cheaper and timely products and services compared to state-owned enterprises (SOEs). Given Aqaba's limited resources and the knowledge that optimal resource allocation can be achieved through private sector participation (PSP), there is no doubt that commercial, for-profit activities ought to be left to PSP. For this reason and to avoid the potential conflict of interest that stems from being the regulator and the developer at the same time, the decision was made to create ADC.[102]

---

[99] Bechtel, *Draft Business Plan for the Aqaba Development Company*, infrastructure development activities, section 5, p. 3.

[100] Bechtel, *Draft Business Plan for the Aqaba Development Company*, financial projections, section 10, p. 5.

[101] AZEM, USAID and Nathan Associates, *Jordan: Aqaba Special Economic Zone – Regional Economic Development Plan Volume III – Fiscal Conditions for Regional Development*, 27 June 2006, p. 24.

[102] AZEM, USAID and Nathan Associates, *ASEZA and ADC*, p. 2.

Stripped of most of its property and its main source of income (the sale of land) – the AZEM report notes that the establishment of ADC deprived ASEZA of capital revenue averaging about JD8 million per year[103] – ASEZA was now to 'take responsibility for socio-economic and government processes, and ADC ... for infrastructure and business enablers'.[104] In short, all not-for-profit activities were to remain with ASEZA, while all for-profit activities were privatised under ADC. The Bechtel report specifies in this regard that ASEZA is to remain responsible for the provision of a 'clean and safe environment', the development of 'pleasant parks and recreation facilities', the guarantee of 'safety and security', the provision of 'attractive investment incentives', as well as '[a]ttract[ing] good schools and universities [as well as] quality health care and hospitals'.[105] Characteristically, Bechtel recommended that ASEZA should 'attract' and not provide what were once central social rights of health and education. In light of this drastic reduction of the public sector, even if ASEZA ever reintroduced elections, they would – given the limited role and responsibilities of ASEZA – hardly have any meaningful emancipatory potential.

While the eventual transfer of ASEZA's land and property to ADC did indeed eliminate what the Bechtel report had called the 'ASEZA funding conflict'[106] (selling land to fund itself), it only did so by creating a new funding gap. ASEZA was thus advised 'to find other sources of income to balance its costs and revenues over the next few years'.[107] In particular, the Bechtel report suggested changes to the customs and tax payments that ASEZA had to return to the treasury of the central government, and/or increasing governmental funding for ASEZA operations. This brought into question the initial reasoning behind the establishment of the ASEZ as a supposed 'economic development engine' and cash machine for the central government. While one USAID report in 2008 had still envisaged an increase of ASEZA's revenue share with the Jordanian central government up to 100 per cent by the end of the ACED programme in 2014,[108] the actual revenue share by the end of the ACED II programme had declined from

---

[103] AZEM, USAID and Nathan Associates, *ASEZA and ADC*, p. 9.

[104] Bechtel, *Draft Business Plan for the Aqaba Development Company*, executive summary, p. 8.

[105] For all quotations see Bechtel, *Draft Business Plan for the Aqaba Development Company*, executive summary, table 2, p. 8.

[106] Bechtel, *Draft Business Plan for the Aqaba Development Company*, executive summary, p. 3.

[107] Bechtel, *Draft Business Plan for the Aqaba Development Company*, impact on ASEZA, section 12, p. 5.

[108] ACED, USAID and AECOM, *Performance Monitoring Plan*, 26 February 2008, p. 15.

the initial 75 per cent to only 50 per cent.[109] Further, what had previously been dubbed a 'funding conflict' – that is, the selling and managing of land by ASEZA for its own benefit – was now, in the framework of the private company ADC, nothing but an 'economic benefit' in the shape of an 'economic rate of return ranging between 24 percent and 29 percent'[110] for ADC's shareholders. While the Jordanian central government benefits from both its revenue share agreement with ASEZA (despite the reduced percentage) and the profits as ADC shareholder, these proceeds not only appear to be counterbalanced by the income foregone, but also come at considerable socio-economic costs. I will discuss these aspects in the following section.

Attempting to help ASEZA in its socio-economic responsibilities, USAID also implemented its own economic development component. In 2006, the AZEM project commissioned an Aqaba Public Transport Network Plan,[111] with the objective of consolidating two existing bus stations. Providing a good example for the extent to which USAID viewed Aqaba as entering a post-politics era, it chose an Israeli business consultant as developer of the plan, and not a local Jordanian one. A Palestinian-Jordanian former employee of a USAID programme in Aqaba could only comment with sarcasm on USAID's choice: 'Ironic isn't it? Me being Jordanian of Palestinian origin. The USA [USAID] loves the idea of this'.[112] In line with this desire to help Jordan move 'beyond politics', USAID not only ignored the political sensitivity of its choice of consultants, but in a much broader manner helped ASEZA to insulate all economic matters from anything considered political, as I illustrate in the following.

Lifetime Partnerships with Investors and the Place of the Poor

ADC, after all, is a profit maximizer.[113]

The marginalisation of 'people-focused activities' in the ASEZ, and the further restriction of any future possibilities that public life in the zone

[109] ACED II, USAID and AECOM, *Final Report*, November 2014, p. 18. In 2004 the share was reduced to 50 per cent. While initially only intended for the period 2004–2008, the 50 per cent share still appears to be operational.
[110] For both quotations see Bechtel, *Draft Business Plan for the Aqaba Development Company*, impact on ASEZA, section 12, p. 8.
[111] Adiv, A. and Cannell, A., *Aqaba Public Transport Network Plan – Final Report*, AZEM, Nathan Associates and USAID for ASEZA and ADC, PowerPoint presentation, 19 June 2006.
[112] Email contact with Muhammad, former employee of a USAID programme in Aqaba, 2 March 2013.
[113] AZEM, USAID and Nathan Associates, *ASEZA and ADC*, p. 7.

might be governed by democratic values occurred on several interrelated levels. One is the transformation of former socio-economic rights into 'socio-economic enablers' that are now dependent on the forces of the market, and another the redirection of financial profits from the public to the private sector. Both have been discussed in the previous sections. To better grasp the extent to which large parts of Aqaba's population were actively excluded from the kind of economic development envisaged and realised by ASEZA, ADC and USAID, it is necessary to explore in more depth some of the effects of Aqaba's neoliberal transition on the local population. Especially insightful in this regard is the development of the al-Shalālah district, which is located in the old city centre of Aqaba and directly overlooked the old port before the latter's relocation to the south of the city. In 2004, al-Shalālah was estimated to be home to about 17,000 people from Jordan, Egypt, Southeast Asia, Iraq and Palestine, among other places. Many of the Palestinian refugees living in al-Shalālah are originally from Gaza and thus not eligible for Jordanian citizenship. Lack of Jordanian identity cards, related ineligibility for state services and widespread informal living conditions were factors which contributed to making the area one of the poorest in Aqaba. The non-public 2004 *Aqaba Community Profile* by the AZEM project of USAID and Nathan Associates paints a particularly dark picture of the area.

Besides a high rate of unemployment, a strong informal economy and many inhabitants' dependence on the nearby port for employment, the authors focus in their description on a whole range of social ills. After noting that '[p]rostitution, drug dealing and weapon smuggling are known to be highly abundant in that area', they continue by detecting 'child abuse, incest, and rape', as well as 'a lot of ignorance and lack of awareness on civilization in general'.[114] Along deeply Orientalist lines, men living in al-Shalālah are described as dangerous and frustrated perpetrators and women as passive victims who urgently need external help: '[t]he women are mistreated and . . . abused by the husband because of his frustration resulting from unemployment and ignorance.' According to the study, the widespread unemployment is again a result of even more 'ignorance, illiteracy, lack of skills, lack of citizenship, and the culture of shame'.[115] It seems clear from such gloomy descriptions that external intervention is urgently required in order to help remedy the socio-economic situation of al-Shalālah.

---

[114] AZEM, USAID and Nathan Associates, *Aqaba Community Profile*, pp. 14, 24.
[115] For both quotations see AZEM, USAID and Nathan Associates, *Aqaba Community Profile*, p. 24.

The key factor that eventually triggered widespread interest in al-Shalālah, however, was none of the above, but instead the area's location and the seeming impossibility of quickly turning its inhabitants into the kind of customers and consumers that would have a place in the ADC/ASEZA/USAID-facilitated 'economic development'. A 2003 US Embassy cable expresses a somewhat more pertinent assessment:

> Shalala, the poorest neighborhood in Aqaba, occupies prime real estate over-looking the city and the Red Sea. Accordingly, ASEZA plans to move its inhabitants, many of whom are squatters living in creaky, rusty shanties, to land outside of the AIIE [Aqaba International Industrial Estate]. The move would ostensibly open up the hilltop for development and bring the Shalalans closer to much-needed jobs that may materialize as the industrial park grows.[116]

For the USA, ASEZA and ADC, the simple reference to a 'poor neighbourhood' that occupied 'prime real estate' was sufficient to justify its relocation. Implicitly, it had been clear since the very beginning of the 'ASEZA vision' that the desired separation of 'economic development' from everything deemed to be 'political', including all those people who could not be readily transformed into affluent consumers, would leave no space for the residents of al-Shalālah. Financed by a loan of the Abu Dhabi Fund, after an initial failed attempt at forceful eviction in 2007, the inhabitants were eventually relocated in 2010 to the al-Karāmah (Arabic for 'dignity') district close to the AIIE on the outskirts of Aqaba. In parallel, the privatisation of the port, which had begun in 2006 with the creation of the Aqaba Container Terminal (ACT) – a joint venture between ADC and Danish APM Terminals – led to long-anticipated major layoffs (a 2008 report funded by the World Bank recommended the dismissal of up to 65 per cent of the port staff).[117] While the large-scale dismissal of port workers demonstrated ADC's success in what Bechtel had termed 'insulat[ing itself] from the management of "people" issues related to Port operations so that ADC can focus on value added activities',[118] for al-Shalālah it simply meant even greater unemployment and socio-economic marginalisation.

Illustrating the violent spatial rearticulations that lie at the very core of neoliberalism, and which enabled the neoliberal transition of Aqaba – as shown by Debruyne[119] – the city's landscape became increasingly reordered by citizens' ability to function as consumers in the global market.

---

[116] US Embassy Amman cable, 'Mixed signals out of Aqaba', 13 January 2003, *Wikileaks*, 03Amman244.

[117] US Embassy Amman cable, 'Aqaba faces the challenges of growth'.

[118] Bechtel, *Draft Business Plan for the Aqaba Development Company*, infrastructure development activities, section 5, p. 5.

[119] Debruyne, *Spatial Rearticulations of Statehood*, especially pp. 163–231.

For instance, a 2009 strike by 3,000–4,000 port workers who faced the imminent loss of jobs and affordable housing (which was part of their contract) was violently suppressed by Jordanian Gendarmerie forces.[120] As a result of Aqaba's neoliberal transition, the all-encompassing governing principle was now the 'maximization of asset values',[121] as remarked in the Bechtel report. This had become most apparent in the successful 'liberation' of the prime real estate formerly 'occupied' by the residents of al-Shalālah, since it had cleared the way for 'maintaining a focus on the creation of financial value for ADC's shareholders',[122] as Bechtel put it, in this once 'economically-depressed, teeming community called Shalala',[123] as described by the US Embassy. In 2011 the first infrastructure work commenced in al-Shalālah and the area of the old port for the $10 billion Marsa Zayed project of the UAE-based Al-Maabar real estate and investment firm, which had bought the area for a total of $500 million. The project, dubbed 'the vibrant heart of Aqaba', is one of a range of large-scale luxury tourism and real estate projects that turn formerly public spaces into closed-off gated communities for affluent customers from the Arabian Gulf, Europe and the US.[124]

While, at first sight, the 'life-time partnerships' that Bechtel proposed ADC should offer to investors such as Al-Maabar, Saudi Oger (the implementer of the Saraya Aqaba project), APM Terminals, Parsons Brinckerhoff International and the like contrast starkly with the ASEZA-implemented relocation of al-Shalālah's residents into the desert at the outskirts of the city, and with USAID's focus on 'self-help' in its community development projects, it is important to realise that the former required and led directly to the latter. Illustrating the kind of 'social authoritarianism'[125] that Robinson describes as a result of neoliberal 'democracy promotion', the former residents of al-Shalālah had effectively lost both their cheap housing and their jobs in the old port. While this had in important ways enabled the neoliberal transition of Aqaba, it was hard for the former residents of al-Shalālah to see what former US DoS official Mary had termed 'the other side where there is opportunity for all to benefit'.

---

[120] For more information see Debruyne, *Spatial Rearticulations of Statehood*, pp. 195–198.
[121] Bechtel, *Draft Business Plan for the Aqaba Development Company*, ADC strategy, section 2, p. 1.
[122] Bechtel, *Draft Business Plan for the Aqaba Development Company*, ADC strategy, section 2, p. 2.
[123] US Embassy Amman cable, 'Aqaba authorities confront social, regional challenges'.
[124] Other projects include the $500 million Tala Bay project, the $1 billion Saraya Aqaba project, the $1.4 billion Ayla Oasis project and the $1.5 billion Red Sea Astrarium project.
[125] Robinson, *Promoting Polyarchy*, p. 376.

In response to continuous socio-economic problems, USAID established so-called neighbourhood enhancement teams which engaged in street beautification and neighbourhood clean-up campaigns. After ASEZA, ADC and USAID had initially helped to insulate economic development from 'people' issues, USAID was thus now trying to again mobilise the 'local community' – but through a discourse of competition rather than one of socio-economic rights. In its neighbourhood-development activity, USAID fundamentally relied on the notion of neoliberal self-government, and on the idea that the further inclusion of Aqaba's poor into the market economy would constitute the desired solution to the problem.

In light of the gradual transformation of socio-economic rights into projects dependent on corporate goodwill, one USAID document described the effects of the city's transition:

In Aqaba, development seems to revolve around high-end tourism and elite residential projects. The Aqaba community feels alienated and they have serious concerns as to whether the benefits of the construction and development will flow back to them. With all this transformation, it seems that the Aqaba community must find ways to maximize their economic and social benefits in a future that is planned for them by others.[126]

Instead of attempting to protect inalienable socio-economic rights of decent and affordable education, health and housing by strengthening the role of the public sector, USAID viewed the expansion of capitalist social relations as a force of democratic emancipation and hence sought only to further incorporate Aqaba's poor into the market. Besides introducing a grants programme for local civil society organisations (CSOs), which were now to be responsible for the provision of social services to all those marginalised by the socio-economic changes, USAID also established an annual CSO excellence award. With the objective of ensuring the quality of the services now provided by local CSOs, USAID thus also introduced the CSO world to the market pressures of constant competition.[127]

As a consequence of Aqaba's growing population, and as a side effect of the many high-end real estate projects, the housing costs in the city rose quickly. In addition, not all of the former residents of al-Shalālah had actually been provided with housing in al-Karāmah, further contributing to a growing shortage of low-income housing.[128] The problem could

---

[126] ACED, USAID and AECOM, *Skills Gap and Training Needs Analysis for Tourism and Supporting Services*, 15 July 2008, p. 3.
[127] ACED, USAID and AECOM, *Aqaba Community and Economic Development (ACED) Program – Community Development*, PowerPoint presentation, March 2010, slide 19.
[128] Debruyne, *Spatial Rearticulations of Statehood*, p. 194.

hardly be addressed through USAID's local community and neighbour-hood enhancement or corporate social responsibility projects. Already in 2003, the Bechtel report had both predicted this growing issue of housing affordability and questioned the likelihood of the kind of trickle-down effects initially forecasted by ASEZA officials:

> Housing affordability will be a major issue in the future in the ASEZ. Workers at the upper end of the income scale (managers, professionals, technicians) will have the incomes needed to purchase new homes. However, those in the lower income brackets will not be able to afford newly built housing units. Because the size of the housing demand is so much larger than the existing housing units, there will be very little trickle down housing available for workers in the lower salary ranges. If suitable living accommodations are to be provided in ASEZ, it will be necessary to undertake a subsidized low-income housing program.[129]

USAID's AZEM team was however rather sceptical of the desirability of such a low-income housing programme. While Amman-based staff of USAID Jordan believed that the Aqaba programmes directly reinforced the promotion of democratic values, the following condescending remarks in an unpublished concept paper developed for the management of ASEZA and ADC offer a striking example of the local USAID staff's perception of their work:

> Traditionally, low-income housing has been provided by the public sector. However, past experience shows that it has not been cost effective, if not counter productive, in that such facilities eventually become run down and infested with crime, drugs and other social ills. Moreover, tenants are invariably dissatisfied with the amenities provided by the government, regardless of how adequate they maybe [sic].[130]

The envisaged '"holistic" development of the ASEZ',[131] which the Bechtel report had mentioned as one of the reasons for ADC's establishment, had thus not only failed to materialise, but it also seems that it had never really been a genuine objective for the staff of ASEZA, ADC or USAID.

'The Culture of Jordanians'

Despite the absence of trickle-down effects, increasing income disparities, the growing gap between rich and poor, a lack of popular accountability

---

[129] Bechtel, *Draft Business Plan for the Aqaba Development Company*, economic projects for the ASEZ, appendix F, p. 31.
[130] AZEM, USAID and Nathan Associates, *ASEZA and ADC*, p. 8.
[131] Bechtel, *Draft Business Plan for the Aqaba Development Company*, executive summary, p. 3.

and an ever-advancing privatisation of public goods, space and property to the benefit of an affluent class of primarily external businessmen and investors, the US Embassy nevertheless insisted that ASEZA 'has proven itself to be a model for economic growth in Jordan'.[132] Referring to a number of macroeconomic benchmarks (among other things, the large amount of overall investment and GDP per capita growth at double the national rate) that fundamentally ignore the growing socio-economic disparities and the democratic unaccountability in the ASEZ, the US Embassy viewed what it called the transition of a 'once sleepy port town into a bustling tourist and commercial center'[133] as a major success.

While the US Embassy was fully aware of 'the disconnect between residents and both the governing structure and the economic opportunities ... [as well as] the conflict between haves and have nots', overcoming these issues was deemed simply to require the adoption of 'political and public relations' targets,[134] besides ASEZA's existing economic targets. This approach conveniently allowed the discursive preservation of the analytical separation between politics and economics, as suggested by liberal theory, and the related relegation of all negative effects of Aqaba's neoliberal transition into the sphere of political culture:

In the absence of effective channels for the airing and addressing of local grievances, this most economically advanced of Jordanian cities leaves its poorest residents with only traditional relationship-based tools. USAID-funded projects are helping to bridge this gap, but overcoming the political culture is proving to be a slow and difficult task.[135]

Such a view of course ignores that rather than a somehow inadequate political culture, or an insufficient marketisation, it was actually the unprotected integration of Aqaba into global capitalism that had both exacerbated existing vulnerabilities and created new dependencies. The effects of Aqaba's neoliberal transition were thus diametrically opposed to democratic ideals of socio-economic equality. And even if ASEZA might in future reintroduce democratic procedures, these would have practically no emancipatory and empowering potential, due to the extent to which formerly public assets have been privatised and matters of socio-economic development separated from that which is deemed to be 'people' issues.

---

[132] US Embassy Amman cable, 'Aqaba faces the challenges of growth'.
[133] US Embassy Amman cable, 'Developing Aqaba – the gateway to Jordan', 13 May 2007, *Wikileaks*, 07Amman2017.
[134] For both quotations see US Embassy Amman cable, 'Aqaba faces the challenges of growth'.
[135] US Embassy Amman cable, 'Aqaba faces the challenges of growth'.

While the establishment of ASEZA and ADC had created enormous financial value – in the sense of introducing formerly state-owned property and companies into the market – this had only been possible due to the total abandonment of public values of social equality and evenly distributed economic opportunity as governing principles. It is true that, despite operating as a private company, ADC is still government-owned and that a future 'value realization'[136] – as the corporate language of the Bechtel report puts it – would likely lead to substantial one-off profit for the public treasury. In 2003 Bechtel estimated the future value of ADC in 2013 to be between JD225 million and JD1,413 million.[137] Besides the substantial range of ADC's estimated value – indicating that the financial profit for the public treasury if it sold its shares would depend quite considerably on market developments far beyond the control of the Jordanian state – it is important to recall that the envisaged future complete privatisation of ADC would also mean the ultimate withdrawal of the Jordanian state as a public actor from the city of Aqaba.

A potential full privatisation in the future is unlikely to be of major concern to the population of Aqaba, however, as the transition to private sector management principals in the governance of the city had already occurred under government ownership (with the help of USAID, Bechtel and BearingPoint). Summing up, it is clear that Aqaba's integration into the world market occurred in a fundamentally uneven and unequal manner. Instead of the initially envisaged 50 per cent share of overall investment, by 2008 the tourism sector accounted for 70 per cent of all investment in the ASEZ (this does not take into account the $10 billion Marsa Zayed project).[138] The job market does not, therefore, provide the local population with many options beyond working in the hospitality sector as waiters, cleaners and the like, serving the affluent foreign tourists who can afford the luxury resorts of Saraya, Ayla Oasis, Tala Bay and Marsa Zayed. Fully aware of the mismatch between jobs on offer and those desired, USAID organised a number of 'career awareness' activities, in order to make sure that also the local population would realise its new place in the city.

Finally, despite the profusion of neoliberal reform, the latter had neither triggered any political liberalisation nor contributed to increasing socio-economic justice, equality or 'opportunity for all to benefit'. Quite the contrary, the neoliberal transition of Aqaba has so far led to a radical

---

[136] Bechtel, *Draft Business Plan for the Aqaba Development Company*, funding options, section 11, pp. 21–24.
[137] Bechtel, *Draft Business Plan for the Aqaba Development Company*, funding options, section 11, p. 23.
[138] US Embassy Amman cable, 'Aqaba development update'.

remaking of Jordanian sovereignty in the service of free trade and international business elites. Taken together, one may thus perhaps best characterise Aqaba's neoliberal transition, like Harvey, as a project aimed at reconstituting and/or reinforcing the class power of capitalist elites.[139] In Aqaba, the promotion of procedural democracy then amounts to little more than the desperate upholding of radically depleted ideals of democracy in a fundamentally undemocratic context of growing socio-economic injustice. The framing of neoliberal reform in a language of mutually reinforcing effects between democracy and economic growth then needs to be interpreted as primarily serving the purpose of morally legitimising exploitation and the further deepening of inequalities.

This chapter has explored the interaction of US and European efforts at 'democracy promotion' with the consolidation and further advance of neoliberalism in the context of Jordan. I have suggested that the two are sufficiently closely intertwined to justify the use of the term 'neoliberal democracy promotion'. Discussing the example of Aqaba's neoliberal transition, I have argued that such efforts at neoliberal 'democracy promotion' are part of a wider imperial project benefiting international business elites and the financial interests of the Jordanian regime. I have demonstrated that neoliberal reforms in Aqaba neither reinforce nor require forms of democratic accountability. Instead, the privatisation of formerly public goods and the marketisation of the social sphere only increased human vulnerabilities and left no space for the city's poor. While socio-economic rights became increasingly diluted and dependent on corporate goodwill, the benefits of the privatisation of state assets primarily accrued to Jordanian elites and a predominantly external stratum of investors and corporate entities.

As neoliberal 'democracy promotion' merely seeks to deepen market dynamics, it was shown to further increase the marginalisation of all human life that cannot readily be made to function as an economically relevant customer and consumer. Finally, I have suggested that the increasing insulation of economic development from human life – based on an analytical separation of politics and economics – is part of an imperial project aimed at the restoration of class power and the facilitation of deeply political and controversial projects. The models of neoliberal economic development that were being promoted have been shown to be either directly opposed to ideals of democracy or to empty them of practically all their emancipatory potential, as they operate based on various forms of violent exclusion, and/or exploitation. Just as the generation of exports in the QIZs depends on the exploitation of cheap

---

[139] Harvey, 'Neoliberalism as creative destruction'.

predominantly Southeast Asian labour, the creation of financial value in Aqaba was enabled by the relocation of the population of al-Shalālah.

Illustrating the deeply political rather than technical nature of Aqaba's neoliberal transition is the fact that it went hand in hand with an advance of specific security arrangements. As remarked in one US Embassy cable, the newly built port of Aqaba is 'capable of handling two U.S. cruiser-class warships or one U.S. JFK class aircraft carrier'.[140] This demonstrates a certain convergence of the infrastructure of the market on the one hand and that of US security interests on the other.[141] Changing the perspective from an investigation of economic support deemed to contribute to processes of democratisation to an exploration of security support deemed to contribute to democracy in Jordan, the following chapter will further investigate such linkages and forms of interaction. Overall, I suggest that both US security support and neoliberal 'democracy promotion' effectively reinforce a new type of neoliberal security state. While such a state can indeed also be democratic in form and procedure to some extent, the emancipatory potential of such procedures is drastically reduced, given the growing socio-economic inequalities and the deeply Orientalist descriptions of Jordanians themselves.

---

[140] US Embassy Amman cable, 'Scenesetter for the visit to Jordan of General Abizaid, Commander U.S. Central Command 28–29 March 2006', 28 March 2006, *Wikileaks*, 06Amman2234.

[141] See Khalili, L., 'The infrastructural power of the military: the geoeconomic role of the US Army Corps of Engineers in the Arabian Peninsula', *European Journal of International Relations*, Vol. 24, No. 4, 2018, pp. 911–933.

6   Securing Jordan

The Moralisation of Commercial Security and the Marketisation of Orientalism

> As for our common defense, we reject as false the choice between our safety and our ideals.[1]

The idea that democracy and security reinforce each other is one of the guiding principles for US support to Jordan.[2] The 2010 US National Security Strategy thus states that

> The United States supports the expansion of democracy and human rights abroad because governments that respect these values are most just, peaceful, and legitimate. We also do so because their success abroad fosters an environment that supports America's national interests.[3]

Accordingly, the 2013–2017 USAID country development strategy for Jordan defines its objective as to 'improve prosperity, accountability, and equality for a stable, democratic Jordan'.[4] Considering Jordan's remarkable level of authoritarian stability, the history of US security support to the country and the US efforts at 'democracy promotion' discussed in previous chapters, I investigate in this chapter the ways in which efforts at

---

[1] Obama, B. (President of the USA), Inaugural address, 20 January 2009, available at: https://obamawhitehouse.archives.gov/blog/2009/01/21/president-barack-obamas-inaugural-address.

[2] As the United States is by far the biggest source of security support for Jordan, I focus in this chapter on an analysis of US-Jordanian security cooperation and its effects on efforts at 'democracy promotion'. The argument that the primacy of train-and-equip programmes does not address the issue of lacking democratic control is however also valid in regard to EU-funded security support programmes, such as the €1.2 million 'Strengthening the Jordanian Gendarmerie' project launched in 2011, implemented by France and financed by the EU.

[3] President of the United States, National Security Strategy (Washington, DC: The White House, May 2010), p. 37.

[4] USAID, *Jordan Country Development Cooperation Strategy 2013–2017*, 2015, p. 12, available at: www.usaid.gov/jordan/documents/cdcs.

security support interact with ideals and conceptions of democracy, as well as Jordanian politics.[5]

Following the territorial advances of the so-called Islamic State in 2014 and 2015, Jordan, which already in 2011 ranked as the third largest recipient of US military aid,[6] quickly benefited from even more US assistance.[7] Research on the nature and effects of US-Jordanian military collaboration remains scarce, however. While Moore, Tell, Baylouny, Amara, Collombier and Marshall, among others, have provided analyses of the General Intelligence Directorate (GID),[8] Jordan's security sector,[9] of militarised liberalisation,[10] of Jordan's emerging military-industrial complex[11] and of the linkages between neoliberalism and Jordanian authoritarianism,[12] the processes and technologies involved in US-Jordanian military collaboration and the challenges they pose for democracy have so far been inadequately explored. Although Jordan is regularly dubbed 'an oasis of stability',[13] it is rarely asked what this stability means and how it is achieved. Considering claims about war's virtuous goals,[14] and about US military assistance making Jordan safe, secure and 'ready for democracy', I investigate in this chapter what exactly this stability and readiness entail for those living in and/or fleeing to Jordan. In other words, how does US-Jordanian military collaboration (re)produce highly problematic biopolitical judgements about the

---

[5] This chapter is in part based on Schuetze, B., 'Simulating, marketing, and playing war: US-Jordanian military collaboration and the politics of commercial security', *Security Dialogue*, Vol. 48, No. 5, 2017, pp. 431–450. See also Schuetze, B., 'Jordan's KASOTC: privatising anti-terror training', *Al Jazeera*, 17 July 2017, available at: www.aljazeera.com /indepth/opinion/2017/07/jordan-kasotc-privatising-anti-terror-training-170717074832 979.html.

[6] US Department of State, 'Foreign military financing account summary, 2015', available at: https://2009–2017.state.gov/t/pm/ppa/sat/c14560.htm.

[7] In 2016, US military aid to Jordan amounted to $463 million.

[8] Moore, P., 'A political-economy history of Jordan's intelligence directorate', unpublished article, 2018.

[9] Tell, N., 'Jordanian security sector governance: between theory and practice', Geneva Centre for Democratic Control of Armed Forces (DCAF), conference paper, July 2004.

[10] Baylouny, A.M., 'Militarizing welfare: neo-liberalism and Jordanian policy', *Middle East Journal*, Vol. 62, No. 2, Spring 2008, pp. 277–303.

[11] See Amara, J., 'Military industrialization and economic development: Jordan's defense industry', *Review of Financial Economics*, Vol. 17, No. 2, 2008, pp. 130–145; Marshall, S., 'Jordan's military-industrial complex and the Middle East's New Model Army'. *Middle East Research and Information Project*, Vol. 43, No. 267, 2013, pp. 42–45.

[12] Collombier, V., *Private Security: Not a Business Like Any Other* (Arab Reform Initiative, Thematic Studies: Arab Securitocracies and Security Sector Reform, 2011).

[13] USAID, *Strategic Statement Jordan 2007–2011*, undated, available at: http://pdf.usaid.gov /pdf_docs/Pdacn487.pdf.

[14] Der Derian, J., *Virtuous War: Mapping the Military-Industrial-Media-Entertainment Network* (New York: Routledge, 2009).

worth of human subjects?[15] And how does this fundamentally anti-democratic and divergent valuation of life help to further the entrenchment of processes of commercialisation and militarisation, as well as create deadly realities?

As I explore the politics of commercial security through the example of a US-funded military training centre in Jordan, my objective is twofold. First, I intend to contribute to filling the gap in the empirical research mentioned above. Second, I aim to discuss the ways in which the politics of commercial security and contemporary militarism at the King Abdullah II Special Operations Training Centre (KASOTC) operate via the simultaneous blurring of boundaries between business and security, public and private, real and simulated, and via the reinforcement of boundaries between those securing, those being secured and those being secured against. While this blurring of boundaries has the crucial effect of deepening old and establishing new commercial security markets by providing them, among other things, with a façade of virtuousness, this reinforcement of boundaries helps to determine the kind of intervention needed, where and by whom. Based on a biopolitical reading of the ways in which marginalised groups are constructed as invalid subjects of security or as security threats, I explore the construction of marketable images of 'the enemy' – that is, the marketisation of imagined moral hierarchies – as a central component in the interaction of processes of militarisation and commercialisation. I suggest that the politics of commercial security at KASOTC revolves around the hierarchical integration of different identity groups depending on their ability to market the deeply problematic conceptions of different value attached to their and/or other human lives. US-Jordanian military collaboration at KASOTC is then shown to be marked by a vivid interaction of governance through both market policies and moral politics.

This is highly relevant to a study of external attempts at 'democracy promotion' in Jordan, as the growing dominance of 'the market' in the country's security sector challenges 'dearly held notions of who can use force, when, where, how, against whom, and for what purposes',[16] and thus further reduces the level of public control. Also, the presentation of war as something to be played and experienced gradually replaces deliberative questions about war, which are key to any understanding of democracy, with a fundamentally anti-democratic interest in the consumption of war.[17] I argue that US security support has created a situation in which security support becomes business, and business an

---

[15] Berndtsson J. and Stern, M, 'Private security guards: authority, control and governance?', in: Abrahamsen, R. and Leander, A. (eds.) *Routledge Handbook of Private Security Studies* (New York: Routledge, 2016), p. 55.

[16] Berndtsson and Stern, 'Private security guards', p. 58.

act of securing Jordan. Within this process of securing Jordan, Jordanians increasingly appear either as security threats or as mere passive objects waiting to be secured. Just as KASOTC only simulates a Jordanian reality, for a significant part of the Jordanian population the security provided by the USA and its supposedly reinforcing effects on processes of democratisation are likewise of a simulated, rather than real, nature.

Taking my cue from Bilgin's critique of the Western-centrism of international security studies,[18] I inquire into the ways in which non-Western insecurities are produced, and investigate how these may result directly from, and be reinforced by, the marketisation of deeply Orientalist ways of knowing. I rely on the growing body of literature on commercial security, militarism and militarisation, which concerns itself with the normalisation of war.[19] While he refrains from using the term militarism, Der Derian provides another study of this normalisation of war in his seminal book *Virtuous War*, in which he argues, using the example of US war preparation and war-making, that contemporary war is ascending to the level of the virtuous. Discussing the US military's technological superiority, Der Derian describes the 'technical capability and ethical imperative to threaten and, if necessary, actualize violence from a distance'[20] and the associated virtualisation of the enemy as key dynamics behind the construction of 'Virtuous War'. With the deadly realities of war displaced from public sight,[21] it can be made to appear as a bloodless, humanitarian and hygienic undertaking[22] that is easily merged with entertainment,[23] business[24] and education.[25]

---

[17] See Stahl, R., *Militainment, Inc.: War, Media, and Popular Culture* (New York: Routledge, 2010), pp. 72, 140.

[18] Bilgin, P., 'The "Western-centrism" of security studies: "blind spot" or constitutive practice?', Security Dialogue, Vol. 41, No. 6, 2010, pp. 615–622.

[19] See for example Kuntsman, A. and Stein, R.L., Digital Militarism: Israel's Occupation in the Social Media Age (Stanford: Stanford University Press, 2015).

[20] Der Derian, *Virtuous War*, p. xxxi.

[21] See Der Derian, *Virtuous War*, p. 165, McSorley, K. (ed.), War and the Body: Militarisation, *Practice* and *Experience* (London: Routledge, 2013); Stahl, *Militainment*, p. 26; Higate, P., 'The private militarized and security contractor as geocorporeal actor', International Political Sociology, Vol. 6, No. 4, 2012, pp. 355–372.

[22] Der Derian, *Virtuous War*, p. xxxi.

[23] Stahl, *Militainment* and Stahl, R., 'Have you played the war on terror?', Critical Studies in Media Communication, Vol. 23, No. 2, 2006, pp. 112–130.

[24] Abrahamsen and Williams, M.C., 'Securing the city: private security companies and non-state authority in global governance', International Relations, Vol. 21, No. 2, 2007, pp. 237–253; Higate, 'The private militarized and security contractor as geocorporeal actor'.

[25] Stavrianakis, A. 'In arms' way: arms company and military involvement in education in the UK', ACME: An International E-Journal for Critical Geographies, Vol. 8, No. 3, 2009, pp. 505–520.

The turning of war into an interactive event to be consumed and played, rather than deliberated,[26] in combination with the simulation of 'Virtuous War' creates a new reality. In this reality, the reliance on a rhetoric of peace serves to morally justify the perpetual use of violence against identity groups perceived as security threats.[27] As a consequence, a number of researchers have emphasised the importance of critically investigating the kind of bio-political judgements concerning the worth of human subjects that distinguish between those who can play and consume war and those who must suffer its deadly realities.[28] Helpful in this regard is Amar's investigation of the ways in which certain identities are spotlighted as sources of insecurity, or 'hypervisibilized'.[29] While Amar links this to a radically new form of moralised human security governance, at KASOTC the problematisation of certain identities as sources of insecurity has itself become marketised, and thereby absorbed by the neoliberal governance paradigm that Amar claims is losing ground in the Global South.[30]

In short, while Amar suggests that the new human security paradigm governs 'through moral politics not market policies', I argue that US-Jordanian military collaboration at KASOTC operates through both the moralisation of market policies (providing commercialised security with an ethical imperative along the lines of Der Derian) and the marketisation of moral politics (deploying Amar's 'hypervisibilization' of certain identities as a means to create new markets). The case of KASOTC thus encourages us to question whether a clear line can be drawn between a 'new' human security and an 'old' neoliberal mode of governance. Further, considering that Der Derian's empirical focus in 'Virtuous War' is on military centres in the US and Europe – thereby giving an unfortunate impression of the Global South as the passive target of a virtuous war designed by others[31] – a study of US-Jordanian military collaboration at KASOTC promises interesting insight into the ways in

---

[26] Stahl, *Militainment.*   [27] Der Derian, *Virtuous War*, p. 42.

[28] See, for instance, Graham, S., 'Technologies of exception: urban warfare and US military technoscience', conference lecture at the Symposium 'Archipelago of Exceptions. Sovereignties of Extraterritoriality' CCCB, 10–11 November 2005, available at: www .publicspace.org/en/text-library/eng/b022-technologies-of-exception-urban-warfare-and-us-military-technoscience; Abrahamsen and Williams, 'Securing the city'; Eichler, M., 'Citizenship and the contracting out of military work: from national conscription to globalized recruitment', Citizenship Studies, Vol. 18, No. 6–7, 2014, pp. 600–614; Stahl, R., 'Life is war: the rhetoric of biomimesis and the future military', *Democratic Communiqué*, Vol. 26, No. 2, 2014, pp. 122–137.

[29] Amar, P., The Security Archipelago: Human-Security States, Sexuality Politics, and the End of Neoliberalism (London: Duke University Press, 2013), p. 17. See also Graham, 'Technologies of exception'.

[30] Amar, *The Security Archipelago*, p. 16.

[31] For a similar critique see Amar, *The Security Archipelago*, p. 20.

which the lines of separation reinforced by contemporary militarism do not follow clear Orientalist positionalities. As Orientalist fantasies are marketised and shown to be a central element of intersecting dynamics of commercialisation and militarisation, I suggest that a genuine critique of those biopolitical judgements necessarily needs to take place within a larger critique of the neoliberal economic logics that demand the creation of marketable images of 'the enemy'.

While the financing of KASOTC, according to *Jane's*, the 'world's largest special forces training facility of its kind',[32] constitutes only one example of US-Jordanian security collaboration, the official confirmation that it is 'the centrepiece'[33] of US-Jordanian counterterrorism and intelligence cooperation demonstrates that an in-depth analysis of it also allows for a better understanding of US-Jordanian security cooperation at large.

'Security and Democracy: One Reinforces the Other'

> [E]verywhere where the notion of security becomes omnipotent . . . it is the system of deterrence that grows, and around it grows the historical, social, and political desert.[34]

During his 2012 appearance on *The Daily Show* with Jon Stewart, King Abdullah II had only to briefly list Jordan's neighbouring states for both host and audience to immediately conclude that in Jordan the very nature of politics was somehow inherently different. The powerful effect of this contextualisation and framing of Jordan within an environment of chaos and instability allowed King Abdullah II to portray himself throughout the remainder of the show 'as the sage and patient monarch trying to guide his people through the treacherous waters of democracy'.[35] The very same primacy of security concerns is also reflected in statements by 'democracy promoters' and diplomats working in the country. 'Democracy promoter' Robert described Jordan as 'a tough environment' and reminded me that 'this is a complicated part of the world. Lots of people have died here',[36] while diplomat Oliver told me that the 'threat of

---

[32] Oliver, D., 'World's largest special forces training centre unveiled in Jordan', *IHS Jane's, International Defence Digest, Jordan*, 5 June 2009.

[33] US Embassy Amman cable, 'Scenesetter for the visit to Jordan of Lieutenant General Buchanan, Commander 9th Air Force and U.S. Central Command Air Forces', 12 January 2006, *Wikileaks*, 06Amman234.

[34] Baudrillard, J., *Simulacra and Simulation*, tr. Glaser, S. (Ann Arbor: University of Michigan Press, 1994), p. 33.

[35] Kifah and Jennifer (pseudonym), 'Jon Stewart's theater of the absurd', *Jadaliyya*, 2 October 2012.

[36] Interview with Robert, 'democracy promoter' working in Jordan, Amman, 24 September 2012.

terrorism is considered high' in Jordan and that diplomats 'get danger pay here'.[37]

Framing Jordanian politics along these lines effectively allows 'democracy promoters' to avoid having to think through what democracy would actually mean in the country, as the predominance of security concerns enables the constant postponement of promises of democratisation to a seemingly attainable but yet distant future. As short-term security concerns remain paramount, 'democracy promoters' conveniently need not reflect on the potential long-term consequences of uncomfortable facts, such as how the practicalities of an imagined Jordanian democracy could potentially conflict with East-Bank Jordanian ideals of self-determination.

Despite this, few of the interviewed employees of Western(-funded) institutions active in Jordan went as far as admitting that the extent to which security concerns permeate Jordanian politics renders efforts at 'democracy promotion' inherently limited. One 'democracy promoter' stated that while working in the country, considering the extent to which the Jordanian regime maintains a tight grip on civil society, she had not known how to spend the available budget. She further apparently told her supervisor that 'you pay me to fail'.[38] The case of the Foundation for the Future (FFF) is also illustrative. It had its headquarters in Amman, but during the period of my research did not fund any major project in the country due to fears of coming under pressure from the regime if it tried to support local efforts at democratisation, and doubts about the strength of local NGOs and their alleged independence from the regime. A Western diplomat who had spent a considerable time in the country was similarly aware of the predominance of security concerns, and openly stated that 'we ask ourselves whether it is still worth the effort to put money in democracy promotion projects'.[39] Along the same lines, an employee of a Western-funded NGO explained: 'I don't feel guilty [about] not funding democracy activities here. We're not missing a big opportunity'. He added that 'if you do democracy promotion properly, it creates backlashes in stability', further remarking that 'Jordan is more complicated. If you make a real democracy, it means they [Palestinian-Jordanians] take over – they already control the economy'.[40]

[37] Interview with Oliver, Western diplomat based in Jordan, Amman, 29 January 2013.
[38] Interview with Helen, 'democracy promoter' with work experience in Jordan, Washington, DC, 30 May 2013.
[39] Interview with Thomas, Western diplomat based in Jordan, Amman, 22 November 2012.
[40] Interview with Philippe, employee of a Western-funded NGO based in Jordan, Amman, 14 March 2013.

The vast majority of the 'democracy promoters' interviewed could not, however, see any fundamental contradictions in their work. Instead, they widely referred to images of democracy and security as balancing, or as reinforcing, each other. Michael insisted that 'in theory, there should not necessarily be a contradiction [in] having [both] security and development interests'. He further said that only 'if a regime one is trying to help sees a contradiction then there is one' [*sic*]. He thus portrayed possible inconsistencies as being fundamentally external to the project of 'democracy promotion' itself, as security interests are deemed to 'affect public statements, but not projects on the ground'.[41] 'Democracy promoter' Adam argued that

it is important to continue [to] promote democracy to maintain internal stability ... As [long] as you maintain the balance you can move ahead ... If [the] balance was more security and no democracy it would be no balance and there would not be peace – like in Egypt or Syria ... The [Kantian idea of] democratic peace is correct.[42]

This image of 'democracy promotion' as an equilibrium-seeking project raises the uncomfortable but important question of whether 'too much' democracy would – contrary to what is suggested by the democratic peace hypothesis – actually ultimately be threatening to security.

As democracy is thus implicitly recognised as a potential threat to stability, the project of 'democracy promotion' turns into a security programme. Accordingly, it was not difficult for Adam to openly acknowledge that '[o]f course. Western stability interests and Jordanian democracy contradict each other'.[43] Within the perceived balance of democracy and security, 'democracy promotion' is effectively subordinated to security concerns. 'Democracy promoter' Robert explained:

I think the reason you might see protests die down a little is people are saying, 'Hey, we have got to keep stability for now, OK'. So I'm not justifying a slow-down. I'm trying to understand what people themselves are saying ... Now – this isn't going to go on forever. Syria is going to resolve itself sooner or later – maybe not sooner. And Jordan is going to be faced with the same unrepresentative political system. It's not a representative political system – we all know that. It's not a democracy. It's a quasi-democracy. Freedom House says it's not free. We know that. That's why we're here ... So should the West be pushing really hard? You know, I think the West ... I think, particularly with Jordan, we should be

---

[41] Interview with Michael, 'democracy promoter' working in Jordan, Amman, 21 November 2012.
[42] Interview with Adam, 'democracy promoter' working in Jordan, Amman, 14 October 2012.
[43] Interview with Adam, 'democracy promoter' working in Jordan, Amman, 14 October 2012.

providing support, we should be looking for openings and the policymakers at the top level are going to have to decide what priority this is going to take at this time. I'm not going to say democracy promotion should be number one.[44]

Just as Robert simply left the question of possible contradictions between security and democracy to 'the policymakers at the top level', other diplomats and 'democracy promoters' interviewed also failed to see contradictions or refused to admit them as it would undermine their presence and ethics, and instead they largely saw interests of security and democracy as mutually reinforcing. Regarding Jordanian security services' handling of protests in late 2012, and considering the US training that they receive, diplomat Oliver explained that the 'police handled protests very well . . . I don't know, but [I] like to think that [the] US can take credit for that'.[45]

Nevertheless, 'democracy promoters' working in Jordan are acutely aware of the extent to which the Jordanian security establishment represents an obstacle to their everyday efforts at 'democracy promotion'. Robert consequently argued that what is required is 'a huge process of moving security out of politics . . . if they want to move to parliamentary government'.[46] This succinctly reflects the view expressed by many US 'democracy promoters' in Jordan, that the security concerns of the Jordanian regime are problematic, while US security support and security interests are instead seen as reinforcing of democracy. Michael, for instance, stated that 'without security interests, there would not be a democracy and governance portfolio or, if at all, then only with a $2 million budget and not $20 million as it is now'.[47]

'Democracy promoters' like Robert and Michael thus viewed the role of US security support to Jordan, significantly, as helping to replace the 'undemocratic' interests of the Jordanian security establishment with the 'pro-democratic' ones of the US security apparatus. As Michael explained, 'it is critical if [a] former *mukhābarāt* [Arabic for 'secret service'] guy goes to the NCHR [National Centre for Human Rights] . . . But if a former CIA guy moves to democracy promotion . . . '.[48] The image conveyed here is one in which US 'democracy promoters', US security interests and Jordanian NGOs and human rights organisations all stand

---

[44] Interview with Robert, 'democracy promoter' working in Jordan, Amman, 24 September 2012.

[45] Interview with Oliver, Western diplomat based in Jordan, Amman, 29 January 2013.

[46] Interview with Robert, 'democracy promoter' working in Jordan, Amman, 24 September 2012.

[47] Interview with Michael, 'democracy promoter' working in Jordan, Amman, 21 November 2012.

[48] Interview with Michael, 'democracy promoter' working in Jordan, Amman, 24 January 2013.

united on the side of democracy. Asked about the possibility of more fundamental contradictions, Washington, DC-based US Department of State (DoS) official John explained the wider US approach to Jordan:

[I]n terms of security, our view of things is that we want to use [Jordan] as a platform to build and project security from – like in Germany and Japan after the Second World War . . . Building democracy in these countries was integral to this . . . Similarly, in Jordan, there's a long process of building democracy . . . It's not antagonistic in our mind.[49]

The strong dominance of security concerns has led many Jordanians to see freedom and stability as mutually contradictory, however: 'It's either freedom or stability – [on the] radio it is presented as such'.[50] Along the same lines, political activist Zaid explained that

the Jordanian regime over the past twelve years has been trying to convince the people – and it successfully convinced people – that security in Jordan . . . is pretty much a gift. It's a royal gift to the people . . . You're going to have to appreciate it and give up democracy because you have security.[51]

As security concerns and appreciation of this 'royal gift' permeate almost every sphere of public life, there is little need for the regime itself to be overtly active in order to press this dichotomised agenda. According to Zaid, the secret service and the police 'don't need to fund an organisation. They get it for free. People believe in the agenda of the intelligence [service]. They volunteer even'.[52]

The Amman hotel bombings in 2005 were of instrumental importance in furthering this 'security first' agenda, and in coalescing Jordanians' appreciation of (public) security, the regime's concerns for (regime) security and US security concerns related to the 'war against terror'. In a 2006 US Embassy cable, then US ambassador David Hale explained that the

excellent collaborative relations [between the USA and Jordan in the war against terror] . . . ha[ve] been further strengthened in the aftermath of the suicide bombing attacks at three hotels in Amman on 9 November 2005. Some here call the attacks 'Jordan's 9–11'. Jordan's population united behind the King's strong condemnation of the attacks and his intent to strike back. Public opinion shifted dramatically against UBL [Usama Bin Laden] and Zarqawi, who previously enjoyed favorable ratings, though public opinion remains opposed to

---

[49] Interview with John, US DoS official, Washington, DC, 18 June 2013.
[50] Interview with Bushra, Jordanian employee of a Western 'democracy promotion' NGO active in Jordan, Amman, 9 October 2012.
[51] Interview with Zaid, political activist, Amman, 17 October 2012.
[52] Interview with Zaid, political activist, Amman, 17 October 2012.

U.S. actions in Iraq. This may give the GoJ [Government of Jordan] increased
leverage in gaining internal support for security measures.[53]

Due to its internalisation by a large part of the Jordanian public, the
security first agenda – pursued by the Jordanian regime, reinforced by
US security interests and to varying degrees also endorsed by 'democracy promoters' – appears to represent the Jordanian people's democratic will. Discussing the slow or inexistent progress of Jordanian
democratisation, 'democracy promoter' Adam remarked that 'people
do appreciate that there is no violence',[54] thus suggesting that as
Jordanians appear to be asking for security first, the lack of actual
democratisation becomes a somewhat lesser concern. With security
a matter of concern for 'democracy promoters', 'democracy promotion'
itself transforms into a security programme, as ideals of democracy and
security increasingly seem to become one and the same. This conceptual
blurring became obvious in DoS official James's response to a question
about the interaction of US security and democracy interests in Jordan.
He maintained that '[s]ecurity and democracy – we've got to do both of
them at the same time … One reinforces the other … If they're not
secure and stable, everything else goes out of the window'.[55] It is
important to note that such claims about democracy and security
being mutually reinforcing rest on a fundamental disregard for the
ways in which external provision of security support is actually
undertaken.

Instead of attempting to restructure control over the security sector and
roll back the military's prerogatives – which Diamond describes as
a necessity for the consolidation of democracy[56] – or containing the
regime's use of the state's security apparatus, US-Jordanian security
cooperation effectively takes the form of direct regime support.
Accordingly, individuals active in the security sector are much more
doubtful about supposedly mutually reinforcing effects between 'democracy promotion' and security assistance. The lack of communication
between the two fields already indicates that the effects of 'democracy
promotion' and security support might be much less aligned than many
'democracy promoters' typically like to assume.

---

[53] US Embassy Amman cable, 'Scenesetter for the Conus visit of General Khalid Sarayreh',
8 June 2006, *Wikileaks*, 06Amman4124.
[54] Interview with Adam, 'democracy promoter' working in Jordan, Amman, 14 October
2012.
[55] Interview with James, US DoS official, Washington, DC, 18 June 2013.
[56] Diamond, L. Developing Democracy: Toward Consolidation (Baltimore: Johns
Hopkins University Press, 1999), p. 113.

Despite the lack of communication with their counterparts in the sphere of security support,[57] most Western 'democracy promoters' and diplomats either could not 'see any discrepancies'[58] between 'democracy promotion' and security interests, thought that security interests 'positively affect democracy promotion'[59] or explained that the security focus of Western states is 'both an enabling and a constraining factor' for 'democracy promotion' in Jordan.[60] Those interviewed and active in the field of US-Jordanian security cooperation, however, were decidedly more sceptical of such assertions. Discussing US 'democracy promotion' in the Middle East, Jack, an American employee of the US-funded Special Forces training centre discussed later in this chapter, explained that

democracy is spelt differently wherever you might go . . . So for the US to try to impose democracy as defined . . . by the US, to me is difficult, because not all nations understand it, nor will they embrace it . . . I mean, [under] Mubarak – as bad as he was – Egypt was calm. [Under] Gaddafi, Libya was calm . . . US efforts at democratising these areas have not been very successful . . . [I]n many cases, these countries in this part of the world have had some sort of conflict for thousands of years . . . Their history goes back so far – you're not going to change it. But you can maybe moderate it . . . that's the term. Sometimes I don't understand what the hell we're doing.[61]

Jack's statement is remarkably similar to the ideas of his best-known predecessor in the field of Western security support/cooperation with Jordan, the British commander of the Arab Legion between 1939 and 1956, John Bagot Glubb. Also expressing his doubts about Western claims of moral superiority, Glubb asserted that '[t]he West . . . does not enjoy any generally admitted preëminence in morals; consequently attempts to introduce Western standards of morality into other countries is likely to provoke opposition'.[62] At this point it is important to note that

[57] Upon my inquiring whether it would be possible to meet a Defense Attaché Officer (DAO), I was told that 'DAO doesn't like to meet with non-military', which of course also includes all US staff engaged in 'democracy promotion'. According to one US Embassy employee, who preferred to remain anonymous, the US Embassy in Amman has approximately 700 employees, most of the US staff (according to him in total around 100) being DAOs responsible for the coordination of US training and the provision of equipment to the Jordanian security services, among other things.

[58] Interview with Stefan, 'democracy promoter' working in Jordan, Amman, 29 January 2013.

[59] Interview with Oliver, Western diplomat based in Jordan, Amman, 29 January 2013.

[60] Interview with Michael, 'democracy promoter' working in Jordan, Amman, 21 November 2012.

[61] Interview with Jack, KASOTC staff member, ViaGlobal, Yajūz, 26 March 2013.

[62] J.B. Glubb, quoted in: Massad, Jo.A., *Colonial Effects: The Making of National Identity in Jordan* (New York: Columbia University Press, 2001), p. 113.

the argument underlying the above two quotations (that is, that 'Arabs are not ready for democracy') is merely the flipside of the argument that 'Arabs need us to democratise them'.

Just as the strong criticism of 'democracy promotion' by individuals active in the security sector suggests that security support may not be quite as reinforcing of 'democracy promotion' as argued by 'democracy promoters', some of the unintended consequences of security support to Jordan further increase such doubts. In some ways it thus seems that parts of the Jordanian security sector, with which the US military cooperates so closely in order to be better placed to respond to regional security threats, are ironically themselves viewed by the US as a security threat. A 2007 US Embassy cable indicated that US representatives were concerned about the Jordanian military's position *vis-à-vis* the regime itself. The cable elaborated on incidents in 2006, when 'senior JAF officers, including general officers, openly criticized King Abdullah in front of official Americans'.[63] According to the cable, the remarks 'were notable as the first time in recent memory that Jordanian soldiers have questioned their monarch within earshot of official Americans'.[64] The tensions between the Jordanian regime and parts of its security establishment became even more obvious when in May 2010, in an unprecedented move, the National Committee of Military Veterans publicly accused the regime of trying to solve the Palestinian question at the expense of East Bank Jordanians.[65] Strongly criticising Queen Rania – herself of Palestinian origin – and other high-level Palestinian-Jordanians, the military veterans' open letter raised major questions regarding the loyalty of the organisation, which comprises 140,000 ex-soldiers, to the regime itself.[66]

In light of this incident, one well-connected 'democracy promoter', who had previously worked in Jordan, went as far as to state that in Jordan 'the most dangerous part of society is these retired military association guys'.[67] The idea that US support to Jordanian security services would both stabilise and 'prepare' Jordan for democracy is thus revealed as an illusion, as parts of the Jordanian security sector itself seem to be much more concerned with guarding and protecting Jordanian national identity

[63] US Embassy Amman cable, 'Jordan's security services', 7 March 2007, *Wikileaks*, 07Amman1031.

[64] US Embassy Amman cable, 'Jordan's security services'.

[65] National Committee of Retired Army Personnel, 'Statement on defending state, identity against Israel's "alternative homeland" – retired army', *Ammonnews*, 5 March 2010, available at: http://en.ammonnews.net/article.aspx?articleNO=7683.

[66] Vogt, A., 'Jordan's eternal promise of reform', Internationale Politik und Gesellschaft, No. 4, 2011, p. 63.

[67] Interview with Helen, 'democracy promoter' with work experience in Jordan, Washington, DC, 30 May 2013.

than with maintaining 'stability', which may ultimately be highly contradictory.

Most of the 'democracy promoters' interviewed were aware of the extent to which the Jordanian security services constituted an obstacle to their work. Adam admitted that 'if you strengthen the security apparatus, you close space'.[68] Emphasising professionalism as a value in and of itself was one way to overlook such contradictions. Helen thus stressed that 'Jordan is better off having a professional military ... They don't set up roadblocks'.[69] The technocratic job of training and equipping the Jordanian police, military and secret service can thus be described as unproblematic and as fully compatible with a wider 'democracy promotion' agenda. This, however, hinges significantly on seeing repression as purely a result of a lack of awareness of democratic principles. However, tight control of civil society actors, repression of political activists and direct intervention in Jordanian politics are much more central to the role of the Jordanian security services in the Jordanian state and society. Instead of reinforcing processes of democratisation, US security support for the Jordanian security apparatus thus directly supports Jordanian authoritarianism.

The Jordanian Security Services

> If the [democratic] façade wasn't there, we'd still support [Jordan]. We also support Bahrain ... But I don't want to minimise the commitment to democracy promotion. It is a real objective, but stability takes precedence when ranking objectives ... We would support them up until they do something horrific, and sometimes they do something horrific ... But you can strengthen institutions and parties.[70]

In August 2014, King Abdullah II made an important effort to 'mov[e] security out of politics', a step which the previously quoted 'democracy promoter' Robert described as a necessity for processes of democratisation in the country. In what the king characterised as the beginning of 'a crucial new phase of reforms',[71] he directed the Jordanian government to expand the authority of the Independent

---

[68] Interview with Adam, 'democracy promoter' working in Jordan, Amman, 14 October 2012.

[69] Interview with Helen, 'democracy promoter' with work experience in Jordan, Washington, DC, 30 May 2013.

[70] Interview with Michael, 'democracy promoter' working in Jordan, Amman, 21 November 2012.

[71] King Abdullah II, letter to Prime Minister Ensour, official translation, Amman, 13 August 2014. The complete letter can be found in *Jordan Times*, 'His Majesty directs gov't to activate Defence Ministry, expand IEC's role', 16 January 2015, available at:

Election Commission (IEC) to include the management of municipal elections, and to activate the Ministry of Defence (MoD) – a position that since 1970 has been inseparable from that of the prime minister. In response to the king's directives, then Prime Minister Abdullah Ensour implemented two constitutional amendments with the support of parliament: first, the expansion of the role of the IEC, and second, granting the king exclusive authority to appoint the chairman of the Joint Chiefs of Staff (commander of the army) and the director of the GID, in order to ensure that both 'remain professional and apolitical, as they have always been known to be'.[72] While the king in practice already appointed the two positions – upon prior nomination by the prime minister – the constitutional amendments were widely recognised as an attempt to take security- and military-related matters 'out of politics'.

This move is in many ways representative of the kind of reforms carried out by the regime, as it simultaneously appears to be an act of both political liberalisation and political de-liberalisation. The amendments thus opened the way for 'fair and transparent' future elections and a possible parliamentary government (until now the king has appointed the cabinet in consultation with the prime minister), while at the same time emptying such procedural steps of great parts of their democratic substance. If a political party is ever to form a parliamentary government, the two most important positions in the Jordanian security sector would still remain beyond its remit.

The king's insistence on being the sole person responsible for the appointment of these two positions, the commander of the army and the director of the GID, points to two fundamental characteristics of the Jordanian security sector: the lack of civilian and parliamentary oversight and control and the deeply political and crucial role the sector plays both as support base for the regime and as protector of Jordanian nationalism. Instead of limiting the regime's use of its security services, or increasing the security sector's accountability to the Jordanian people, US security support to Jordan draws the country into a subcontractor-like role within regional US imperial strategy, and directly reinforces deeply problematic processes of militarisation and commercialisation that only further reduce the chances of popular control over the country's security sector.

---

www.jordantimes.com/news/local/his-majesty-directs-gov%E2%80%99t-activate-defence-ministry-expand-iec%E2%80%99s-role.

[72] Prime Minister Ensour, letter to King Abdullah II, official translation, Amman, 13 August 2014. The complete letter can be found in *Jordan Times*, 'His Majesty directs gov't to activate Defence Ministry, expand IEC's role'.

The latter primarily consists of the Jordanian Armed Forces (JAF); the GID; the Public Security Directorate (PSD), which is Jordan's national police force; the Gendarmerie, which is a militarised police force responsible for riot control and the security of diplomatic missions; and the Special Operations Forces, which were headed by King Abdullah II 1993–1999. It is worth mentioning the King Abdullah Design and Development Bureau (KADDB), which was created in 1999 as an independent government entity within the JAF and effectively constitutes the latter's military-industrial arm. By 2010, the KADDB was operating as a limited private shareholding company with a turnover of over $100 million and expected to reach $300–400 million within two years.[73] In the words of its then chairman, '[u]nfortunately, when there is more conflict, we become more active and make more money'.[74]

While, in theory, Jordan's security sector comes under civil and parliamentary control, in practice all authority lies with the king. Despite the director of the GID reporting in principle to the prime minister, and the PSD being linked to the Ministry of Interior (MoI), both are in reality accountable only to the king, who, according to the constitution, also acts as supreme commander of the armed forces.[75] The KADDB board of directors reports directly to the private office of the king through the head of the JAF.[76] The limited role of civilian and parliamentary oversight is further exacerbated by the absence of a parliamentary committee specifically tasked with overseeing the security sector, by the annual defence budget being presented to parliament as a block item and by the untraceability of the GID budget in the state budget.[77] Further, as remarked by Tell, 'the fact that most security procurements are externally funded by foreign aid limits the role that the parliament is able to play'.[78] Given the lack of any meaningful civilian oversight, US support for the Jordanian security services reinforces the fundamentally undemocratic notion that Jordanian sovereignty ultimately lies with the king. In 2017, Jordan's

---

[73] Marcopolis, 'Largest real estate developer in Jordan', interview with Dr Moayad Samman, 8 November 2010, available at: www.marcopolis.net/largest-real-estate-developer-in-jordan.htm.

[74] Marcopolis, 'Largest real estate developer in Jordan'.

[75] Tell, 'Jordanian security sector governance', pp. 5, 8.

[76] Tell, 'Jordanian security sector governance', p. 4. For more information on KADDB see Debruyne, P., *Spatial Rearticulations of Statehood: 'Jordan's Geographies of Power under Globalization'* (Ghent: Ghent University, PhD thesis, 2014), in particular p. 317. Also see Amara, 'Military industrialization and economic development', pp. 130–145.

[77] Tell, 'Jordanian security sector governance', pp. 9–10.

[78] Tell, 'Jordanian security sector governance', p. 18.

defence budget reached a total of JD2.3 billion (approximately $3.3billion) and represented approximately 28 per cent of total public spending.[79]

The impressive size of the Jordanian security sector, which has been dominated by East Bank Jordanians since 1970/1971,[80] is closely related to the integral role played by the Jordanian army in the making of the Jordanian state. In this regard, Vatikiotis goes as far as to say that the army effectively created the country.[81] As the 'security sector in Jordan perceives itself as the guardian, protector, and stronghold of Jordanian nationalism in the face of a demographic or political Palestinian takeover',[82] as Tell argued, and is thus of crucial importance for the stability and perceived legitimacy of the Hashemite monarchy, it was the only sector that continued to grow in times of structural adjustment and economic crisis.[83] As the onset of economic liberalisation increasingly marginalised the regime's traditional pillar of support – the East Bank population, for whom identification as 'Jordanian' was often closely intertwined with state employment[84] – the militarisation of economic liberalisation represented the most practical way for the regime to ensure the future of Jordanian authoritarianism.[85]

Aided by substantial US military financing, the Jordanian regime was thus able to gradually replace its former support base with a strengthened military that had previously only constituted a part of that base. Considering the Jordanian security sector's dependence on US funding, which is again closely linked to regional instability, it is understandable that Baylouny should describe the potential for regional peace and a reduction of the military's size and the country's foreign aid as 'a threat to Jordan's stability'.[86] The Jordanian security services are then best understood as fulfilling a hybrid role as provider of employment opportunities for

[79] Central Bank of Jordan, *Annual Report 2017 [at-Taqrīr as-sanawīy 2017]*, p. 104, available at: www.cbj.gov.jo/EchoBusV3.0/SystemAssets/5c395f60-ea7f-4da5-8897-d046f33b75 f4.pdf.

[80] Abu-Odeh, A., Jordanians, Palestinians & the Hashemite Kingdom in the Middle East Peace Process (Washington, DC: United States Institute of Peace Press, 1999), p. 51.

[81] Vatikiotis, P.J., Politics and the Military in Jordan: A Study of the Arab Legion 1921–1957 (London: Frank Cass & Co., 1967), p. 137.

[82] Tell, 'Jordanian security sector governance', p. 15. See also National Committee of Retired Army Personnel, 'Statement on defending state, identity against Israel's "alternative homeland"'.

[83] Baylouny, 'Militarizing welfare', p. 301.

[84] Brand, L.A., 'Palestinians and Jordanians: a crisis of identity', *Journal of Palestine Studies*, Vol. 24, No. 4, Summer 1995, p. 48.

[85] Baylouny, 'Militarizing welfare', p. 303.

[86] Baylouny, 'Militarizing welfare', p. 303. See also, Moore, 'A political-economy history of Jordan's intelligence directorate', p. 10.

economically marginalised East Bankers, as guardian of Jordanian nationalism and as a protector of state and regime against internal and external threats. In a leaked US Embassy cable the deputy chief of mission in Amman described the role of the GID as follows:

Charged with regime security and stability, GID seeks to monitor all forms of communication in the country, track political movements and religious organizations, and monitor the presence and activities of foreigners. GID disrupts what are deemed as anti-regime activities through the use of threats, harassment, detention/arrest, and prosecution.[87]

It is difficult to overestimate the extent to which the GID controls and intervenes in Jordanian politics and society. The former head of the GID, Muhammad Raqqad, publicly acknowledged rigging the 2007 and 2010 elections.[88] Beyond attending events organised by local and international NGOs (such as the political parties fair discussed in Chapter 2), the intelligence services are also directly linked to select NGOs. Further, political activists are regularly threatened or, depending on the intelligence agenda, directly encouraged to participate in protests against the government.

The intelligence services are also known to check the appointment of every university professor, ambassador and important editor.[89] A *New York Times* article quotes the former head of the GID and MP Mahmoud Kharabsheh as saying that

[s]ome Parliament members allow the mukhabarat [Arabic for 'intelligence'] to intervene in how they vote because they depend on them for help in getting reelected . . . They enter into 90 percent of the political decisions in this country . . . It's a carrot and stick . . . They tell the M.P.s that whatever they want in the future, they will support them. It is well understood that they will turn against any M.P. who fails to do what they ask.[90]

Moreover, military-dominated state security courts regularly charge political activists under terrorism provisions, and try protestors and journalists accused of subverting the system of government or insulting the king.[91]

---

[87] US Embassy Amman cable, 'Jordan's security services'.

[88] *Dunyā al-Waṭan*, 'Raqqad acknowledges the illegitimacy of MPs – 2007 and 2010 elections forged' [*I'tirāfāt al-bāshā al-Raqqād tuṭīḥ bi-sharʿīyat an-nuwwāb . . . al-intikh ābāt fī-l-ʿāmain 2007 wa 2010 muzawwarah*], 19 December 2011, available at: www .alwatanvoice.com/arabic/content/print/229399.html.

[89] MacFarquhar, N., 'Heavy hand of the secret police impeding reform in Arab world', *New York Times*, 14 November 2005, available at: www.nytimes.com/2005/11/14/world/ middleeast/heavy-hand-of-the-secret-police-impeding-reform-in-arab-world.html.

[90] M. Kharabsheh, quoted in: MacFarquhar, 'Heavy hand of the secret police impeding reform in Arab world'.

[91] See, among others, Human Rights Watch, World Report 2013 (New York: Human Rights Watch, 2013), pp. 563–564. In November 2014 the deputy head of the Muslim Brotherhood, Zaki Bani Irsheid, was arrested after he had criticised the UAE on Facebook.

In a 2010 report the UN Committee against Torture accused the GID and the PSD 'of a widespread and routine practice of torture and ill-treatment of detainees'.[92] In addition, state security courts and military tribunals shield security personnel alleged to be responsible for human rights violations from legal accountability, to the extent that a UN mission in 2006 noted 'total impunity for torture and ill-treatment'.[93] A 2006 report by Amnesty International focusing on the GID described it as 'the primary instrument of abuse of political detainees'.[94] Finally, several reports suggest the existence of a secret CIA detention facility in the al-Jafr prison in the southern Jordanian desert.[95]

While the US DoS' *Jordan 2013 Human Rights Report* criticises 'mistreatment and allegations of torture by security and government officials with impunity',[96] it is important to note that US cooperation with the Jordanian security agencies being criticised is extremely close. By 2009 the USA was conducting more than twenty joint exercises annually with Jordanian forces,[97] who not only consult with the USA regarding all their international arms transfers,[98] but even accept CIA personnel being 'virtually embedded'[99] at GID headquarters, which the CIA liaison officer in Amman is free to access unescorted.[100] In addition to direct secret financial assistance to the GID,[101] a US DoS report also notes that in 2006 alone 300

---

[92] UN Committee against Torture, *Concluding Observations of the Committee against Torture – Jordan*, 44th session, 26 April–14 May 2010, p. 1.

[93] Nowak, M., *Report of the Special Rapporteur on Torture and Other Cruel, Inhuman or Degrading Treatment or Punishment – Mission to Jordan* (United Nations: Human Rights Council, 5 January 2007), p. 5.

[94] Amnesty International, Jordan: 'Your Confessions Are Ready for You to Sign': Detention and Torture of Political Suspects (London: Amnesty International, 23 July 2006), p. 3, available at: www.amnesty.org/en/documents/MDE16/005/2006/fr/.

[95] See for instance Pearlstein, D. and Patel, P., Behind the Wire: An Update to Ending Secret Detentions (New York: Human Rights First, 2005), p. 10.

[96] US DoS, Jordan 2013 Human Rights Report (Washington, DC: US DoS, Bureau of Democracy, Human Rights and Labor, 2013), p. 1.

[97] US Embassy Amman cable to Washington, DC, 'Jordan-U.S. security dialogues', 25 November 2009, *Wikileaks*, 09Amman2579.

[98] US Embassy Amman cable to Washington, DC, 'Scenesetter for the Conus visit of General Khalid Sarayreh'.

[99] Former CIA official quoted in: Silverstein, K., 'U.S. partnership with Jordan was targeted', *Los Angeles Times*, 12 November 2005, available at: www.seattletimes.com/nation-world/us-partnership-with-jordan-was-targeted/.

[100] Warrick, J., 'Jordan emerges as key CIA counterterrorism ally', *Washington Post*, 4 January 2010, available at: www.washingtonpost.com/wp-dyn/content/article/2010/01/03/AR2010010302063.html.

[101] Silverstein, 'U.S. partnership with Jordan was targeted'.

Jordanians participated in the US Counterterrorism Fellowship Program, which aims at strengthening bilateral relations with Jordan

by exposing members of its military to democratic principles and ... rais[ing] awareness and respect for human rights ... Additionally, the ... Program taught the country's military personnel how to combat terrorism while respecting the rule of law, human rights, and civil rights.[102]

While US security support to Jordan is claimed to contribute to processes of democratisation, the primary focus is clearly on technical train-and-equip programmes that do nothing to change Jordanian security services' role as a principal barrier to processes of democratisation in the country. The close US-Jordanian relationship – in 2006 the Jordanian government first presented its draft strategic defence review to the US military, before formally presenting it to the king[103] – also appears to be a somewhat contentious point among members of the Jordanian military. The head of the influential and powerful National Committee of Retired Army Personnel called the stationing of 900 US soldiers in Jordan in 2012 a 'black day' and 'a return of colonialism'.[104] Apart from such criticism of US policy in moments when the close cooperation between the two militaries becomes publicly known, the Jordanian security services appear to have mostly accepted their role as a regional subcontractor for US imperialism.

The immense significance that the JAF leadership attaches to close US-Jordanian military cooperation was perhaps most vividly expressed in its reaction to the 2005 Al-Qaeda bombing of three Amman hotels, which killed sixty people. A 2006 US Embassy cable acknowledged that

[t]he JAF leadership sent a very strong signal in terms of the importance of our relationship by remaining in Washington to finish the Joint Military Commission (JMC) despite the hotel suicide attacks in Amman, which occurred during the initial day of JMC meetings in November 2005.[105]

---

[102] US DoS, Supporting Human Rights and Democracy: The U.S. Record 2006 (Washington, DC: US DoS, Bureau of Democracy, Human Rights and Labor, 2006), p. 166.

[103] US Embassy Amman cable to Washington, DC, 'U.S.-Jordan joint military committee meets', 22 November 2006, *Wikileaks*, 06Amman8549.

[104] Ali Habashneh, quoted in: *Al-Quds*, 'Washington deploys American special forces and battleships to Aqaba in preparation of a rapid intervention' [*Washington tanshur qūwwāt amīrikīyah wa sufunan ḥarbīyah fī-l-'Aqaba isti'dādan li-t-tadakhkhul as-sarī'*], 15 July 2013, available at: https://arabsolaa.com/articles/view/126327.html.

[105] US Embassy Amman cable, 'Scenesetter for the Conus visit of General Khalid Sarayreh'.

While not necessarily reflecting the position of the JAF leadership as a whole, the following episode from 2006 provides another insightful illustration of the way in which individual JAF officers view the priorities of their work. When the US coordinator for counterterrorism asked the commander of Jordan's Counterterrorism Battalion at a meeting whether his units were prepared for out-of-country deployments, the latter

> enthusiastically replied that he could have CT [counterterrorism] forces ready to deploy to Iraq or Syria in six to twelve hours. He said his battalion understands and supports U.S. policy, and that his men's language and cultural skills make them uniquely qualified for deployments abroad.[106]

By early 2015 the officer's desire for a more interventionist regional role of the Jordanian army had largely been fulfilled, as units of the Royal Jordanian Air Force were participating in air strikes against bases of the so-called Islamic State in both Syria and Iraq. In addition, Jordan has in recent years assigned up to 850 troops, including special operations forces and GID officers, to support the US war in Afghanistan,[107] and operated a military field hospital in Iraq. Further, Jordanian forces have not only trained American soldiers in situational and cultural awareness,[108] but also the newly established Iraqi National Police and, on US and Israeli request, also the forces of the Palestinian Authority, thereby helping to reduce the costs of the occupation.[109] Besides training the police forces of other countries, Jordan also directly rents out its own gendarmerie units, for example in Bahrain.[110] Both Bahrain and the US reimburse Jordan for the military services provided, which once again demonstrates the country's position as a regional subcontractor for US imperialism and a supporter of authoritarian regimes in the region.[111]

---

[106] US Embassy Amman cable, 'Ambassador Crumpton's visit to Jordan's 71st Counterterrorism Battalion', 2 March 2006, *Wikileaks*, 06Amman1511.

[107] US Embassy Amman cable, 'Jordan: preview of Afghanistan support offer in upcoming Washington meetings', 22 January 2010, *Wikileaks*, 10Amman219.

[108] US Embassy Amman cable, 'Scenesetter for the Conus visit of General Khalid Sarayreh'.

[109] US Embassy Amman cable, 'Jordan: preview of Afghanistan support offer'.

[110] See *Bahrain Mirror*, '*Bahrain Mirror* publishes important document regarding Jordanian police: 499 policemen are costing Bahrain 1.8 million dollar per month', 3 April 2014, available at: www.bahrainmirror.com/news/14724.html. In January 2015, a member of the Jordanian Gendarmerie allegedly 'passed away in Bahrain while working in a joint training mission with Bahraini security forces'. At the same time heavy protests were taking place in Bahrain. See *Jordan Times*, 'King receives family of gendarmerie killed in Bahrain', 14 January 2015, available at: www.jordantimes.com/news/local/king-receives -family-gendarme-killed-bahrain.

[111] In 2005 alone the US provided Jordan $97 million in coalition support funds for costs incurred in connection with the US occupation of Iraq. US Embassy Amman cable, 'Scenesetter for the Conus visit of General Khalid Sarayreh'.

In order to facilitate the training of Jordanian and foreign military and police, the Jordanian security services run an extensive network of training facilities, all of which have been established with US funding and are also used by US forces. The cluster of known US-funded security/military training centres includes the Peace Operations Training Center (POTC) in az-Zarqā', a battle simulation center (BSC), the Jordan International Police Training Center (JIPTC) east of Amman and the King Abdullah II Special Operations Training Center (KASOTC) north of Amman. In the following section I provide an in-depth analysis of the latter as an example of US security support to Jordan.

US-Jordanian Military Collaboration and KASOTC

Most of the US foreign military financing (FMF) funds that Jordan receives are used to equip the Jordanian army with US-produced weapons, and to finance various military construction projects. One such project was the King Abdullah II Special Operations Training Center, which was funded in 2005 through USD99 million in supplemental FMF resources.[112] The centre is located several kilometres north of Amman in an area called Yajūz[113] (Arabic for 'permissible') and is better known under its acronym KASOTC.

KASOTC was constructed by the US Army Corps of Engineers and General Dynamics but is owned by the JAF. Following US President Bush's authorisation in 2005, the US Army Corps of Engineers contracted American International Contractors Inc. (AICI) for the construction of the project, with additional contracts given to the US Company General Dynamics Information Technology and US-based Stanley Consultants.

KASOTC exemplifies the function of modern Jordan within the US regional security strategy, which in many ways resembles that of the state of Transjordan for the British in the 1920s and '30s.[114] Just as the Arab Legion was a product of British colonialism and the work of British colonial officers, KASOTC is the product of US imperialism and the work of the US Army Corps of Engineers and General Dynamics. Where in the newly established state of Transjordan, British colonial officers were training the Arab Legion in order to

---

[112] Sharp, J.M., *Jordan: Background and U.S. Relations*, CRS, Washington, DC, 1 April 2013, pp. 9, 14.

[113] Yajūz is both the name for the main artery connecting Amman and az-Zarqā' and is used to refer to urban settlements along that road.

[114] See also Robins, P., *A History of Jordan* (Cambridge: Cambridge University Press, 2004), p. 204.

discipline and stabilise an area that was deemed 'ungovernable'[115] in Massad's words, in KASOTC a group of former soldiers, predominantly Americans, is training the special forces of the Jordanian army and other regional allies and US soldiers to help rule the Middle East, which is still deemed to be as 'ungovernable' as the Transjordan of the 1920s. Furthermore, just as the Arab Legion was commanded and funded by the British but remained at Abdullah's service, KASOTC was initially funded through the US Department of Defense (DoD), is managed by the US private company ViaGlobal, but owned by the JAF, which remains at Abdullah II's service.

For US army sources it is important to emphasise that KASOTC is 'owned and operated by the Jordanian government'.[116] The same applies for Jordanian government officials. While the US army had deployed a total of 2,300 US military personnel to Jordan by late 2016, a permanent US army presence would be the subject of strong public protest. The sensitivity of the topic is reflected in the assurances of Jordanian government officials such as former Prime Minister Ensour that there are no foreign army training centres in the country.[117] And while KASOTC is indeed formally not a US army training centre, in its day-to-day operation it comes close to one.

A 2006 US Embassy cable raises doubts about the Jordanian government's supposed independence in KASOTC's day-to-day running: 'The release of the remaining $91 m is contingent on the approval of the political-military agreement by both sides. This agreement concerns the use of the facility, release of tactics, techniques and procedures, and other sensitive issues'.[118] Three months later, the US Ambassador to Jordan reported that the Jordanian government had accepted the suggested arrangement.[119] While the exact provisions are not known, the centre should best be understood as a hybrid entity. KASOTC employee Jack explained:

It's a privately held company. There are three elements of KASOTC. First of all, you have the facility ... Then you have KASOTC as the company, which is

---

[115] Massad, *Colonial Effects*, p. 26.
[116] Aleandre, R. and Lanham, D., 'King Abdullah Special Operations Training Center (KASOTC) provides capabilities for coalition forces', *Army AL&T*, October–December 2009, p. 64.
[117] Prime Minister Abdullah Ensour, paraphrased in Neimat, K., 'Government vows to salvage economy, revamp political life', *Jordan Times*, 15 April 2013, available at: www.vista.sahafi.jo/art.php?id=b2ec8d140085a3809f7c43b68ad32aa48b443315.
[118] US Embassy Amman cable, 'Scenesetter for the visit to Jordan of Lieutenant General Buchanan'.
[119] US Embassy Amman cable, 'GoJ agrees to KASOTC arrangement', 5 April 2006, *Wikileaks*, 06Amman2403.

responsible for taking care of the facility. Then you have ViaGlobal group, which is a US company, which we work for, that is hired by the Jordanian Armed Forces to operate, manage and maintain KASOTC, the company and the facility.[120]

KASOTC's business development manager, William, simply called it a 'very unique sort of arrangement'. He further admitted:

It works a little different than a standard maybe American capitalist type of business. But really the only challenges [are] our business processes and understanding how to implement them … we get *incredible* support from *any* of the security forces. Really anything KASOTC wants to do, we pretty much can.[121]

According to KASOTC employee Jack,[122] by 2013, 60 per cent of KASOTC's revenues came from the training of US soldiers and 20 per cent from the training of Jordanian forces (in light of the ongoing war in Syria, by 2014 all JAF border guards and Jordanian law enforcement received compulsory training at KASOTC).[123]

KASOTC's General Director Toney, business development manager William and staff member Jack were at the time of my research among ten to twelve ViaGlobal staff members working at the facility. Based on a contract with the JAF, the responsibilities of the ViaGlobal staff include the provision of training and assistance in the management of the centre. ViaGlobal, a limited liability company based in Maryland, USA, has since 2005 'designed, managed, and operated the King Abdullah II Special Operations Training Center'.[124] The US insistence on KASOTC being run as a commercial business, and not directly by the US military, was of course instrumental for maintaining the façade that there is no direct US involvement. As KASOTC is managed by ViaGlobal, the US government can easily point to the allegedly apolitical nature of the business and further argue that all retired US military staff employed by ViaGlobal are contracted by the JAF and not the United States.

However, ViaGlobal, KASOTC and the JAF are entangled in such a way that instead of ViaGlobal and its staff being service providers for the JAF, the relationship seems to have become inverted. In addition to the ViaGlobal staff members who help to manage KASOTC,

---

[120] Interview with Jack, KASOTC staff member, ViaGlobal, Yajūz, 26 March 2013.

[121] Interview with William, KASOTC business development manager, ViaGlobal, Yajūz, 24 March 2013.

[122] Interview with Jack, KASOTC staff member, ViaGlobal, Yajūz, 26 March 2013.

[123] *IHS Jane's Intelligence Review*, 'Jordan responds to the Islamic State threat', 29 October 2014.

[124] ViaGlobal, 'Tactical training', available at: www.viaglobalgroup.com/expertise/#tactical.

approximately one hundred JAF personnel work at the facility. Even though the latter play a major role in operating the centre, it is the US private company ViaGlobal and the Jordanian private company KASOTC that make the profits from its day-to-day running. While the exact profit-sharing agreement between KASOTC and ViaGlobal is not known, the JAF personnel working at the facility seem to have become service providers for US and Jordanian private sector interests. Despite KASOTC officially being owned by the JAF, the business structure of the centre as a tax-exempt Jordanian for-profit corporate entity requires that JAF units who want to use KASOTC for training purposes must pay like any other customer. However, as the JAF is not only a customer, but after all also the owner of the centre, 'they get a discount'.[125]

When US, Jordanian and other special forces, border guards and law enforcement units come to train at KASOTC they are exposed to what the construction manager of the US Army Corps of Engineers imagines to be 'an environment that will be just like what they might encounter with terrorists, including the sights and sounds of the battlefield'.[126] This 'typical terrorist environment' is created with the help of 'thousands of individual sound effects and more than 100 separate smell effects',[127] as well as fog generators and rooftop explosions. Mirroring Jordan's well-known Palestinian and Syrian refugee camps, such as Wiḥdāt, Baqaʿah and Zaʿtarī, KASOTC houses its own refugee camp. While this is of course void of refugees, simulations of their living environment and what might happen in it are highly present at the centre.

The controllable and safe refugee camp experience that KASOTC offers to its customers is further complemented by the largest mock city in existence, a sniper range and experiences revolving around an artificial Afghan village, and a real Airbus 300.[128] In the words of the engineer who oversaw KASOTC's construction, 'These areas look like typical village, city and countryside settings, using Middle Eastern architecture . . . This

[125] Interview with William, KASOTC staff member, ViaGlobal, Yajūz, 26 March 2013.

[126] US Army Corps of Engineers construction manager, quoted in Kibler, J., 'Construction progressing on the special operations training center in Jordan', *Special Operations Technology (SOTECH)*, Vol. 6, No. 2, March 2008.

[127] Mahon, T., 'General Dynamics ramps up urban training work', *Training & Simulation Journal*, December 2007–January 2008, p. 10.

[128] KASOTC, 'Home of the Annual Warrior Competition', 2014, available at: www .kasotc.com/KASOTC_Site/Home.html; KASOTC, 'Where advanced training meets advanced technology', 2011, available at: www.kasotc.com/KASOTC_Site/Home_file s/KASOTC%20Downloaded.pdf, p. 17.

Figure 6.1 KASOTC's military operations on urban terrain (MOUT) area. Available at: www.kasotc.com/DetailsPage/KASOTC_EN/Photo AlbumDetailsEN.aspx?ID=9. © KASOTC.

training area also offers a refugee camp and a building that can be used as an embassy or palace'.[129] (see Figure 6.1)

The establishment of KASOTC as a US-funded military training centre owned by the JAF and managed by a private US business, and the centre's simulation of seemingly typical security threats illustrate well the blurring of lines that a growing body of literature has observed between military and civilian,[130] public and private,[131] as well as real and simulated.[132] This has the effect of creating new markets for a military sector that is increasingly concerned with the biopolitical and the disciplining of social formations.[133]

[129] US Army Corps of Engineers construction manager, quoted in Kibler, 'Construction progressing on the special operations training center in Jordan'.
[130] McDonald, K., 'Grammars of violence, modes of embodiment and frontiers of the subject', in: McSorley, K. (ed.), *War and the Body: Militarisation, Practice and Experience* (London: Routledge, 2013), p. 149.
[131] Abrahamsen and Williams, 'Securing the city', p. 242.
[132] Stahl, 'Life is war', p. 129.
[133] See Eichler, 'Citizenship and the contracting out of military work', pp. 600–614; Stavrianakis, 'In arms' way', pp. 505–520; Stahl, 'Life is war', pp. 122–137.

As argued by Stavrianakis and Selby,[134] it is, however, important to note that despite a gradual merging of public and private, processes of militarisation remain predominantly state-based. In the case of KASOTC, this is apparent in the fact that, the centre's seemingly apolitical commercial nature notwithstanding, its customer base is almost exclusively made up of US and Jordanian soldiers.

While a blurring of boundaries is a central characteristic of the commercialisation of security, the latter manifests itself via a simultaneous reinforcement of imagined moral hierarchies. In US-Jordanian military collaboration at KASOTC these appear to be shaped by what I call the marketisation of Orientalism. Perceptions of *protector* (US military), *protected* (Jordan) and source of insecurity (terrorists) thus increasingly merge with the functions of service provider (ViaGlobal employee), customer (JAF soldiers training at KASOTC) and those unable to be either (refugees). Rather than the end of neoliberalism, as suggested by Amar,[135] at KASOTC we can thus observe a vivid interaction of governance through market policies and moral politics.

Simulating War

After I contacted the centre in March 2013, William, then KASOTC's business development manager, invited me to visit and attend the opening ceremony of the Fifth Annual Warrior Competition. The Warrior Competition is KASOTC's key annual marketing event, bringing together special forces teams from around the world to compete in a number of disciplines. Upon my arrival at the centre I was taken to an airfield-like structure on which stands had been set up in front of an Airbus 300 as though for a military parade. The official programme leaflet featured the competition's emblem which, reminiscent of the blurring of lines between entertainment and militarism, consists of the profile of a warrior closely resembling images of the Spartans in the American action film *300*. (see Figure 6.2)

In addition to some introductory words by King Abdullah II and former US Brigadier General and General Director of KASOTC, Frank Toney, the leaflet also included advertisements by (primarily) US and European weapons and military equipment producers. In fact, the event was almost completely financed through the profits gained from such

---

[134] Stavrianakis, A. and Selby, J., Militarism and International Relations: Political *Economy, Security* and *Theory* (Abingdon: Routledge, 2013), p. 8.

[135] Amar, *The Security Archipelago*.

Figure 6.2 The emblem of KASOTC's Annual Warrior Competition. Available at: http://warriorcompetition.com/. © KASOTC.

sponsors and was purely a PR exercise to gain new customers. The competition thus provided a good example of the processes, not of democratisation, but of commercialisation that US-Jordanian security cooperation sets in motion, and of the ways in which US security support helps to deepen existing markets and establish new ones for the US defence industry. While neoliberal arguments about the efficiency of the market have led to such processes of commercialisation, the market has, as also suggested by Eichler, 'merely furthered the global and coercive reach of US militarization'.[136] This again has clear implications for who or what is secured and how.[137]

One advertisement by the US company Falcon Defense Group, for a close-quarters combat automatic shotgun, particularly caught my attention. In addition to stating: 'Proudly Supporting the Hashemite Kingdom of Jordan Since 2001!' it featured the slogan 'Don't Fight Fair! ... If You Find Yourself In A Fair Fight – Your Tactics Suck!'[138] As I was wondering whether the slogan was invoking the Spartans' slaughtering of the Persian hordes in *300*, or whether it was in open defiance of the Geneva Convention, the JAF band had already ended its performance of the royal anthem, which was now followed by a Qur'ān recital by the official JAF *imām*. After some welcoming

---

[136] Eichler, 'Citizenship and the contracting out of military work', p. 610.
[137] Abrahamsen and Williams, 'Securing the city', p. 239.
[138] KASOTC, Fifth Annual Warrior Competition, official programme, 2013, p. 25.

remarks in Arabic by Jordanian Military Commander Colonel Al-Magableh, KASOTC's General Director Frank Toney officially welcomed in English the competitors, guests and the JAF General Ziad Majali:

> Our Warrior Competition is an internationally recognized engagement between the forces for good; designed to build work relationships … and forge a bond between warriors; so when required these partnerships can effectively and efficiently support each other in confronting the forces of evil.[139]

Before coming to KASOTC, Toney had not only served as senior advisor to all Iraqi counterterrorism forces, but had also led a DoS programme for the democratisation of the Nigerian Armed Forces, thereby well illustrating the virtuous goals increasingly claimed for contemporary war-making and war-preparation.

Der Derian reminds us in this regard that contemporary US war-preparation and war-making are marked by the interaction of an unparalleled technological and a claimed ethical superiority. The former not only enables the actualisation of violence from a distance, thereby letting 'the enemy' appear absent ('forces of evil'), but in doing so it also provides war with a façade of virtuousness. Virtuous war is then much less about preparing for an imagined reality of war than it is about simulating war as bloodless, humanitarian and hygienic.[140] This simulation of war as a virtuous undertaking is an important precondition for the global marketing of war. As processes of military commercialisation and virtualisation intersect, war's deadly realities are not only increasingly hidden from sight, but war also takes on new forms of meaning when divergent ascriptions of value to different lives are marketised, a phenomenon I will explore in more depth later. The growing base of customers ready to consume and play war at KASOTC then directly depends on the simulation of war's enemies as absent and of its goals as virtuous.

In attempting to deconstruct said simulation, an exploration of military training centres outside the Global North is particularly insightful, as war's virtuous simulations and its deadly realities are, in a Global South context, often in much closer proximity than in the US and European military centres discussed by Der Derian. Also, a closer analysis of military centres outside the Global North helps us to challenge descriptions that view people in the Global South largely as passive targets of a virtuous war designed by others.[141]

[139] KASOTC, Fifth Annual Warrior Competition, official programme, 2013, p. 3.
[140] Der Derian, *Virtuous War*, p. xxxi.
[141] See also Amar, *The Security Archipelago*, p. 20.

Figure 6.3 Simulating war at KASOTC. Available at: www.kasotc
.com/DetailsPage/KASOTC_EN/PhotoAlbumDetailsEN.aspx?I
D=8. © KASOTC.

KASOTC's Warrior Competition provides a good illustration of the
kind of moral claims advanced by actors in the field of commercial
security.[142] A demonstration of some of the military capabilities that
can be trained at the centre followed Toney's speech, including the
enactment of a hostage situation involving KASOTC's Airbus 300, an
air assault including several helicopters, snipers shooting at targets that
released coloured smoke upon impact and trained dogs stopping a fleeing
prisoner. (see Figure 6.3)

What stood out most in this spectator-friendly demonstration of contemporary war was the strange interplay of aestheticised violence and the
near-total absence of the latter's effects on 'the enemy'.[143] Considering the
obvious absence of any demonstration of the horrors of war's effects on the
body of 'the enemy', the viewer might, from where I was sitting, have got
the impression that KASOTC was 'designed ultimately to save lives', as
stated by a leading General Dynamics employee.[144]

KASOTC's presentation of US security support, Jordanian security
services and the centre's simulations of war – condensed into easily
digestible and film-like action sequences – stands in stark contrast to

[142] See also Bacevich, A.J., The New American Militarism: How Americans *Are Seduced* by
War (New York: Oxford University Press, 2013), p. 24.
[143] See Kuntsman and Stein, *Digital Militarism*, p. 13.
[144] Quoted in Mahon, 'General Dynamics ramps up urban training work', p. 10.

the role of the Jordanian GID and PSD in torturing political detainees, as well as in the CIA's rendition and detention programme.[145] It is thus important to see KASOTC not just as simulating an as-typical-as-possible 'terrorist environment', but also as attempting to persuade us of the neatness (coloured smoke instead of blood), clarity (forces of good vs forces of evil) and humanitarian idealism ('designed to save lives') that supposedly lie at the core of the project of securing Jordan, and that are an inherent requirement for the mutually reinforcing construction of security support and various virtuous goals, such as democratisation.

Even if only cursorily, a *New York Times* article[146] pointedly challenged KASOTC's vision of humanitarian wars by aptly juxtaposing the aforementioned virtuous goals with the embodied practices of war that critical research on militarism increasingly places at the centre of analysis.[147] It thus described how one US participant said of his teammate that he was 'not a competitor – he's a killer' and how the latter told 'tales about blood-splattered Iraqi swimming pools'.[148] At KASOTC it is not the practice of war that matters, however, but its simulation. The transformation of war into 'virtuous war' relies heavily on this displacement of the realities of war and, as part of this, on the absence of 'the enemy'.

KASOTC's refugee camp and its Afghan village were consequently absent from the presentation, just as the performing units also refrained from demonstrating their skills in crowd control and dispersal, which are also among those that can be trained at the centre.[149] I did not see KASOTC's refugee camp during my visit, as it seems likely that the staff of the centre – having quite literally constructed it as a site of security concerns – are acutely aware of the political sensitivity of simulating *the refugee* as a security threat in a country whose population predominantly hails from a refugee background. In many ways, the exclusion of the Afghan village and KASOTC's refugee camp from the official ceremony thus appears to be characteristic of how US-Jordanian military collaboration attempts to uphold an impression of moral authority. Such claims of moral

[145] UN Committee against Torture, *Concluding Observations of the Committee against Torture – Jordan*, p. 1.

[146] Eells, J., 'Sleep-away camp for postmodern cowboys', *New York Times*, 19 July 2013, available at: www.nytimes.com/2013/07/21/magazine/sleep-away-camp-for-postmodern-cowboys.html.

[147] McSorley, *War and the Body*; Higate, 'The private militarized and security contractor as geocorporeal actor', pp. 355–372; Stahl, *Militainment*.

[148] Eells, 'Sleep-away camp for postmodern cowboys'.

[149] KASOTC, 'Where advanced training meets advanced technology', p. 8.

Figure 6.4 The participants in KASOTC's Annual Warrior Competition in front of KASOTC's Airbus 300. Available at: http://warriorcompetition .com/DetailsPage/DetailsPage_EN/PhotoAlbumDetailsEN.aspx?I D=27. © KASOTC.

authority indeed abound. A 2006 DoS report noted that '[o]ne of the primary purposes of the US military education and training in the country is to strengthen bilateral relations by exposing members of its military to democratic principles'.[150]

Once the smoke from the demonstration had settled, the participating teams were presented (see Figure 6.4). William seemed to have done an impressive job, as the competition had attracted over thirty teams – a record. Among the participating 'forces for good' were six Jordanian teams (Gendarmerie, PSD, Royal Guard, Special Forces, GID and Airborne 30), five American, five Lebanese, three Palestinian, two Iraqi, as well as one or more teams from Algeria, Bahrain, Canada, China, France, Greece, Kazakhstan, Kuwait, Malaysia, the Netherlands, Russia, Saudi-Arabia and Switzerland. While KASOTC's paying customers are predominantly US soldiers, and special forces units from close regional allies, the range of participating nations in KASOTC's prime marketing event suggests that the commercialisation of contemporary

---

[150] US DoS, Supporting Human Rights and Democracy, p. 166.

militarism goes hand in hand with a global marketing of conceptions of 'the enemy'. Before exploring this in more depth, I will now investigate the central question of who or what US-Jordanian military cooperation at KASOTC actually secures.

Responding to Reid-Henry's call 'to bring the economic back into the picture' in order to arrive at 'a more critical mapping of . . . the geographical indexing of life',[151] I will explore in more depth the processes of commercialisation triggered by US-Jordanian military collaboration at KASOTC. I will begin by focusing on KASOTC's then business development manager, followed by a critical discussion of the self-conception of ViaGlobal. I argue that what is ultimately secured at KASOTC and by ViaGlobal is not primarily the personal security of Jordanians, but corporate business interests, as well as deeply problematic conceptions of the value of human lives. While the creation of new security markets depends on the blurring of boundaries mentioned above, the commercialisation of security is also shown to reinforce old and create new boundaries that help to determine who plays what role in these new security markets. Both processes are fundamentally anti-democratic, as notions of public control only lose further ground and ideals of equality are radically undermined.

Privatising Security

In the previous section, I suggested that the simulation of moral claims enables the further marketing of war as something to be consumed and played on a global scale. In this section, I argue that the blurring of boundaries at KASOTC goes hand in hand with a simultaneous and deeply anti-democratic reinforcement of boundaries between those securing, those being secured and those being secured against.

Later in the day I went to KASOTC's outdoor sports field, where some of the participants in the Annual Warrior Competition were playing football while others trained at the nearby shooting ranges. To the sound of intermittent gunfire, I asked William to tell me more about himself. As my other interviewees had asked to remain anonymous, I offered him the same arrangement. William, however, did not deem any such measure necessary; he merely remarked, 'You're after the facts!',[152] and willingly answered my questions. Despite his offer,

---

[151] Reid-Henry, S., 'Spaces of security and development: an alternative mapping of the security-development nexus', Security Dialogue, Vol. 42, No. 1, 2011, p. 102.

[152] Interview with William, KASOTC business development manager, ViaGlobal, Yajūz, 24 March 2013.

I decided to keep him anonymous. Having spent a year working for a US company that produces lasers for firearms, he had gone back into the Marine Corps and eventually made the transition from a US marine to KASOTC's business development manager.

While he provides an excellent example of 'professional continuity',[153] a clear distinction between the two spheres was very important to William. In response to my initial offer to refer to him as 'someone involved in security cooperation', he not only replied that it was fine to quote him personally, but also corrected me that 'it's not security, but business'. Similarly, when I expressed my surprise about the presence of Chinese and Russian teams at a US-financed training centre, he reminded me, 'It does not have anything to do with the US. This is Jordan'. In William's eyes, not only had US security support become a supposedly apolitical business affair, but Jordan itself was not much more than a business opportunity, as in his last statement 'Jordan' could easily have been replaced by 'business'.

When I asked him about the impact of the war in Syria, he simply repeated: 'I'm a business development guy. I don't know … The country is safe and secure. I'm not even seeing problems. In my opinion, from [the perspective of] a typical citizen, it hasn't affected security – economics yes – but I've not seen anything'. Of course, William is neither a 'typical citizen', nor as far removed from the field of US-Jordanian security cooperation as he claimed. A journalist who briefly joined our conversation by KASOTC's football field triggered a stronger reaction. When he remarked that he thought the Syrian opposition had been trained at KASOTC, William responded: 'Where did you hear this? … No, no, no. There's no way … This is a commercial business. This is not a Jordanian military base. We're … a company like any other company. We would never train any of the …'.[154] Interestingly, for William, the main reason why Syrian rebels were not being trained at KASOTC was the centre's commercial nature. While irregular forces could in his opinion be trained at Jordanian military bases, he considered this impossible at a supposedly 'neutral' commercial business, such as KASOTC. If Syrian rebels had indeed not been trained at KASOTC, their chances of eligibility might perhaps have been greater had they established a corporate entity. The German firearm producer Sig Sauer has

---

[153] Higate, P., '"Switching on" for cash: the private militarised security contractor as geo-corporeal actor', in: McSorley, K. (ed.), *War and the Body: Militarisation, Practice and Experience* (London: Routledge, 2013), p. 106.

[154] Interview with William, KASOTC business development manager, ViaGlobal, Yajūz, 24 March 2013.

already shown interest in registering such a corporate team at KASOTC's Annual Warrior Competition and the US company International Defense Systems has already done so.[155]

But what are the effects of this blurring of boundaries between military assistance and business development, and between William's work as a soldier and as a manager? And how does this relate to persistent attempts at demarcation ('it's not security, but business')? A number of critical scholars of militarism have discussed the difficulties of distinguishing between public and private,[156] citizen and soldier,[157] home front and battlefield,[158] as well as war and non-war.[159] But why was it, in light of this evident blurring of boundaries, so important to William to give an impression of the opposite? In order to better understand the imagined and real separations that contemporary US-Jordanian military collaboration at KASOTC reinforces and is premised upon,[160] it is helpful to discuss in more depth the background of ViaGlobal, the private company that manages KASOTC. Its website provides an informative starting point.

Until it was updated in early 2017, the site featured a photographic background featuring two men.[161] One, a soldier, is facing – and thus giving the impression of *protecting* – what seems to be a generic business district in a Western city, while the other, a businessman, is facing – and thus giving the impression of *managing* – a remote desert area patrolled by a few army vehicles. The two photos blend into each other and, while of course part of ViaGlobal's corporate message, in many ways symbolise the nature of the company's work, as well as the blurring of boundaries between *military* and *business*, and the mutual contamination of the two fields. The image conveys a world in which *business* – which, in the case at hand, gained a strong foothold in the Jordanian security sector due to US insistence on the structure of KASOTC as a commercial entity – needs to be secured by *the military*, just as the unknown desert needs to be managed and made understandable by *the businessman*.

The clarity of the roles and spheres that the photo invokes (*the soldier* and *the businessman, the desert* and *the business district*), however, also indicates that all blurring notwithstanding, the politics of commercial

---

[155] Eells, 'Sleep-away camp for postmodern cowboys'.
[156] Abrahamsen and Williams, 'Securing the city', pp. 242–243.
[157] Stahl, 'Have you played the war on terror?' p. 125.   [158] Stahl, 'Life is war', p. 133.
[159] McDonald, 'Grammars of violence, modes of embodiment and frontiers of the subject', p. 139.
[160] See also Graham, 'Technologies of exception'.
[161] An archived version of the old background photo on ViaGlobal's website can be viewed at: https://web.archive.org/web/20150510233129/http://viaglobalgroup.com:80/.

security calls for fundamentally different interventions in different contexts.[162] Paraphrasing Dalby, one may then note that the blurring of military and business goes hand in hand with a reinforcement of boundaries between zones of peace that must be protected and zones of violence that must be managed.[163] The simultaneous blurring and demarcation of boundaries, illustrated by William's professional background (US soldier and ViaGlobal employee) and comments ('it's not security, but business'), and the photo on ViaGlobal's website, serves a clear purpose. While the former opens up new commercial security markets, the latter helps to determine what kind of intervention is (or is not) deemed necessary, where and by whom. Potential training for Syrian rebels is thus a deeply problematic political intervention, while US security support to Jordan becomes an apolitical business affair.

ViaGlobal's self-conception allows us to gain a more detailed understanding, not only of the roles played by the different actors involved in US-Jordanian military collaboration at KASOTC, but also of the ways in which the merging of business and security at the centre reinforces highly dichotomous ascriptions of agency. Having previously been the soldier who protected *business*, William was now the business development manager who managed *the desert*. While the two spheres are portrayed as linked and blurring into each other – the ViaGlobal employee can easily jump from one to the other and understand, protect and manage both – this permeability only applies to ViaGlobal's soldier-cum-businessman. Although the latter appears to have a semblance of agency,[164] those protected by US-Jordanian military collaboration appear to be mere passive customers of the services provided.

Both the urban business and the desert background in the photo are – apart from the ViaGlobal employee – void of any obvious depictions of human beings. What is secured by the soldier and managed by the businessman then seems to be an abstract notion of business and an abstract notion of the unknown, rather than human lives. While the erasure of clear boundaries is a key characteristic of Der Derian's 'virtuous war',[165] as well as Stahl's 'interactive war',[166] it is important to realise that this blurring goes hand in hand with a reinforcement of 'the

---

[162] For the central role that such assumptions of 'difference' play in intervention, see Sabaratnam, M., 'Avatars of Eurocentrism in the critique of the liberal peace', *Security Dialogue*, Vol. 44, No. 3, 2013. pp. 259–278.
[163] In Stavrianakis and Selby, *Militarism and International Relations*, p. 38.
[164] Stahl argues that militarism actually 'plays the citizen'. Stahl, *Militainment*, p. 47.
[165] Der Derian, *Virtuous War*.   [166] Stahl, *Militainment*.

distance between those who have and those who have not',[167] between those able to protect and those requiring protection. While the moralisation of commercial security discussed in the first two sections of this chapter is marked by the blurring of boundaries and has the effect of presenting the centre as virtuous, apolitical and 'saving lives', the marketisation of moral politics is, in turn, marked by the reinforcement of deeply problematic and strongly contrasting conceptions about the role of human subjects.

Below the photo, ViaGlobal's website states that the company 'provides expert programs, consulting services, and other assistance to US Government and Intelligence clients'.[168] Ultimately, of course, this means that in ViaGlobal's own words, the JAF is nothing but a customer of US government and intelligence services. While this might seem like an over-interpretation of the information given on the company's website, the nature of US-Jordanian security cooperation demonstrates that such a description is not that far from the truth. The notion that ViaGlobal and KASOTC are, due to their nature as commercial businesses, simply somehow inherently apolitical is highly misleading. All four board members of ViaGlobal are former US army staff, including – at the time of my field research – a former US Navy Seal who, according to ViaGlobal, had 'participated in nearly all conflicts and major combat operations since Vietnam'.[169]

As I asked KASOTC employee Jack about the hybrid nature of the centre and the assistance provided by JAF soldiers in its operation, he explained in more detail the centre's blurring of the public-private distinction, as well as the hierarchical relations between *protector*/service provider and *protected*/customer that the latter set in motion:

JACK: We've got about one hundred Jordanian Armed Forces personnel on the facility.
AUTHOR: That are also contracted by ViaGlobal . . .?
JACK: Not yet [*laughs*].

[167] Der Derian, *Virtuous War*, p. xxxiv.
[168] ViaGlobal, 'Careers, 2015', available at: www.viaglobalgroup.com/careers/. On the homepage, this formulation has been adjusted to 'and other assistance to US Government and private clients'. ViaGlobal, homepage, available at: www.viaglobalgroup.com/.
[169] ViaGlobal, 'The Board, Captain Steve Fitzgerald (USN, Ret.)'. The original ViaGlobal link is no longer active. A cached version may be found at: https://web.archive.org/web/20170111023756/www.zoominfo.com/p/Steve-Fitzgerald/911564693.

AUTHOR: So they are working for the Jordanian Armed Forces at the moment?

JACK: In support of KASOTC.

AUTHOR: And paid by?

JACK: By the Jordanian Armed Forces.

AUTHOR: ... But they – you say they will be contracted?

JACK: There's a goal to do that. We're against it. I'm against it, as ...

AUTHOR: Why?

JACK: Because it's ... [a] bad choice of work ... I mean why would a contractor pay the salaries of a military force? They're not even a military force, they're a mercenary force at this point – to some degree. Where do the loyalties lie? Who to work for? Who do they take directions from? ... How do they take directions from the JAF if we're paying them? It doesn't make sense.

AUTHOR: ... But there are discussions that ViaGlobal is going to contract them or is going to pay them?

JACK: Not ViaGlobal. KASOTC.

AUTHOR: ... But KASOTC is operated by ViaGlobal ... So ViaGlobal would have an indirect say? ...

JACK: [*no response and then change of topic*].

Despite some remaining ambiguities, the above dialogue allows for some interesting conclusions. First, it is worth noting that Jack himself had been in the US military for several decades before his retirement and in 2013 was working for a private US company – ViaGlobal. While from the Jordanian standpoint it would be more than legitimate to wonder whether his loyalty was with his previous employer – the US army – or with his current contracting authority – the JAF – Jack could only see possible conflicts of interest with regard to the Jordanian soldiers who might be contracted by KASOTC or ViaGlobal.

Second, and more importantly, among the JAF, KASOTC, ViaGlobal and, considering the central role of the United States in the establishment of KASOTC, presumably also among US army representatives at the US Embassy in Amman, a discussion seems to have taken place about the possibility of JAF personnel being either contracted indirectly (by KASOTC the company, which again is managed by ViaGlobal) or directly by the US company ViaGlobal. While US-Jordanian military collaboration at KASOTC may contribute to the strengthening of the Jordanian military's coercive capacity, the potential privatisation of JAF soldiers would of course represent a serious erosion of Jordanian sovereignty and control over the country's security sector. It can hardly be argued that this process does not directly undercut efforts at supporting Jordanian democratisation.

One can recapitulate then that the blurring of military and business in US-Jordanian military collaboration at KASOTC reinforces new lines of biopolitical separation concerning the crucial question of who secures, who is secured and who is secured against. While these separations are informed by Orientalist notions of who or what constitutes a security threat ('the refugee' as a threat and Arab cities as 'typical terrorist environment'), we can also observe a marketisation of such Orientalist assumptions at KASOTC.

Playing War

Although the reinforcement of imagined moral hierarchies at KASOTC occurs via the 'hypervisibilization'[170] of certain identities, it would be wrong to refer to KASOTC as illustrating the emergence of a new form of moralised human security governance and the potential end of neoliberalism, as explored by Amar in Egypt and Brazil. Instead, one can observe at KASOTC a vivid interaction of governance through moral politics *and* market policies. The problematisation of Arab living environments as 'typical terrorist environments' and of refugees as generic source of insecurity is thus itself being marketised at the centre. KASOTC then provides us with an example of neoliberalism's absorption of Amar's 'hypervisibilization' of certain identities under the wider objective of creating new commercial security markets, rather than the potential end of neoliberalism. This is fundamentally anti-democratic, as Jordan's security sector is increasingly governed based on the principles of the market, rather than on notions of public control. Also, deeply problematic and Orientalist assumptions of difference are effectively perpetuated.[171]

At KASOTC, the roles of *protector* (US military) and service provider (ViaGlobal), *protected* (Jordan) and customer (JAF soldiers), and security threat (terrorists) and marginalised (refugees) increasingly coincide. The opening up of new commercial security markets at KASOTC then seems to depend directly on images of Jordanians as either passive objects waiting to be secured, or as security threats. Finally, the semblance of agency that US-Jordanian military collaboration at the centre provides to the soldier-cum-businessman has no deliberative meaning, as it only amounts to the opportunity to observe and/or organise simulations of war, or to play at interactive war. Deliberative questions about how and why refugees, for instance, are turned into security threats to begin with are, however, fundamentally evaded.[172]

---

[170] Amar, *The Security Archipelago*, p. 17.
[171] Sabaratnam, 'Avatars of Eurocentrism in the critique of the liberal peace', p. 260.
[172] Stahl, 'Have you played the war on terror?', pp. 112–130.

The evolution of the privatisation and commercialisation of military training at KASOTC and its effects can best be illustrated through a focus on William's predecessor as KASOTC's business development manager, Charles K. Redlinger. CK, as he prefers to be called, worked as US General David Petraeus' security manager at the multinational security transition command in Baghdad before coming to KASOTC. When he left the centre in 2012, CK established the private company MissionX, which offers what it calls tactical adventures, corporate leadership programmes and consulting to the film industry. Naturally, the services offered by the private company KASOTC are also open to other private companies, such as MissionX. The latter thus provides us with yet another illustration of the close interaction of processes of commercialisation and militarisation.

Within its tactical adventures portfolio, for a fee of USD20,000, MissionX offers a 'Special Operations Adventure Experience'. This is conducted at KASOTC and, according to MissionX's own description, is 'so intense and extreme that the lines between reality and fantasy are blurred'.[173] On arrival at KASOTC, participants are issued with special forces equipment, combat uniforms and weapons, and become part of 'realistic war-game scenarios', during which they 'step into a role as an elite unit member charged with undertaking a variety of daring and risky missions'.[174] As war is turned into a consumable and interactive event, dreams of killing fuelled by what Stahl aptly calls 'Militainment',[175] a neoliberal emphasis on greater efficiency and 'contemporary neoliberal desires for self-actualization'[176] closely intertwine. Now head of his own private business, CK appears to have fulfilled the expectations behind KASOTC, as outlined in the previously quoted statement by KASOTC's General Director Toney, and seems to have forged strong bonds with other warriors. This, however, predominantly applies to CK's previous work as US Special Forces soldier, rather than to his role as a ViaGlobal employee working on behalf of the JAF. In 2013 for instance, CK and MissionX donated one 'Special Operations Adventure Experience' to an auction in support of US special operations charities.[177]

[173] MissionX, 'Special operations adventure – Jordan – Mission details', available at: www.missionx.com/special-operations.html.
[174] MissionX, 'Adventures', available at: www.missionx.com/adventures.html.
[175] Stahl, *Militainment*.
[176] McSorley, K., 'Conclusion: rethinking war and the body', in: McSorley, K. (ed.), *War and the Body: Militarisation, Practice and Experience* (London: Routledge, 2013), p. 234.
[177] ITS Tactical, 'Silent professional auction: a special operations forces charity event', 2013, available at: www.itstactical.com/centcom/news/silent-professional-auction-a-special-operations-forces-charity-event/.

Considering the price of its adventure programme, MissionX primarily targets investment bankers, actors and other affluent professionals.[178] Illustrating Hardt and Negri's observation that 'war seems to have seeped back and flooded the entire social field',[179] the 'Special Operations Adventure Experience' is also promoted as a learning experience. MissionX thus additionally runs, in cooperation with the London-based company Fieri, what it calls a leadership programme. This seems to be more or less the same as the 'Special Operations Adventure Experience', but is described in more corporate language as 'a new and unique approach to commercial leadership development'.[180] Providing the ultimate blending of military and business, Fieri explains that if you play war at KASOTC you can 'explore various styles of leadership'. MissionX assists in the normalisation of war and writes that participation in the programme will help participants 'learn how to empower [their] managers and employees'.[181]

Just as ViaGlobal employees like William or CK can manage *the desert*, as well as protect *business*, the manager or investment banker who participates in the programme conducted by Fieri and MissionX can motivate his team of bankers or traders in London or New York and properly handle a shotgun and seek cover in an Afghan village or an Arab *sūq*. How precisely these dynamics – enabled by the initial US financing of KASOTC – reinforce values of democracy and security remains questionable. The politics of commercial security at KASOTC thus primarily revolves around the hierarchical integration of different identity groups, based on their ability to market the deeply problematic conceptions of different value attached to their own and/or other human lives. Finally, CK and MissionX are not just helping investment bankers realise their fantasies of playing war in the Middle East,[182] they are also (re)shaping images and the material realities of Jordan.

As its third field of activity, MissionX offers technical advice and training to the film industry. A US Embassy cable remarks in this regard that over recent years Jordan has increasingly marketed itself by reference

---

[178] *Out Dare Adventures*, 'MissionX – What is it and why do I want it', *Out Dare Adventures*, 6 February 2013, available at: www.outdareadventures.com/missionx-what-is-it-and-why-do-i-want-it/.

[179] Hardt, M. and Negri, A., Multitude: War and Democracy in the Age of Empire (London: Penguin Books, 2005), p. 7.

[180] Fieri, 'Fieri MissionX', available at: http://fieri.biz/off-site/.

[181] MissionX, 'Leadership development', available at: www.missionx.com/leadership-development.html.

[182] See also Kuntsman and Stein, *Digital Militarism*, p. 95.

to 'its ability to double as Iraq',[183] one of the key selling points being the use of JAF personnel and equipment at minimal cost. Besides working as advisors for films produced with the support of the JAF, MissionX also offers stunt training for action movie performers, which is then partly conducted at KASOTC. In an online promotional video, CK and his UK stunt coordinators, as well as a team of Jordanian action movie performers trained by MissionX, demonstrate their skills. At the beginning of the film one of the instructors explains that 'some guys already have the basics . . . an idea of performance, how to throw a punch safely . . . Some guys need more work than others, but we're feeling good'.[184]

Most of the aspiring Jordanian actors do indeed seem to already 'have the basics' and know the role of an Arab in the film industry, as during the remainder of the five-minute film they demonstrate their skills, convincingly choking or beating each other, as well as at shooting, getting shot and looking scary enough for the viewer to find it sufficiently 'realistic'. While most of the Jordanian actors get shot at some point, CK does not. Both the Jordanian stunt actors and CK know their place. Having previously organised the Warrior Competition as a ViaGlobal employee on behalf of KASOTC and the JAF, CK has recently again been involved in organising the competition, only now in his capacity as co-founder of MissionX. Apart from assisting KASOTC in running the sixth Annual Warrior Competition in 2014, he has also worked recently as military consultant for the sci-fi thriller *Monsters: The Dark Continent*.

From Simulations of War to Its Deadly Realities

The processes of commercialisation and militarisation triggered by US security support fundamentally limit the space that could potentially come within the reach of democratic procedures. I have demonstrated in this chapter that US-Jordanian security cooperation gradually shifts control over the Jordanian security sector away from the Jordanian state and into the hands of the international private sector. The concomitant creation of new business opportunities for Jordanian elites, international military adventure entrepreneurs and the international weapons industry allows for new ways of retaining authoritarian power and reproducing deeply Orientalist images of Jordan. Within these, the agency of Jordanians remains clearly confined, so that Jordan itself appears to

---

[183] US Embassy Amman cable, 'Opportunities for Jordan's growing film industry', 7 August 2007, *Wikileaks*, 07Amman3326.
[184] MissionX, 'Jordanian movie action performers hone craft at KASOTC', promotional video, available at: www.missionx.com/film–tv.html#prettyPhoto/0/.

constantly require external intervention in order for abstract notions of democracy, economic development and security to seemingly become realised. The kind of security that is promoted by US security support is then primarily the security of the Jordanian regime, US geostrategic interests and private businesses. For the Jordanian population at large, the security promoted appears much more simulated than real, as it is either constructed as a security threat or as a passive object waiting to be secured.

A popular theme in research on commercial security is the blurring of boundaries.[185] This chapter provides ample evidence of the existence of such blurred boundaries in US-Jordanian military collaboration at KASOTC. Various scholars of commercial security have, however, also called for more attention to the ways in which deeply problematic biopolitical judgements reinforce lines of separation.[186] Based on a discussion of the ways in which certain identities are hypervisibilised, Amar suggests that we are witnessing the emergence of a new type of human security governance and the potential end of neoliberalism.[187] This chapter has identified at KASOTC numerous examples of such a deeply anti-democratic divergent ascription of value to different lives, including a clear distinction between the seemingly apolitical customer, who simulates, markets and plays war, and marginalised groups, who are simulated as a threat and/or excluded. The politics of commercial security at KASOTC are thus shown to revolve around the hierarchical integration of different identity groups depending on their ability to market the deeply problematic conceptions of different value attached to their own and other human lives.

Regarding the simultaneous blurring and reinforcement of boundaries, I have argued that the former has the crucial effect of establishing new and of deepening old commercial security markets, while the latter helps to determine who plays what role in these. In contrast to Amar, I have suggested that, at KASOTC, both processes occur in close association. Thus, my findings do not support the thesis of an emerging new type of moralised human security governance that gradually replaces an old neoliberal mode. Rather, we can observe at

---

[185] McDonald, 'Grammars of violence, modes of embodiment and frontiers of the subject', p. 149; Abrahamsen and Williams, 'Securing the city', p. 242; Stahl, 'Life is war', p. 129.

[186] Dalby, S., 'Challenging cartographies of enmity: empire, war and culture in contemporary militarization', in: Stavrianakis, Anna and Selby, Jan (eds.), *Militarism and International Relations: Political Economy, Security and Theory* (Abingdon: Routledge, 2013), p. 38. Berndtsson and Stern, 'Private security guards', p. 55. Reid-Henry, 'Spaces of security and development', p. 102.

[187] Amar, *The Security Archipelago*, p. 17.

KASOTC both the moralisation of market policies and the market-isation of moral politics.

The deeply problematic conceptions about the different worth of human subjects that were shown to be reproduced by US-Jordanian military collaboration at KASOTC are then not external to processes of commercialisation in the military sphere, but instead lie at their very core. With market policies and moral politics so intimately intertwined, the politics of commercial security at KASOTC does not simply reproduce conventional Orientalist lines of separation. Rather, one can observe a gradual merging of the roles of *protector* and service provider, *protected* and customer, and *protected against* and marginalised. While contemporary warfare attempts to make this latter category appear absent, war's virtuous simulations and its deadly realities are – particularly in a Global South context – often in close proximity.

In June 2016, a suicide bomber killed several Jordanian soldiers only a few hundred kilometres from KASOTC in the remote desert region of Rukbān. In response, Jordan quickly declared its entire north-eastern border region a closed 'military zone'. Unlike at KASOTC, the implicit labelling of all refugees in the area as potential terrorists had very real implications in Rukbān. Tens of thousands of Syrian refugees were thus suddenly left stranded in the desert by Jordanian border guards, all of whom had, since 2014, received compulsory training at KASOTC. While it is impossible to draw a direct causal link, KASOTC's simulation of the refugee as a security threat nevertheless seems in important ways to have preceded and engendered precisely the kind of reality that it intended to model and prepare for.[188] In short, within only a few years the simulation of the refugee as a terrorist at KASOTC had become a deadly reality in Rukbān. For the countless discourses and practices that construct refugee populations as security threats, KASOTC's refugee camp had thus proven to be more real than real refugee camps. Paraphrasing Der Derian,[189] one may conclude that the biopolitical judgements that were shown to be inscribed in US-Jordanian military collaboration at KASOTC and that simulated the refugee as terrorist might indeed have helped to actually invent the refugee as terrorist.[190]

Finally, I have demonstrated that processes of commercialisation in US-Jordanian military collaboration directly presuppose, create and reinforce marketable images of 'the enemy'. These fundamentally revolve around the creation of non-Western insecurities, which means the relegation of marginalised lives to a position of lesser value and agency, and the

---

[188] Der Derian, *Virtuous War*, p. 15.   [189] Der Derian, *Virtuous War*, p. 109.
[190] See Bilgin, 'The "Western-centrism" of security studies', pp. 615–622.

elevation of others to that of manager, *protector* and customer. The processes of commercialisation and militarisation triggered by US-Jordanian military collaboration are deeply anti-democratic, as notions of public control lose ground and deliberative questions about war are replaced by consumerist desires to play war and simultaneously enhance one's corporate leadership skills.

7 Imperial Coercion, Liberal Intervention and the Rise of Populist Politics

While this book has focused on US and European policy in Jordan, it has also provided a vivid illustration of what greater US and European policy presence in the Global South means. As one of the largest recipients of US and European foreign aid worldwide, Jordan is thus not just a case study, but a state of the art. I have argued that even though US and European policy in Jordan comes under the cloak of a universally applicable morality that claims the surmounting of authoritarianism as its objective, its effect is not very different from traditional modes of imperial support for authoritarian regimes, except for making resistance against it all the harder.

In *Promoting Democracy, Reinforcing Authoritarianism*, I have investigated what US and European 'democracy promoters' in Jordan *actually do* when they promote democracy. Against the backdrop of the remarkable stability of the authoritarian regime in Jordan, I have inquired into the often unforeseen and contradictory consequences of external attempts at 'democracy promotion' and into the kind of power (re)produced by them. I have discussed 'democracy promotion' through a focus on practice, which allows for an empirically grounded illustration of the different ways in which interventions in the name of democracy actually reinforce and perpetuate exactly those hierarchies of power they initially set out to overcome. I have shown that Jordanian authoritarianism is so stable not despite, but in part directly because of, US and European efforts at 'democracy promotion' in the country. As the idea of 'democracy promotion' itself fundamentally relies on seeming universal moral hierarchies, the maintenance of the latter has been shown to be at the very centre of the project. This occurs via the depoliticisation of the structural dynamics of power that underlie Jordanian authoritarianism, via the technocratisation of questions of democracy and the subordination of the political context in which the 'democracy promotion' interventions take place to a seemingly decontextualised level of 'the universal'. While these processes create the necessary space and the practical distance that allows for the emergence of the universally deployable democracy expert,

I have demonstrated that the *kind* of democracy that the latter promotes is practically void of any emancipatory potential.

I have shown that the narrow focus that 'democracy promoters' give to the promotion of procedural democracy is entirely reconcilable with various political, economic and social modes of authoritarian governance. The effect of 'democracy promotion' in Jordan is thus seemingly one of uniting authoritarianism with notions of democracy, while in the process emptying the latter of practically all its emancipatory meaning. The procedural conceptual closure and the associated taming of the power of democracy effectively help to stabilise and reinforce abstract moral, as well as real political and economic, hierarchies of power. The *kind* of democracy that is promoted presents no challenge to the maintenance of deeply authoritarian power structures.

Instead, it constitutes a complementary counterpart of an elite project aimed at the further deepening of class power and the enforcement of Western security interests. Within these processes, Jordanians appear, along deeply Orientalist lines, either as passive and unknowing objects that require urgent external support (in the form of democracy training, institutional support, awareness training, security support, etc.) or as a source of danger that needs to be secured against (civil society actors deemed to be too political, the imagined refugee-terrorist, etc.).

Such Orientalist images play a major role in the reinforcement of imagined moral hierarchies. They help in the continuous (re)construction of 'the Jordanian' as a passive object, whose alleged inability to function democratically, and lack of knowledge and awareness of democracy, seemingly requires constant external interventions. While the structural barriers that prevent further emancipatory processes of democratisation remain largely ignored and/or directly perpetuated by the 'democracy promotion' project, those alleged barriers that the project does address are both the result of and the enabling factor for the proclaimed universal superiority of narrow procedural conceptualisations of democracy. The effect of US and European efforts at 'democracy promotion' in Jordan is thus to help maintain the appearance of the liberal democratic dream as a constant point of reference – seemingly realisable but ultimately unattainable – on the horizon of Jordanian politics. The very moral hierarchies that 'democracy promotion' interventions intend to overcome are thus only further reinforced, now behind a façade of constant democratisation.

This book adopted a two-pronged approach that pays close attention to both ideational and material factors in the reproduction of 'democracy promotion' as a process of domination. It has thus tried to overcome the dichotomy in much critical research on the topic between constructivist approaches that tend to ignore the specific understandings of economy and security that underlie efforts at 'democracy promotion' on the one hand and critical political economy approaches that tend to downplay the role of human agency on the other. The book has demonstrated the different agency- and structure-related mechanisms through which 'democracy promotion' is perpetuated. These include, among others, its functioning as a process that seemingly (re)confirms desired self-understandings as 'liberal', 'democratic' and 'modern' *vis-à-vis* 'the Jordanian non-democratic other'.

I have also emphasised the predominance of the procedural within external attempts at 'democracy promotion', which effectively turns unintended consequences into mere reminders of the project's incompleteness and thus of the need for further improvements. Other dynamics include 'democracy promotion's' roles as facilitating a project of neoliberal restructuring and as providing Western imperialism with a moral purpose. Finally, by combining ideational and material factors, this book opens doors to move beyond strictly discourse- or structure-focused approaches in the study of 'democracy promotion' and the politics of intervention.

The most important insight of this book is that US and European attempts at 'democracy promotion' in Jordan are not just window dressing, but are directly reinforcing authoritarian power in the country and as such are neither external to nor alleviate the processes of domination associated with neoliberal restructuring and security support to an authoritarian state.

In late May and early June of 2018, Jordan once again witnessed several days of anti-regime protests. Protestors not only demanded the reversal of price hikes on fuel and electricity and the repeal of an income tax draft law that would have increased taxation on lower earners, but also the dismissal of Prime Minister Hani al-Mulki and more meaningful public participation in political and economic decision-making processes.[1] Perhaps one of the most striking features of these protests – at least for those with an interest in the politics of intervention – was the fact that they were led, at least initially, by what are perhaps the only major established political institutions in Jordan that have remained immune to external assistance: Jordan's professional associations.[2]

As demonstrated throughout this book, it is for very good reasons that the arenas provided by the US and European 'democracy promotion'

---

[1] See Moore, P., 'The fiscal politics of rebellious Jordan', *Middle East Report Online*, 21 June 2018; and Ababneh, S., 'Do you know who governs us? The damned Monetary Fund', *Middle East Report Online*, 30 June 2018.

[2] See Schuetze, B., 'Confronting authoritarianism vs. disciplining democracy: the recent protests in Jordan and US attempts at democracy promotion', *Jadaliyya*, 30 July 2018.

project in Jordan play no role in popular protests against authoritarian rule. Instead, the objectives of the Jordanian regime, on the one hand, and US and European policy in Jordan, on the other, align closely as both sides attempt to make Jordanians' democratic demands compatible with authoritarian stability. While I have argued that external efforts at 'democracy promotion' in Jordan are part of a wider strategy of authoritarian upgrading, it is also important to keep in mind that challenges to authoritarian rule of course nevertheless persist, as illustrated by the protests in summer 2018. I thus strongly caution against any deterministic approaches regarding the (im)possibility of processes of democratisation in the country.[3] Nevertheless, the paternal guiding hands of US and European 'democracy promoters' have never been behind any meaningful challenges to authoritarian rule in the country in the past, and nor are they likely to be in the future. This raises several important questions for the future (study) of 'democracy promotion' at large.

If external efforts at 'democracy promotion' are part of a wider strategy of control and domination, how are its effects any different from the openly coercive imperial control traditionally applied by Western states? Given that 'democracy promotion' is emblematic of the liberal international order, what does the current rise of populist movements mean for the future of 'democracy promotion'? What role did the 'democracy promotion' project – via the effective reinforcement of assumptions of cultural difference – play in the current rise of populist politics? Or, in other words, how does the rising populism all over the world impact on the 'democracy promotion' project, and how have US and European attempts at 'democracy promotion' also contributed to said rise of populist politics?

In this book I have argued that liberalism, liberal intervention and 'democracy promotion' are heavily complicit in various forms of structural violence. I have demonstrated that liberal interventions in the name of democracy reinforce imagined moral hierarchies, fundamentally undermine democratic values and reproduce authoritarian power behind a façade of slow but gradual democratisation, while simultaneously perpetuating deeply Orientalist notions that serve as an extremely efficient rationale for an ongoing politics of intervention. Further, my findings point to the precarious nature of the oft-invoked binary between authoritarian and democratic modes of governance. If, as I have argued, 'democracy promotion' reinforces authoritarian practices, scholars need to move beyond said binary to investigate further the ways in which

---

[3] See Ryan, C.R., *Jordan and the Arab Uprisings: Regime Survival and Politics beyond the State* (New York: Columbia University Press, 2018), p. 9.

different authoritarian and democratic practices may be interlinked. Cavatorta has in this context spoken of a gradual global convergence of governance around liberal-authoritarian forms of rule.[4]

Simultaneous processes of authoritarian upgrading and democratic downgrading have prepared the way for the rise of populist politics all over the world, Trump, Putin, Erdogan, Duterte and Bolsonaro being only some of the most notable examples. As a consequence, 'democracy promotion' is increasingly coming under populist pressure both in 'target' countries and 'at home'. Just as Russia, the UAE and Egypt, among others, have shut down the offices of US and European institutions engaged in 'democracy promotion', Trump's approach to 'democracy promotion' oscillates between disinterest and the large-scale cutting of foreign aid. Finally, rising powers such as Brazil and India show a decided disinclination to the idea of 'democracy promotion' abroad.[5]

But what exactly does the growing national populist pressure on the 'democracy promotion' project mean for researchers with an interest in interventions in the name of 'democracy', and for political activists struggling to resist authoritarian power? Despite his strong critique of 'democracy promotion', Guilhot argues that 'a hegemony built on the notion of democracy and human rights is ... highly preferable to a hegemonic system regulated only by national interests and geopolitical calculations'.[6] While such an interpretation is also regularly found among US and European 'democracy promoters', Jordanian NGO employees and Jordanian politicians, this book suggests a somewhat more cautious response.

Although the means of external social control have undergone important changes during recent decades, I have demonstrated that these have not only failed to fundamentally alter deeply authoritarian dynamics of power, but actually – in the case of Jordan – even led to their reinforcement. As shown throughout this book, the introduction of ethical norms to the foreign policies of Western states in no way impedes or limits the enforcement of US and/or European geopolitical calculations in the region, within which the protection of the stability of a number of authoritarian regimes features prominently. Rather, I have demonstrated that the framing of Western foreign policies under a narrative of 'democracy

---

[4] Cavatorta, F., 'The convergence of governance: upgrading authoritarianism in the Arab world and downgrading democracy elsewhere?', *Middle East Critique*, Vol. 19, No. 3, Fall 2010, pp. 217–218.

[5] Stuenkel, O., 'Rising powers and the future of democracy promotion: the case of Brazil and India', *Third World Quarterly*, Vol. 34, No. 2, 2013, pp. 339–355.

[6] Guilhot, N., *The Democracy Makers: Human Rights and International Order* (New York: Columbia University Press, 2005), p. 14.

promotion' has elevated the pursuit of national interests, including external support for authoritarian regimes, to a new level of efficiency.

This is primarily due to the fact that the narrative manages to deprive those who resist authoritarianism of their hitherto exclusive position as advocates for democratic change. It is thus very difficult for political activists to challenge authoritarian modes of governance that adopt the language of procedural democracy since, with the help of the latter, mechanisms of control and domination have only been further refined and internalised. While a politics of domination has traditionally relied on the open threat and/or use of violence, culturalist narratives of being 'not yet ready' for democracy, economic exploitation and processes of militarisation now have very similar effects and remind us of the difficulty of clearly separating coercive and consensual means of social control.

Although contemporary support for Jordanian authoritarianism comes under the cloak of a universally applicable morality that claims the surmounting of authoritarianism as its objective, its effect is not particularly different from traditional modes of imperial support for authoritarian regimes, except for making resistance against it all the harder. It is thus much more insightful to inquire into the continuities that link Western imperialism, liberal interventionism and populism, rather than giving a flawed impression of distinct and self-contained ideologies and/or eras. While US foreign assistance worldwide has been drastically reduced under the Trump administration, US aid to Jordan, including funds dedicated to 'democracy promotion', remain consistently high (some are even further increasing).[7] Just as the 'democracy promotion' project does not represent a clear break from past imperialism, populist politics is not to be seen as fully separate from contemporary liberalism either, despite the pressure it puts on the latter. The recognition of certain continuities between imperialism, liberalism and populism is important in so far as it cautions against the romanticisation of contemporary liberal interventions and reminds us that imperial coercion and 'democracy promotion' are part of the same politics of control and domination.

If Jordanian authoritarianism is in part reproduced by practices of US and European 'democracy promotion' that traverse Jordan's national borders, resistance against authoritarian practices in Jordan also needs to acknowledge this transregional dimension. One of the goals of this

---

[7] US foreign assistance worldwide amounted to approximately USD 31 billion in 2016, compared to USD 18 billion for 2018. See the map of foreign assistance worldwide at: www.foreignassistance.gov/explore. The annual amounts of US 'democracy, human rights and governance' assistance to Jordan requested amounted to USD 25 million in 2013, USD 28 million in 2014, USD 28 million in 2015, USD 47 million in 2016, USD 35 million in 2017, USD 40 million in 2018 and USD 42 million in 2019.

book was thus to lay bare some of the modes of transregional authoritarian reinforcement in Jordan. Ultimately, in order to be effective, resistance against Jordanian authoritarianism must occur both in and beyond Jordan's national borders, and should not occur via, but in opposition to, an external policy of 'democracy promotion'.

The strategy that I have pursued in this book in order to demonstrate the structural violence inherent in 'democracy promotion' is one of constant contextualisation. I began by drawing on the work of Hopgood and by arguing that the typically liberal belief in an objective moral authority is fundamentally premised on the absence of context. Informed by Wedeen's notion of culture as 'processes of meaning-construction',[8] I investigated what 'democracy promoters' *actually do* when they promote democracy and, in doing so, laid bare some of the micropolitics of domination which, rather than testifying to the supposed incompleteness of the liberal project, actually lie at its core. At a more general level, this book calls for the study of moral interventions at large through a focus on their often unintended consequences and thus on the ways in which they often perpetuate precisely those moral hierarchies they initially set out to overcome. Important studies pursuing such an approach include those conducted on the topic of 'development aid' by Ferguson and on human rights reporting by Hopgood.[9]

Hopgood's observation that abstract moral authority relies on the absence of context of course brings up the question of whether conceptions of moral authority can be contextualised at all. While I have argued that the universal moral authority claimed by 'democracy promotion' is necessarily compromised the very moment 'democracy promoters' engage with the political context of their 'target' countries, it is important to note that this does not imply that moral behaviour in itself is impossible. Instead, I suggest that conceptions of morality are only meaningful when they are contextualised. The contextualisation of morality may of course take fundamentally different shapes depending on the context in which it occurs, however. First and foremost, this is a reminder of the importance of context sensitivity as opposed to any attempt at universalisation. Liberalism's ability to shape the world in its image has thus always been highly limited and should not be idealised in hindsight. To take morality seriously ultimately means to accept the multiplicity of

---

[8] Wedeen, L., 'Conceptualizing culture: possibilities for political science', *The American Political Science Review*, Vol. 96, No. 4, December 2002, p. 717.

[9] Ferguson, J., *The Anti-Politics Machine: 'Development,' Depoliticization, and Bureaucratic Power in Lesotho* (Minneapolis: University of Minnesota Press, 1994); Hopgood, S., *Keepers of the Flame: Understanding Amnesty International* (London: Cornell University Press, 2006).

modernities and to reassert the importance of the contextual over the universal.

Can an altered 'democracy promotion' project address these concerns? Can 'democracy promotion' ever be adequately reformed for it to become the emancipatory project that it claims to be? These questions run parallel to a quickly growing body of literature that concerns itself with questions of coloniality and decolonisation.[10] Based on the empirical data discussed in this book and in light of the conceptual anchoring of 'democracy promotion' in deeply Western-centric and Orientalist ways of knowing, I am decidedly sceptical about the possibility of adequately reforming or decolonising 'democracy promotion'. Instead, I view the 'democracy promotion' project as inextricably linked to a politics of control and domination.

Drawing on Ferguson, I argue that a fundamental transformation of the 'democracy promotion' project is highly unlikely to come about via internal reform.[11] Instead, 'democracy promotion' is currently coming under growing external populist pressure. This is not due to a lack of internal reform, however, but to the contradictory nature of the liberal project itself. Attempts to universalise deeply romanticised and strongly Western-centric conceptions of moral authority have thus, far from attaining their claimed objective, ultimately only strengthened fundamentally illiberal dynamics. Ironically, the current rise of populist politics is thus in at least some aspects the result of past liberal interventions and the different forms of structural violence and socio-economic exclusion and processes of depoliticisation associated with it. Finally, given the reinforcing effects that US and European attempts at 'democracy promotion' have on authoritarian practices and structures of power in Jordan, the waning power of global liberalism and the potential gradual decline of the global 'democracy promotion' project is not necessarily a loss worth mourning.

[10] See, for instance, Sabaratnam, M., 'IR in dialogue ... but can we change the subjects? A typology of decolonising strategies for the study of world politics', *Millennium: Journal of International Studies*, Vol. 39, No. 3, 2011, pp. 781–803 and De Jong, S., Icaza, R. and Rutazibwa, O.U. (eds.), *Decolonization and Feminisms in Global Teaching and Learning* (London: Routledge, 2018).

[11] Ferguson, *The Anti-Politics Machine*, pp. 279–288.

Sources and Bibliography

Interviews and Meetings

Note: Approximately 160 interviews were conducted in Jordan (September 2012–March 2013 and January 2015–February 2015), Washington, DC (May 2013–June 2013) and Brussels (May 2015). Due to regular requests for anonymisation, the list below includes only the organisational and institutional affiliation of the respective interviewee(s).

Jordanian state institutions and state-owned or -operated entities:
Anti-Corruption Commission (ACC)
Aqaba International Industrial Estate (AIIE)
Aqaba Special Economic Zone Authority (ASEZA)
Executive Privatisation Commission (EPC)
Independent Electoral Commission (IEC)
Jordan Development Zones Company (JDZ)
Jordan Enterprise Development Corporation (JEDCO)
King Abdullah II Special Operations Training Center (KASOTC)
Ministry of Planning and International Cooperation (MoPIC)
Ministry of Political Development (MoPD)
Parliament
Royal Court
Royal Institute for Inter-Faith Studies (RIIFS)
University of Jordan (UoJ)
Jordanian civil society:
Agricultural Engineers Association
Al-'Arab Al-Yawm
Al-Ghad
Al-Hayat Centre for Civil Society Development
Al-Quds Center for Political Studies
Amman Center for Peace and Development (ACPD)
AmmanNet
Center for Defending Freedom of Journalists (CDFJ)
Centre for Strategic Studies (CSS)
Dhabaḥtūnā national campaign for student rights
Ḥibr (www.7iber.com)
Ḥirāk
Identity Center
Islamic Action Front (IAF)
Mizan Law Group
National Centre for Human Rights (NCHR)

National Current Party (aṭ-Tayyār al-Waṭaniy)
Phenix Centre
Researchers and academics
Tamkeen Center for Legal Aid and Human Rights
Young Entrepreneurs Association (YEA)

US state institutions:

Department of State (DoS)
Middle East Partnership Initiative (MEPI)
USAID – Jordan and Washington, DC offices
US Embassy in Jordan

US quasi-governmental organisations, companies, associations, think tanks and research centres:

American Bar Association (ABA) – Amman
Atlantic Council
Brookings Institute
Carnegie Endowment for International Peace
Center for American Progress
Center for International Private Enterprise (CIPE)
Center for Strategic and International Studies (CSIS)
Council on Foreign Relations (CFR)
Creative Associates International
Democracy International (DI)
Development Alternatives Incorporated (DAI)
Family Health International 360 (FHI 360)
International Foundation for Electoral Systems (IFES)
International Republican Institute (IRI)
International Youth Foundation (IYF)
Management Systems International (MSI)
National Democratic Institute (NDI)
National Endowment for Democracy (NED)
Open Society Foundations (OSF)
Partners for Democratic Change
Washington Institute for Near East Policy (WINEP)

European state institutions:

Dutch Embassy in Jordan
EU Delegation in Jordan
EU EOM in Jordan
EuropeAID
European Commission
European External Action Service (EEAS)
German Embassy in Jordan
Gesellschaft für Internationale Zusammenarbeit (GIZ)
UK Embassy in Jordan

European quasi-governmental organisations, companies, associations, think tanks and research centres:

Election Observation and Democratic Support Project (EODS)
European Endowment for Democracy (EED)

Friedrich Ebert Foundation (FES)
Friedrich Naumann Foundation for Freedom (FNF)
Konrad Adenauer Foundation (KAS)
Other organisations and institutions:
Foundation for the Future (FFF)
International Monetary Fund (IMF)
United Nations Development Programme (UNDP)

Speeches, Reports, Public Statements, Internal Documents, Newsletters and Laws

ACED, USAID and AECOM, *Aqaba Community and Economic Development (ACED) Program – Community Development*, PowerPoint presentation, March 2010.

ACED, USAID and AECOM, *Performance Monitoring Plan*, 26 February 2008.

ACED, USAID and AECOM, *Skills Gap and Training Needs Analysis for Tourism and Supporting Services*, 15 July 2008.

ACED II, USAID and AECOM, *Final Report*, November 2014.

Adiv, Aaron and Cannell, Alan, *Aqaba Public Transport Network Plan – Final Report*, AZEM, Nathan Associates and USAID for ASEZA and ADC, PowerPoint presentation, 19 June 2006.

Al Urdun Al Jadid Research Center, *Civil Society Index* – Analytical Country Report: *Jordan 2010, the Contemporary Jordanian Civil Society: Characteristics, Challenges and Tasks* (Amman: Civicus, Foundation for the Future and UNDP, 2010), available at: www.civicus.org/downloads/CSI/Jordan.pdf.

Amnesty International, *Jordan: 'Your Confessions Are Ready for you to Sign': Detention and Torture of Political Suspects* (London: Amnesty International, 23 July 2006), available at: www.amnesty.org/en/documents/MDE16/005/2006/fr/.

ASEZA, 'Investment incentives', available at: www.aqabazone.com/Pages/view page.aspx?pageID=56.

AZEM and USAID, *Overview of the AZEM Project*, PowerPoint presentation, 1 June 2006.

AZEM, USAID and Nathan Associates, *Aqaba Community Profile*, June 2004.

AZEM, USAID and Nathan Associates, *ASEZA and ADC: Building a New Partnership – a Concept Paper*, 14 October 2004.

AZEM, USAID and Nathan Associates, *Jordan: Aqaba Special Economic Zone – Regional Economic Development Plan Volume III – Fiscal Conditions for Regional Development*, 27 June 2006.

Baskin, Gershon and Al Qaq, Zakaria (eds.), *Israeli-Palestinian-Jordanian Trade: Present Issues, Future Possibilities* (Jerusalem: Israel/Palestine Center for Research and Information (IPCRI), Center for International Private Enterprise (CIPE) and Konrad Adenauer Foundation (KAS), April 1998).

Bechtel, *Draft Business Plan for the Aqaba Development Company*, 31 August 2003.

Bolle, Mary J., Prados, Alfred and Sharp, Jeremy, *Qualifying Industrial Zones in Jordan: A Model for Promoting Peace and Development in the Middle East?*, CRS Report RS22002, Congressional Research Center, Washington, DC, 26 January 2005.

Bush, George W., 'A distinctly American internationalism', speech at the Ronald Reagan Presidential Library, Simi Valley, California, 19 November 1999.

Bush, George W., 'The future of Iraq', speech at the American Enterprise Institute, Washington, DC, 26 February 2003.

Carter Center, *Study Mission Report on Jordan's 2013 Parliamentary Elections*, 14 February 2013, available at: www.cartercenter.org/news/pr/jordan-021 413.html.

Commission of the European Communities, *Communication from the Commission on EU Election Assistance and Observation*, COM(2000) 191 final (Brussels: European Commission, April 2000).

Constitution of the Hashemite Kingdom of Jordan, available at: www.refworld .org/pdfid/3ae6b53310.pdf.

Denoeux, Guilain (MSI), Wilcox, Oliver (USAID) and Zawaneh, Zayyan (MSI), *Jordan Democracy and Governance Assessment*, USAID Center for Democracy and Governance and USAID/Jordan, August 2003, available at: http://pdf .usaid.gov/pdf_docs/pnadd348.pdf.

European Commission, *Commission Implementing Decision of 11.6.2014 Modifying Decision C(2010) 7441 on the Annual Action Programme 2010 in favour of the Kingdom of Jordan for the 'Support to Democratic Governance' Programme* (Brussels: European Commission, 11 June 2014).

European Commission, *Communication from the Commission to the European Parliament, the Council, the European Economic and Social Committee and the Committee of the Regions – The Roots of Democracy and Sustainable Development: Europe's Engagement with Civil Society in External Relations* (Brussels: European Commission, 12 September 2012).

European Commission, *Handbook for European Union Election Observation* (Brussels: European Commission, 2009).

EEAS and European Commission, *Programming of the European Neighbourhood Instrument (ENI) – 2014–2020 – Single Support Framework for EU support to Jordan (2014–2017)*, available at: https://ec.europa.eu/neighbourhood-enlarge ment/sites/near/files/single_support_framework_2014-2020.pdf.

ENPI, *Jordan – National Indicative Programme 2011–2013*, available at: https://ec .europa.eu/europeaid/sites/devco/files/nip-jordan-2011-2013_en.pdf.

ENPI, *Jordan – Strategy Paper 2007–2013 & National Indicative Programme 2007–2010*, available at: https://ec.europa.eu/europeaid/sites/devco/files/csp-ni p-jordan-2007-2013_en.pdf.

EU Delegation in Jordan, *Action Fiche for Jordan – Democratic Governance*, available at: https://ec.europa.eu/neighbourhood-enlargement/sites/near/files/c201 07441_aap_jordanie_2010_ad1.pdf.

EU Election Observation Mission, *Final Report: Parliamentary Elections 2013*, 2013.

FES, *Comprehensive Guide to Civil Society Organisations in Jordan 2010* (Amman: FES and Phenix Center, 2010).

FES, *Guide to Political Life in Jordan 2007–2011* (Amman: FES and Phenix Center, 2008).

FES and RSS, *The Future of Jordan's Qualified Industrial Zones (QIZs)*, Amman, 2013.

FHI 360, *Jordan Civil Society Program – October 5, 2008–October 4, 2013: Final Report* (Washington, DC: FHI 360, submitted to USAID Jordan, 3 January 2014).

Finkel, Steven E. et al., *Deepening Our Understanding of the Effects of US Foreign Assistance on Democracy Building – Final Report* (USAID, Vanderbilt University, University of Pittsburgh, Latin American Public Opinion Project and Hertie School of Governance Berlin, 28 January 2008).

Human Rights Watch, *World Report 2013* (New York: Human Rights Watch, 2013).

ICNL, Law of Societies (No. 51 of 2008) as Amended by Law No. 22 of 2009, unofficial translation by the ICNL.

IDEA, *Electoral System Design: The New International IDEA Handbook* (Stockholm: International IDEA, 2005).

Identity Center, *Map of the Political Parties and Movements in Jordan* (Amman: Netherlands Institute for Multiparty Democracy and Embassy of the Kingdom of the Netherlands, 2013–2014).

Institute for Global Labour and Human Rights, *Sexual Predators and Serial Rapists Run Wild at Wal-Mart Supplier in Jordan: Young Women Workers Raped, Tortured and Beaten at the Classic Factory* (Pittsburgh: Institute for Global Labour and Human Rights, June 2011).

International Crisis Group, *Popular Protest in North Africa and the Middle East (IX): Dallying with Reform in a Divided Jordan* (Amman/Brussels: Middle East/ North Africa Report No. 118, 12 March 2012).

International Human Rights Network, *Human Rights NGO Capacity Building – Iraq: Next Steps Report* (Oldcastle, Ireland: IHRN, 2005).

IRI, *Jordan Parliamentary Elections January 23, 2013, Final Report*, 2013.

IRI, *Pre-election Assessment Statement*, 3 December, 2012.

Jordan Independent Electoral Commission Law No. 11, 2012.

KASOTC, *5th Annual Warrior Competition* (KASOTC, official program, 24–28 March 2013).

King Abdullah II, 'Each playing our part in a new democracy', Royal Hashemite Court, Amman, third discussion paper, 2 March 2013, available at: https://kingabdullah.jo/en/discussion-papers/each-playing-our-part-new-democracy.

King Abdullah II, 'Goals, achievements and conventions: pillars for deepening our democratic transition', Royal Hashemite Court, Amman, fifth discussion paper, 13 September 2014, available at: https://kingabdullah.jo/en/discussion-papers/goals-achievements-and-conventions-pillars-deepening-our-democratic-transition.

King Abdullah II, 'Making our democratic system work for all Jordanians', Royal Hashemite Court, Amman, second discussion paper, 16 January 2013, available at: https://kingabdullah.jo/en/discussion-papers/making-our-democratic-system-work-all-jordanians.

King Abdullah II, 'Our journey to forge our path towards democracy', Royal Hashemite Court, Amman, first discussion paper, 29 December 2012, available at: https://kingabdullah.jo/en/discussion-papers/our-journey-forge-o ur-path-towards-democracy.

King Abdullah II, 'Towards democratic empowerment and active citizenship', Royal Hashemite Court, Amman, fourth discussion paper, 2 June 2013, available at: https://kingabdullah.jo/en/discussion-papers/towards-democratic-emp owerment-and-active-citizenship.

King Abdullah II, *The Daily Show* with Jon Stewart, 25 September 2012.

King Abdullah II, 'To the Jordanian people RE: elections' success', Royal Hashemite Court, Amman, letter, translated from Arabic, 29 January 2013, available at: https://kingabdullah.jo/en/letters/letter-jordanian-people-elections.

Marks, Daniel (managing editor), *Executive Jordan* (Amman: Gulf Media Consulting, 2007).

Merloe, Patrick, *Promoting Legal Frameworks for Democratic Elections: An NDI Guide for Developing Election Laws and Law Commentaries* (Washington, DC: National Democratic Institute (NDI), 2008).

MoPIC and EU Programme Administration Office (PAO), *Support to Human Rights and Good Governance Programme – Draft Final Report – Narrative and Financial (June 2005–May 2012)*, 2013.

National Agenda Steering Committee, *National Agenda: The Jordan We Strive For, 2006–2015* (Amman: National Agenda Steering Committee, 2005), available at: www.nationalagenda.jo/Portals/0/EnglishBooklet.pdf.

NDI, *Final International Election Observation Report on the Jordanian Parliamentary Elections, November 9, 2010*, 2011.

NDI, *Final Report on the Jordanian Parliamentary Elections, January 23, 2013*, 2013.

NDI, *Pre-Election Assessment Delegation Statement Regarding Jordan's 2013 Legislative Elections*, 19 November 2012.

NDI and USAID, 'Ana Usharek – Empowering youth at Jordanian universities to play an informed role in Jordan's political & decision-making processes', Newsletter, Edition 5, April 2014.

NDI and USAID, 'Ana Usharek – Empowering youth at Jordanian universities to play an informed role in Jordan's political & decision-making processes', Newsletter, Edition 6, December 2014.

NDI and USAID, 'I participate – Empowering youth at Jordanian universities to play an informed role in Jordan's political & decision-making processes program newsletter', Newsletter, Edition 1, June 2012.

NDI Jordan, 'Welcome to the Republic of Ibar', document for training purposes, undated.

Nowak, Manfred, *Report of the Special Rapporteur on Torture and Other Cruel, Inhuman or Degrading Treatment or Punishment – Mission to Jordan* (United Nations: Human Rights Council, 5 January 2007).

Nuland, Victoria (Spokesperson, US DoS), 'Daily press briefing', *DoS*, Washington, DC, 25 January 2013.

Obama, Barack (President of the USA), Inaugural address, 20 January 2009, available at: https://obamawhitehouse.archives.gov/blog/2009/01/21/presi dent-barack-obamas-inaugural-address.

Pearlstein, Deborah and Patel, Priti, *Behind the Wire: An Update to Ending Secret Detentions* (New York: Human Rights First, 2005).

President of the United States, *National Security Strategy* (Washington, DC: The White House, May 2010).

Sharp, Jeremy M., *Jordan: Background and U.S. Relations*, CRS, Washington, DC, 1 April 2013.

Toner, Mark C. (Deputy Spokesperson, US DoS), 'Daily press briefing', DoS, Washington, DC, 15 November 2012.

UN, *Declaration of Principles for International Election Observation* (New York: United Nations, October 2005).

UN Committee against Torture, *Concluding Observations of the Committee against Torture – Jordan*, 44th session, 26 April–14 May 2010.

USAID, *Democracy and Governance: A Conceptual Framework* (Washington, DC: Office of Democracy and Governance, USAID, technical publication series, November 1998).

USAID, *Strategic Statement Jordan 2007–2011*, undated, available at: http://pdf .usaid.gov/pdf_docs/Pdacn487.pdf.

USAID, *Jordan Country Development Cooperation Strategy 2013–2017*, 2015, available at: www.usaid.gov/jordan/documents/cdcs.

USAID, *USAID/Jordan Country Strategy 2010–2014* (Washington, DC, March 2010).

USAID, *USAID Strategy on Democracy, Human Rights and Governance* (Washington, DC: USAID, June 2013).

USAID Jordan, 'Civil Society Program', USAID Jordan, Democracy & Governance Sector – Project Profile, April 2012.

USAID Jordan, 'Rule of Law Program', USAID Jordan, Democracy & Governance Sector – Project Profile, April 2012.

USAID Jordan, *United States Support for the City of Aqaba*, April 2004.

US DoS, *Jordan 2013 Human Rights Report* (Washington, DC: US DoS, Bureau of Democracy, Human Rights and Labor, 2013).

US DoS, *Supporting Human Rights and Democracy: The U.S. Record 2006* (Washington, DC: US DoS, Bureau of Democracy, Human Rights and Labor, 2006).

Williamson, Winkie and Hakki, Huda, *Mapping Study of Non-State Actors in Jordan* (The European Union's MED – Mediterranean Programme for the Hashemite Kingdom of Jordan, July 2010).

World Bank, *Hashemite Kingdom of Jordan Development Policy Review: Improving Institutions, Fiscal Policies and Structural Reforms for Greater Growth Resilience and Sustained Job Creation – Volume 1: Synthesis*, Poverty Reduction and Economic Management Department, Middle East and North Africa Region, 30 June 2012.

Zoellick, Robert B., 'Global trade and the Middle East: reawakening a vibrant past', remarks at the World Economic Forum, Amman, 23 June 2003.

Arabic-Language Sources

Al-Quds, 'Washington deploys American special forces and battleships to Aqaba in preparation of a rapid intervention' [*Washington tanshur qūwwāt amīrikīyah wa sufunan ḥarbīyah fī-l-ʿAqaba isti ʿdādan li-t-tadakhkhul as-sarī*], 15 July 2013, available at: https://arabsolaa.com/articles/view/126327.html.

Central Bank of Jordan, *Annual Report 2017 [at-Taqrīr as-sanawīy 2017]*, available at: www.cbj.gov.jo/EchoBusV3.0/SystemAssets/5c395f60-ea7f-4da5-8897-d0 46f33b75f4.pdf.

CSS, *Democracy in Jordan – 2006 [ad-Dimuqrātiyah fi-l-Urdun – 2006]* (Amman: CSS – University of Jordan, 2006), available at: http://jcss.org/Photos/634751 946970442902.pdf.

Dhabahtūnā, *Fourth Annual Report of the National Campaign for Student Rights [At-taqrīr as-sanawīy ar-rābiʿ li-l-ḥamlah al-waṭanīyah min ajl ḥuqūq aṭ-ṭalabah]*, 5 February 2012, available at: www.thab7toona.org.

Dhabahtūnā, *Study on the Politics of Higher Education and Medical Faculties – February 2013 [Dirāsah ḥawl siyāsat at-taʿlīm al-ʿālī wa-l-kulliyāt aṭ-ṭibbīyah – shubbāṭ 2013]*, available at: www.thab7toona.org.

Dunyā al-Waṭan, 'Raqqad acknowledges the illegitimacy of MPs – 2007 and 2010 elections forged' [*Iʿtirāfāt al-bāshā al-Raqqād tuṭīḥ bi-sharʿīyat an-nuwwāb . . . al-intikhābāt fī-l-ʿāmain 2007 wa 2010 muzawwarah*], 19 December 2011, available at: www.alwatanvoice.com/arabic/content/print/229399.html.

Hashemite University, 'Instructions for student societies in the Hashemite University' [*Taʿlīmāt al-jamʿīyāt al-ʿilmīyah aṭ-ṭullābīyah fī-l-jāmiʿah al-hāshimīyah*], undated, available at: https://hu.edu.jo/Regulations/student/%D 8%AF%D9%84%D9%8A%D9%84%20%D8%A7%D9%84%D8%B7%D8 %A7%D9%84%D8%A8.htm.

Hashemite University, 'Student disciplinary procedures system, 2003' [*Niẓām taʿdīb aṭ-ṭalaba fī-l-jāmiʿah al-hāshimīyah – niẓām raqm 107 li-sanah 2003*], available at: https://hu.edu.jo/Regulations/student/%D8%AF%D9%84%D9%8A%D9%84 %20%D8%A7%D9%84%D8%B7%D8%A7%D9%84%D8%A8.htm.

Kheitan, Fahed, 'If only they had not realised the void' [Laytahā lam taftun li-l-farāgh], *Al-Ghad*, 27 April 2014.

NDI Jordan, Anā Ushārik programme, 'Human Rights' [ḥuqūq al-insān], undated.

NDI Jordan, Anā Ushārik programme, 'Introduction to democracy' [madkhal ilā ad-dimuqrāṭīyah], undated.

NDI Jordan, Anā Ushārik programme, 'The electoral process' [al-ʿamalīyah al-intikhābīyah], undated.

NDI Jordan, Anā Ushārik programme, 'The role of media in the democratic process' [dawr al-iʿlām fī-l-ʿamalīyah ad-dimuqrāṭīyah], undated.

NDI Jordan, Anā Ushārik programme, 'The role of political parties in the democratic process' [dawr al-aḥzāb as-siyāsīyah fī-l-ʿamalīyah ad-dimuqrāṭīyah], undated.

US Embassy Cables Published by WikiLeaks

(accessible via https://cablegatesearch.wikileaks.org/search.php)

'Ambassador Crumpton's visit to Jordan's 71st Counterterrorism Battalion', 2 March 2006, *Wikileaks*, 06Amman1511.

'Aqaba authorities confront social, regional challenges', 1 April 2004, *Wikileaks*, 04Amman2554.

'Aqaba development update', 3 April 2008, *Wikileaks*, 08Amman1000.

'Aqaba faces the challenges of growth', 14 August 2008, *Wikileaks*, 08Amman2383.

'Developing Aqaba – the gateway to Jordan', 13 May 2007, *Wikileaks*, 07Amman2017.

'GoJ agrees to KASOTC arrangement', 5 April 2006, *Wikileaks*, 06Amman2403.

'Jordan: preview of Afghanistan support offer in upcoming Washington meetings', 22 January 2010, *Wikileaks*, 10Amman219.

'Jordan's security services', 7 March 2007, *Wikileaks*, 07Amman1031.

'Jordan-U.S. security dialogues', 25 November 2009, *Wikileaks*, 09Amman2579.

'Mixed signals out of Aqaba', 13 January 2003, *Wikileaks*, 03Amman244.

'Opportunities for Jordan's growing film industry', 7 August 2007, *Wikileaks*, 07Amman3326.

'Scenesetter for the Conus visit of General Khalid Sarayreh Commander of the Jordanian Armed Forces', 8 June 2006, *Wikileaks*, 06Amman4124.

'Scenesetter for the visit to Jordan of General Abizaid, Commander U.S. Central Command 28–29 March 2006', 28 March 2006, *Wikileaks*, 06Amman2234.

'Scenesetter for the visit to Jordan of Lieutenant General Buchanan, Commander 9th Air Force and U.S. Central Command Air Forces', 12 January 2006, *Wikileaks*, 06Amman234.

'U.S.-Jordan joint military committee meets', 22 November 2006, *Wikileaks*, 06Amman8549.

Websites

ASEZA, 'Investment incentives', available at: www.aqabazone.com/Pages/view page.aspx?pageID=56.

CIPE, available at: www.cipe.org.

EU-JDID, @EUJDID, Twitter, available at: https://twitter.com/EUJDID/status/ 909131685874331648.

Fieri, 'Fieri MissionX', available at: http://fieri.biz/off-site/.

Freedom House, *Freedom in the World – Jordan*, available at: https://freedom house.org/report/freedom-world/2015/jordan#.Vceu3PlR2uI.

GJU, Ana Usharek Initiative at GJU – Amman, 11 November 2012, available at: www.gju.edu.jo/page.aspx?type=n&lng=en&id=292.

Graham, Stephen, 'Technologies of exception: urban warfare and US military technoscience', conference lecture at the Symposium 'Archipelago of Exceptions. Sovereignties of Extraterritoriality' CCCB, 10–11 November 2005, available at: www.publicspace.org/en/text-library/eng/b022-technolo gies-of-exception-urban-warfare-and-us-military-technoscience.

IRI andMiddle East Marketing Research Consultants (MEMRC), 'National priorities, governance and political reform in Jordan', *National Public Opinion Poll No. 9*, 17–20 July 2012, available at: www.iri.org/sites/default/files/2012% 20September%2024%20Survey%20of%20Jordanian%20Public%20Opinio n,%20July%2017–20,%202012.pdf.

ITS Tactical, 'Silent professional auction: a special operations forces charity event', 2013, available at: www.itstactical.com/centcom/news/silent-profes sional-auction-a-special-operations-forces-charity-event/.

Jerusalem Summit 2004, Gen. (Ret.) Mansour Abu Rashid, available at: www.jerusalemsummit.org/eng/short.php?speaker=190&summit=31.

King Abdullah II, Royal Hashemite Court, Initiatives – The Democracy Empowerment Programme, undated, available at: http://kingabdullah.jo/inde x.php/en_US/initiatives/view/id/107.html.

KASOTC, 'Home of the Annual Warrior Competition', 2014, available at: www.kasotc.com/KASOTC_Site/Home.html.

KASOTC, 'Where advanced training meets advanced technology', 2011, available at: www.kasotc.com/KASOTC_Site/Home_files/KASOTC%20Downloaded.pdf.

Marcopolis, 'Largest real estate developer in Jordan', interview with Dr Moayad Samman, 8 November 2010, available at: www.marcopolis.net/largest-real-es tate-developer-in-jordan.htm.

MissionX, 'Adventures', available at: www.missionx.com/adventures.html.

MissionX, 'Jordanian movie action performers hone craft at KASOTC', promotional video, available at: www.missionx.com/film–tv.html#prettyPhoto/0/.

MissionX, 'Leadership development', available at: www.missionx.com/leader ship-development.html.

MissionX, 'Special operations adventure – Jordan – mission details', available at: www.missionx.com/special-operations.html.

NDI Jordan, promotional video, 30 October 2013, available at: www.youtube .com/watch?v=AIH_I-fCj6k.

NDI, @NDI, Twitter, 7 November 2017, available at: https://twitter.com/NDI/ status/927922558225272834.

Out Dare Adventures, 'MissionX – What is it and why do I want it?', 6 February 2013, available at: www.outdareadventures.com/missionx-what-is-it-and-why-do-i-want-it/.

UNDP Jordan, Electoral assistance in Jordan: a project funded by the European Union and implemented by UNDP, Brief/Background, available at: www.jo .undp.org/content/jordan/en/home/operations/projects/d.

UNRWA, 'Where we work', available at: www.unrwa.org/where-we-work/jordan.

USAID, Democracy and Governance – Overview, 28 February 2011, available at: http://jordan.usaid.gov/printme.aspx?webUrl=/en/OurWork/ProgramAr.

US Census Bureau, 'Foreign trade, trade in goods with Jordan', available at: www.census.gov/foreign-trade/balance/c5110.html.

US DoS, 'Foreign military financing account summary, 2015', available at: https://2009–2017.state.gov/t/pm/ppa/sat/c14560.htm.

US Government, Map of foreign assistance worldwide, available at: www.foreign assistance.gov/explore.

Al-Lawziyīn, 'Yā bayraqunā al-ʿālī' ('Our high flag'), translation of the lyrics, available at: www.allthelyrics.com/forum/showthread.php?t=115600.

ViaGlobal, 'Careers, 2015', available at: www.viaglobalgroup.com/careers/.

ViaGlobal, 'Tactical training', available at: www.viaglobalgroup.com/expertise/ #tactical.

ViaGlobal, The Board, Captain Steve Fitzgerald (USN, Ret.). The original ViaGlobal link is no longer active. A cached version may be found at: https://web.archive.org/web/20170111023756/www.zoominfo.com/p/Steve-F itzgerald/911564693.

Newspapers, Magazines and News Agency Reports

Aleandre, Rod and Lanham, David, 'King Abdullah Special Operations Training Center (KASOTC) provides capabilities for coalition forces', *Army AL&T*, October–December 2009, pp. 62–65.

Atalla, Munir, 'Silver lining of the Jordanian elections', *Open Democracy*, 28 January 2013, available at: www.opendemocracy.net/en/silver-lining-of-jordanian-elections/.

Bahrain Mirror, '*Bahrain Mirror* publishes important document regarding Jordanian police: 499 policemen are costing Bahrain 1.8 million dollar per month', 3 April 2014, available at: www.bahrainmirror.com/news/14724.html.

Democracy Digest, 'Jordan's Islamists step up anti-election campaign', 16 January 2013, available at: www.thenational.ae/world/mena/jordanian-islamists-step-up-anti-election-threats-1.467561.

Eells, Josh, 'Sleep-away camp for postmodern cowboys', *New York Times*, 19 July 2013, available at: www.nytimes.com/2013/07/21/magazine/sleep-away-camp-for-postmodern-cowboys.html.

Fahim, Kareem, 'Loyalists to dominate Jordan's new parliament', *New York Times*, 24 January 2013, available at: www.nytimes.com/2013/01/25/world/middleeast/jordan-elections-favor-government-loyalists.html?ref=world&_r=0.

Greenfield, Danya, 'Optimism after Jordan's election', *Foreign Policy*, 25 January 2013, available at: https://foreignpolicy.com/2013/01/25/optimism-after-jordans-election/.

Habib, Randa, 'Jordan tribes break taboo by targeting queen', *Ma'an News Agency*, 9 February 2011, available at: www.maannews.com/Content.aspx?id=358567.

Hazaimeh, Hani, 'Jordan makes tangible progress in reforms – EU', *Jordan Times*, 13 May 2010.

Hazaimeh, Hani, 'UK, US commend polls, pledge more support', *Jordan Times*, 26 January 2013.

Husseini, Rana, 'Ensour encourages women to participate in elections', *Jordan Times*, 6 January 2013, available at: www.vista.sahafi.jo/art.php?id=dc9ba71cd69485a8eaccfc8d29b47a000fa011b0.

IHS Jane's Intelligence Review, 'Jordan responds to the Islamic State threat', 29 October 2014.

Jordan Times, 'His Majesty directs gov't to activate Defence Ministry, expand IEC's role', 16 January 2015, available at: www.jordantimes.com/news/local/his-majesty-directs-gov%E2%80%99t-activate-defence-ministry-expand-iec%E2%80%99s-role.

Jordan Times, 'Jordan a model for the region – US ambassador', 7 January 2004.

Jordan Times, 'King receives family of gendarmerie killed in Bahrain', 14 January 2015, available at: www.jordantimes.com/news/local/king-receives-family-gendarme-killed-bahrain.

Jordan Times, 'Parliamentary elections the defining moment in Jordan Spring – king', 8 August 2012, available at: https://kingabdullah.jo/en/news/parliamentary-elections-defining-moment-jordan-spring-king.

Kibler, Joan, 'Construction progressing on the special operations training center in Jordan', *Special Operations Technology (SOTECH)*, Vol. 6, No. 2, March 2008.

Kuttab, Daoud, 'Islamists boycott fails in Jordan's elections', *Huffington Post*, 24 January 2013, available at: www.huffpost.com/entry/post_b_2539174?g uccounter=1&guce_referrer=aHR0cHM6Ly93d3cuZ29vZ2xlLmZyLw&gu ce_referrer_sig=AQAAADVGqSr2NfbPDMA9iTd_MWgXnLyodinVsTqe z8fvXbeE4dNcAzbtT644iPGyIrlgYghatCLWI9nwALbKi_GWpwmPHorY ZSnrZL-gyK4VncZN03Lv5D5Ja2sj8EuCmNkdxHCMqh5yR1V9Q5NYhp wRXhj6fcGlCNZWyP0d51AUcGLc.

MacFarquhar, Neil, 'Heavy hand of the secret police impeding reform in Arab world', *New York Times*, November 2005, available at: www.nytimes.com/20 05/11/14/world/middleeast/heavy-hand-of-the-secret-police-impeding-refor m-in-arab-world.html.

Mahon, Tim, 'General Dynamics ramps up urban training work', *Training & Simulation Journal*, December 2007–January 2008, p. 10.

National Committee of Retired Army Personnel, 'Statement on defending state, identity against Israel's "alternative homeland" – retired army', *Ammonnews*, 5 March 2010, available at: http://en.ammonnews.net/article.aspx?articleNO=7683.

Neimat, Khaled, 'Government vows to salvage economy, revamp political life', *Jordan Times*, 15 April 2013, available at: www.vista.sahafi.jo/art.php? id=b2ec8d140085a3809f7c43b68ad32aa48b443315.

Oliver, David, 'World's largest special forces training centre unveiled in Jordan', *IHS Jane's, International Defence Digest, Jordan*, 5 June 2009.

Schenker, David, 'Saving Jordan's King Abdullah must be a U.S. priority', *The Wall Street Journal*, 20 March 2013, available at: www.wsj.com/articles/ SB10001424127887323829504578267951332697058.

Schuetze, Benjamin, 'Jordan's KASOTC: privatising anti-terror training', *Al Jazeera*, 17 July 2017, available at: www.aljazeera.com/indepth/opinion/2017/0 7/jordan-kasotc-privatising-anti-terror-training-170717074832979.html.

Silverstein, Ken, 'U.S. partnership with Jordan was targeted', *Los Angeles Times*, 12 November 2005, available at: www.seattletimes.com/nation-world/us-part nership-with-jordan-was-targeted/.

Sweis, Rana F., 'In Jordan, progress in small steps', *New York Times*, 30 January 2013, available at: www.nytimes.com/2013/01/31/world/middleeast/in-jordan-progress-in-small-steps.html.

Warrick, Joby, 'Jordan emerges as key CIA counterterrorism ally', *Washington Post*, 4 January 2010, available at: www.washingtonpost.com/wp-dyn/content/ article/2010/01/03/AR2010010302063.html.

Zoellick, Robert B. (US Trade Representative), 'Countering terror with trade', *Washington Post*, 20 September 2001, available at: www.washingtonpost.com/ archive/opinions/2001/09/20/countering-terror-with-trade/aa1e3f27-f069-4b6 6-b752-8d141876d0b7/.

Unpublished PhD Theses

Debruyne, Pascal, *Spatial Rearticulations of Statehood: 'Jordan's Geographies of Power under Globalization'* (Ghent: Ghent University, PhD thesis, 2014).

Wilson, J. Zoë, *Wishful Thinking, Wilful Blindness and Artful Amnesia: The UN and the Promotion of Good Governance, Democracy and Human Rights in Africa* (Halifax: Dalhousie University, PhD thesis, 2004).

Secondary Sources

Ababneh, Sara, 'Do you know who governs us? The damned Monetary Fund', *Middle East Report Online*, 30 June 2018.

Ababsa, Myriam (ed.), *Atlas of Jordan: History, Territories and Society* (Beirut: Presses de l'IFPO, 2013).

Abdel Rahman, Maha, 'The politics of 'uncivil' society in Egypt', *Review of African Political Economy*, Vol. 29, No. 91, March 2002, pp. 21–35.

Abrahamsen, Rita, *Disciplining Democracy: Development Discourse and Good Governance in Africa* (London: Zed Books, 2000).

Abrahamsen, Rita and Leander, Anna, *Routledge Handbook of Private Security Studies* (New York: Routledge, 2016).

Abrahamsen, Rita and Williams, Michael C., 'Securing the city: private security companies and non-state authority in global governance', *International Relations*, Vol. 21, No. 2, 2007, pp. 237–253.

Abu-Dalbouh, Walid, 'Jordan and the Euro-Mediterranean Partnership', in: Fernández, Haizam Amirah and Youngs, Richard (eds.), *The Euro-Mediterranean Partnership: Assessing the First Decade* (Madrid: Real Instituto Elcano and FRIDE, 2005), pp. 139–147.

Abu-Odeh, Adnan, *Jordanians, Palestinians & the Hashemite Kingdom in the Middle East Peace Process* (Washington, DC: United States Institute of Peace Press, 1999).

Abu-Rish, Ziad, 'Jordan, liberalism, and the question of boycott', *Jadaliyya*, 9 November 2010.

Abu-Rish, Ziad, 'Romancing the throne: *The New York Times* and the endorsement of authoritarianism in Jordan', *Jadaliyya*, 3 February 2013.

Achcar, Gilbert, *The People Want: A Radical Exploration of the Arab Uprising* (London: Saqi Books, 2013).

Aksartova, Sada, 'Why NGOs? How American donors embraced civil society after the Cold War', *The International Journal of Not-for-Profit Law*, Vol. 8, No. 3, May 2006, pp. 15–20.

Alaime, Mathieu, 'Aqaba an extra-territorial city', in Ababsa, Myriam (ed.), *Atlas of Jordan: History, Territories and Society* (Beirut: Presses de l'IFPO, 2013), pp. 407–410.

Albrecht, Holger and Schlumberger, Oliver, '"Waiting for Godot": regime change without democratization in the Middle East', *International Political Science Review*, Vol. 25, No. 4, October 2004, pp. 371–392.

Alford, William P., 'Review: exporting "the pursuit of happiness"', *Harvard Law Review*, Vol. 113, No. 7, 2000, pp. 1677–1715.

Allinson, Jamie, *The Struggle for the State in Jordan: The Social Origins of Alliances in the Middle East* (London: I.B. Tauris, 2016).

Amar, Paul, *The Security Archipelago: Human-Security States, Sexuality Politics, and the End of Neoliberalism* (London: Duke University Press, 2013).

Amara, Jomana, 'Military industrialization and economic development: Jordan's defense industry', *Review of Financial Economics*, Vol. 17, No. 2, 2008, pp. 130–145.

Amin, Samir, 'The issue of democracy in the contemporary third world', in: Gills, Barry, Rocamora, Joel and Wilson, Richard (eds.), *Low Intensity Democracy: Political Power in the New World Order* (London: Pluto Press, 1993), pp. 59–79.

Anderson, Lisa, 'Democracy in the Arab world: a critique of the political culture approach', in: Brynen, Rex, Korany, Bahgat and Noble, Paul (eds.), *Political Liberalization and Democratization in the Arab World* (Boulder: Lynne Rienner, 1995), pp. 77–92.

Anderson, Lisa, 'Searching where the light shines: studying democratization in the Middle East', *Annual Review of Political Science*, Vol. 9, 2006, pp. 189–214.

Ayers, Alison J., 'Demystifying democratisation: the global constitution of (neo) liberal polities in Africa', *Third World Quarterly*, Vol. 27, No. 2, 2006, pp. 321–338.

Bacevich, Andrew J., *The New American Militarism: How Americans Are Seduced by War* (New York: Oxford University Press, 2013).

Bank, André and Schlumberger, Oliver, 'Jordan: between regime survival and economic reform', in: Perthes, Volker (ed.), *Arab Elites: Negotiating the Politics of Change* (Boulder: Lynne Rienner, 2004), pp. 35–60.

Bank, André and Sunik, Anna, 'Parliamentary elections in Jordan, January 2013', *Electoral Studies*, Vol. 34, 2014, pp. 376–379.

Barkawi, Tarak and Laffey, Mark (eds.), *Democracy, Liberalism, and War* (London: Lynne Rienner, 2001).

Baudrillard, Jean, *Simulacra and Simulation*, tr. Glaser, Sheila (Ann Arbor: University of Michigan Press, 1994).

Bayart, Jean-François, 'Civil society in Africa', in: Chabal, Patrick (ed.), *Political Domination in Africa: Reflections on the Limits of Power* (Cambridge: Cambridge University Press, 1986), pp. 109–125.

Baylouny, Anne Marie, 'Militarizing welfare: neo-liberalism and Jordanian policy', *Middle East Journal*, Vol. 62, No. 2, Spring 2008, pp. 277–303.

Bellin, Eva, 'Civil society: effective tool of analysis for Middle East politics?', *PS: Political Science and Politics*, Vol. 27, No. 3, September 1994, pp. 509–510.

Berman, Sheri, 'Civil society and the collapse of the Weimar Republic', *World Politics*, Vol. 49, No. 3, April 1997, pp. 401–429.

Berman, Sheri, 'The past and future of social democracy and the consequences for democracy promotion', in: Hobson, Christopher and Kurki, Milja (eds.), *The Conceptual Politics of Democracy Promotion* (Abingdon: Routledge, 2012), pp. 68–84.

Berndtsson Joakim and Stern, Maria, 'Private security guards: authority, control and governance?', in: Abrahamsen, Rita and Leander, Anna (eds.), *Routledge Handbook of Private Security Studies* (New York: Routledge, 2016), pp. 51–60.

Bicchi, Federica, 'Want funding? Don't mention Islam: EU democracy promotion in the Mediterranean', *CFSP Forum*, Vol. 4, No. 2, March 2006, pp. 10–12.

Bilgin, Pinar, 'The "Western-centrism" of security studies: "blind spot" or constitutive practice?', *Security Dialogue*, Vol. 41, No. 6, 2010, pp. 615–622.

Bouillon, Markus, 'Walking the tightrope: Jordanian foreign policy from the Gulf crisis to the peace process and beyond', in: Joffé, George (ed.), *Jordan in Transition: 1990–2000* (London: Hurst & Co, 2002), pp. 1–22.

Bourdieu, Pierre, *Acts of Resistance: Against the Tyranny of the Market*, tr. Nice, Richard (New York: The New Press, 1998).

Brand, Laurie A., 'Palestinians and Jordanians: a crisis of identity', *Journal of Palestine Studies*, Vol. 24, No. 4, Summer 1995, pp. 46–61.

Bridoux, Jeff and Kurki, Milja, 'Cosmetic agreements and the cracks beneath: ideological convergences and divergences in US and EU democracy promotion in civil society', *Cambridge Review of International Affairs*, Vol. 28, No. 1, 2015, pp. 1–20.

Brown, Michael E. et al. (eds.), *Debating the Democratic Peace* (London: MIT Press, 1997).

Brown, Nathan J. (ed.), *The Dynamics of Democratization: Dictatorship, Development, and Diffusion* (Baltimore: The Johns Hopkins University Press, 2011).

Brown, Wendy, 'American nightmare: neoliberalism, neoconservatism, and de-democratization', *Political Theory*, Vol. 34, No. 6, December 2006, pp. 690–714.

Brownlee, Jason, *Democracy Prevention: The Politics of the U.S.-Egyptian Alliance* (Cambridge: Cambridge University Press, 2012).

Bruff, Ian, 'The rise of authoritarian neoliberalism', *Rethinking Marxism*, Vol. 26, No. 1, 2014, pp. 113–129.

Brumberg, Daniel, 'Democratization in the Arab world? The trap of liberalized autocracy', *Journal of Democracy*, Vol. 13, No. 4, October 2002, pp. 56–68.

Brynen, Rex, 'Economic crisis and post-rentier democratization in the Arab world: the case of Jordan', *Canadian Journal of Political Science*, Vol. 25, No. 1, March 1992, pp. 69–97.

Brynen, Rex, Korany, Bahgat and Noble, Paul (eds.), *Political Liberalization and Democratization in the Arab World* (Boulder: Lynne Rienner, 1995).

Büger, Christian and Villumsen, Trine, 'Beyond the gap: relevance, fields of practice and the securitizing consequences of (democratic peace) research', *Journal of International Relations and Development*, Vol. 10, No. 4, 2007, pp. 417–448.

Bush, Sara S., *The Taming of Democracy Assistance: Why Democracy Promotion Does Not Confront Dictators* (Cambridge: Cambridge University Press, 2015).

Busse, Matthias and Gröning, Steffen, 'Assessing the impact of trade liberalization: the case of Jordan', *Journal of Economic Integration*, Vol. 27, No. 3, September 2012, pp. 466–486.

Buzan, Barry, Wæver, Ole and De Wilde, Jaap, *Security: A New Framework for Analysis* (London: Lynne Rienner, 1998).

Carapico, Sheila, *Political Aid and Arab Activism: Democracy Promotion, Justice, and Representation* (New York: Cambridge University Press, 2014).

Carothers, Thomas, *Aiding Democracy Abroad: The Learning Curve* (Washington, DC: Carnegie Endowment for International Peace, 1999).

Carothers, Thomas and De Gramont, Diane, *Development Aid Confronts Politics: The Almost Revolution* (Washington, DC: Carnegie Endowment for International Peace, 2013).

Cavatorta, Francesco, 'The convergence of governance: upgrading authoritarianism in the Arab world and downgrading democracy elsewhere?', *Middle East Critique*, Vol. 19, No. 3, Fall 2010, pp. 217–232.

Cavatorta, Francesco and Durac, Vincent, *Civil Society and Democratization in the Arab World: The Dynamics of Activism* (Abingdon: Routledge, 2011).

Challand, Benoît, *Palestinian Civil Society: Foreign Donors and the Power to Promote and Exclude* (London: Routledge, 2009).

Chandler, David, 'Back to the future? The limits of neo-Wilsonian ideals of exporting democracy', *Review of International Studies*, Vol. 32, No. 3, July 2006, pp. 475–494.

Chandrasekaran, Rajiv, *Imperial Life in the Emerald City: Inside Baghdad's Green Zone* (London: Bloomsbury Publishing, 2006).

Clark, Janine, 'Questioning power, mobilization, and strategies of the Islamist opposition: how strong is the Muslim Brotherhood in Jordan?', in: Albrecht, Holger (ed.), *Contentious Politics in the Middle East: Political Opposition under Authoritarianism* (Gainesville: University Press of Florida, 2010), pp. 117–137.

Collombier, Virginie, *Private Security: Not a Business Like Any Other* (Arab Reform Initiative, Thematic Studies: Arab Securitocracies and Security Sector Reform, 2011).

Conry, Barbara, 'Loose cannon: the National Endowment for Democracy', *Cato Institute*, Washington, DC, Foreign Policy Briefing No. 27, 8 November 1993.

Dalby, Simon, 'Challenging cartographies of enmity: empire, war and culture in contemporary militarization', in: Stavrianakis, Anna and Selby, Jan (eds.), *Militarism and International Relations: Political Economy, Security and Theory* (Abingdon: Routledge, 2013), pp. 33–44.

Dana, Tariq, 'The structural transformation of Palestinian civil society: key paradigm shifts', *Middle East Critique*, Vol. 24, No. 2, 2015, pp. 191–210.

De Jong, Sara, Icaza, Rosalba and Rutazibwa, Olivia U. (eds.), *Decolonization and Feminisms in Global Teaching and Learning* (London: Routledge, 2018).

Der Derian, James, *Virtuous War: Mapping the Military-Industrial-Media-Entertainment Network* (New York: Routledge, 2009).

Diamond, Larry, *Developing Democracy: Toward Consolidation* (Baltimore: Johns Hopkins University Press, 1999).

Diamond, L., 'Introduction: political culture and democracy', in: Diamond, Larry (ed.), *Political Culture and Democracy in Developing Countries* (Boulder: Lynne Rienner, 1993), pp. 1–33.

Diamond, Larry, 'Universal democracy?', *Policy Review*, No. 119, 2003, pp. 3–25.

Diamond, Larry, Linz, Juan and Lipset, Seymour M., *Democracy in Developing Countries: Latin America, Volume 4* (Boulder: Lynne Rienner, 1989).

Diamond, Larry and Plattner, Marc F. (eds.), 'Introduction', in: *The Global Resurgence of Democracy* (Baltimore: Johns Hopkins University Press, 1996), pp. ix–xxxii.

Doyle, Michael W., 'Kant, liberal legacies, and foreign affairs', in: Brown, Michael E. et al. (eds.), *Debating the Democratic Peace* (London: MIT Press, 1997), pp. 3–57.

Durkheim, Emile, *The Elementary Forms of the Religious Life*, tr. Swain, Joseph (London: George Allen, 1915).

Eichler, Maya, 'Citizenship and the contracting out of military work: from national conscription to globalized recruitment', *Citizenship Studies*, Vol. 18, No. 6–7, 2014, pp. 600–614.

El-Anis, Imad, *Jordan and the United States: The Political Economy of Trade and Economic Reform in the Middle East* (London: I.B. Tauris, 2011).

Elliott, Cathy, *Democracy Promotion as Foreign Policy: Temporal Othering in International Relations* (New York: Routledge, 2017).

Farsakh, Leila, 'Democracy promotion in Palestine: Aid and the "de-democratization" of the West Bank and Gaza', Birzeit University, 2012, available at: http://rosaluxemburg.ps/wp-content/uploads/2015/03/Leila-Farsakh.pdf.

Ferguson, James, *The Anti-Politics Machine: 'Development,' Depoliticization, and Bureaucratic Power in Lesotho* (Minneapolis: University of Minnesota Press, 1994).

Finkel, Steven E. et al., 'The effects of U.S. Foreign assistance on democracy building, 1990–2003', *World Politics*, Vol. 59, No. 3, April 2007, pp. 404–440.

Fukuyama, Francis, 'The end of history?', *The National Interest*, Vol. 16, Summer 1989, pp. 3–18.

Gallie, Walter B., 'Essentially contested concepts', *Proceedings of the Aristotelian Society, New Series*, Vol. 56, 1955–1956, pp. 167–198.

Gills, Barry, Rocamora, Joel and Wilson, Richard (eds.), *Low Intensity Democracy: Political Power in the New World Order* (London: Pluto Press, 1993).

Greenwood, Scott, 'Jordan's "New Bargain": the political economy of regime security', *Middle East Journal*, Vol. 57, No. 2, Spring 2003, pp. 248–268.

Guazzone, Laura and Pioppi, Daniela (eds.), *The Arab State and Neo-Liberal Globalization: The Restructuring of State Power in the Middle East* (Reading: Ithaca Press, 2012).

Guilhot, Nicolas, *The Democracy Makers: Human Rights and International Order* (New York: Columbia University Press, 2005).

Gylfason, Thorvaldur, Martinez-Zarzoso, Inmaculada and Wijkman, Per Magnus, 'Can free trade help convert the "Arab Spring" into permanent peace and democracy?', *Defence and Peace Economics*, Vol. 26, No. 3, 2015, pp. 247–270.

Hamid, Shadi, 'The struggle for Middle East democracy', *Cairo Review of Global Affairs*, Vol. 1, 2011, pp. 18–29.

Hanieh, Adam, '"Democracy promotion" and neo-liberalism in the Middle East', *State of Nature*, Vol. 3, Spring 2006, available at: http://links.org.au/node/224.

Hanieh, Adam, *Lineages of Revolt: Issues of Contemporary Capitalism in the Middle East* (Chicago: Haymarket Books, 2013).

Hann, C., 'Introduction – political society and civil anthropology', in: Hann, Chris and Dunn, Elizabeth (eds.), *Civil Society: Challenging Western Models* (London: Routledge, 1996), pp. 1–26.

Hann, Chris and Dunn, Elizabeth (eds.), *Civil Society: Challenging Western Models* (London: Routledge, 1996).

Hardt, Michael and Negri, Antonio, *Multitude: War and Democracy in the Age of Empire* (London: Penguin Books, 2005).

Harvey, David, 'Neoliberalism as creative destruction', *Annals of the American Academy of Political and Social Science*, Vol. 610, NAFTA and Beyond: Alternative Perspectives in the Study of Global Trade and Development, March 2007, pp. 22–44.

Hassan, Oz, *Constructing America's Freedom Agenda for the Middle East: Democracy and Domination* (London: Routledge, 2013).

Heydemann, Steven, 'Breaking through Jordan's apathy barrier?', *United States Institute of Peace*, 22 January 2013.

Heydemann, Steven, 'In the shadow of democracy: review article', *Middle East Journal*, Vol. 60, No. 1, Winter 2006, pp. 146–157.

Heydemann, Steven, 'Upgrading authoritarianism in the Arab world', The Saban Center for Middle East Policy at the Brookings Institution, Analysis Paper Number 13, October 2007, available at: www.brookings.edu/wp-content/upl oads/2016/06/10arabworld.pdf.

Higate, Paul, 'The private militarized and security contractor as geocorporeal actor', *International Political Sociology*, Vol. 6, No. 4, 2012, pp. 355–372.

Higate, Paul, '"Switching on" for cash: the private militarised security contractor as geo-corporeal actor', in: McSorley, Kevin (ed.), *War and the Body: Militarisation, Practice and Experience* (London: Routledge, 2013), pp. 106–127.

Hobson, Christopher and Kurki, Milja (eds.), *The Conceptual Politics of Democracy Promotion* (Abingdon: Routledge, 2012).

Hobson, Christopher and Kurki, Milja, 'Introduction: the conceptual politics of democracy promotion', in: Hobson, Christopher and Kurki, Milja (eds.), *The Conceptual Politics of Democracy Promotion* (Abingdon: Routledge, 2012), pp. 1–15.

Hopgood, Stephen, *Keepers of the Flame: Understanding Amnesty International* (London: Cornell University Press, 2006).

Horkheimer, Max, Adorno, Theodor W. and Noerr, Gunzelin Schmid (eds.), *Dialectic of Enlightenment: Philosophical Fragments*, tr. Jephcott, Edmund (Stanford: Stanford University Press, 2002).

Huntington, Samuel P., *Political Order in Changing Societies* (London: Yale University Press, 1968).

Huntington, Samuel P., *The Third Wave: Democratization in the Late Twentieth Century* (Norman: University of Oklahoma, 1993).

Hyde, Susan D., *The Pseudo-Democrat's Dilemma: Why Election Observation Became an International Norm* (Ithaca: Cornell University Press, 2011).

Jad, Islah, 'NGOs: between buzzwords and social movements', *Development in Practice*, Vol. 17, No. 4/5, August 2007, pp. 622–629.

Joffé, George (ed.), *Jordan in Transition: 1990–2000* (London: Hurst & Co., 2002).

Kamat, Sangeeta, 'NGOs and the new democracy: the false saviors of international development', *Harvard International Review*, Vol. 25, No. 1, Spring 2003, pp. 65–69.

Kant, Immanuel, *Perpetual Peace*, tr. Smith, Campbell M. (London: George Allen & Unwin, 1795/1917).

Kardoosh, Marwan A., 'The Aqaba Special Economic Zone, Jordan: a case study of governance', University of Bonn, Center for Development Research, 2005.

Kardoosh, Marwan A., 'Qualifying Industrial Zones and sustainable development in Jordan', Jordan Center for Public Policy Research and Dialogue, February 2005.

Karmel, Ezra J., 'How revolutionary was Jordan's Hirak? What the Incognito participation of Palestinian-Jordanians in Hirak tells us about the movements', Identity Center, Amman, June 2014, available at: http://identity-center.org/sit es/default/files/How%20Revolutionary%20Was%20Jordan%27s%20Hira k__0.pdf.

Khakee, Anna, Khalaf, Mona, Lutterbeck, Derek, Hourani, Hani and Al-Taher, May, 'A long-lasting controversy: Western democracy promotion in Jordan', Mediterranean Academy of Diplomatic Studies and Al Urdun Al Jadid Research Center (UJRC), Malta and Amman, 2009.

Khalili, Laleh, 'The infrastructural power of the military: the geoeconomic role of the US Army Corps of Engineers in the Arabian Peninsula', *European Journal of International Relations*, Vol. 24, No. 4, 2018, pp. 911–933.

Kienle, Eberhard, 'Democracy promotion and the renewal of authoritarian rule', in: Schlumberger, Oliver (ed.), *Debating Arab Authoritarianism: Dynamics and Durability in Nondemocratic Regimes* (Stanford: Stanford University Press, 2007), pp. 231–249.

Kifah and Jennifer (pseudonyms), 'Jon Stewart's theater of the absurd', *Jadaliyya*, 2 October 2012.

Kirby, Owen H., 'Want democracy? Get a king', *The Middle East Quarterly*, December 2000, pp. 3–12.

Knowles, Warwick, *Jordan since 1989: A Study in Political Economy* (London: I.B. Tauris, 2005).

Krämer, Gudrun, 'Good counsel to the king: the Islamist opposition in Saudi Arabia, Jordan, and Morocco', in: Kostiner, Joseph (ed.), *Middle East Monarchies: The Challenge of Modernity* (Boulder: Lynne Rienner, 2000), pp. 257–288.

Kreitmeyr, Nadine, 'Neoliberal co-optation and authoritarian renewal: social entrepreneurship networks in Jordan and Morocco', *Globalizations*, Vol. 16, No. 3, 2019, pp. 289–303.

Kuntsman, Adi and Stein, Rebecca L., *Digital Militarism: Israel's Occupation in the Social Media Age* (Stanford: Stanford University Press, 2015).

Kurki, Milja, 'Democracy and conceptual contestability: reconsidering conceptions of democracy in democracy promotion', *International Studies Review*, Vol. 12, No. 3, 2010, pp. 362–386.

Langohr, Vickie, 'Too much civil society, too little politics: Egypt and liberalizing Arab regimes', *Comparative Politics*, Vol. 36, No. 2, January 2004, pp. 181–204.

Lenner, Katharina and Turner, Lewis, 'Learning from the Jordan Compact', *Forced Migration Review*, No. 57, February 2018, pp. 48–51.

Li, Tania Murray, *The Will to Improve: Governmentality, Development, and the Practice of Politics* (London: Duke University Press, 2007).

Lipset, Seymour M., 'Some social requisites of democracy: economic development and political legitimacy', *The American Political Science Review*, Vol. 53, No. 1, March 1959, pp. 69–105.

Lust-Okar, Ellen M., 'The decline of Jordanian political parties: myth or reality?', *International Journal of Middle East Studies*, Vol. 33, No. 4, 2001, pp. 545–569.

Lust-Okar, Ellen, 'Elections under authoritarianism: preliminary lessons from Jordan', *Democratization*, Vol. 13, No. 3, June 2006, pp. 456–471.

Lust-Okar, Ellen, *Structuring Conflict in the Arab World: Incumbents, Opponents, and Institutions* (Cambridge: Cambridge University Press, 2005).

Lynch, Marc, *State Interests and Public Spheres: The International Politics of Jordan's Identity* (New York: Columbia University Press, 1999).

Mansfield, Edward D. and Snyder, Jack, *Electing to Fight: Why Emerging Democracies Go to War* (Cambridge: MIT Press, 2005).

Markakis, Dionysis, *US Democracy Promotion in the Middle East: The Pursuit of Hegemony* (London: Routledge, 2016).

Marshall, Shana, 'Jordan's military-industrial complex and the Middle East's New Model Army', *Middle East Research and Information Project*, Vol. 43, No. 267, 2013, pp. 42–45.

Martínez, José Ciro, 'Jordan's self-fulfilling prophecy: the production of feeble political parties and the perceived perils of democracy', *British Journal of Middle Eastern Studies*, Vol. 44, No. 3, 2017, pp. 356–372.

Martínez, José Ciro, 'Leavening neoliberalization's uneven pathways: bread, governance and political rationalities in the Hashemite Kingdom of Jordan', *Mediterranean Politics*, Vol. 22, No. 4, 2017, pp. 464–483.

Massad, Joseph A., *Colonial Effects: The Making of National Identity in Jordan* (New York: Columbia University Press, 2001).

McDonald, Kevin, 'Grammars of violence, modes of embodiment and frontiers of the subject', in: McSorley, Kevin (ed.), *War and the Body: Militarisation, Practice and Experience* (London: Routledge, 2013), pp. 138–151.

McSorley, Kevin, 'Conclusion: rethinking war and the body', in: McSorley, Kevin (ed.), *War and the Body: Militarisation, Practice and Experience* (London: Routledge, 2013), pp. 233–244.

McSorley, Kevin (ed.), *War and the Body: Militarisation, Practice and Experience* (London: Routledge, 2013).

Mitchell, Timothy, *Rule of Experts: Egypt, Techno-Politics, Modernity* (Berkeley: University of California Press, 2002).

Moore, Pete, 'A political-economy history of Jordan's intelligence directorate', unpublished article, 2018.

Moore, Pete W., *Doing Business in the Middle East: Politics and Economic Crisis in Jordan and Kuwait* (Cambridge: Cambridge University Press, 2004).

Moore, Pete, 'The fiscal politics of rebellious Jordan', *Middle East Report Online*, 21 June 2018.

Moore, Pete, 'The newest Jordan: free trade, peace and an ace in the hole', *Middle East Research and Information Project*, 26 June 2003.

Moore, Pete W., 'QIZs, FTAs, USAID and the MEFTA: a political economy of acronyms', *Middle East Report*, No. 234, Spring 2005, pp. 18–23.

Moore, Pete W. and Schrank, Andrew, 'Commerce and conflict: U.S. effort to counter terrorism with trade may backfire', *Middle East Policy*, Vol. X, No. 3, Fall 2003, pp. 112–120.

Mouffe, Chantal, 'Democracy in a multipolar world', *Millennium: Journal of International Studies*, Vol. 37, No. 3, 2009, pp. 549–561.

Mouffe, Chantal, *The Democratic Paradox* (London: Verso, 2009).

Müllerson, Rein, *Democracy: A Destiny of Humankind? A Qualified, Contingent and Contextual Case for Democracy Promotion* (New York: Nova Science Publishers, 2009).

Nagel, Thomas, 'Moral conflict and political legitimacy', in: Raz, Joseph (ed.), *Authority* (Oxford: Blackwell, 1990), pp. 300–324.

Neveling, Patrick, 'Export processing zones and global class formation', in: Carrier, James G. and Kalb, Don (eds.), *Anthropologies of Class: Power, Practice and Inequality* (Cambridge: Cambridge University Press, 2015), pp. 164–182.

Oren, Ido, *Our Enemies and US: America's Rivalries and the Making of Political Science* (New York: Cornell University Press, 2013).

Parker, Christopher, 'Tunnel-bypasses and minarets of capitalism: Amman as neoliberal assemblage', *Political Geography*, Vol. 28, No. 2, 2009, pp. 110–120.

Pascucci, Elisa, 'The local labour building the international community: precarious work within humanitarian spaces', *Environment and Planning A: Economy and Space*, Vol. 51, No. 3, 2018, pp. 743–760.

Peters, Anne M. and Moore, Pete W., 'Beyond boom and bust: external rents, durable authoritarianism, and institutional adaptation in the Hashemite Kingdom of Jordan', *Studies in Comparative International Development*, Vol. 44, No. 3, 2009, pp. 256–285.

Petras, James, 'NGOs: in the service of imperialism', *Journal of Contemporary Asia*, Vol. 29, No. 4, 1999, pp. 429–440.

Przeworski, Adam, *Democracy and the Market: Political and Economic Reforms in Eastern Europe and Latin America* (Cambridge: Cambridge University Press, 1991).

Reid-Henry, Simon, 'Spaces of security and development: an alternative mapping of the security-development nexus', *Security Dialogue*, Vol. 42, No. 1, 2011, pp. 97–104.

Robins, Philip, *A History of Jordan* (Cambridge: Cambridge University Press, 2004).

Robinson, William I., 'Globalization, the world system, and "democracy promotion" in U.S. foreign policy', *Theory and Society*, Vol. 25, No. 5, October 1996, pp. 615–665.

Robinson, William I., *Promoting Polyarchy: Globalization, US Intervention, and Hegemony* (Cambridge: Cambridge University Press, 1996).

Rostow, Walt Whitman, *The Stages of Economic Growth: A Non-Communist Manifesto* (New York: Cambridge University Press, 1960).

Rupert, Mark, 'Democracy, peace: what's not to love?', in: Barkawi, Tarak and Laffey, Mark (eds.), *Democracy, Liberalism, and War* (London: Lynne Rienner, 2001), pp. 153–172.

Ryan, Curtis R., 'Civil society and democratization in Jordan', University of Amsterdam and Hivos, Amsterdam and The Hague, Working Paper 7, 2010.

Ryan, Curtis R., *Jordan and the Arab Uprisings: Regime Survival and Politics beyond the State* (New York: Columbia University Press, 2018).

Ryan, Curtis R., *Jordan in Transition: From Hussein to Abdullah* (London: Lynne Rienner Publishers, 2002).

Ryan, Curtis R., 'Jordan's unfinished journey: parliamentary elections and the state of reform', *Project on Middle East Democracy (POMED)*, Policy Brief, March 2013.

Sabaratnam, Meera, 'Avatars of Eurocentrism in the critique of the liberal peace', *Security Dialogue*, Vol. 44, No. 3, 2013, pp. 259–278.

Sabaratnam, Meera, 'IR in dialogue ... but can we change the subjects? A typology of decolonising strategies for the study of world politics', *Millennium: Journal of International Studies*, Vol. 39, No. 3, 2011, pp. 781–803.

Sadiki, Larbi, *The Search for Arab Democracy: Discourses and Counter-Discourses* (London: Hurst Publishers, 2004).

Said, Edward W., *Orientalism* (New York: Vintage Books, 1978).

Salamé, Ghassan (ed.), *Democracy without Democrats? The Renewal of Politics in the Muslim World* (London: I.B. Tauris, 1994).

Schlumberger, Oliver (ed.), *Debating Arab Authoritarianism: Dynamics and Durability in Nondemocratic Regimes* (Stanford: Stanford University Press, 2007).

Schraeder, Peter J., 'The state of the art in international democracy promotion: results of a joint European-North American research network', *Democratization*, Vol. 10, No. 2, Summer 2003, pp. 21–44.

Schmitt, Carl, *The Concept of the Political*, tr. Schwab, George (London: University of Chicago Press, 1996).

Schmitter, Philippe C., 'Review: democracy's third wave – *The Third Wave. Democratization in the Late Twentieth Century* by Samuel P. Huntington', *The Review of Politics*, Vol. 55, No. 2, Spring 1993, pp. 348–351.

Schmitter, Philippe C. and Brouwer, Imco, 'Conceptualizing, researching and evaluating democracy promotion and protection', *European University Institute (EUI)*, Florence, Working Paper no. 99/9, 1999.

Schuetze, Benjamin, 'Confronting authoritarianism vs. disciplining democracy: the recent protests in Jordan and US attempts at democracy promotion', *Jadaliyya*, 30 July 2018.

Schuetze, Benjamin, 'Marketing parliament: the constitutive effects of external attempts at parliamentary strengthening in Jordan', *Cooperation and Conflict*, Vol. 53, No. 2, 2018, pp. 237–258.

Schuetze, Benjamin, 'Misrepresenting the contextual and idealising the universal: how US efforts at democracy promotion bolster authoritarianism in Jordan', Arnold-Bergstraesser-Institut, Working Paper, No. 3, 2016, available at: https://www.arnold-bergstraesser.de/sites/default/files/field/pub-download/ab i_working_paper_3_benjamin_schuetze_misrepresenting_the_contextual_an d_idealising_the_universal_0.pdf.

Schuetze, Benjamin, 'Simulating, marketing, and playing war: US-Jordanian military collaboration and the politics of commercial security', *Security Dialogue*, Vol. 48, No. 5, 2017, pp. 431–450.

Schwedler, Jillian, 'Cop rock: protest, identity, and dancing riot police in Jordan', *Social Movement Studies*, Vol. 4, No. 2, September 2005, pp. 155–175.

Schwedler, Jillian, 'The political geography of protest in neoliberal Jordan', *Middle East Critique*, Vol. 21, No. 3, 2012, pp. 259–270.

Selim, Gamal M., *The International Dimensions of Democratization in Egypt: The Limits of Externally-Induced Change* (London: Springer, 2015).

Shlaim, Avi, *Lion of Jordan: The Life of King Hussein in War and Peace* (London: Allen Lane, 2007).

Smith, Tony, *America's Mission: The United States and the Worldwide Struggle for Democracy in the Twentieth Century* (Princeton: Princeton University Press, 1994).

Smith, Tony, 'From "fortunate vagueness" to "democratic globalism"': American democracy promotion as imperialism', in: Hobson, Christopher and Kurki, Milja (eds.), *The Conceptual Politics of Democracy Promotion* (Abingdon: Routledge, 2012), pp. 210–214.

Snider, Erin A., 'US democracy aid and the authoritarian state: evidence from Egypt and Morocco', *International Studies Quarterly*, Vol. 62, No. 4, 2018, pp. 795–808.

Spiro, David E., 'The liberal peace: and yet it squirms', in: Brown, Michael E. et al. (eds.), *Debating the Democratic Peace* (London: MIT Press, 1997), pp. 351–354.

Stahl, Roger, 'Have you played the war on terror?', *Critical Studies in Media Communication*, Vol. 23, No. 2, 2006, pp. 112–130.

Stahl, Roger, 'Life is war: the rhetoric of biomimesis and the future military', *Democratic Communiqué*, Vol. 26, No. 2, 2014, pp. 122–137.

Stahl, Roger, *Militainment, Inc.: War, Media, and Popular Culture* (New York: Routledge, 2010).

Stavrianakis, Anna, 'In arms' way: arms company and military involvement in education in the UK', *ACME: An International E-Journal for Critical Geographies*, Vol. 8, No. 3, 2009, pp. 505–520.

Stavrianakis, Anna and Selby, Jan (eds.), *Militarism and International Relations: Political Economy, Security and Theory* (Abingdon: Routledge, 2013).

Stuenkel, Oliver, 'Rising powers and the future of democracy promotion: the case of Brazil and India', *Third World Quarterly*, Vol. 34, No. 2, 2013, pp. 339–355.

Sukarieh, Mayssoun and Tannock, Stuart, 'The global securitisation of youth', *Third World Quarterly*, Vol. 39, No. 5, 2018, pp. 854–870.

Tansel, Cemal Burak (ed.), *States of Discipline: Authoritarian Neoliberalism and the Contested Reproduction of Capitalist Order* (London: Rowman & Littlefield International, 2017).

Tell, Nawaf, 'Jordanian security sector governance: between theory and practice', Geneva Centre for Democratic Control of Armed Forces (DCAF), conference paper, July 2004.

Tell, Tariq Moraiwed, *The Social and Economic Origins of Monarchy in Jordan* (New York: Palgrave Macmillan, 2013).

Tempest, Clive, 'Myths from Eastern Europe and the legend of the West', *Democratization*, Vol. 4, No. 1, 1997, pp. 132–144.

Teti, Andrea, 'Democracy without social justice: marginalization of social and economic rights in EU democracy assistance policy after the Arab uprisings', *Middle East Critique*, Vol. 24, No. 1, 2015, pp. 9–25.

Valbjørn, Morten, 'The 2013 parliamentary elections in Jordan: three stories and some general lessons', *Mediterranean Politics*, Vol. 18, No. 2, 2013, pp. 311–317.

Valbjørn, Morten and Bank, André, 'Examining the "post" in post-democratization: the future of Middle Eastern political rule through lenses of the past', *Middle East Critique*, Vol. 19, No. 3, 2010, pp. 183–200.

Vatikiotis, Panayiotis Jerasimof, *Politics and the Military in Jordan: A Study of the Arab Legion 1921–1957* (London: Frank Cass & Co., 1967).

Vogt, Achim, 'Jordan's eternal promise of reform', *Internationale Politik und Gesellschaft*, No. 4, 2011, pp. 61–76.

Volpi, Frédéric and Cavatorta, Francesco (eds.), *Democratization in the Muslim World: Changing Patterns of Power and Authority* (Abingdon: Routledge, 2007).

Wedeen, Lisa, 'Conceptualizing culture: possibilities for political science', *The American Political Science Review*, Vol. 96, No. 4, December 2002, pp. 713–728.

Wiarda, Howard J., *Cracks in the Consensus: Debating the Democracy Agenda in U.S. Foreign Policy* (Washington, DC: Center for Strategic and International Studies (CSIS), 1997).

Wickham, Carrie R., 'Beyond democratization: political change in the Arab world', *PS: Political Science and Politics*, Vol. 27, No. 3, September 1994, pp. 507–509.

Wiktorowicz, Quintan, 'Civil society as social control: state power in Jordan', *Comparative Politics*, Vol. 33, No. 1, October 2000, pp. 43–61.

Wilson, Mary Christina, *King Abdullah, Britain and the Making of Jordan* (New York: Cambridge University Press, 1987).

Wittes, Tamara C. and Yerkes, Sarah E., 'What price freedom? Assessing the Bush administration's freedom agenda', The Saban Center for Middle East

Policy at the Brookings Institution, Analysis Paper, No. 10, September 2006.

Wolff, Jonas and Wurm, Iris, 'Towards a theory of external democracy promotion: a proposal for theoretical classification', *Security Dialogue*, Vol. 42, No. 1, 2011, pp. 77–96.

Yom, Sean L., 'Civil society and democratization in the Arab world', *Middle East Review of International Affairs*, Vol. 9, No. 4, December 2005, pp. 14–33.

Yom, Sean L., 'Tribal politics in contemporary Jordan: the case of the *Hirak* movement', *The Middle East Journal*, Vol. 68, No. 2, Spring 2014, pp. 229–247.

Yom, Sean and Al-Khatib, Wael, 'The politics of youth policymaking in Jordan', in: *POMEPS Studies, No. 31, Social Policy in the Middle East and North Africa* (Washington, DC, October 2018), pp. 41–45, available at: https://pomeps.org/ 2018/08/02/the-politics-of-youth-policymaking-in-jordan/.

Žižek, Slavoj, *In Defense of Lost Causes* (London: Verso, 2008).

Index

Books in the Series